STILL LIFE PAINTING TECHNIQUES

STILL LIFE PAINTING TECHNIQUES

EDITED BY MARY SUFFUDY

Watson-Guptill Publications/New York

First published in 1985 in New York by Watson-Guptill Publications,
a division of Billboard Publications, Inc.,
1515 Broadway, New York, N.Y. 10036

Library of Congress Cataloging in Publication Data

Suffudy, Mary.
Still life painting techniques.

Includes index.
1. Still-life painting—Technique. I. Title.
ND1390.S84 1985 751.42′2435 85-13804
ISBN 0-8230-4986-8 (pbk.)

Distributed in the United Kingdom by Phaidon Press Ltd.,
Littlegate House, St. Ebbe's St., Oxford

Manufactured in U.S.A.

1 2 3 4 5 6 7 8 9/89 88 87 86 85

The artists whose work and teaching are included in this book deserve particular recognition and thanks. Because of their generosity and willingness to be involved in this project, *Still Life Painting Techniques* contains the finest instruction Watson-Guptill has to offer.

I would also like to offer special thanks to Betty Vera and Jay Anning for their invaluable contributions to this book.

Mary Suffudy

Contents

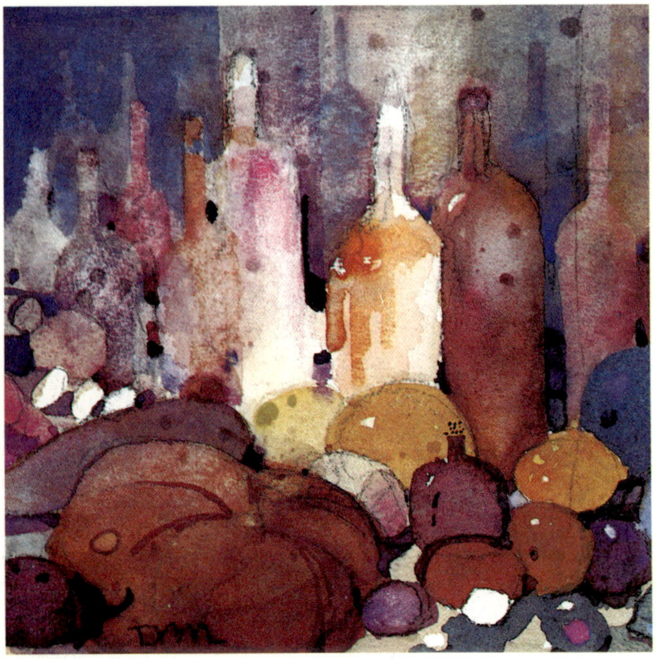

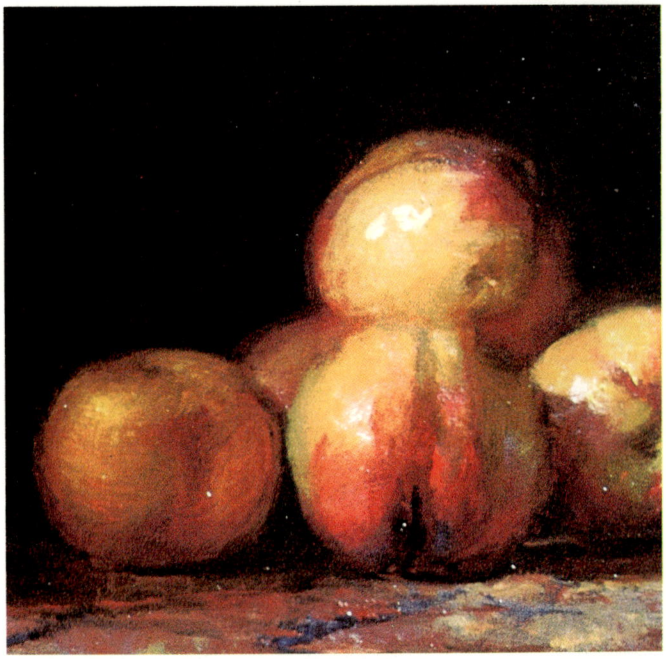

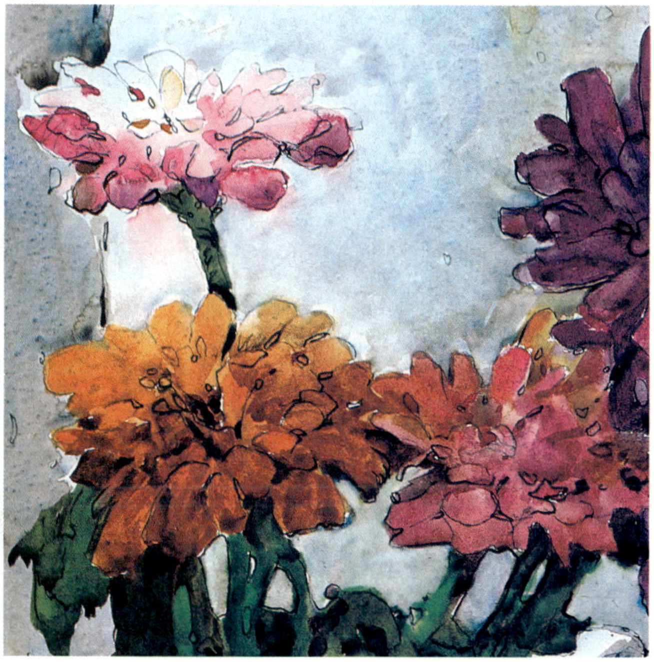

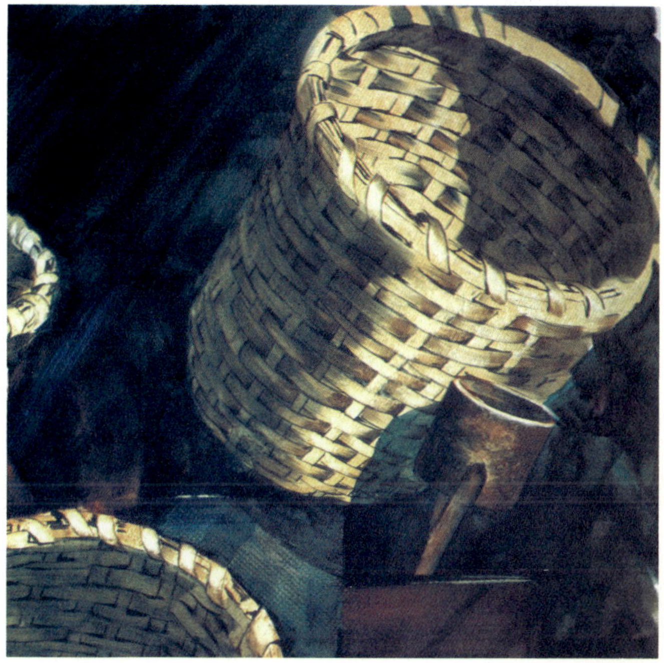

Introduction

The editors at Watson-Guptill have heard time and time again that you, our readers, want more books that show how—not just one—but a *variety* of successful artists work. And so we have responded with an entire series of books that includes *Watercolor Painting Techniques*, *Oil Painting Techniques*, *Pencil Drawing Techniques*, and *Landscape Painting Techniques*—each book packed with selected teachings from some of our very best artists and instructors. It is with great pleasure that we now introduce you to *Still Life Painting Techniques*.

Having even one great art teacher can be inspiring. Having benefit of six great teachers is rare inspiration indeed. By studying the paintings and techniques of this distinguished group of instructors, you can extend your ability to perceive and to create polished works of art that reflect your own personal point of view. In short, this book is really several painting courses rolled into one.

Here is a bit of information about the artists and the books on which *Still Life Painting Techniques* is based.

Charles Reid is an extraordinarily popular artist who does everything well—flowers, still lifes, landscapes, portraits, and figures. Students from across the country flock to his painting workshops. In *Still Life Painting Techniques*, Reid shares his special expertise in painting flowers. Included are passages from *Flower Painting in Watercolor* and *Flower Painting in Oil*. His other books are *Painting What You Want to See*, *Figure Painting in Watercolor*, *Portrait Painting in Watercolor*, and *Pulling Your Paintings Together*.

David Lyle Millard is the author of two of Watson-Guptill's most celebrated books, *The Joy of Watercolor* and *More Joy of Watercolor*. Both books are superb references for the watercolorist who wants to learn how to use color imaginatively and how to paint a variety of subjects with feeling. Excerpts from the books provide instruction on composing still life paintings, creating effective backgrounds, and using color and light.

David A. Leffel paints in a classic, twentieth-century old master style, and for more than a decade he has taught crowded classes at the Art Students League in New York. Excerpts from *Oil Painting Secrets from a Master* (based on notes by his student Linda Cateura) provide insights into handling light and shadow, mastering edges, and choosing different backgrounds.

Georg Shook has won national recognition as an artist, teacher, and lecturer. In *Sharp Focus Watercolor Painting*, which he co-authored with Gary Witt, Shook introduced readers to painting watercolor on the hot-pressed surface. Excerpts that appear in *Still Life Painting Techniques* show how this extremely smooth surface makes it possible for the watercolorist to have ultimate control of textural effects. Passages from *Painting Watercolors from Photographs*, also co-authored by Witt, provide valuable tips on using photographs as valuable aids to creating successful paintings.

Arthur Stern believes that color is the key to painting what you actually see. Passages from his highly regarded, and revolutionary, *How To See Color and Paint It* demonstrate how to observe, identify, mix, match, and paint the colors of the world with remarkable accuracy. The projects shown in *Still Life Painting Techniques* were executed by his students and show how you can learn from an inspiring teacher.

Joseph Dawley is widely respected for his ability to create beautiful realistic images of difficult subjects. Selections from *The Painter's Problem Book* show you how to paint still life subjects as diverse as lettuce, potatoes, oranges, glass, silver, china, and fabric. You'll learn how to handle the problems of textures that are rough, smooth, transparent, and shiny.

This book does indeed provide an invigorating sampling of the ideas and techniques of some of today's best artist/instructors. You will find a variety of painting styles in both watercolor and oil. We at Watson-Guptill hope that *Still Life Painting Techniques* will encourage you to explore the work of these artists in even greater detail, and that you will continue to develop and grow as an artist with a style and philosophy all your own.

PAINTING STILL LIFES IN WATERCOLOR AND OIL

Creative planning is essential to making successful paintings. In this section of the book, David Lyle Millard shows you how to get the best angle on a still life, how to decide what objects to include, how to compose with geometric shapes, and how to compose with color.

From Arthur Stern you'll learn how space influences color and how to see light and shade as colors. What is the best way to handle white shapes, create vibrant darks, mass forms, master edges, create effective backgrounds? David Lyle Millard and David Leffel show you.

Finally, Georg Shook demonstrates how working from photographs can help you make better paintings.

Searching for Form and Pattern

Getting the Best Angle. Look for design when you begin a still life, just as you would when painting a street scene or landscape. Walk around the motif and draw several compositions from different angles first. Here the artist has sketched the same still life from five different points of view (to orient yourself, look at the position of the cutting board in each one). After you've done five sketches like these, try painting watercolors of your best compositions, making each new angle work as a painting. Paint each one in a different watercolor technique—wet over dry washes, wet-in-wet, and so on—using a different combination of colors. Dare to invent and experiment.

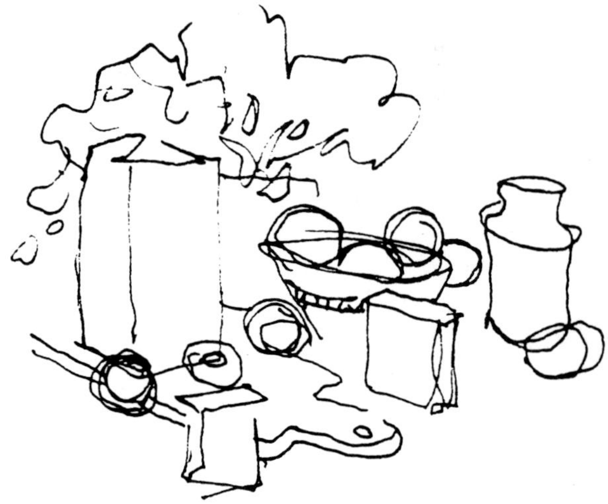

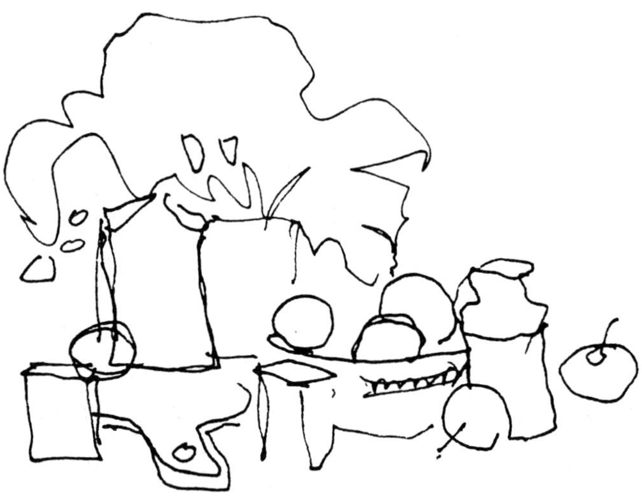

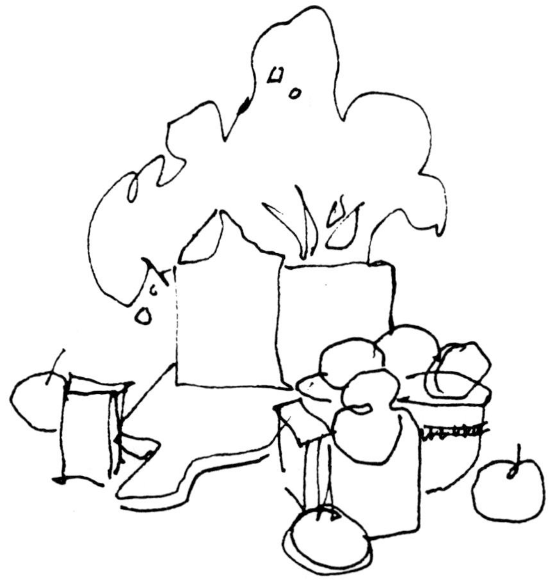

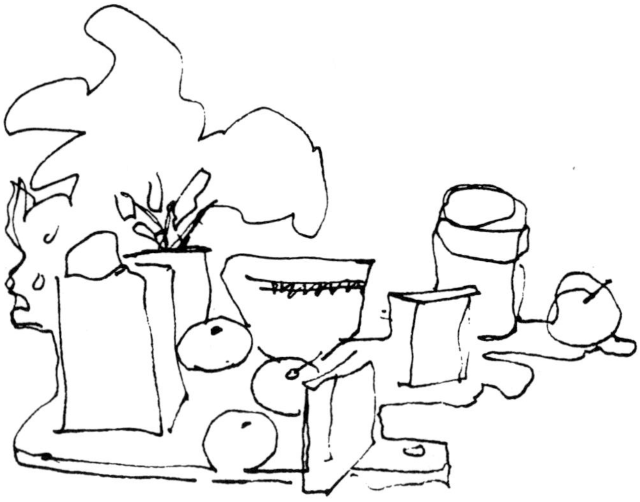

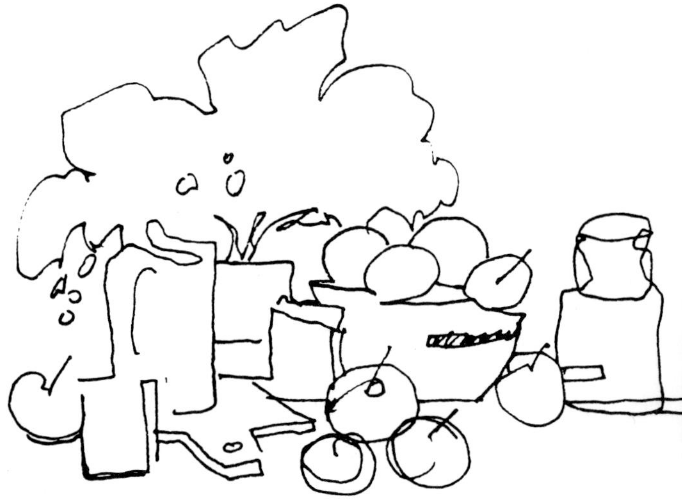

Developing Three-Dimensional Form. In this watercolor sketch, Mr. Millard laid in the background first. Then he started his move from two dimensions to three by painting the shadow side of the objects only. Note the subtle changes where color has been dropped into the monotone wash. Note, also, how the intensity or relative brightness of the color affects its apparent position within the depth of the picture plane: The brighter the color, the closer it appears.

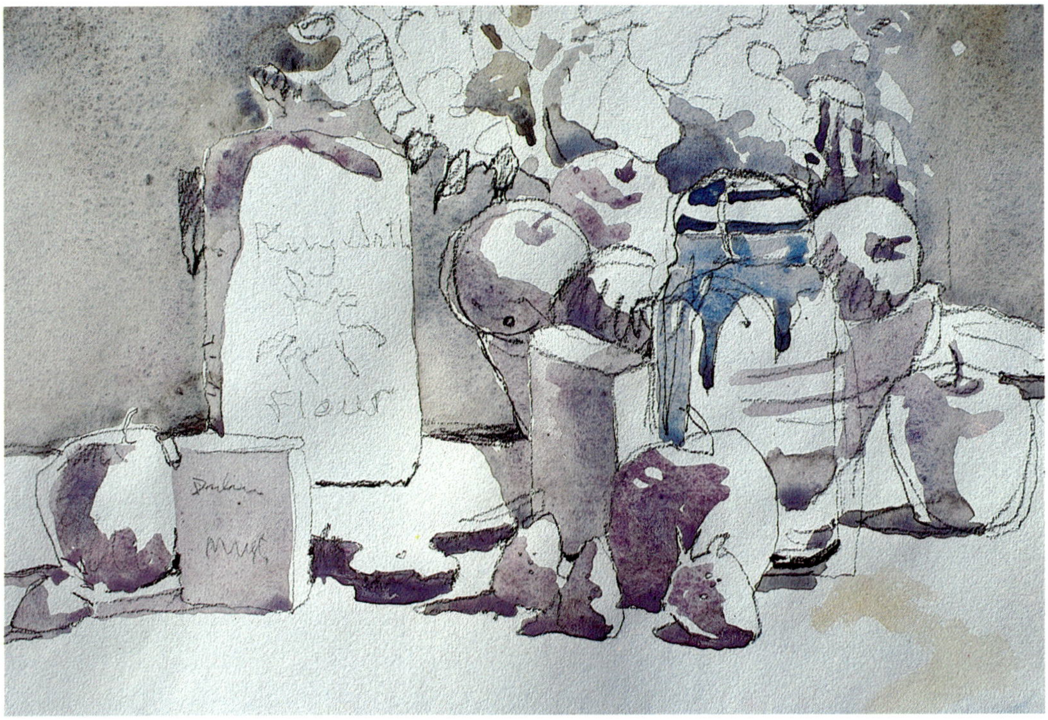

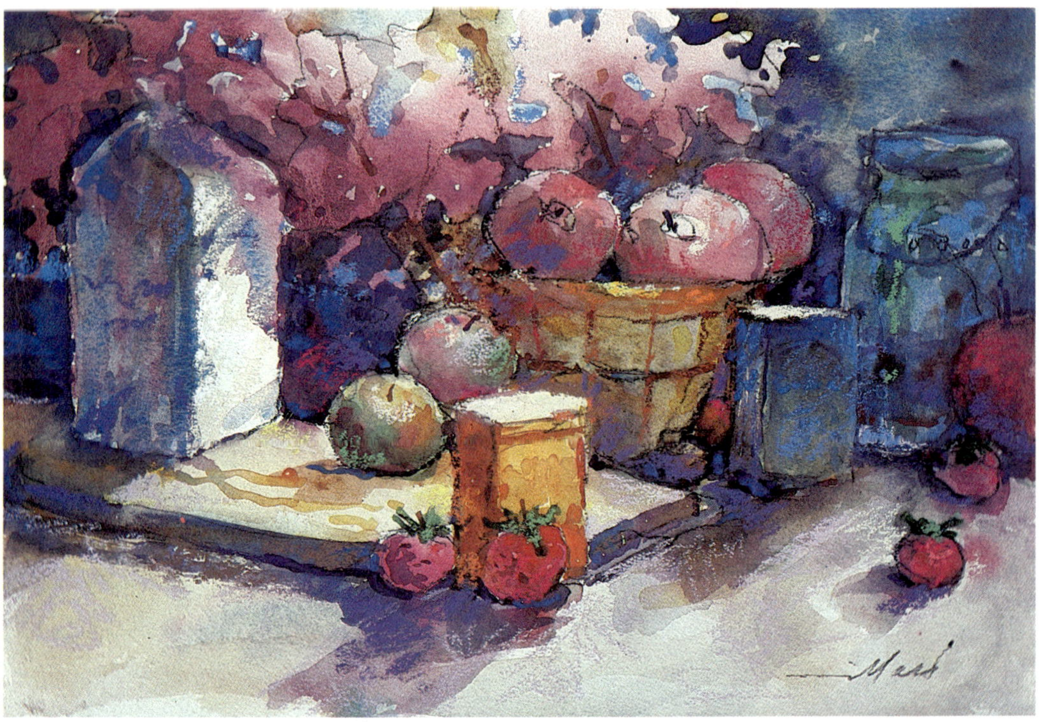

Enhancing Form with Color. Here the artist started with very loose washes and then, after the painting was bone dry, he enhanced the forms with touches of pastel for the sheer brilliance of pure pigment. He added just enough pastel to cause a color vibration, a shimmer, where pure color hits more subdued tone, but he has let the previous color show through.

Deciding How Much to Include

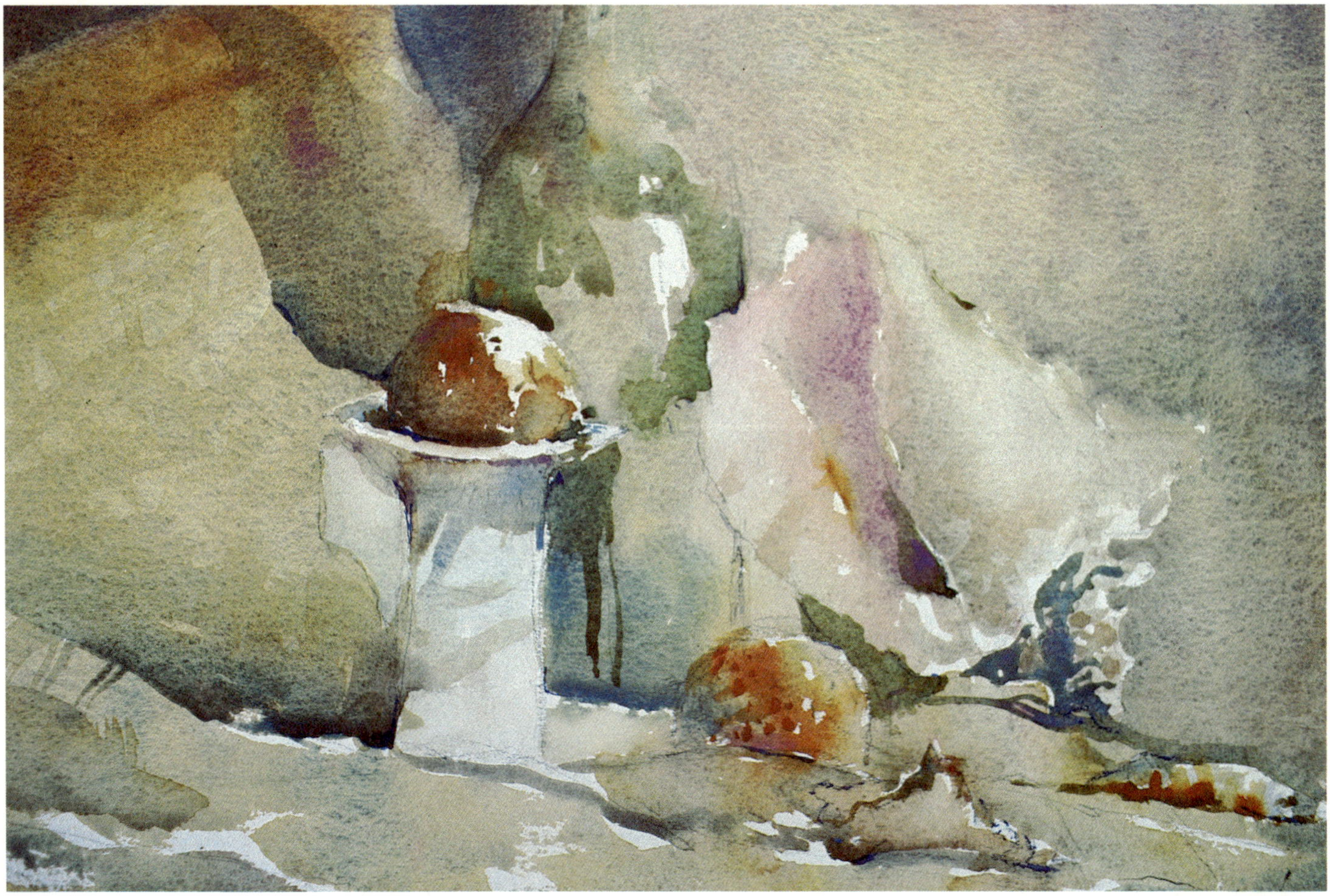

Creating a Geometric Understructure. In these three compositions from the same painting, artist David Millard was determining his emotional response to the setup and deciding how he wanted to emotionally affect the viewer, too. The top illustration shows Mr. Millard's actual painting. Triangular structures form its foundation: A triangle within a triangle within a triangle, so to speak, gives a rhythm to this composition. This is a classical arrangement, with the objects moved back from the edge of the table.

Studying the Finished Painting. Would you crop the painting to this format at right? It definitely has a different feeling. Do you think this "dropped-down" composition creates more excitement?

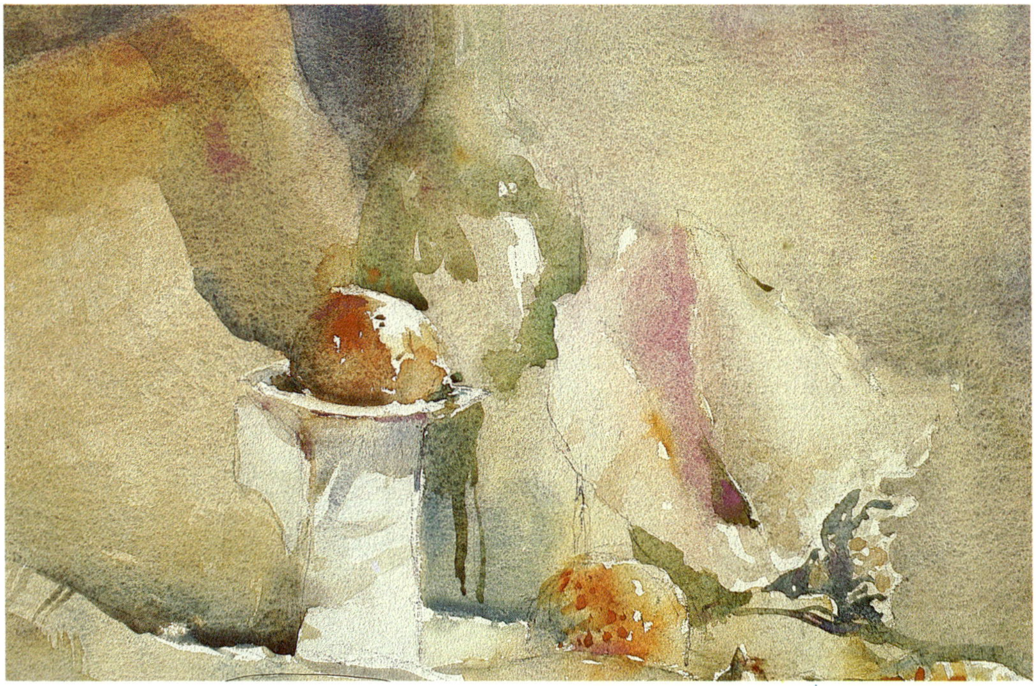

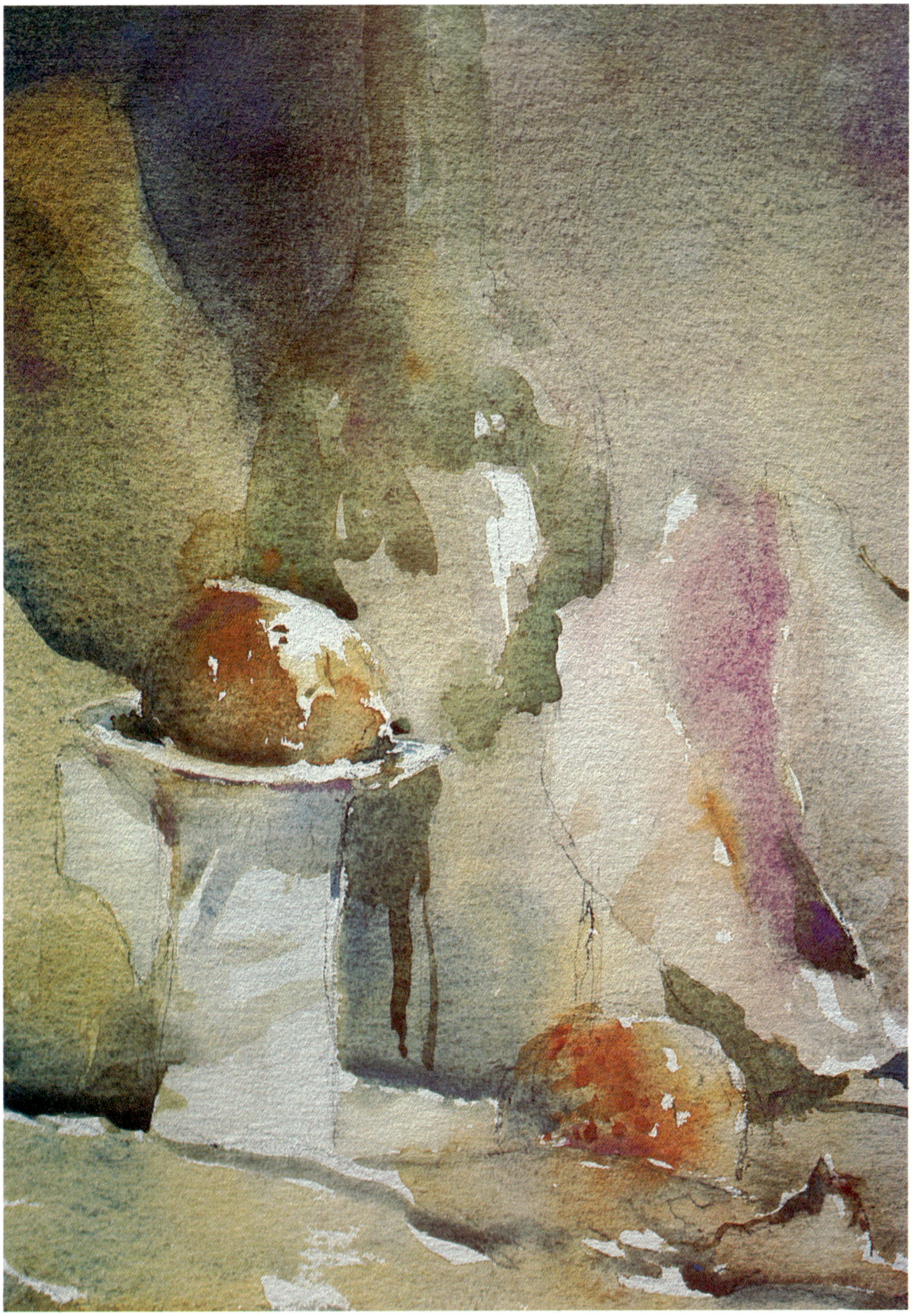

Getting Close. This close to the setup, your viewer participates in your painting in a personal way, detecting techniques, noting that the background wash goes over everything except the selected whites, seeing soft and hard edges and color dropped in wet-in-wet. Look at the way accents are "biting in"—above and below the orange, beside the vase. Note that there are grainy deposits. This format allows the viewer to focus on complementary colors. The design here is quite evident. Do you like a painting that is this intimate?

Composing with Geometric Shapes

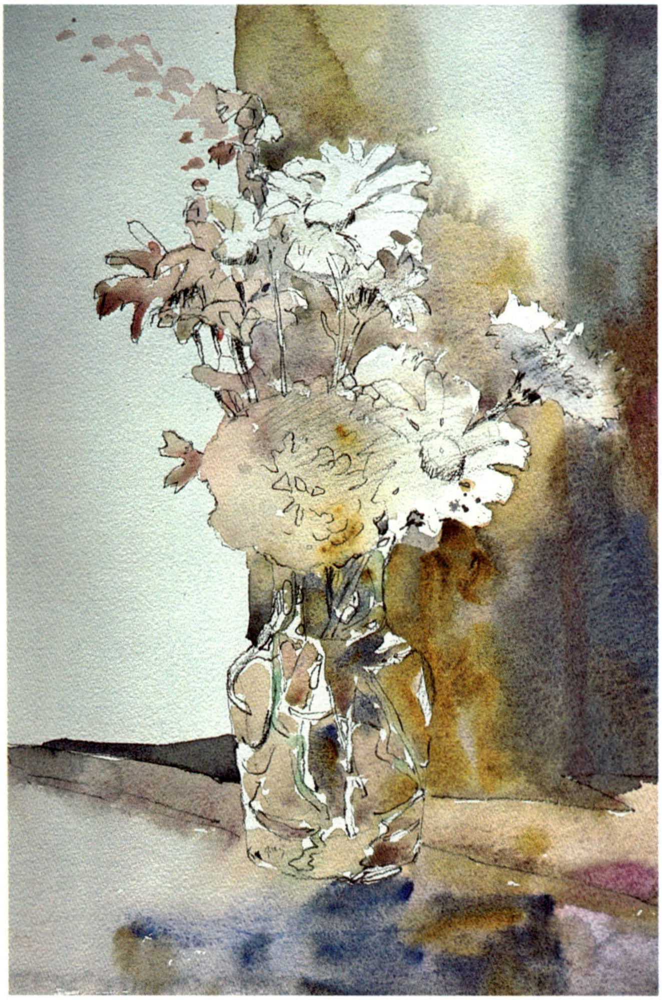

Triangles. You can create an excitement with shapes, just as you can with brilliant colors. These ordinary wildflowers in a common glass jar have been depicted with understated color, in keeping with their simplicity. But this simple floral is dramatic because of the triangles and diagonals: The main group of flowers forms a major rectangle, the white panel at the top left is a major triangle, and there are several small "supporting" triangles. This "invisible structure" allowed the artist to cut loose with a zingy, free wash.

As you arrange flowers for your own still life, think out your composition of accents and angles first. Don't get too stiff or "organized." Be subtle. Only *you* should know where these geometric shapes occur. Take the time to move or rotate the vase, looking at it from all angles with an eye to selecting the best "pose." Also think about where you want to place the white shapes—and plan light direction before you put in the first wash.

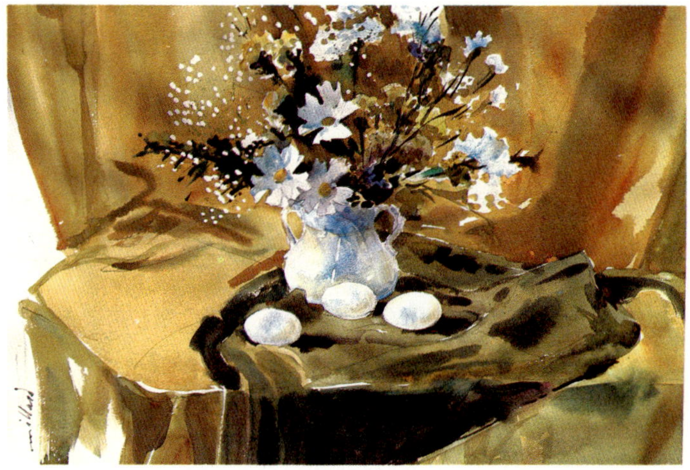

Circles. This floral still life is moving into color but has a limited palette—just browns, blues, and greens. The composition uses a series of circular shapes: The entire bouquet is a circle, as are the centers and rims of the flowers, the pitcher, the pitcher's handle, the eggs, and the dots for the baby's breath. (Here the artist felt it was desirable to block out these tiny areas with masking fluid before applying the varied wet-in-wet wash behind the dots.)

Although this floral is set on a square bridge table, Mr. Millard created more visual excitement by changing the square to a triangular wedge for the top. This in turn encouraged his mind's eye to "see" or invent other wedges or triangles and weave them into the composition along with the circular shapes.

There is a considerable amount of visual motion created by the S-sweep of the backdrop cloth, which moves the eye across the tabletop and down toward the base. This gives a definite feeling that "space" exists behind and around the flowers. The various triangles (indicated in the diagram) serve to give contrast to all of the circles, as well as to direct the eye. The white shape on the left-hand side, where light seems to be entering, was an intuitive choice on the part of the artist. The composition might have worked equally well without it.

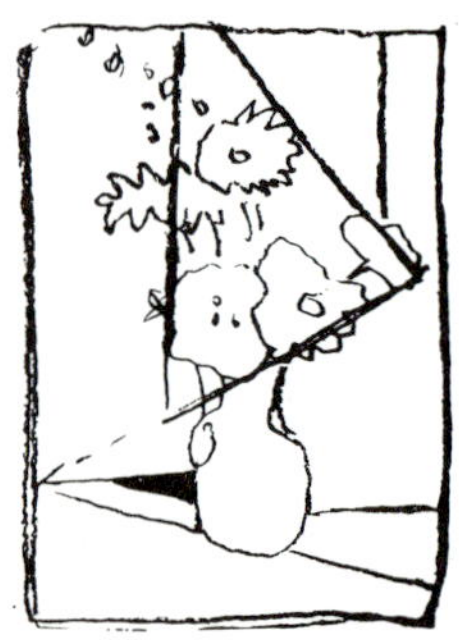

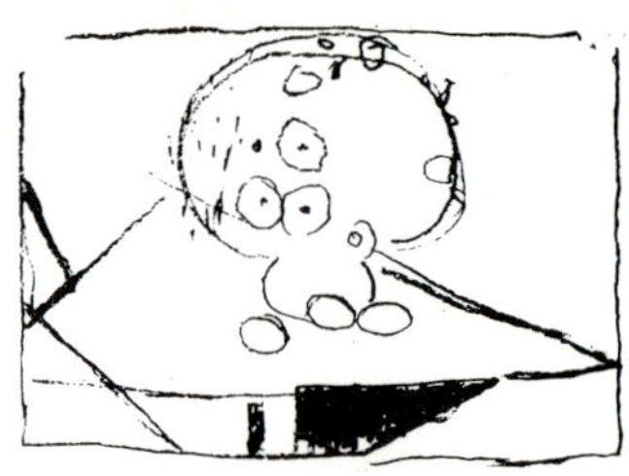

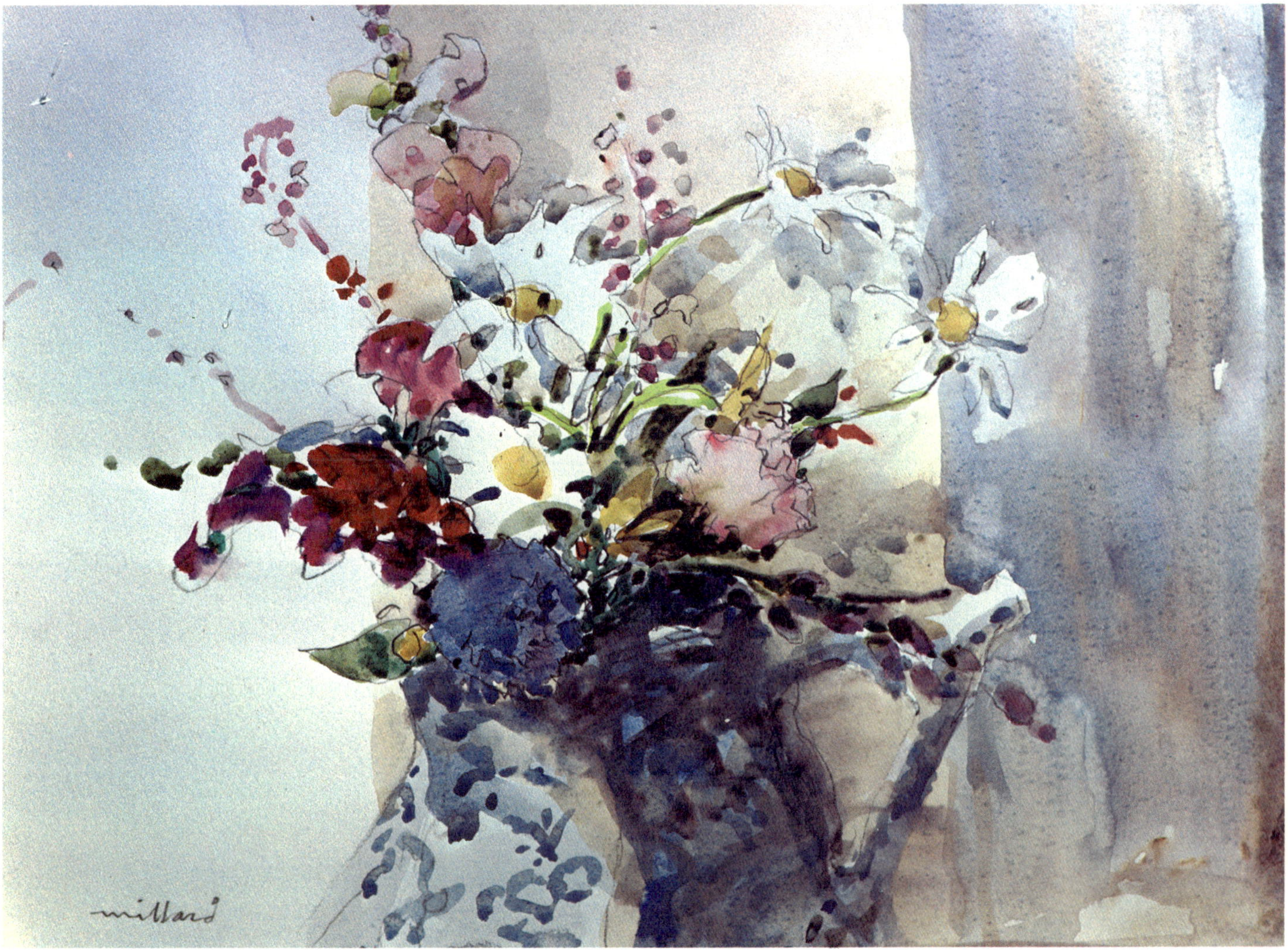

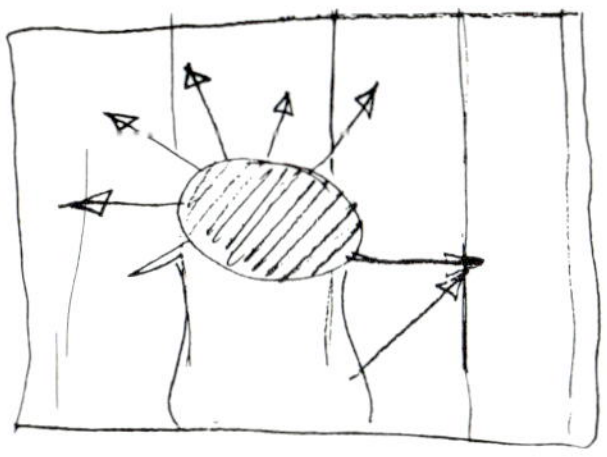

Radiating "Spokes." This floral painting is moving into even more color, with small areas of pinks, reds, yellow, and green in the blossoms. They present a loose appearance and may seem haphazard or straggly at first glance, but in fact you can see that they are quite controlled when you study the underlying geometry. As shown in the diagram, the rich blue tones on the pitcher serve as a dark central core from which color is discharged outward in various directions, like the spokes of a wagon wheel. Even the handle of the pitcher seems to duplicate this radiation of the colored blossoms.

The asymmetrical splay of flowers is complemented and steadied by the three rectangular panels of the background, which, in turn, are graded in tonal value from light on the left to darkest on the right side. This indicates the direction or source of illumination.

The graded tones of the rectangle present a strong contrast to the delicate flowers—not by strength of color, but by the difference in shape. Remember, you can compose with shapes not only *within* the florals but also, at the same time, with the shapes *surrounding* the subject. Composing with shapes need not be a constant discipline in the use of geometrics, but it should make you more aware of shapes when you paint still lifes. Always be on the lookout for any visual device that will make your painting better and thereby make you a better artist.

Composing with Panels and Bands

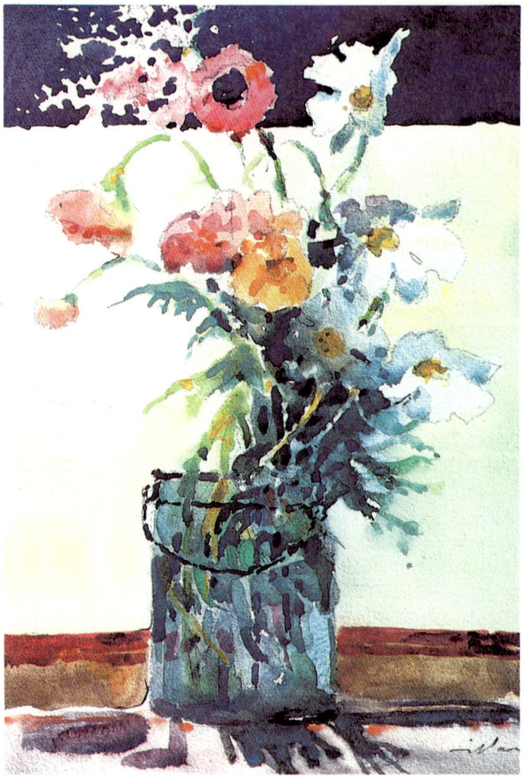

Horizontal Bands. The artist liked the way the brilliantly colored blossoms, with their "bloopy" stems, were grouped on one side of this bouquet, with the four white daisies on the other. This made an unusual vertical division of color. He also liked the "lazy S" shape formed by the flowers. Against this combination, it seemed natural to use horizontal bands at the base—where the wired bottle sat on a multicolored shelf of browns, red, and lavenders—and at the top, where it seemed most appropriate to contrast midnight blue against the yellow panel.

The blue band was painted in *after* the floral was completed. The artist worked this color around the white daisy and then around the imaginary small floral shapes and the red and pink flowers, to make very interesting negative design shapes.

When you do an exercise like this yourself, Mr. Millard suggests following the same order. Do the floral first and complete the painting without the strong horizontal band. Then live with the painting propped up where you can see it for a week. After that you can brush in the band if you still think the painting needs it. Make the color very deep and rich, and paint it in a single wash. The reason for looking at the panel for a week, and then adding the panel, is so that you can develop some emotional response to what is happening in your composition. You will see a great deal of difference between the two versions—in the amount of impact or softness.

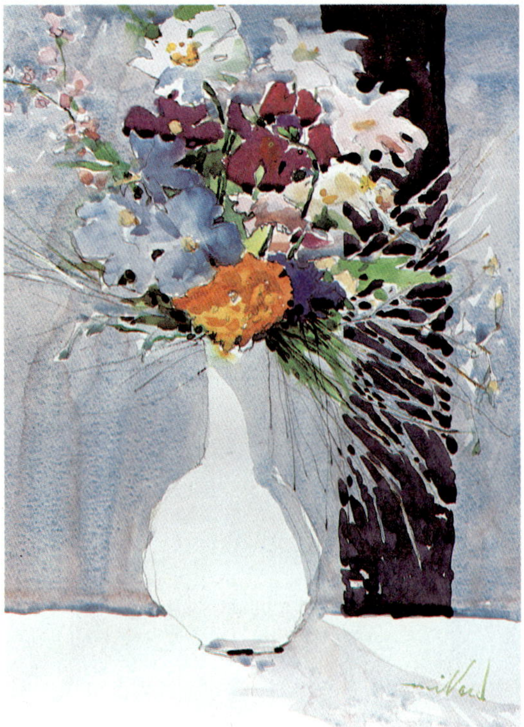

Vertical Band. You can't always just paint what you plop into a jar. This cluster of daisies, cosmos, a marigold, and a bachelor's button was set into a long-necked white vase resting on a brown table. Artist David Millard felt the still life needed more enthusiasm, and so he used his imagination to help raise his watercolor painting from the ordinary. He finds that still lifes are easy to shift around and recompose, and he advises taking inspiration from the great French pastel artist Odilon Redon, who was good with color and composition and was also not above inventing blossoms that existed only in his mind's eye. And that's what is going on here: The top two daisies start white, where they are in the light, and then turn pale blue. The next several daisies below it become pink and the next several to the left, a stronger blue. These colors were invented by the artist. He also invented the needlelike sprigs fanning out from the top of the vase. These pine needles were not painted in the first session, but were added later after the artist thought the painting was finished. The white table was invented.

When the flowers were completed in the first session, Mr. Millard set the sketch aside for a couple of weeks, studying it from time to time. Then he decided to try a vertical panel to give the flowers some punch; they seemed too weak. He decided to try painting in some "fake" pine "needles," the panel "behind" the edge of the flowers, and several dozen negative shapes to see what happened. And it worked!

Two-Color Vertical Band. *Pink Tigers and Rose* is a full-sheet watercolor which the artist painted in the studio from several sketchbook studies. He made each sketch from the same large bouquet, which he turned to achieve several different "profiles." As the vase was rotated, the arrangement of flowers appeared to change. When you paint floral still lifes, it is a good idea to make this "rotating" a standard practice.

When this particular painting was completed, Mr. Millard placed it where he could study it daily. It looked all right to him, but he wanted to wait and watch it for a while. Often, after you have just finished a painting and put down the brush, your own judgment is "off." You have just had such an exciting time—pushing the paint around, delighting in solving the problems at hand, and putting together a great batch of colors that look right and feel right. And your vision may be "colored" by these happy feelings. If you want an opinion of your painting, don't ask a dear friend. Prop it up and keep it "in limbo" and study it, as Mr. Millard did. What do *you* think? You are the one to decide.

Mr. Millard's painting sat for about three months, and he looked at it periodically between painting trips and at odd moments. Then one morning he decided to try placing a panel behind the flowers to create a myriad of negative shapes, threading them vertically through the shadowed flowers on the left-hand side and including a portion of the vase.

He selected a panel with an Oriental brocade of deepest blue-purple with a faded rose-colored border. The strong verticals gave the painting a good deal of authority, a sense of importance that it had not possessed on the first attempt.

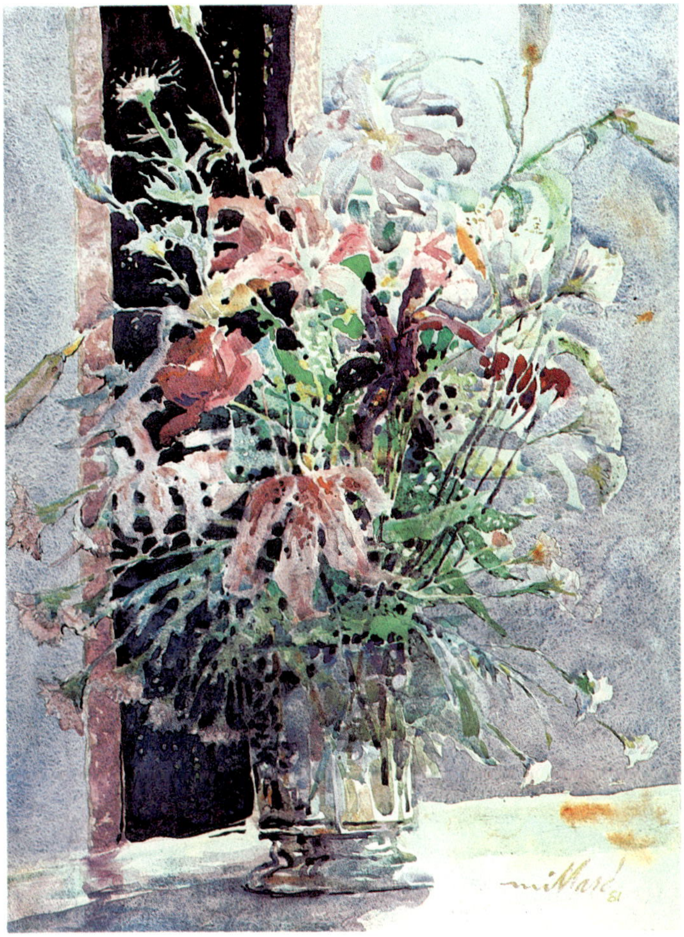

Three Panels. These three panels, themselves quiet in color, support a multicolor riot. They also divide the background into three vertical pieces. The left-hand panel is a light, warm gray with casual, slim stripes of pale emerald green alternating with light streaks of drybrushed cadmium yellow pale. The center panel is a very light, clear yellow with a hint of a greenish-gray cast. This color unifies the variegated colors of all the flowers and stems. The right-hand panel is a combined wash of lavender, pink, and blue. The narrow borders at the left, right, and base are brushed-on variations of gray, green, and yellow.

The artist based his composition on an X format, with the deep colors of the burgundies and red-purples at the extremities. These darker colors—and their shapes—tend to push the eye back into the center, almost like arrows.

The bouquet itself is a kaleidoscope of carefully related colors. There are light, middle, and deep hues of yellows, yellow-oranges, oranges, orange-reds, blue-reds, pinks, and lavenders above the vase—and below, an equally complex and pleasant relationship of more than a dozen green mixtures and nearly as many blue combinations. (The white is the paper itself.) In pulling together such a complex set of relationships, the artist's very best thinking was called for.

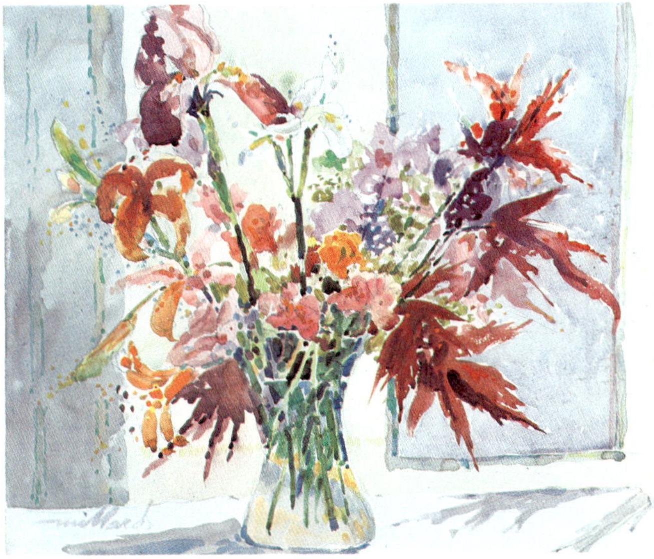

Composing with Color

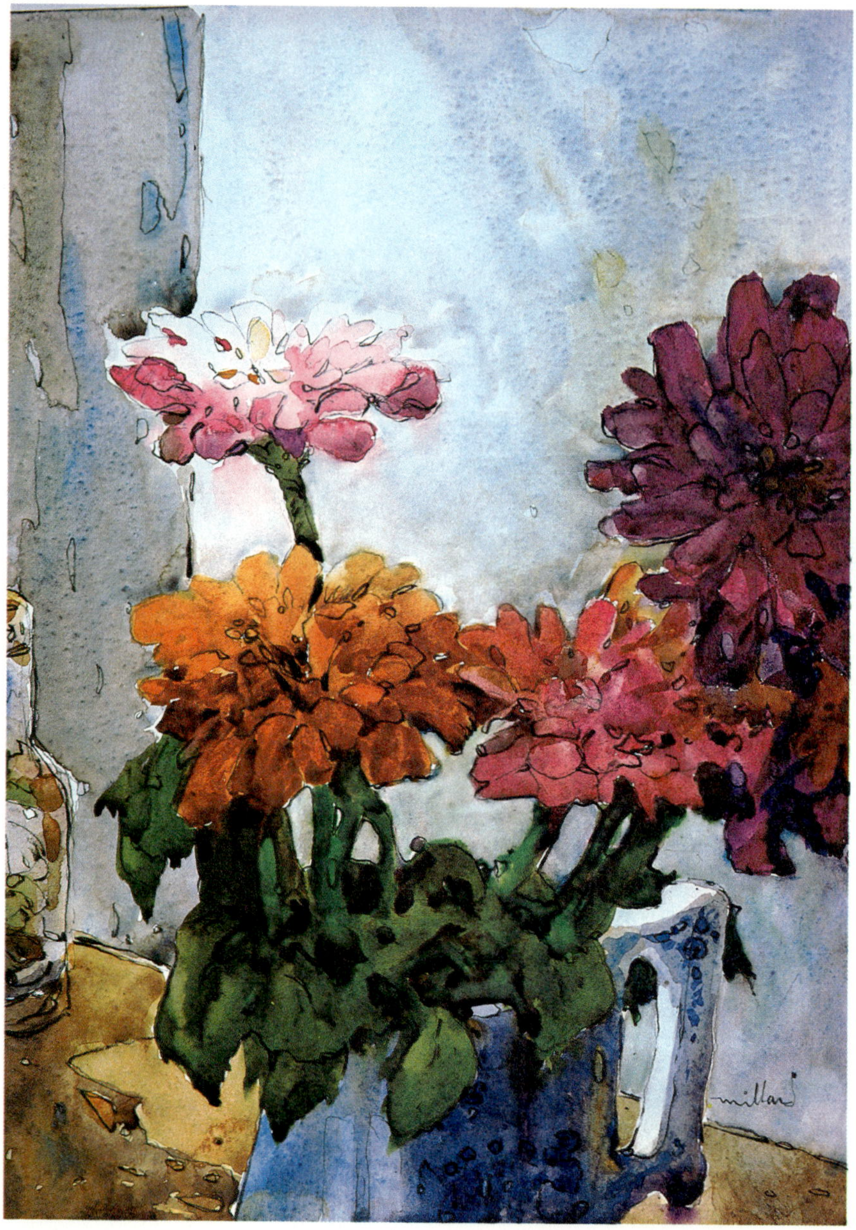

Color and Light. This arrangement of brilliant summer zinnias is all about color relationships: orange next to pink next to fuchsia, moving around the color wheel, with each color influencing the color next to it—which is why the fuchsia zinna contains some orange petals. The famous colorist Josef Albers spent a lifetime playing one color against another, as did Bonnard and the Impressionists.

When Mr. Millard painted these zinnias arranged in an old white earthenware pitcher, they were sitting on a broad windowsill. They were far enough away from the glass so that when the artist focused his eyes on the flowers, the background "went out of focus" and became just a light gray setting. The brightest light was hitting the very top of the pink zinnia, and so he left the white paper and began increasing the depth of color toward the outer petals. He observed that the stem was dark between this pink and the orange of the next blossom, where he darkened the orange into burnt sienna. By the time he had crossed this orange zinnia, it had actually run into four or five petals at the top of the fuchsia zinnia.

The artist created an arc of brilliant color curving upward into the two deep burgundy zinnias on the right. Since these were as high as the first pink flower, there had to be a narrow concentration of light on the first zinnia in order for him to achieve so dark a color on the right.

He achieved the rich green with a heavily pigmented wash of sap green plus burnt sienna. This area duplicates the upper arc and moves the eye toward the light striking the handle of the pitcher. This path of light was made on the leaves and stems by swabbing or lifting off some spots with a damp brush.

When you arrange a floral still life for painting, Mr. Millard suggests cutting the stems to different lengths. Don't make them all the same. Lay the blossoms out flat on a white tablecloth and shift them around, creating color designs and relationships—*then* cut the stems to fit your ideas and put them in the vase. Arrange the stems for good negative shapes, too.

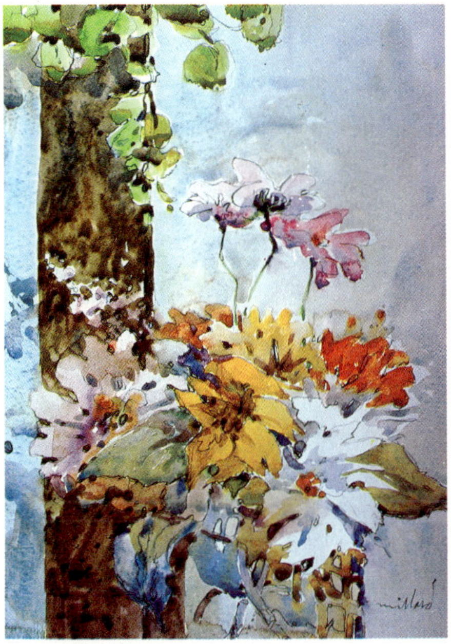

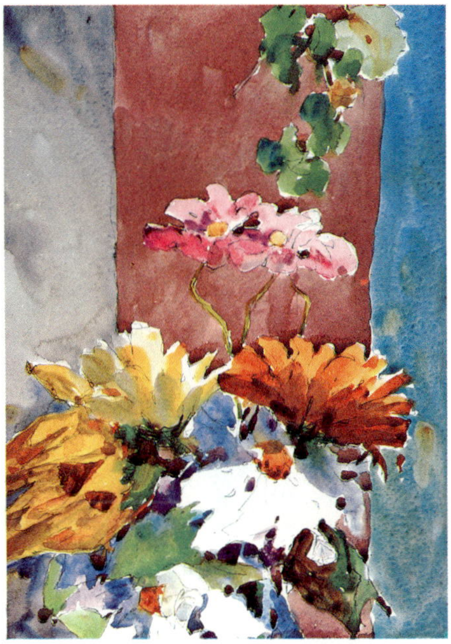

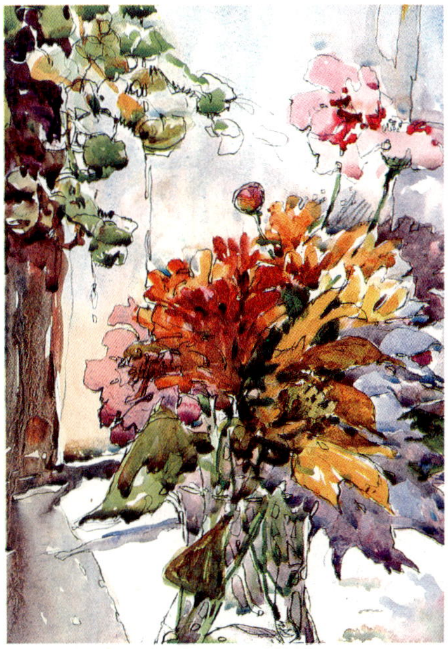

Soft Color Relationships. Often, an artist can get better acquainted with a problem by doing several variations on a theme. This painting is the first of three different compositions that express the delicacy of a few fragile, pale pink cosmos blossoms. Mr. Millard has also decided to dangle some Swedish ivy above them to imply more at the top of the picture than the eye sees. These round green ivy shapes are very compatible with the awkward stems of the cosmos.

The artist decided that there would be certain factors common to all three compositions: 1) The pink cosmos and their awkward stems would be aloof from the rest of the bouquet. 2) Each painting would present the flowers with a very different composition and color treatment. 3) A color panel would be used to establish a hard, linear contrast with the delicate asymmetrical patterns of the different flowers.

Here the artist moved in on the flowers and lopped off the bottom of the vase. The painting has a rather cool quality, with a light, simple background setting the stage for the delicate flowers. The flowers cast a blue-gray shadow on the wall. Note the carefully drawn negative shapes of the stems, and the smaller negatives within the vase and flowers.

Strong Color Impact. In the second painting, the artist zoomed in even closer to the floral setup. He also used stronger color, harder edges, and deeper shadows in the flowers. This time, no vase is visible. The central location of the cosmos has also predetermined the position of the panel. Compare this composition with the first one, where the artist based the size and position of the panel on the interstices of the carbon drawing rather than on its actual contours in the setup and no two panel widths are the same. Here, note the powerful negative shapes in the cosmos and white flowers. The pink cosmos have been placed against a panel of an analogous color—a deeper, smoky pink. The edges of the cosmos are hard on top but soft at the bottom. In these paintings, Mr. Millard was not just concerned with color—he was probing, exploring how he could compose with it.

Color and Negative Shapes. In the third painting, the cosmos are very different, both in color and position. This time the negative shapes surrounding the bouquet have been emphasized, and the edges of the flowers are soft on top and hard at the bottom. Complementaries have been stressed with "invented" lavenders around most of the bouquet. The side panel is composed of "self-mixed" browns, which have been mixed from the floral colors. The shadow on the left implies that the vase is sitting on a tabletop. Note the curve that sweeps from the upper right-hand corner, moves down through the greens, and weaves through the flowers to the leaves at the lower left.

Understanding How Space Influences Color

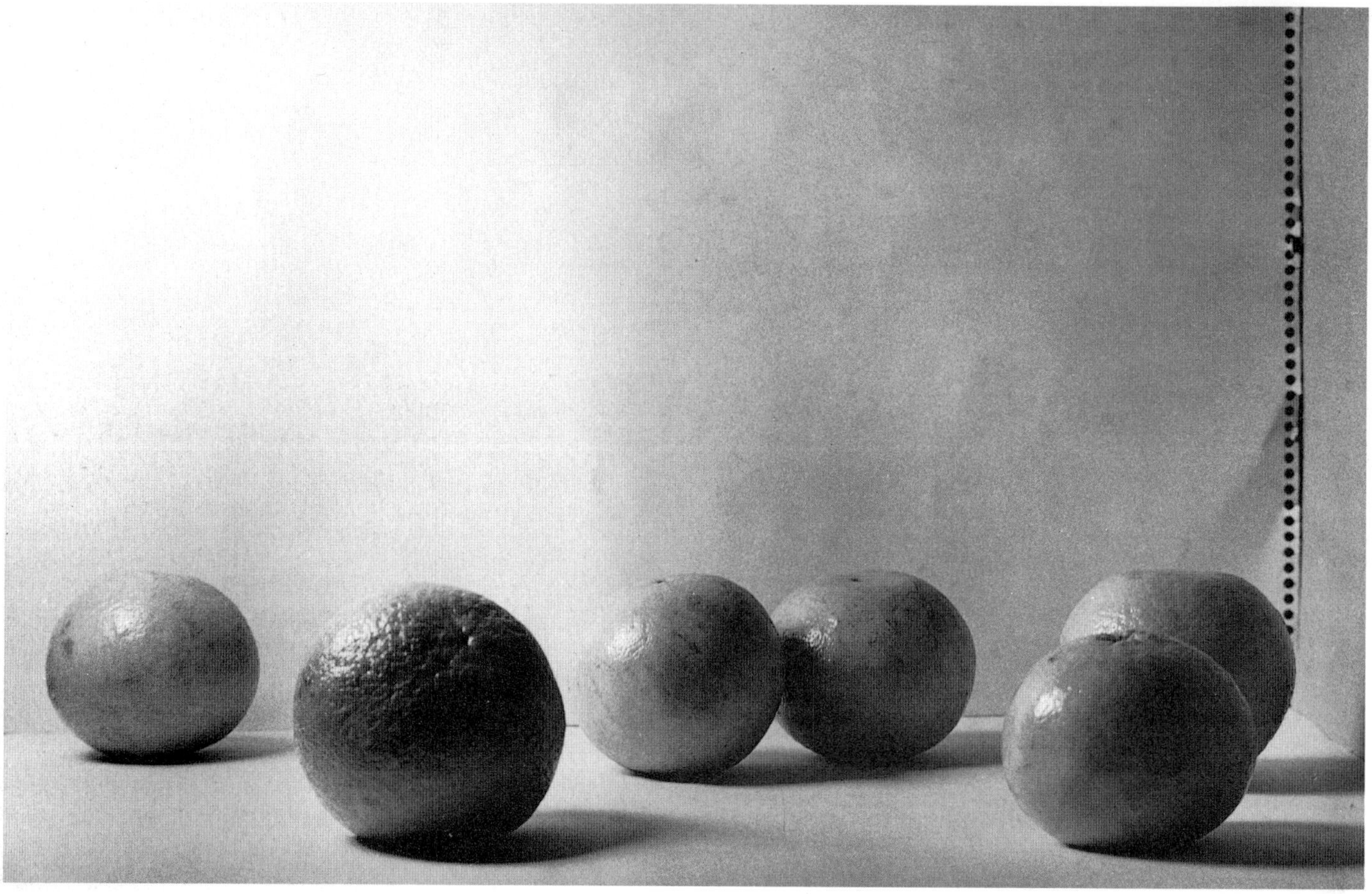

Arranging the Setup. This book includes several of the challenging still life projects Arthur Stern has developed to help his students learn to paint what they really see. The exercise shown here and on pages 22–23 is illustrated with the work of student Alfred Tyrol. As with his other projects included in this book, Mr. Stern cautions that the paintings shown are not intended to be copied; they are to serve only as examples of how your project might look.

To begin this exercise in seeing how spatial relationships affect color, you need to make your own still life setup. Buy a half-dozen oranges that are evenly colored—with no patches of green or yellow—and as alike as possible. Using a large box with the top and two adjacent sides removed, line the floor and left wall of the setup box with white paper, and then line the right wall with pale gray. You should see only the white wall and white floor, not the gray wall. Place a light source at the left, low enough to cast good-sized shadows on the floor of the setup box. As in the photograph, arrange one pair of oranges so that they actually touch, and arrange another pair so that one orange overlaps the other. If some of your oranges do have green or yellow areas, turn them so that those areas face away from you and out of sight. If you prefer not to use a setup box, you can spread your oranges on a white cloth-covered tabletop placed against a white wall instead. Either way, the important thing is to make sure that the oranges aren't surrounded by anything that can influence their color.

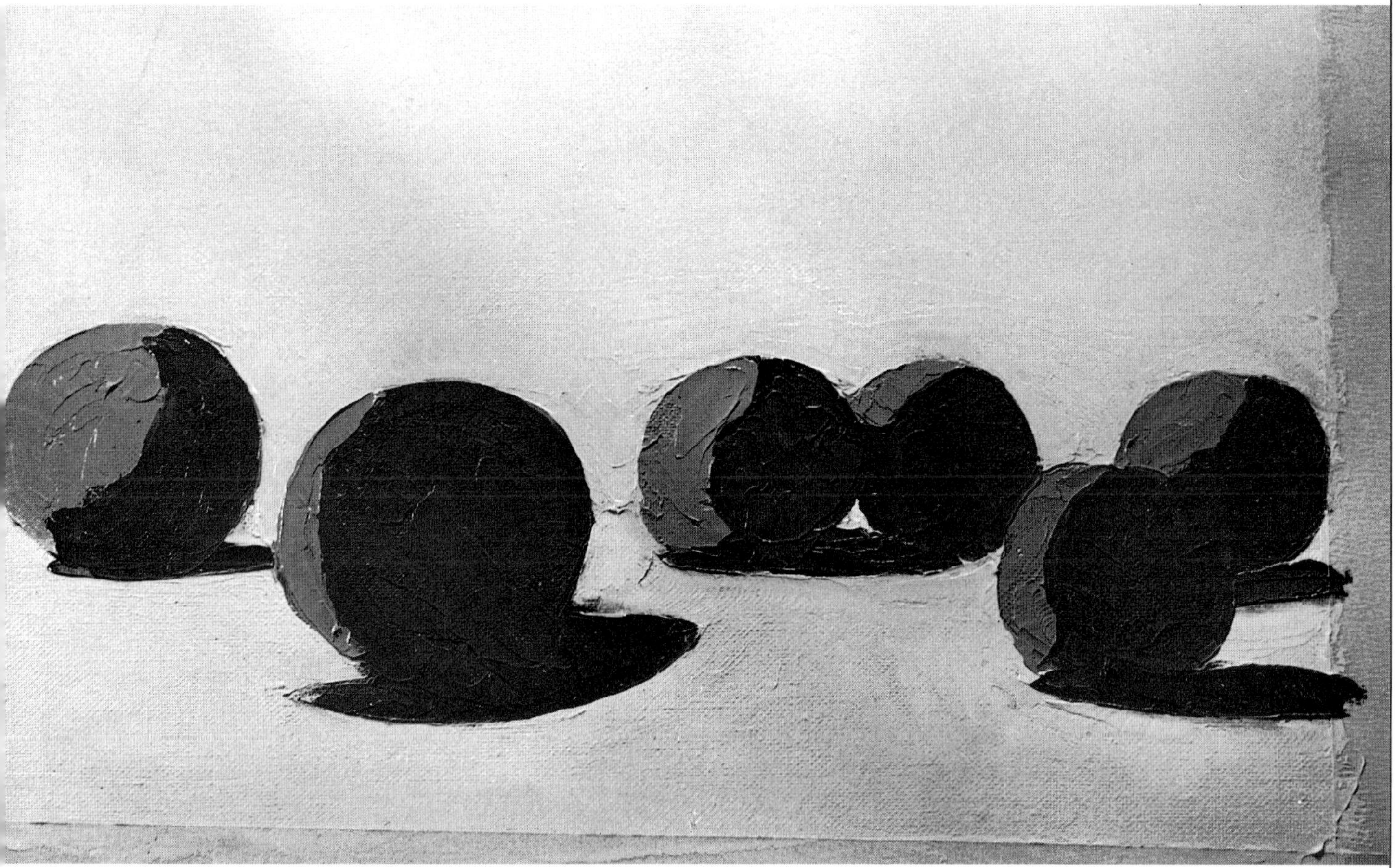

First Statement. This is a fairly spacious composition, and so the student, using oil paint and a palette knife, has worked on a full sheet of canvas paper. He used a 3:4 viewfinder to compose the picture. (A viewfinder is not absolutely necessary, but it is a convenient device to have on hand. You can make your own by using a sharp knife or razor blade to cut a 1½″ × 12″ [38 × 50 mm] window in the center of a 2″ × 16″ [31 × 41 cm] piece of gray or black cardboard. The window will give you a 3:4 proportion.)

This student was able to summarize what he saw in just four colors. First he looked through a spot screen—a small piece of gray cardboard with a hole punched through it—to identify the color of the light side of one of the central oranges. Then he used this color for the light sides of *all* the oranges. In the same way, he used the spot screen to identify the color of the dark side of one central orange, and then he used that color on the shadow sides of all six. The other two colors were the color of the horizontal plane on which the oranges were resting, and the color of the background wall, making a total of four colors the artist laid down: one color for the light sides of the oranges, one for their dark sides and cast shadows, one for the setup floor, and one color for the back wall.

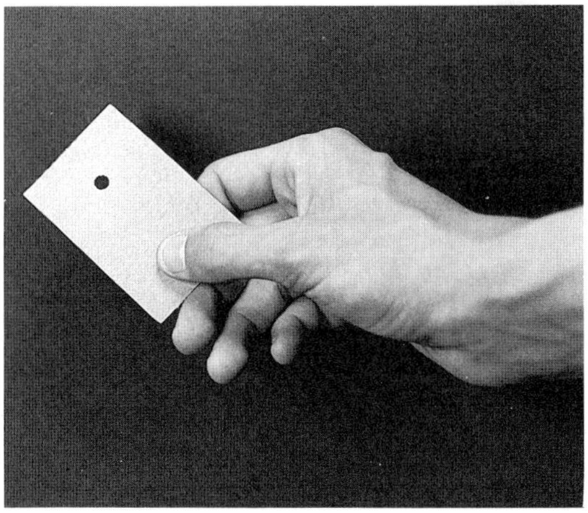

Spot screen.

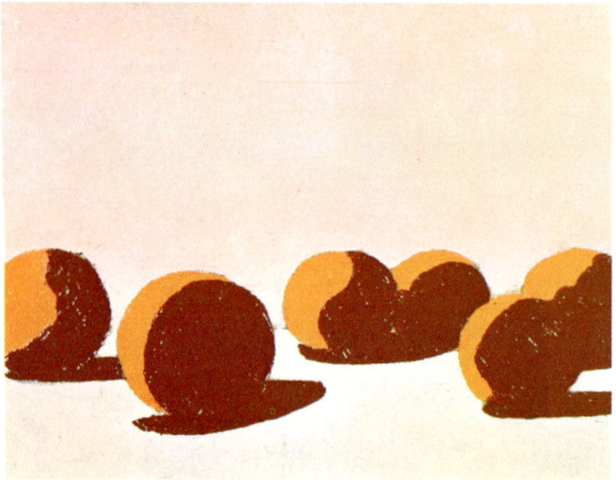

Observations. Using the palette knife to pick up some of the color he had mixed for the light sides of the oranges, the artist looked through the spot screen to compare the color on the knife with the light sides of all six oranges. He was not surprised to discover that all those light sides were different; the color on the knife caught the central orange hue the artist had looked at when he mixed the color. Next he looked at the dark color that he had mixed to paint the shaded sides of the oranges and their cast shadows and he made the same comparisons. The colors of the shaded sides and shadows were all different too. This color matched only the dark side of the *single* orange he had looked at when mixing this dark hue. What accounted for all this variation? It didn't seem to have much to do with the influence of the white wall and floor. The strongest factor seemed to be the distance of the oranges from the light source and from each other. Those closer to the light tended to be lighter, while those farther away were darker. Another factor was the influence of the oranges on one another.

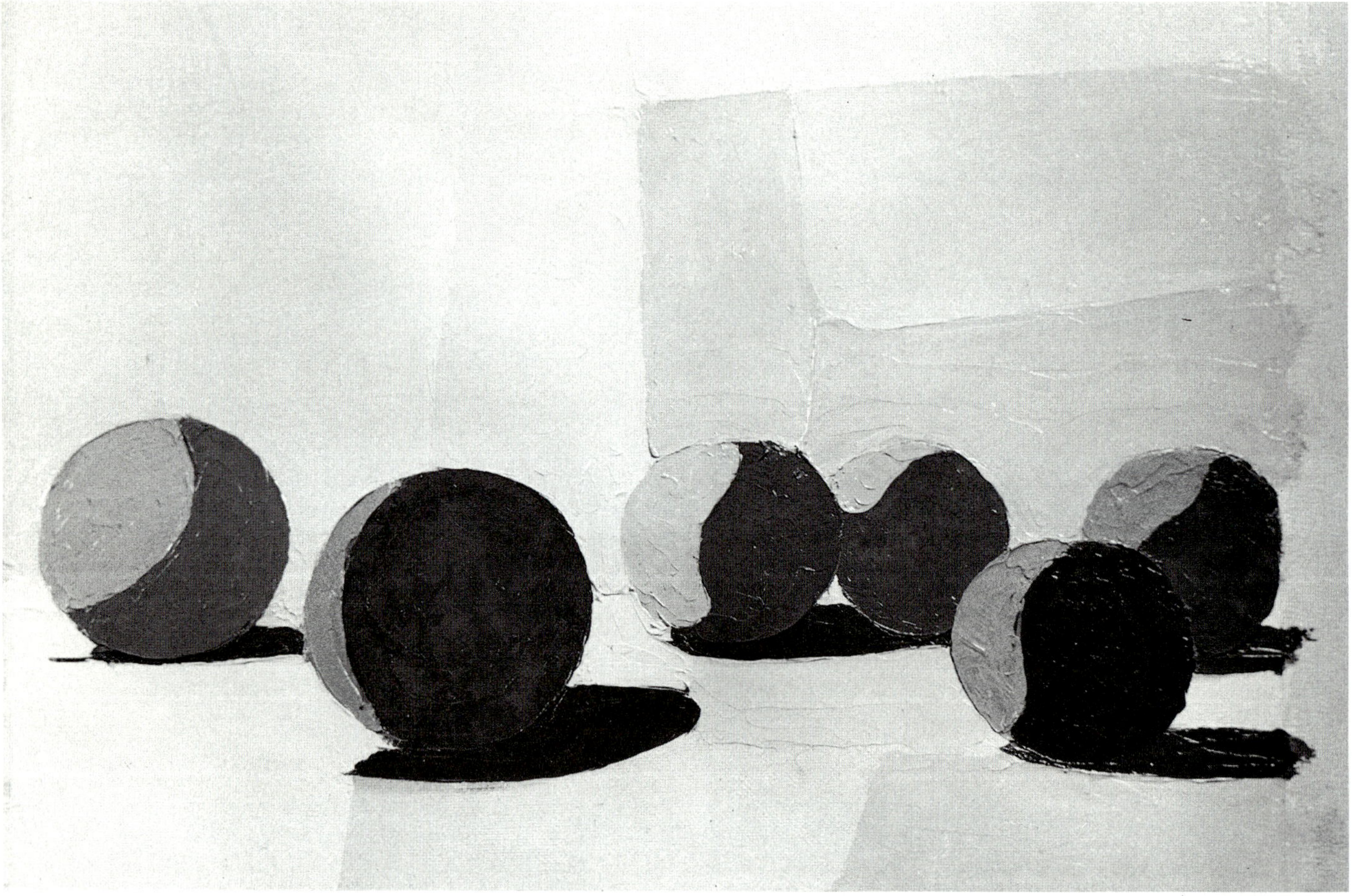

Second Statement. Using what he had learned from his first statement, the student now recorded the color differences more accurately. Although a color photograph of Alfred Tyrol's second statement was unavailable (because he worked directly over this step to obtain his third statement), the color differences he found can be seen easily in this black-and-white photograph. He saw each orange as a unique trio of color spots—light side, dark side, and cast shadow—and gave it some individual character. Now it was obvious to him that even a slight change in the location of any object produces significant changes in hue, luminosity, and intensity within its light side, dark side, and cast shadow. When you paint a still life, you cannot just mix three batches of color and apply them mechanically to all the oranges (or apples or pears) that stand before you.

When you carry your own project forward to a second statement, keep in mind that the light and dark sides of each orange will show themselves to be different from those of the other five. Identify and mix each of these colors with your spot screen. In the first statement, you used the same color to mix the dark side of each orange and its cast shadow on the tabletop; now look for the difference in color between them. Finally, try to separate the supposedly white floor and wall of the setup box into several big color spots that catch the variations in hue, luminosity, and intensity as each plane moves farther away from the source of direct light.

Third Statement, oil, by Alfred Tyrol. Collection of Horace Lilholt.

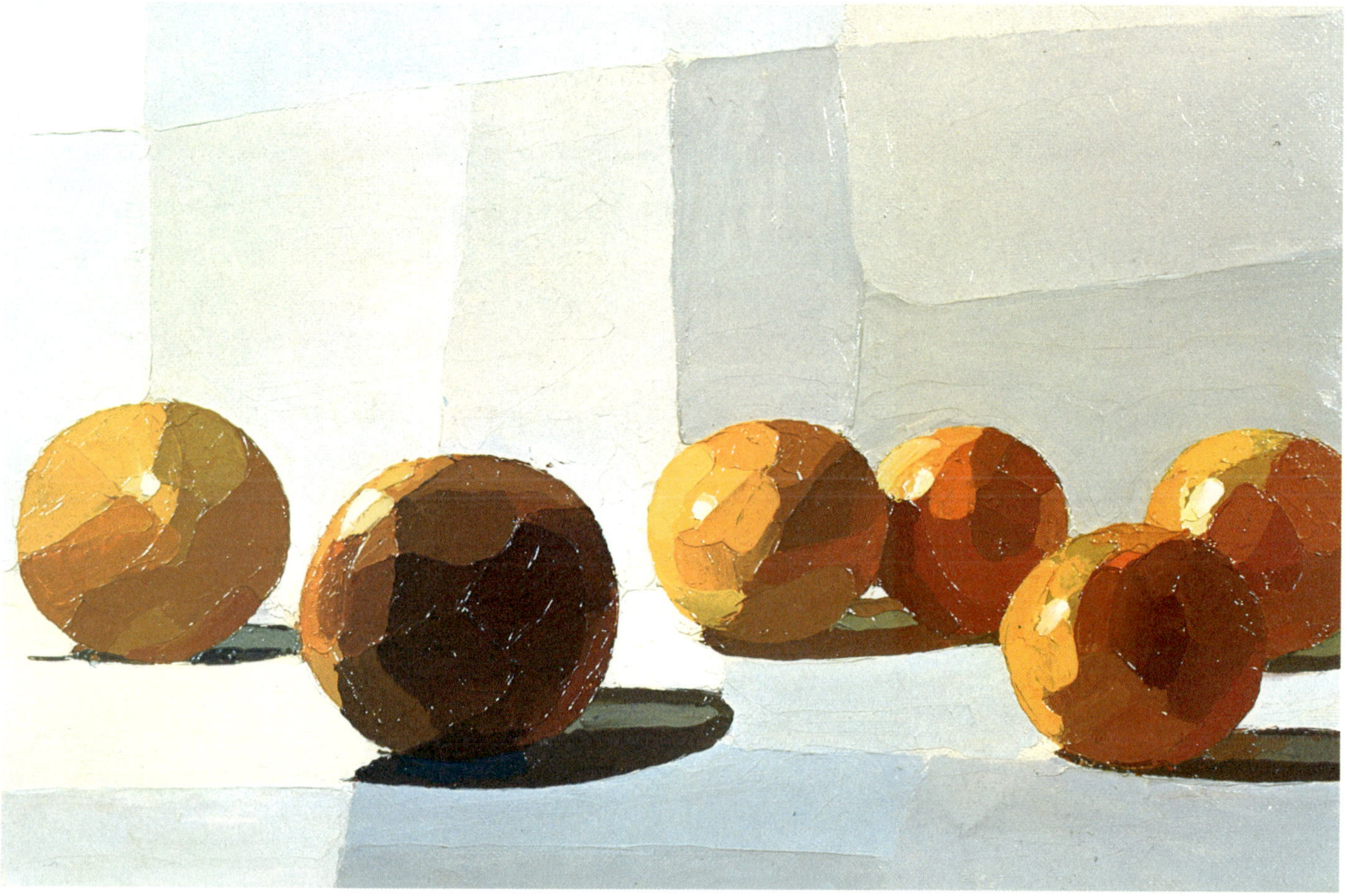

Third Statement. This student still had not done full justice to the richness and complexity of his six models; his second statement was little more than an elaborate first statement. Now he needed to go on to paint a third statement, paying equal attention to the color variations within the lighted sides of the six oranges, the transitional colors that fell between the light and dark sides, and the "lesser lights" reflected in the dark sides and the cast shadows. There can be no predetermined limit to the number of color spots required by such a third statement, but this student has found as many as a dozen different color spots in each of several of the oranges. And there are still more color shots to be found in the wall and floor of the setup box, revealing the subtle gradation of the light.

The function of the third statement is to observe and record *transitional* colors. These are the color spots that fall between the bold, purposely oversimplified color areas identified in the first and second statements. As you paint these transitional colors, you will no longer see too strong a contrast between the light and dark sides of the oranges. Instead, you will see a logical progression of hue, intensity, and luminosity as your eye moves around each form. It's this progression of colors that creates the illusion of three-dimensionality that you begin to see at this stage. In painting your final statement, save the highlights for last. Don't be tempted to paint them pure white, however bright they may look. Like everything else, even each highlight has its own color. Look at each highlight separately and with extreme care, and match its color.

Extra Project. You may wish to try this project again, using a different background color. Pick up the oranges and cover the floor and left wall of the setup box with blue paper, leaving the gray paper on the right wall. Or cover the tabletop with blue, if you are not using a setup box. Then replace the oranges in their same positions, keeping the lamp for your light source where it was, and start again, painting your first, second, and third statements. As you do so, observe how the new background color influences the oranges.

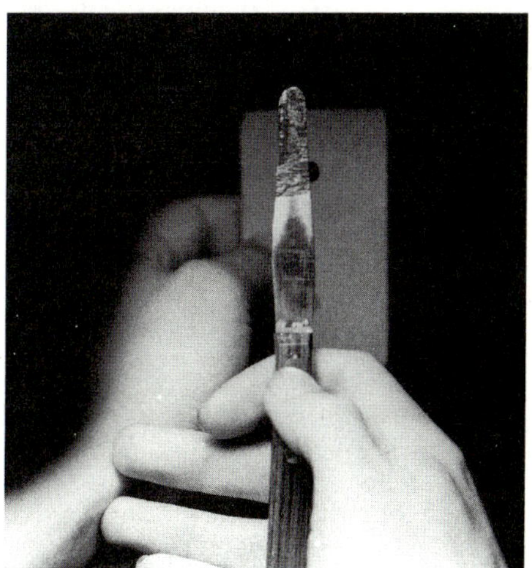

Holding the knife against the spot screen.

Seeing Light and Shade As Colors

Arranging the Setup. The problem that Arthur Stern set up for his students in this project was to paint a series of three statements of a complex white object. A heavy white cloth napkin is ideal for this exercise, if you can find one. (Grandmothers often have them tucked away, or you might try to beg, borrow, or buy one from a restaurant.) Launder and iron the napkin, but don't fold or crease it.

Using a two-sided setup box, line the left wall with red paper, the right wall with blue, and the floor with yellow. The corner of the setup box should be directly in line with your eye; you should see both walls equally. The corner of the box should be in the dead center of your picture, although the napkin will actually cover the line where the walls meet. Pin the center of the napkin at the corner where the left and right walls meet—high enough for the four corners of the napkin to fall just short of the setup-box floor. Allowing some of the underside of the napkin to show, drape the cloth in a few big folds. Arrange a lamp above the napkin, just enough to one side to create areas of light and shade on the folds. The lamp should be close enough for the light to fall directly on the walls and floor of the setup box, to form a strong shadow within the napkin's underside, and to fill the corner of the box with shadow.

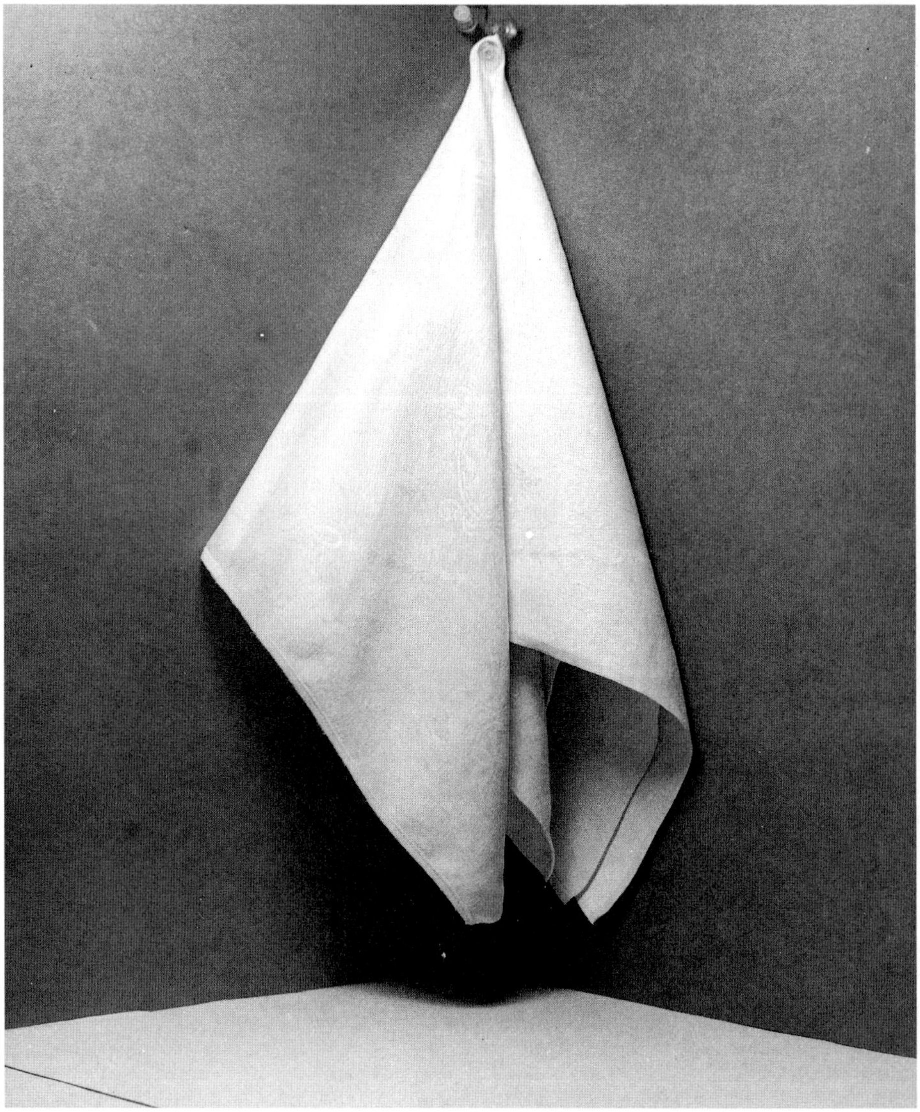

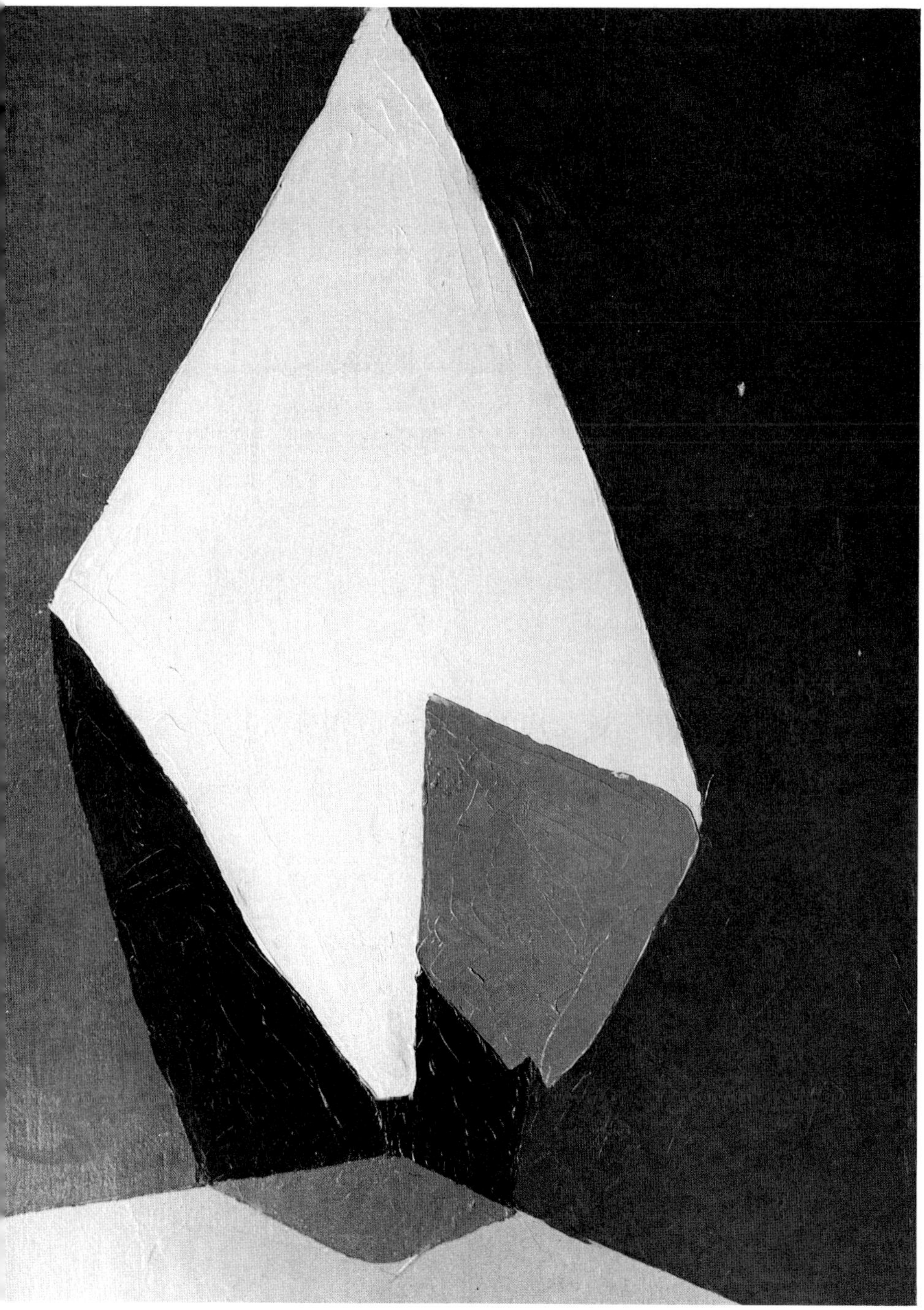

First Statement. For this project, oil painting student Arthur Tyrol used a full sheet of canvas paper, held vertically. He used his 3:4 viewfinder to compose the picture. (You'll find instructions for making a viewfinder on page 21.) As he scanned the napkin with his spot screen, he kept in mind that the purpose of his first statement was to summarize the subject by painting the minimum number of large color spots. As you work from your own setup, don't get caught up in all the small shapes within the shadow area at the bottom of the folded napkin. Try to visualize that area of shadow as a single spot. Ignore the hints of shadow within the large lighted area of the napkin. Paint that big area as a single light color spot. You should be able to summarize the main color areas in eight color spots: two for the walls of the setup box, one for its floor, one for the lighted area of the napkin, one for its dark area, two for the shadows on the walls, and one for the shadow on the floor of the box.

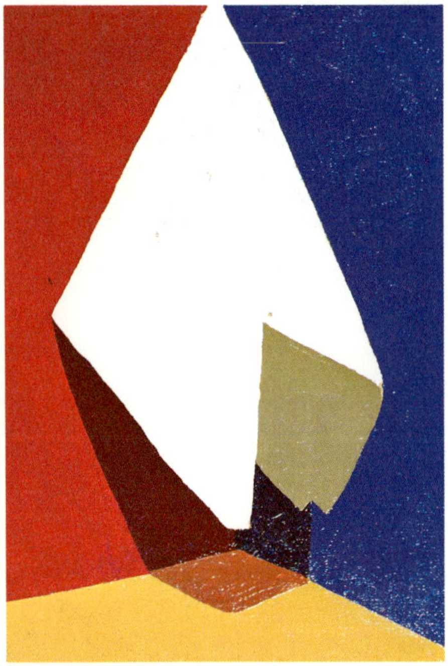

Observations. The first thing this student noticed was that each of the four elements in the setup—the napkin and the three planes of the setup box—divided into two areas: one of light and one of shade. A comparison of each element's light part with its shadow part reveals that light and shade are not simply variations of a single color, but rather two separate colors. You cannot predict that the shadow on the red wall will be a darker red, the shadow on the blue wall a darker blue, the shadow on the yellow floor a darker yellow, or the shaded area of the napkin a "darker" white (whatever that might be). Nor is the napkin likely to be white at all! If you study it through a spot screen (a piece of gray or black cardboard with a hole punched in it), it will appear to be an off-white of some kind—which is really a very light version of one hue or another.

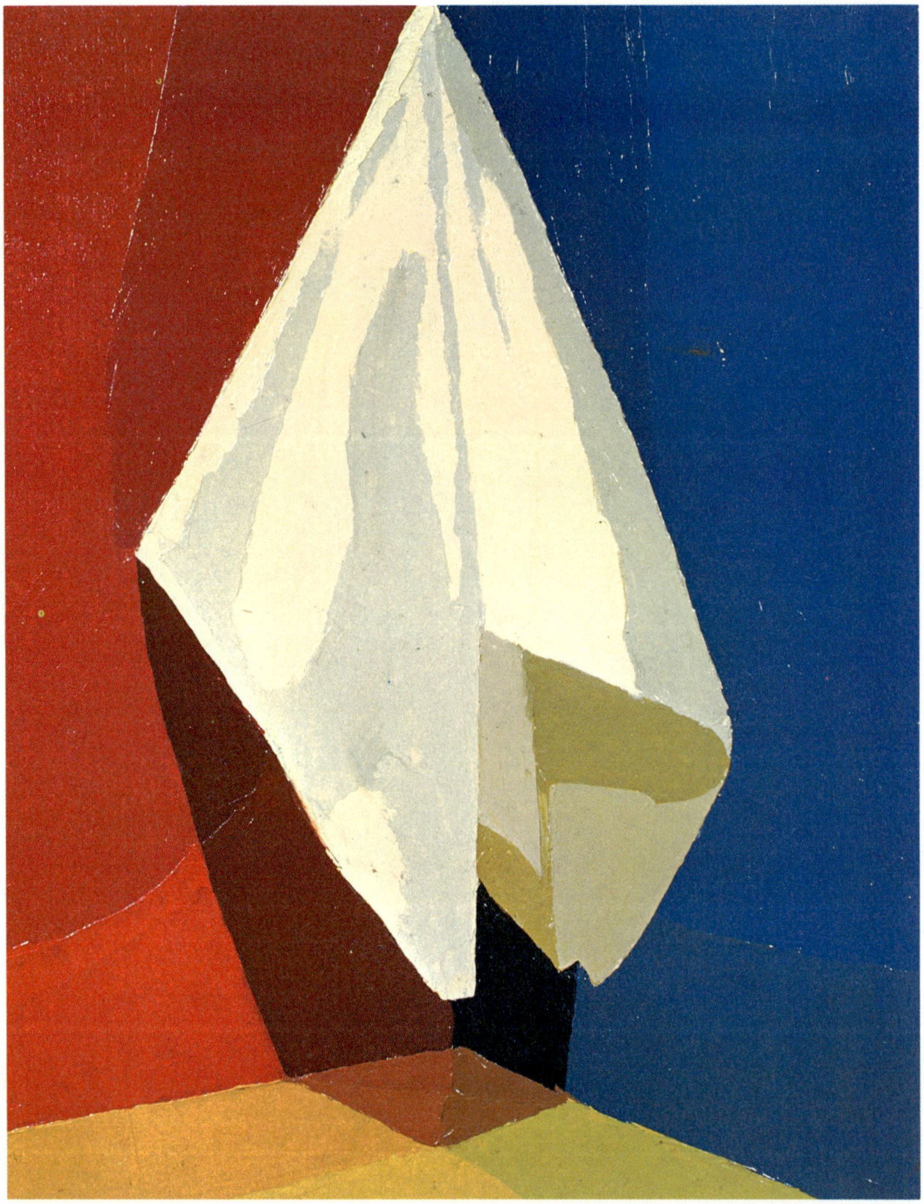

Second Statement. Working on the same sheet of canvas paper, the student moved on to a second statement. Now he began to look for some of the slightly darker areas within the lighted shapes of the napkin, walls, and floor of the setup box. He also began to discover some variations within the small shaded area of the napkin, as well as within the cast shadows on the walls and floor of the box. How many color spots are you going to find when you do your own second statement? It might be about two dozen.

As Mr. Stern's student did, go back and examine your completed second statement. Try to sort out the logic and those various color spots. For example, examine the walls of the setup box and try to identify which color spots are influenced by the adjacent wall, or by the floor, or by both the wall and floor. Other areas are influenced by neither the walls nor the floor but by the direct light. As you go on with other still life projects, you'll begin to be able to predict which color areas will influence one another. But don't try to predict the specific colors. You *must* do this by observation alone.

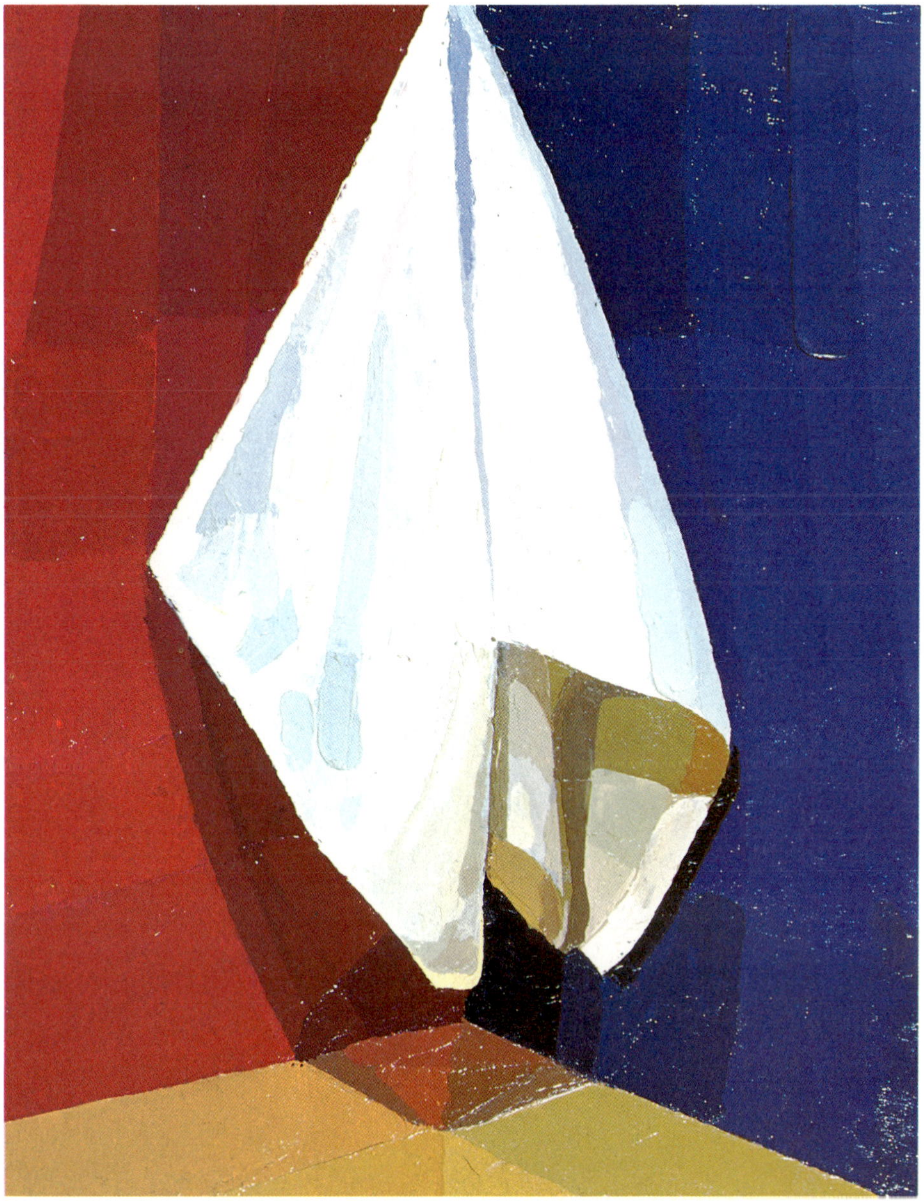

Extra Project. To get further practice in seeing light and shade as colors, try another variation of the napkin setup. This time, take down the white napkin and tack up another piece of cloth that's roughly the same size, but a different color. Keep the lighting and the position of the setup box the same. Paint three statements, revealing how the colors of the setup box influence the new subject, and how its color influences the planes of the box.

Third Statement. You will find, as this student did, that there are still more color spots to be discovered on the walls and floor of the setup box—and, of course, on the napkin—and you'll have to decide how far to take your third and final statement of these three planes. It is fascinating to explore all the very subtle transitional colors within the supposedly white napkin in the third statement shown here. Many of these colors could have been so easily buried under the blanketing effect of the color the student *knew* the napkin to be. He could find them only with the aid of the spot screen. But if these very quiet color spots are observed and recorded correctly, the napkin should look more three-dimensional at this final stage of the project than it did in the first and second statements.

Without consciously attempting to render the pattern of light and shade on the napkin, but by simply recording each color spot you've seen, you should be able to produce a solid and realistic rendering of the soft folds and curving planes of the cloth. This still life exercise should also help you abandon, once and for all, any notion that light and shade are simply lighter and darker versions of a single hue. When light falls on one side of an orange and shade falls on the other, the light side is not just lighter orange, nor is the shade side just darker orange. They are totally different colors.

Using Complementary Color

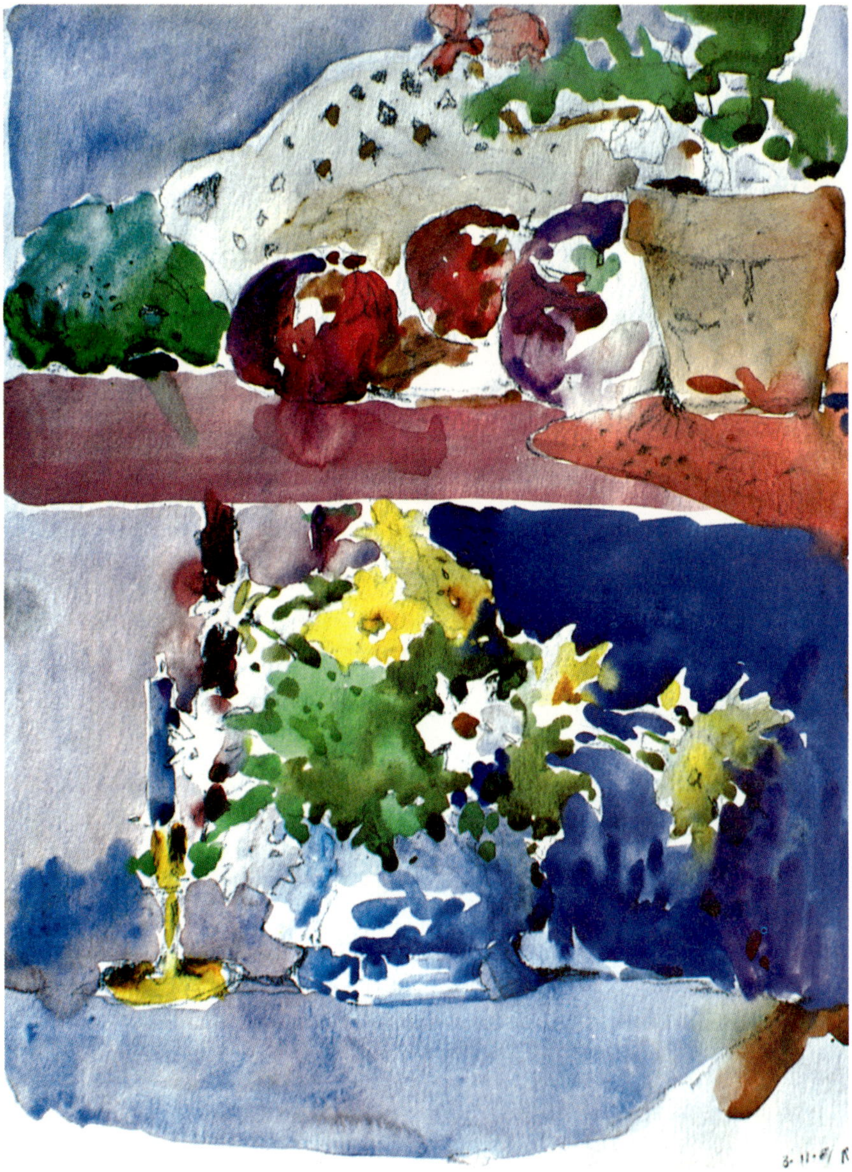

Red and Green. Complementary colors (hues opposite each other on the color wheel) enhance each other, and artist David Millard has done two watercolor sketches using complementaries to create interesting still life compositions. One of the most typical complementary pairs is green and red. In the exercise at the top of this page, the reds range into the red-purples: cadmium red, permanent rose, light red, mauve, and Winsor violet. They follow the arc of the latticed porcelain dish, and they rest on a violet-pink tablecloth. The greens, also following the arc of the dish, range from sap and cobalt greens with a touch of burnt sienna at the top right to sap green and viridian at the base of this upper area of green. The green wash at the lower left starts with cerulean blue and cobalt green and goes into a sap green–viridian combination at the darker bottom, where it nicely complements the pink on which it rests. The blue background was done with a gentle wash of cobalt blue and raw umber, and the tone in the dish is raw sienna with a touch of cobalt violet. This simple still life is made interesting because of the complementary colors.

Orange and Blue/Violet and Yellow. Against a predominantly blue-violet background, the artist has painted the flower centers a complementary orange—cadmium orange with a touch of burnt sienna. The yellow flowers ease into the violet background—another set of complements—and the blue background (ultramarine blue with a touch of ivory black on the left) blends into the shadow color, with a bit of mauve added against the yellow and Davy's gray blossoms. The ultramarine blue also bleeds a bit into the cerulean blue and light red pitcher and tablecloth. Note the gradual transitions within these colors as they move around the color wheel, from purples to red-blues to blue and red mixtures. The tablecloth was wet with clear water and then the artist laid in a weak wash of cobalt violet, wet-in-wet, on the top left of the bouquet. This drizzled down into the tablecloth. Stronger dabs of cobalt violet were placed on the extreme right to balance the bright, deep colors. To integrate the yellow flowers, he added the candlesticks with cadmium orange and burnt sienna. The leaves are cobalt green, and sap greens were put on partially wet-in-wet, with sap green spots worked over a dry base of cobalt green.

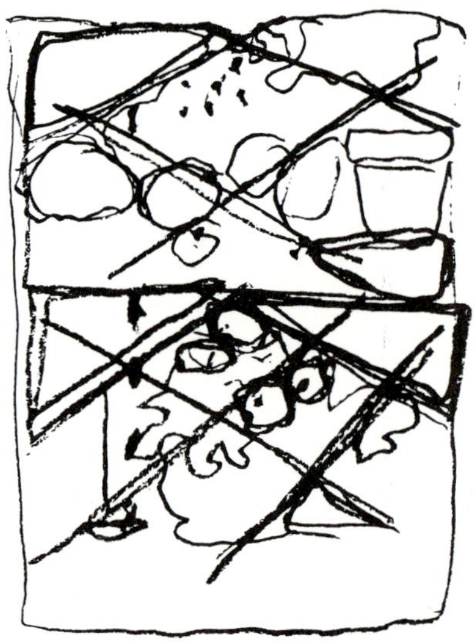

Using Imaginary Color

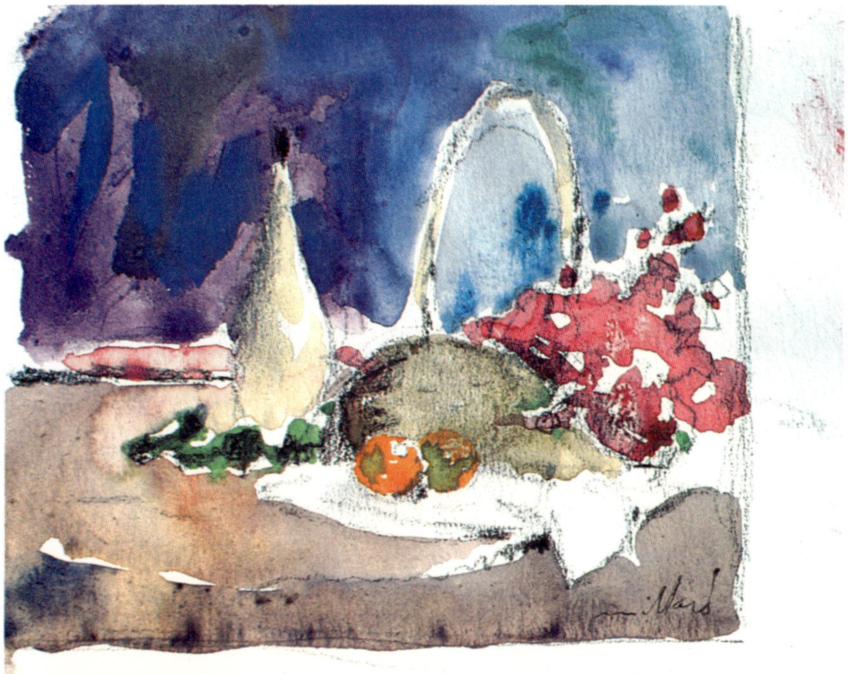

Painting the Setup As It Appears. This simple still life contains just a creamy liqueur bottle, a basket of pink flowers, and an orange. The artist chose an orange instead of an apple in order to get the right color vibrations for his blue background, which was done with a rich blending of washes. Across the upper half of the sketch, starting at the right, he used manganese blue, which moves into cobalt blue, which in turn was blended into ultramarine blue, which was laid over a prior wash of cobalt violet. The tablecloth is a combination of cobalt violet, raw umber, and cadmium orange put on in one fast wash along the upper surface. Where the cloth turns down, he added a little cobalt blue to the first mixture to obtain a soft, shadowy quality.

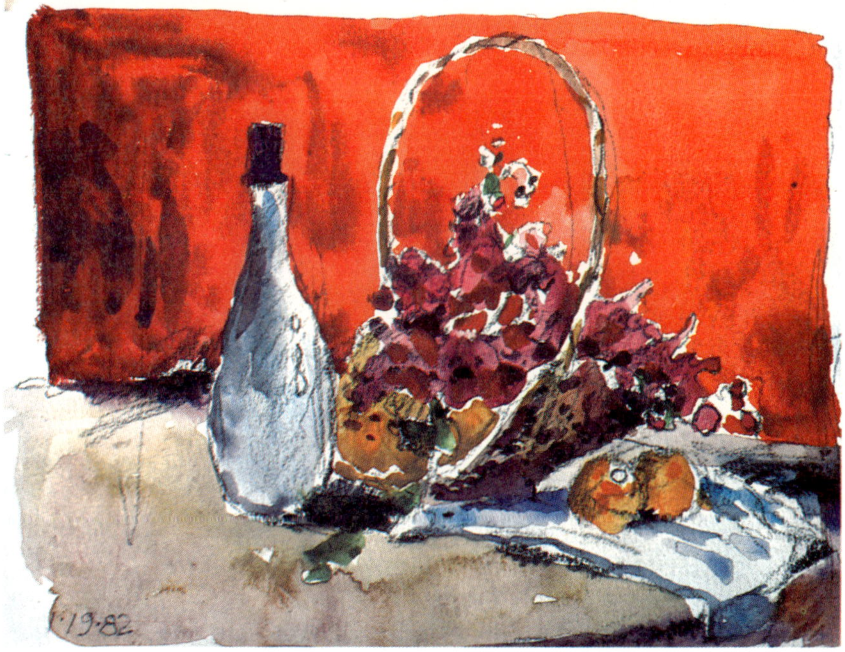

Inventing New Colors. On the lower half of the sketchbook page, the artist shifted gears. In the bottom sketch, he tried a new color combination with the same still life as before. First he redrew the contour lines, this time changing the composition a little with a simple shift in the line of the basket and of the white cloth. This time he painted a series of reds in the background where he had used blue before. Look at what a difference a single change of color makes visually! This is just one of the many inventive color decisions you can make in your own still life painting. The red background, from the left, was mixed with cadmium red deep with alizarin crimson dropped into it wet-into-wet, then cadmium scarlet was added wet-in-wet, then a bit of Chinese orange, and finally, some permanent rose was added at the lower right, above the table.

Mr. Millard also changed the flowers to cobalt violet with some mauve added wet-in-wet; he added more oranges and strengthened their color, and he also deepened the basket color. Notice the cropping of the tabletop and the angle from which the still life is viewed—and the fact that the artist has zoomed in for a closer look.

Using Color and Light

"Pushing" the Light with Receding Darks. You can create moods by the way you light and paint your watercolor florals. Build a platform for your still life models or set up a table or shelf, big and roomy—or a wide board fastened to a windowsill. Then play with light. Try natural light or spotlighted effects within a colored box on a table, like a stage setting—crisp, elegant, bright. In this watercolor by David Millard, the dark "stage wing" on the left (painted with mauve and brown) accepts the purple iris into its shadow, pushing hard on the "spotlighted" white flower.

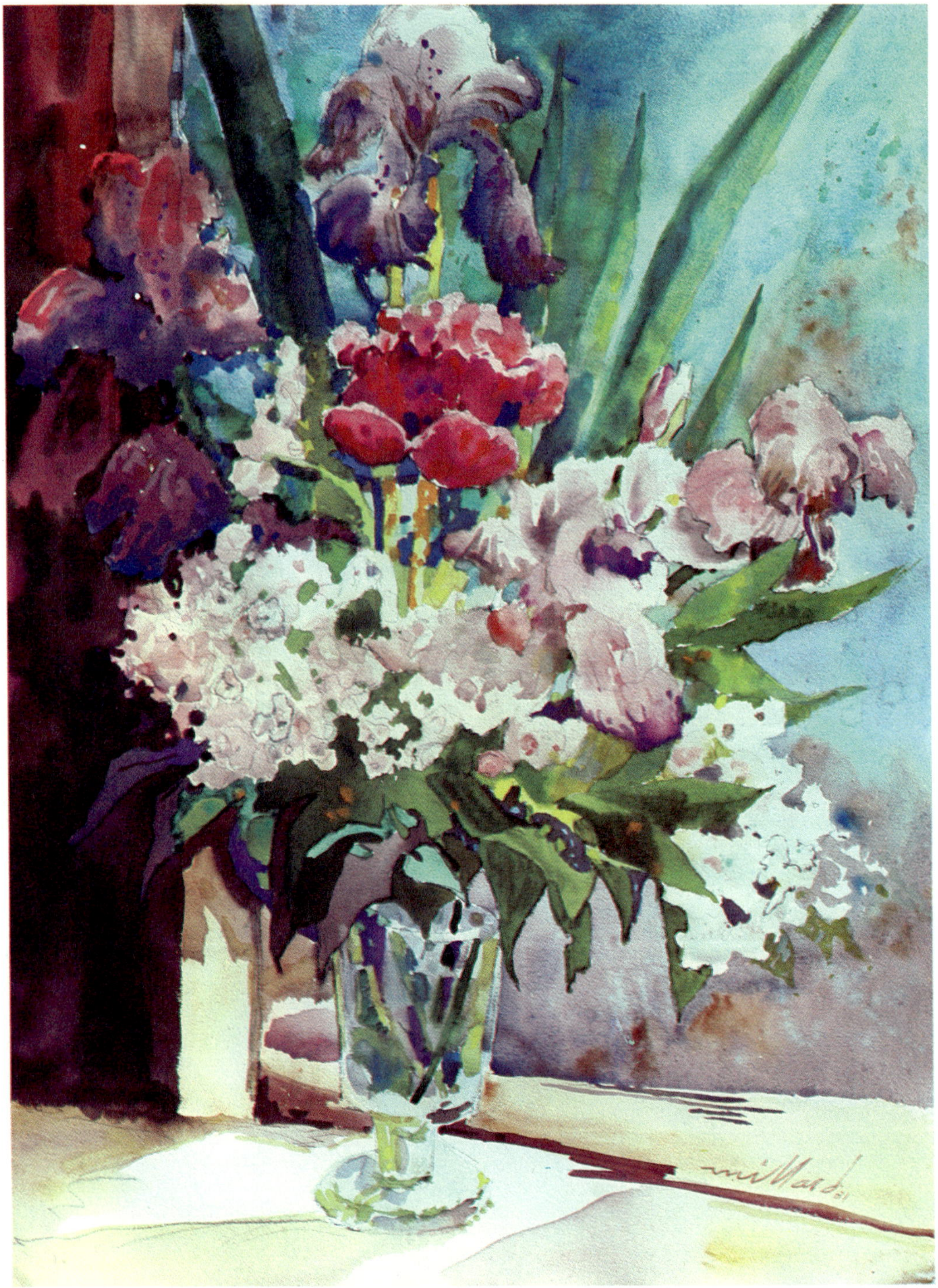

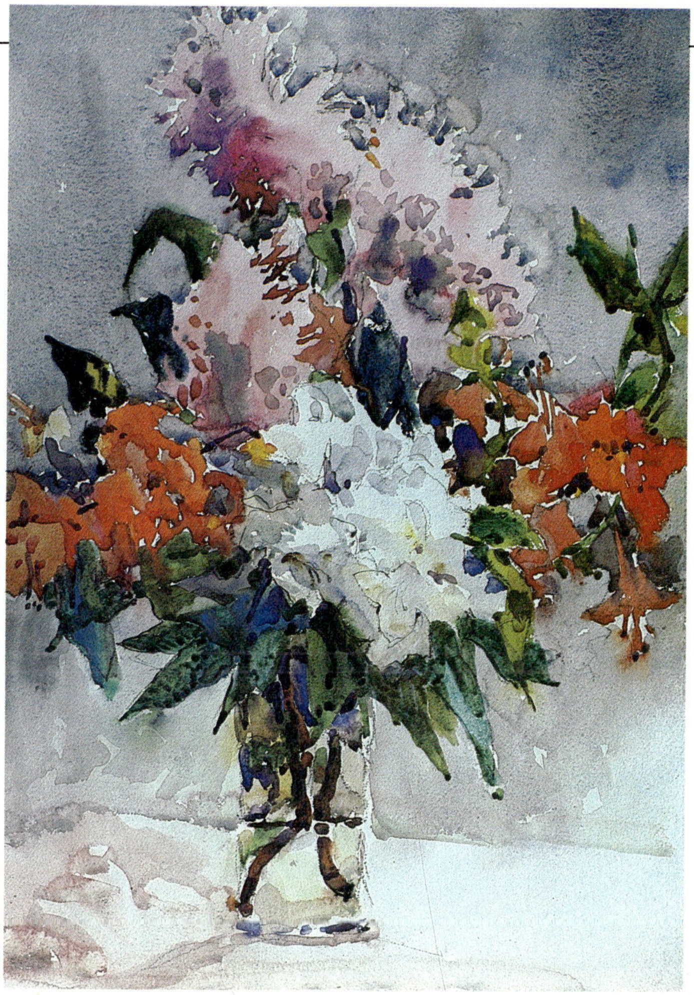

Making Your Colors Brilliant. Here Mr. Millard set off his colors with a soft background of cool gray against the warm flowers and warm gray under the cool leaves. He has kept the background pale and used a multiplicity of related colors within each set: from yellow-oranges to burnt sienna, from mauve and permanent rose to the palest pink, and so on. He arranged cool colors around the warms, and deep contrasting colors around the whites.

Packing Color Around the Whites. Study this closeup to see how the artist handled the flowers. Can you see the soft edge on the left-hand side, and the hard edge on the right? Note that there's no detail where the white is brightest. Now look at the green leaves. Green leaves are not all green, as you might think at first. How many greens can you see here? Within them, the artist has used blues, purples, ochres, and olive.

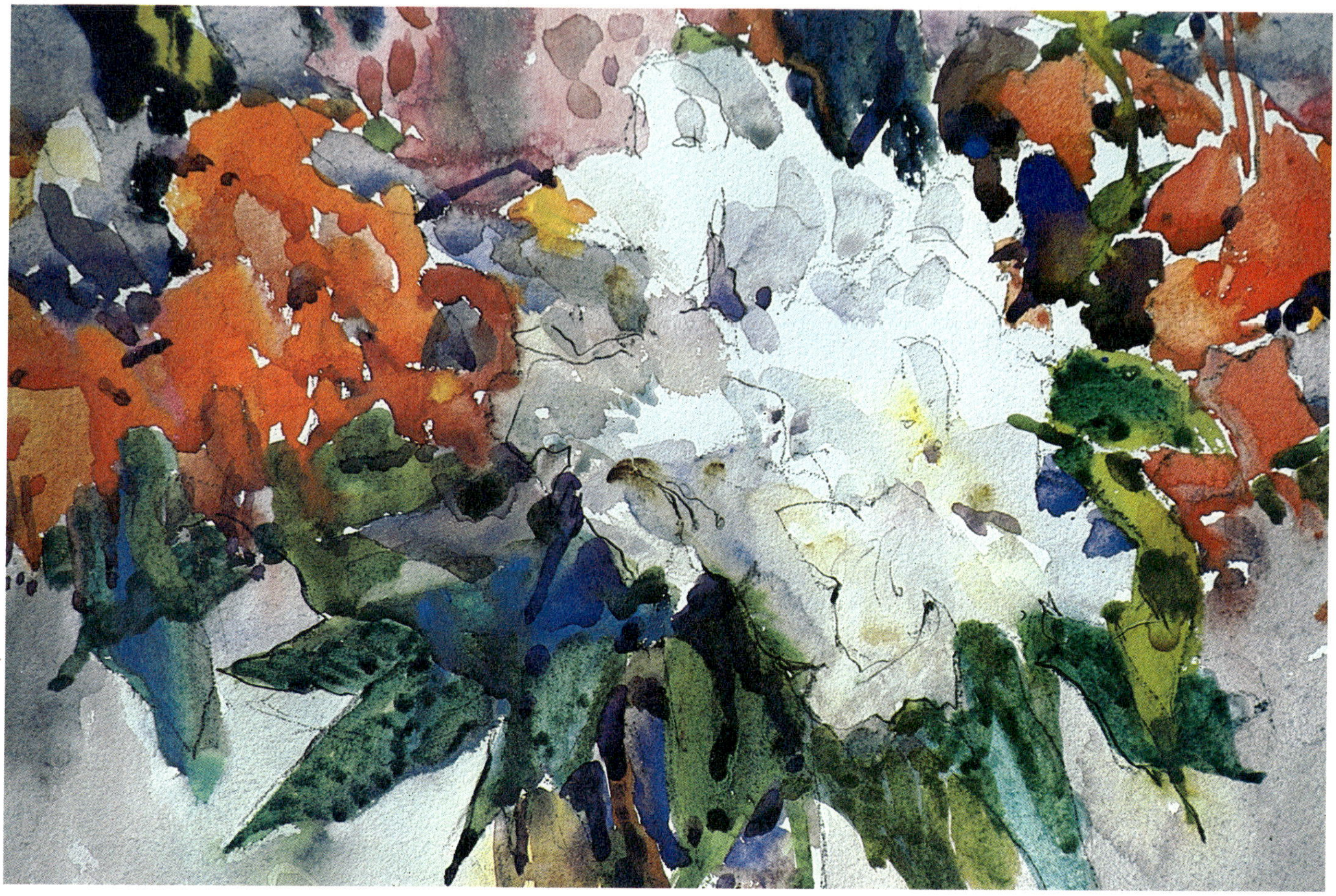

Handling White Shapes

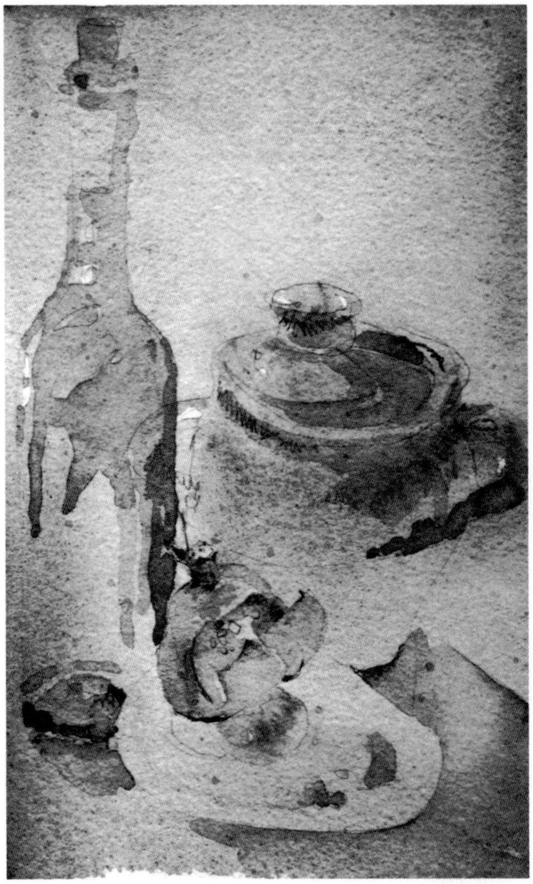

Using a Minimum of White. Here the artist laid his first wash over everything on his contour sketch, toning the entire paper except for a few tiny pieces of white where he wanted just a hint of sparkle. His first wash was airy and felt full of sunlight because of the open, granular quality of the pigments: cobalt violet and raw umber. He mixed a big juicy puddle and worked across the top, left to right. Each time he reached into the puddle for a new load of color, he gave the mixture a good stir so it wouldn't settle.

After the first wash was bone dry, he wet the paper with clear water in the area of the bowl on the plate and the bottom edge of the pomegranate on its plate, and he put in a second wash, wet-in-wet. He used cobalt violet, cobalt blue, and raw umber on the bowl and cobalt violet, alizarin crimson, raw umber, and cadmium orange on the pomegranate.

Then he applied color over the dry first wash for the wine bottle. His mix was raw sienna, Davy's gray, and olive green, applied in a drippy wash that was mostly "tinted water," not heavy pigment. He put it on quickly, holding his work at an angle, and let it run down; he also let it dry at this angle. The third wash is very subtle indeed, consisting of just the darkest bits in the bottle, bowl, and shadows. Notice the see-through quality of the glass bottle, and the way the artist has "lost" and "found" edges.

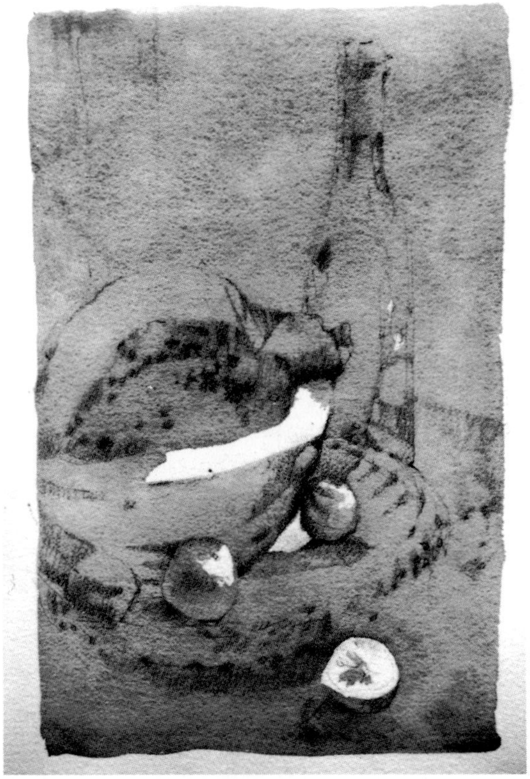

Positive and Negative Whites. In this painting, the large curve of white on the papaya, the bright patches on the tops of three limes, and the tiny "flicks" on the wine bottle are *positive patterns*. However, the piece of white tucked in behind the lime on the paper plate is a *negative shape*. It is important to learn to use positive and negative shapes successfully in your still life compositions. If you want to see examples of effective negative shapes, Mr. Millard suggests looking at works by Degas.

Spatial relationships—between foreground, middleground, and distance—are also quite evident in this grainy watercolor. The eye moves back quickly from the first lime to the front edge of the papaya. From there it drifts back to the wine bottle and sees through the bottle to further depths. There is an illusion of warmth in the center of the big single wash, where raw umber was added wet-in-wet to the background wash. The artist created the background of cobalt violet, ultramarine blue, and raw umber by flooding it over the contour drawing, except on the whites. He added more ultramarine blue to the puddle as the overall wash neared the bottom of the picture. A little raw sienna has been touched onto the top and neck of the bottle over a dry wash. Mr. Millard has kept the luminous quality in the center of the painting by carefully matching the color and values here.

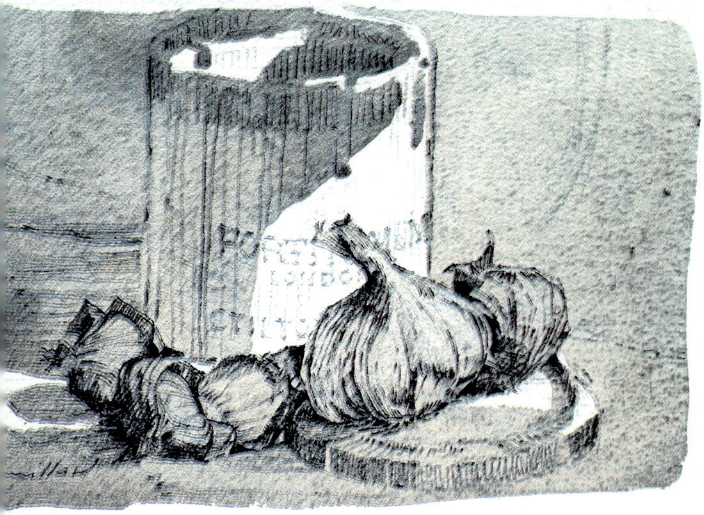

Making Flat Whites Appear Curved. In painting this rustic subject, the artist has left white areas, seeing their individual shapes as an overall part of his design. These light-struck areas follow the forms of objects and also continue the rhythms of the underlying contour drawing, which also follows forms to show volume. The arc of the garlic and shallots moves into the background, repeating the oval curve of the crock.

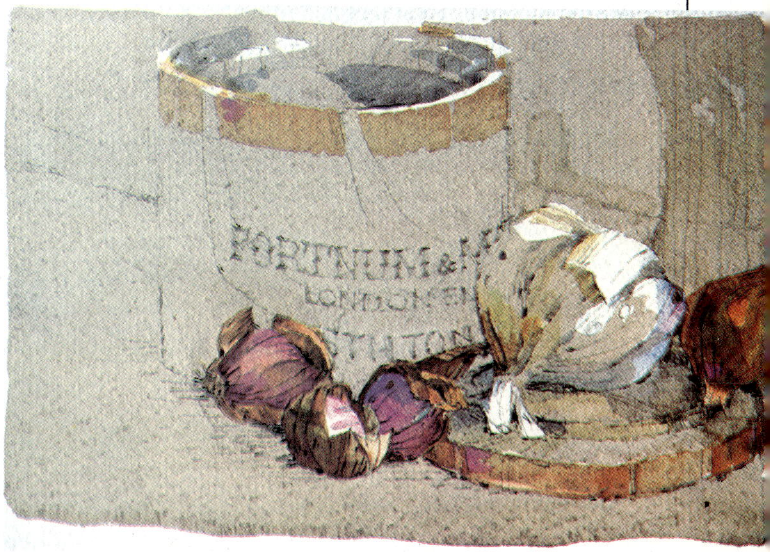

Modeling White Forms with Color. In this colored sketch, the jar lid provides a more important stage setting for the garlic, which has been given a "spotlight" treatment, and there is more luster on the porcelain crock. This time the artist created even more reality in the white shapes. This is a lesson in setting up your still lifes to catch *pieces* of light, rather than full sun. Here the white shapes follow the form. The artist has used the edge of his brush to describe the edges of objects with color.

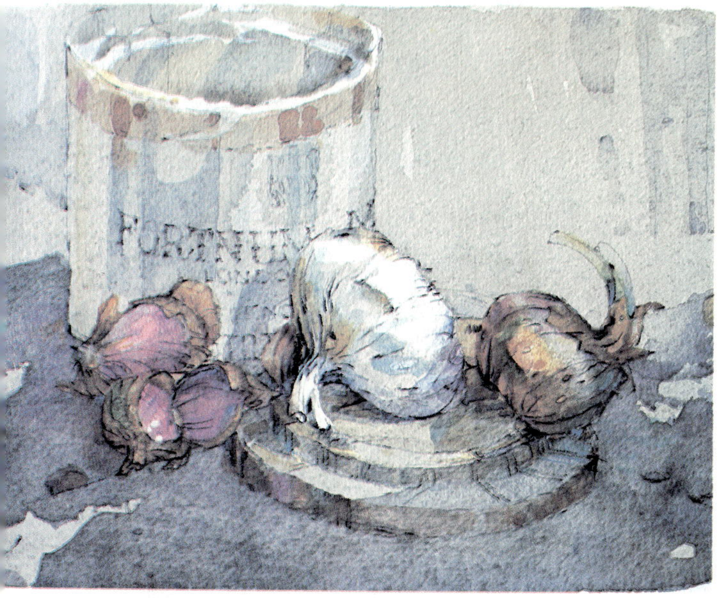

Getting a Three-Dimensional Effect. You can model form by glazing many watercolor washes over one another (apply them only to dry watercolor, and slant the paper to keep the washes clean). Here these deeper washes blend the shallots into the shadows with "lost edges." Harder edges accent the garlic and onion on the jar lid. The onion's shadow follows the form of the garlic. Likewise, the garlic's shadow on the crock. Very deep shadows under its stem really lift the white garlic out into space.

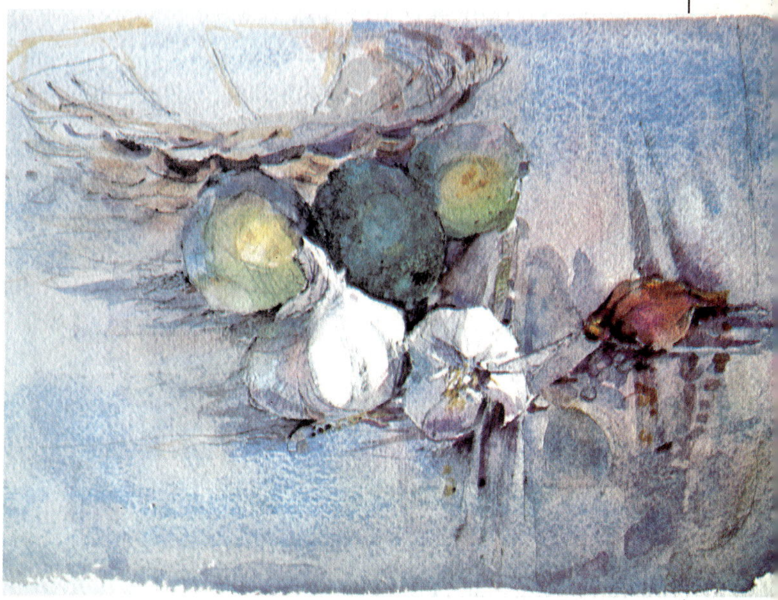

Making the Whites "Sing." The vignette of color surrouding these white objects makes them appear brighter, and the color is intensified and deepened as it moves from the edges of the painting toward the center. The whites here have impact because of the intensity of the deep viridian green lime, outlining the garlic in a hard edge. The outlining continues in the dark streaks and shadows of the background, fragments from a patterned tablecloth.

Making Rich, Vibrant Darks

Building Up Darks with Layered Washes. David Millard decided he would build this painting from pale washes to darker tones and much richer color.

The artist put in the background first, leaving the white areas along the tops of the objects. After this wash was bone dry, he laid in the shadows adding a little local color to the shadow wash. Then he let this dry. If he had gone on to the next wash too soon, the pigment would have begun to "crawl," and he would have had backruns. He worked with his paper at a five-degree angle so that the colors would run to the bottom and his deep tones would remain clear.

Mr. Millard followed this sequence of washes and colors: 1) a background wash of burnt umber and ultramarine blue; 2) a first shadow wash of pale burnt sienna; 3) a second background wash of burnt umber, ultramarine blue, and cobalt violet; 4) a second wash for the object shadows—again, pale burnt sienna; 5) a third wash of local colors for the vegetables, added in a very controlled manner; and 6) a fourth wash for the accents and deep shadows, adding Winsor violet to the burnt umber–ultramarine blue background wash.

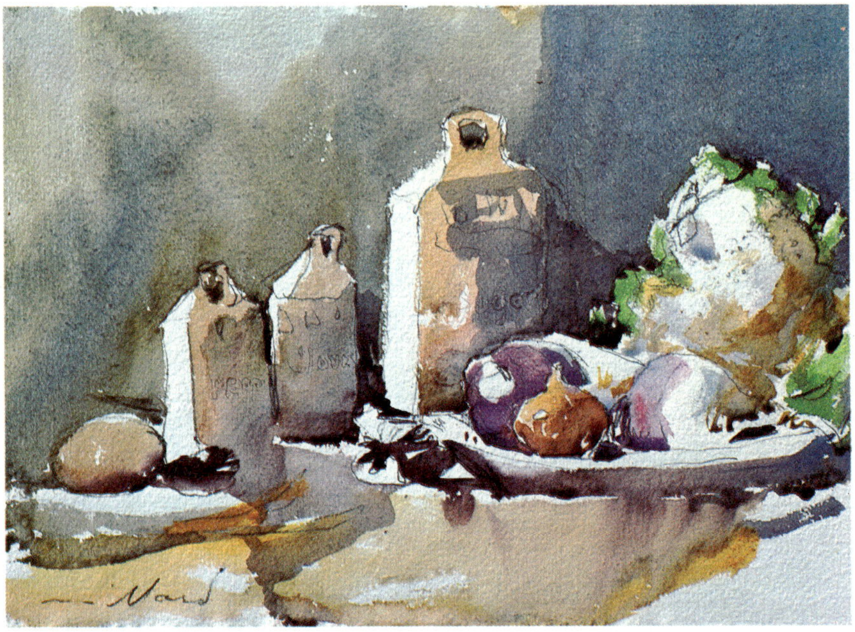

Making Clean, Colorful Darks. You can keep your darker washes clear and clean if you put them on the paper with zest and don't work into them. Aim for crisp, clear brushwork. Think of *alla prima* or "one-shot" washes.

You can obtain a tranquil beauty from what appears to the naive viewer to be just two colors. That white tablecloth is just the white of the paper. Color on this white area was kept luminous, not heavy.

The earth tone in the painting is a combination of raw sienna, raw umber, burnt sienna, and burnt umber plus a few touches of Winsor violet and Venetian red—all analogous, or closely related, colors. The blue tone is made up of manganese blue, cerulean blue, cobalt blue, and ultramarine blue, plus some sap green and viridian—again, analogous colors. Against the overall feeling of tranquility is the constant and carefully planned light and dark pattern: the dark blue pitcher against the light bread and white cloth; the dark negative area running down the left side of the big urn, across the top of the bowl and white cloth; and lastly, the very irregular dark under that oddly shaped crown of dried weeds.

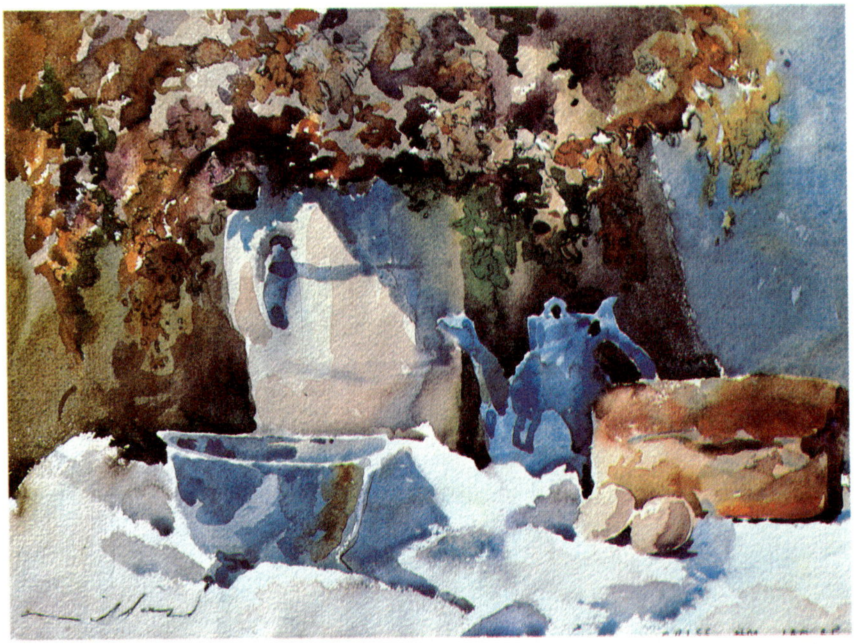

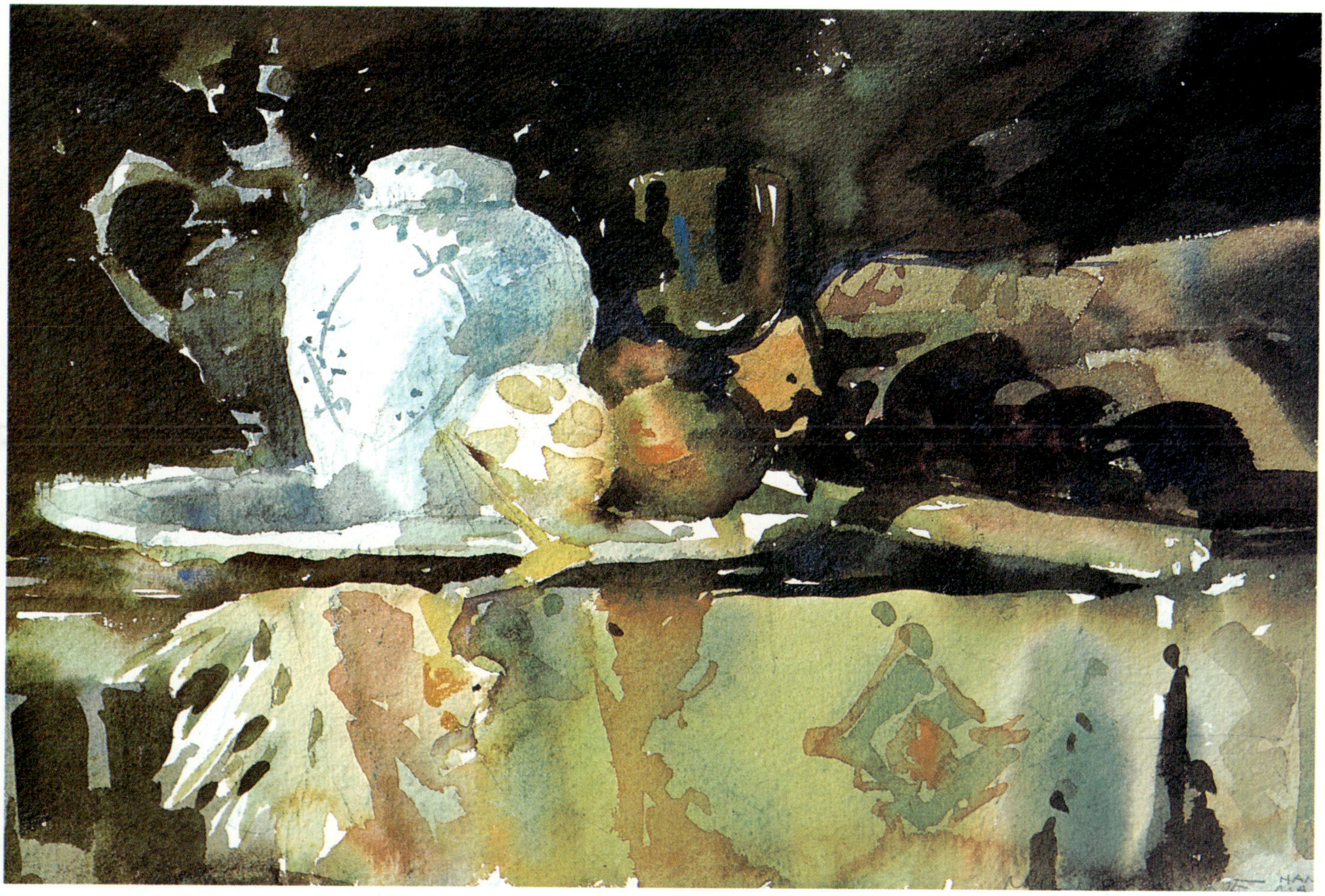

Controlling the Deepest Tones. This watercolor, done in the manner of the old Dutch still life masters, was painted in two sessions. Since the composition was complicated, the artist felt the need of a very controlled, limited palette. The watercolor appears to be painted in only three colors: orange, blue, and green. But there are actually *many* blues, oranges, and greens.

All the objects were painted, and then the painting was put aside to dry at the usual five-degree angle. (This is the way the artist keeps the shadows in the background transparent.) While it was drying, he tried to resolve how he would execute the deep, rich background—a wash of very heavily pigmented sap green and burnt sienna, which he mixed on the paper. The darkest darks, added wet-in-wet, consisted of alizarin crimson and ultramarine blue, mixed into the wet wash. A slightly diluted wash, but not too watery, was added to the pewter pitcher, since it "popped" forward too much after the extremely deep tones went into the background.

Mr. Millard deliberately left small specks of white showing in the background so it wouldn't "go dead." The background wash was put right *over* the glass, except for the carefully placed whites (no masking fluid was used here).

Chiaroscuro Painting

The term *chiaroscuro* literally means "light/dark." In chiaroscuro painting, your eye follows the light. The light gives the picture its flow—it takes the eye from one place to another, and the shadows structure the painting.

A still life artist can work from two basic views. One is the shallow picture plane in which objects are placed across the canvas from left to right, or from right to left. The other is the tipped picture plane, with objects going into the picture at a variety of angles or curves, portraying depth.

When the picture plane is at eye level or close to it, oil painter David Leffel advises placing the most important element, or the center of interest, at the right. With the artist working from dark at the left to light at the right, the picture culminates at the right. To keep the eye—which has followed the light to the right—from going beyond the edge, use a "stopper." The stopper may be a shadow on a fruit peel, or a lone grape. It will hold the eye and keep it from traveling further.

Mr. Leffel suggests beginning a still life painting by placing the center of interest, then painting this focal point with enough tone and mass to be seen precisely. To be worthy of interest, the focal point must have enough light, color, texture, and substance to excite and capture attention.

The artist has used a typical still life setting for the painting shown here: an amber glass at the left, five nectarines in a group, and a small blue-and-white Mexican pitcher to serve as the center of interest on the right. The light comes in gradually from the left to focus on the pitcher at the right. The background is dark: The light on the objects becomes gradually brighter as it goes toward the right, where it bursts into full intensity.

The three small illustrations show how Mr. Leffel blocked in the overall chiaroscuro pattern in the beginning stages of his painting. In this way, he placed the center of interest and established the deepest shadows as well as the movement of light across the painting. To paint the shadow, he began with the darkest dark first—the amber glass—and used a lighter shadow color for the background. Next he placed the shadow on the nectarines, making the shadow here a bit lighter than the shadow on the glass. Then he painted the shadow on the pitcher at the right, using the same shadow value as on the nectarines. Up to this point, he had painted only darks.

Keeping the background soft and shadowy, the artist used a cadmium color to provide transparency. He made the glass in the shadow area somewhat soft-edged. On the first nectarine (from left to right) he painted a little bit of light, with the edge in shadow, to create the illusion of form. On the second fruit he painted a bit more light than on the first one; and on the next he painted more light still, making this nectarine brighter than the previous one. In other words, he was painting a progression of values. Out of the darkness at the left, the light travels across the picture plane. This light, striking the pitcher, also hits the surface before it. As each item gets closer to the pitcher, it is more luminous.

In setting up a still life, you'll create more interest if all the objects do not have light on them. It also helps to have an object darker than the background. In chiaroscuro painting, one way to make an object light is to paint the surrounding area in a lighter tone, not darker. It's like placing a little halo around it. If something looks dark and you want to lighten it, see how much light you can put in an adjacent area.

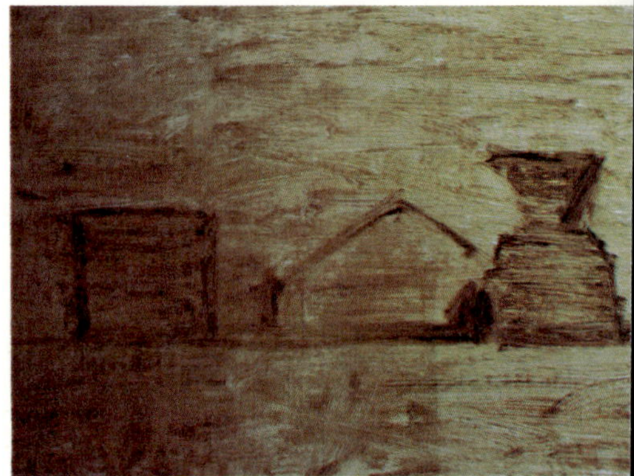

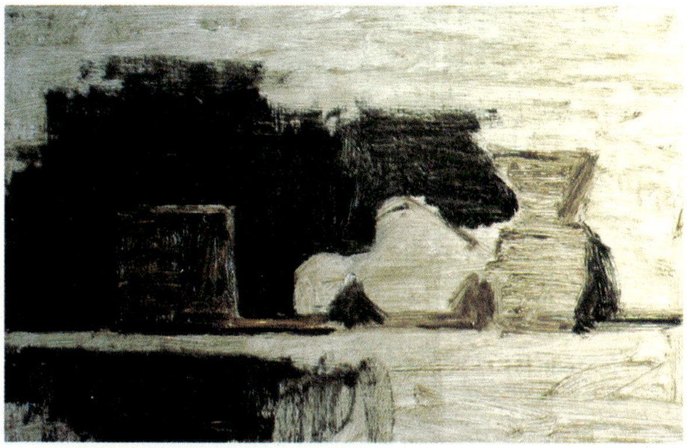

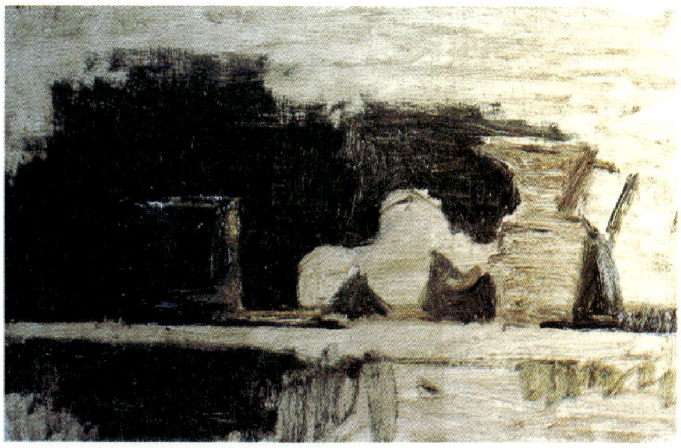

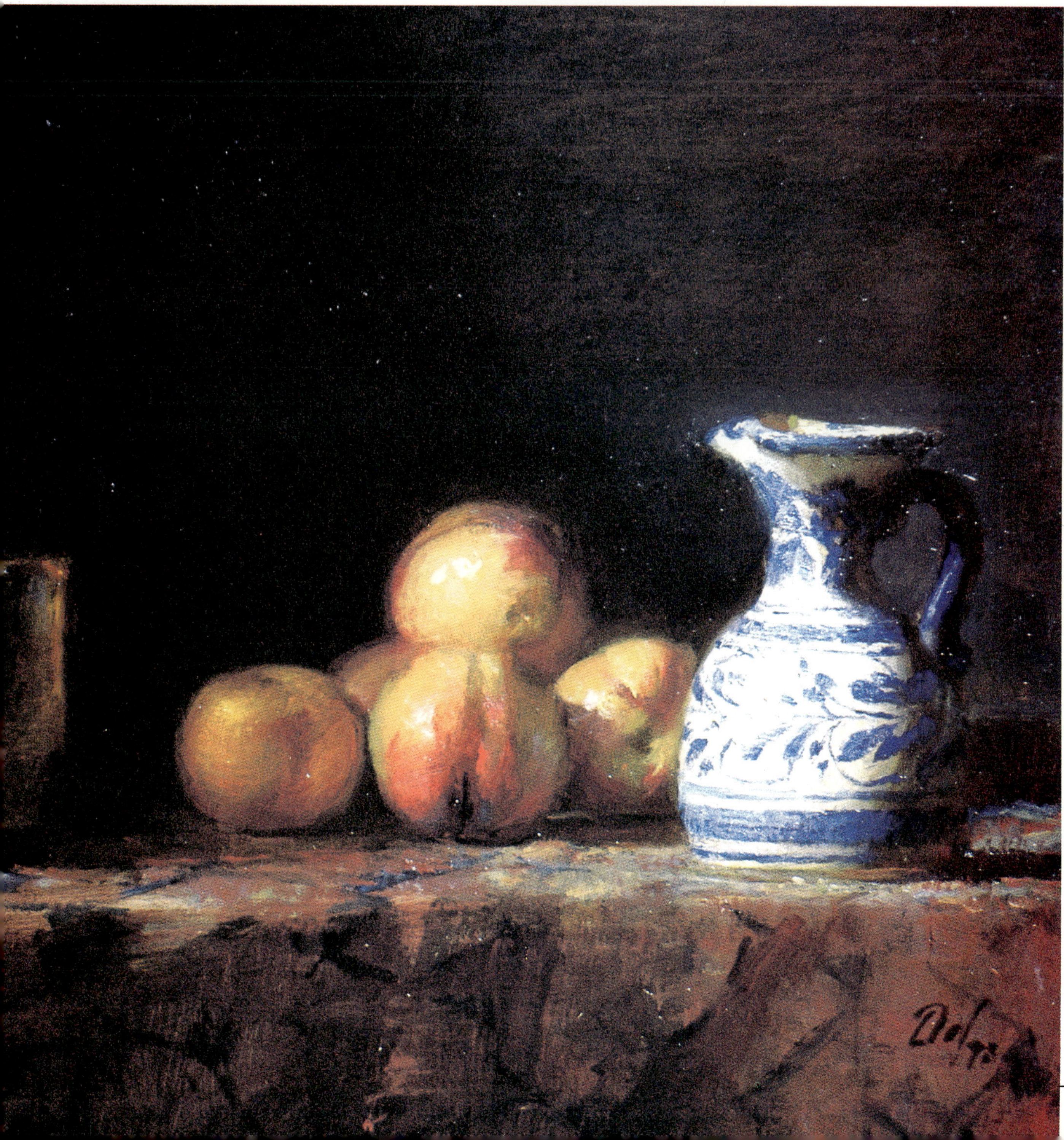

Massing Forms

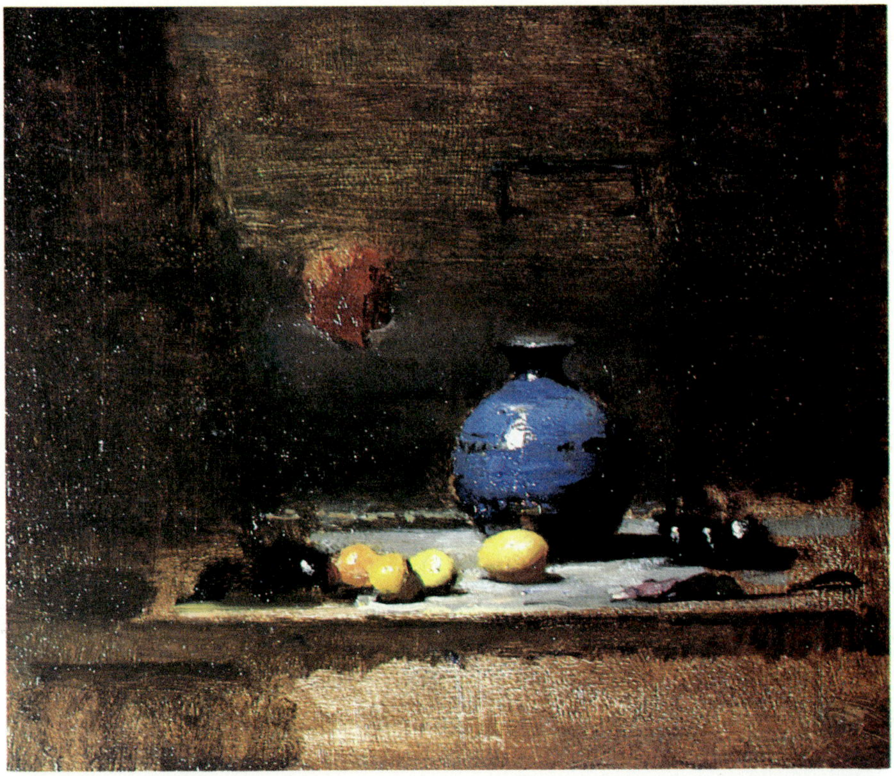

Developing the Concept by Massing. Try to see your subject as a whole rather than in terms of its details. The way to do that is by massing individual details into flat planes of a single value and color. For example, you should see an apple as two planes, a light plane and a shadow plane. Later you can put in the smaller details, such as the stem of the apple, but you shouldn't get involved too early with these minor details.

David Leffel massed the light and shadow areas of the fruit and blue vase in the oil painting at the top of this page. In the next stage, shown below, he went on to develop refinements—such as reflected lights—in the shadows. You should see your entire painting as a whole, he advises, and not just as separate objects. A mass of shadow and a mass of light will give your painting more dimension and weight.

Massing also starts you thinking, early on, about the concept of your painting, because where and how you shape your masses—your strongest lights or your deep shadows, for example—is part of its overall "look." When all your broad masses and planes are in position, you can put in smaller forms, paint small shadows or lights, or soften your edges into a light area. You should always be working from the larger to the smaller, from the whole to the specific.

Mr. Leffel stresses thinking in terms of planes, mass, and dimension rather than line and shading. The way to start is by creating a mass, which gives you a sense of proportion and better idea of size than a line drawing. You need one mass (an object, say) against another mass (space). To see how massing works, try painting a bunch of grapes. Mass the whole cluster, rather than starting with individual grapes. Do a mass for the shadow, another for the light. Then you can begin to suggest individual grapes.

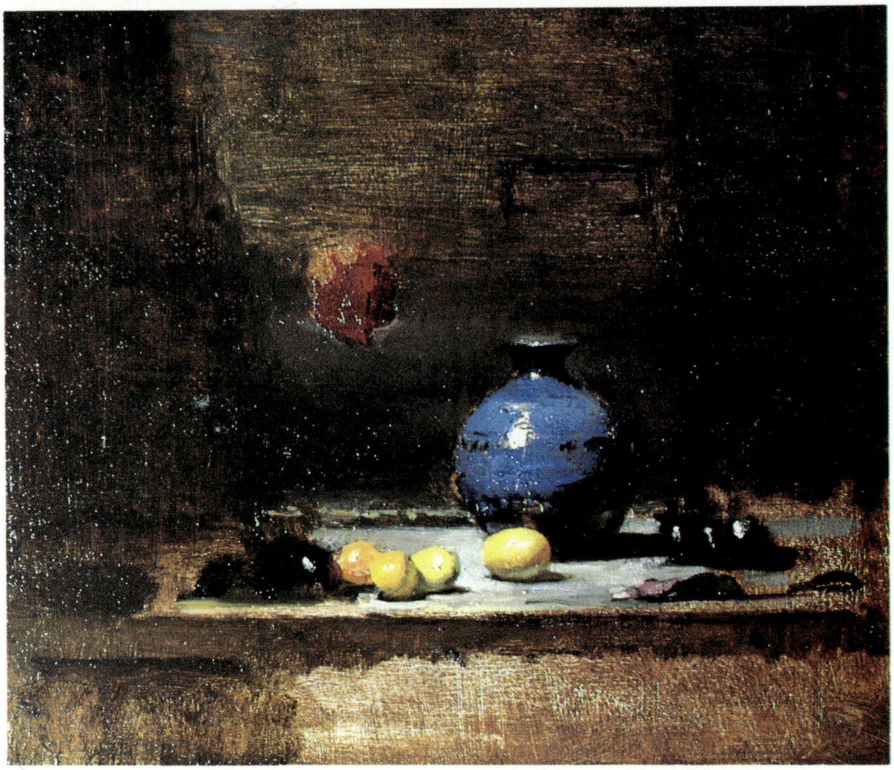

Painting Shadows. The rough drawings on this page explain the procedure Mr. Leffel has followed in his painting. He started with the shadows first because they give the feeling of structure and keep the composition in place. The first step in painting an object is to mass together the shadow on the object and the shadow cast by it, as shown here. Paint both shadows as one shape.

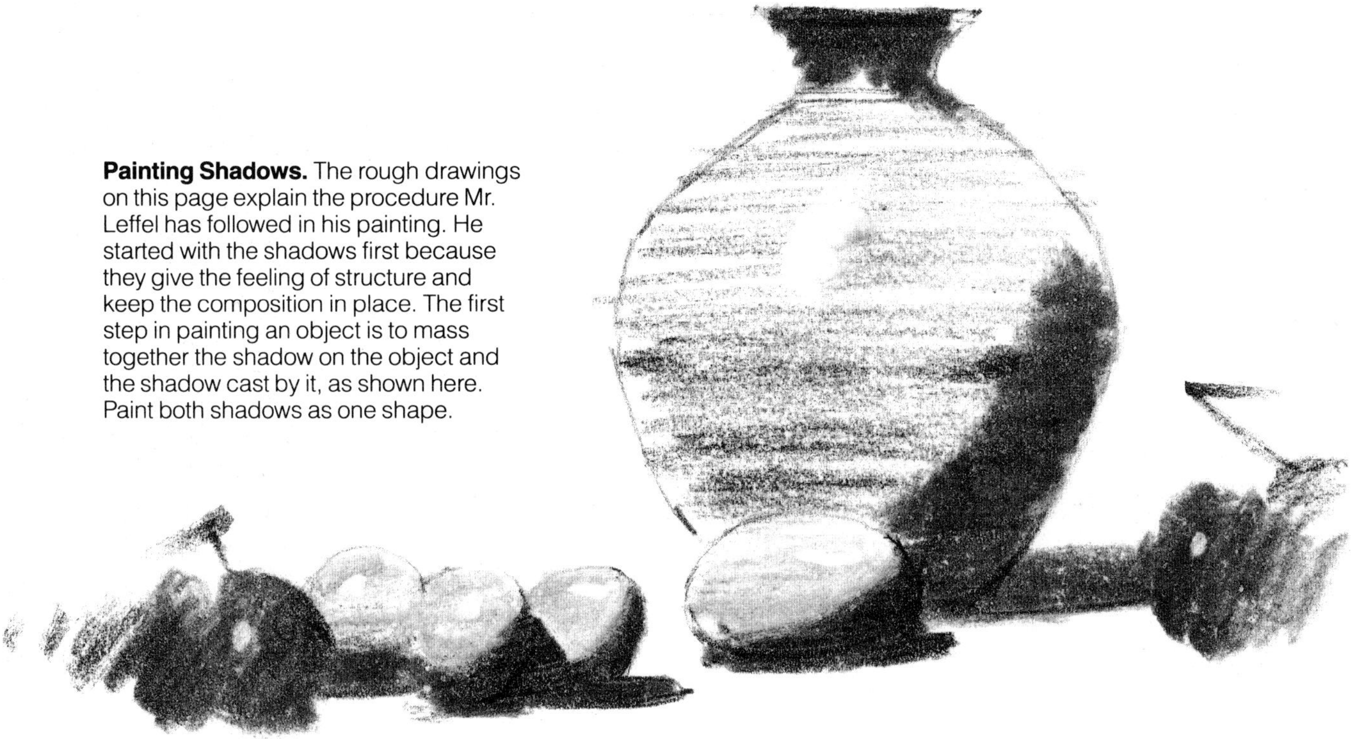

Drawing Reflections. After massing the shadows and cast shadows of objects, you can break up the shadows by adding some reflected light. In the drawing here, these areas have been lifted out with a kneaded eraser.

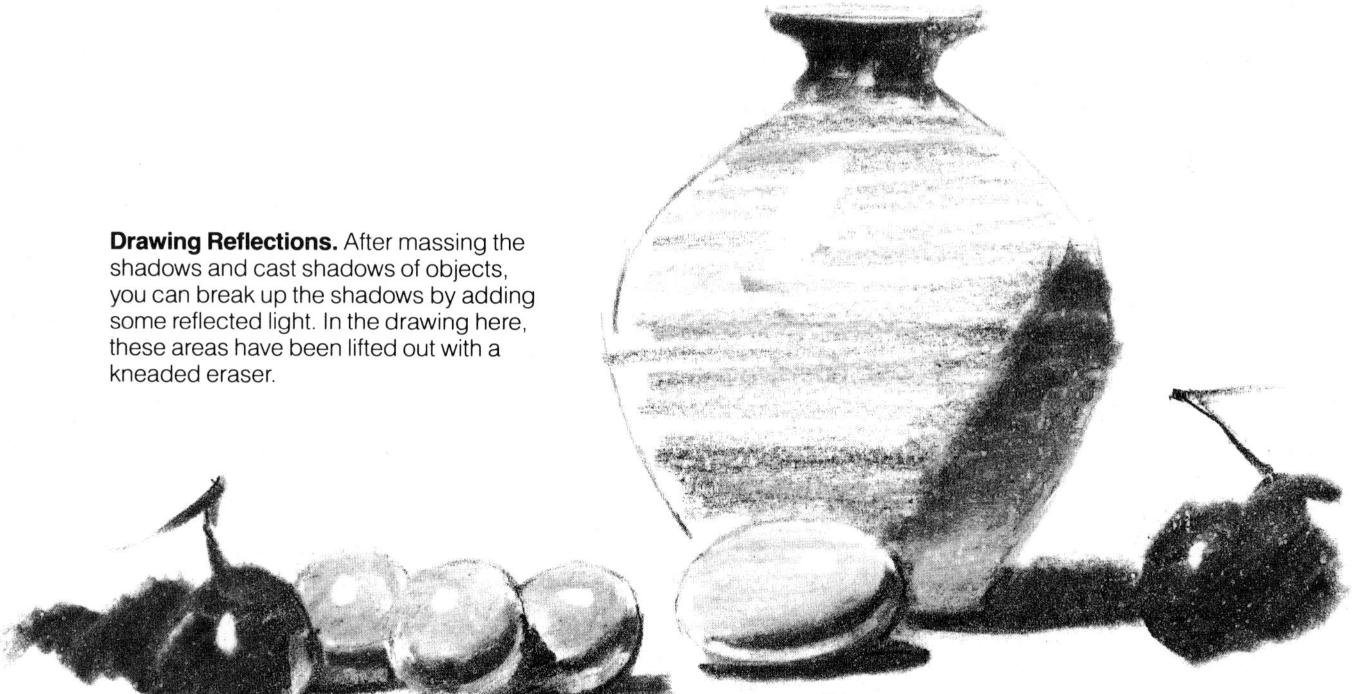

Mastering Edges

Edges can help you convey the illusion of three-dimensional form on a flat canvas. Oil painter David Leffel believes edges are wonderful. You can paint a flat plane, and then, just by varying your edges, you can achieve a dimensional quality.

All objects in your painting have inside edges and outside edges. The inside edge of an object is where the plane or form changes direction. The outside edge is where a form begins and/or ends; it faces the source of light.

There are two other kinds of edges: hard and soft. A hard edge is clear and distinct, whereas a soft edge is fuzzy. A soft edge creates continuity. The softer the edge, the duller the look. A hard edge defines where something ends. The harder the edge, the more riveting your painting is in that area. Compare the edges in the two details, shown on this page, from Mr. Leffel's still life painting.

An important lesson to learn in trying to portray a three-dimensional form is that the eye will automatically focus on the cleanest, sharpest thing it sees. In addition, a hard, thin edge tells the viewer that the object it sees is not round or dimensional, for only very thin things—such as leaves or sheets of writing paper—have such sharp edges.

When an artist paints a hard edge where an object meets a background, that edge will be a strong place of focus. It follows, then, that if the focal point is away from the edge, that is, inside the material, the mind's eye is not conscious of edges, and the illusion conveyed is that of form or mass. Therefore, you have to draw attention away from the edge and give the eye a new focal point. How do you accomplish this? You can eliminate the outside edge by dragging two wet layers of paint (the light and the shadow) together, blending their edges. Edges on the lighted side do not start darker. When light hits surface, the edges are as brightly lit as the inside. To keep the far edge of an object from becoming a focal point, lighten the background where the edge and background meet.

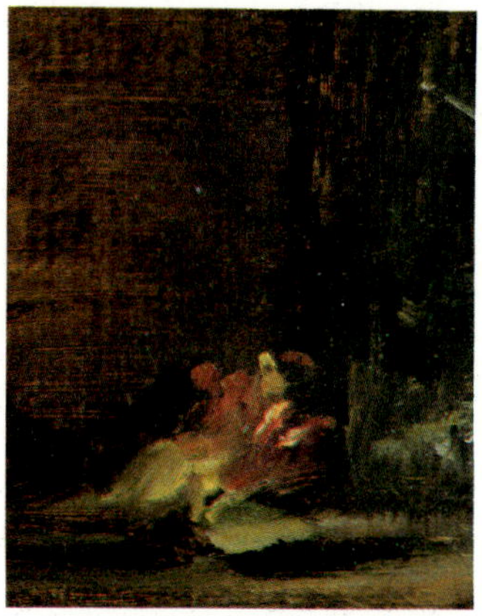

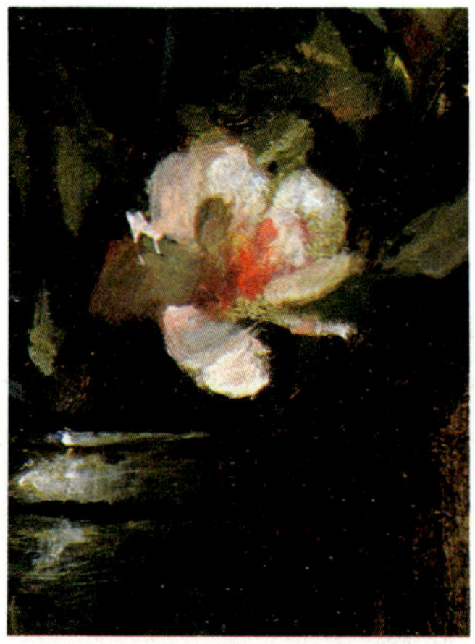

***Carnations in Pewter*, oil, 12″ × 14″ (30.5 × 35.5 cm), by David Leffel. Private collection.**

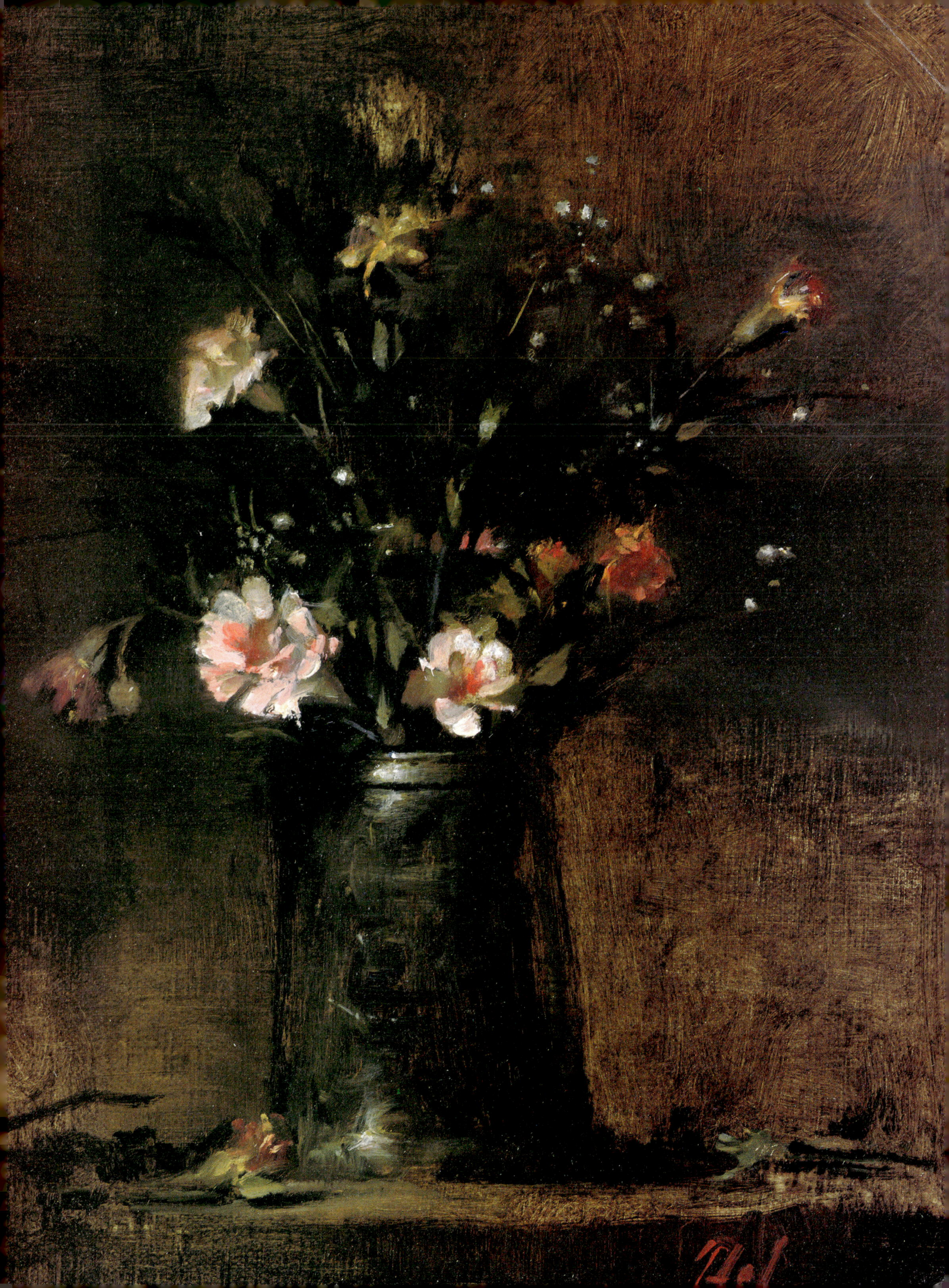

Painting Backgrounds

The term *background*, as oil painter David Leffel uses it here, has to do with aesthetics, not picture planes. Thus, everything that you don't want to emphasize, everything that is not in the light, is part of the background. In order for one section of an object to recede, something else on it has to come forward. Everything works in relationship to everything else.

When your background seems too colorful and your fruit still life seems lost, try neutralizing the background. You'll see that the fruit will come forward.

Mr. Leffel suggests two ideas for painting backgrounds: they can be warm in relation to the subject, or cool.

Here is how to create a warm background: After you've decided on the shadow color and value of the element or elements in the foreground, weaken the color and/or lighten the value and paint this as your background.

The following method can be used to develop a cool background: Decide on the essential shadow color and the local color of your subject, and then decide on a cool, grayed color that will describe the turning planes of the object. Paint this color as your background, and the viewer will immediately identify it as air or space. To cool your background color, use raw umber or burnt umber with a little cobalt blue added.

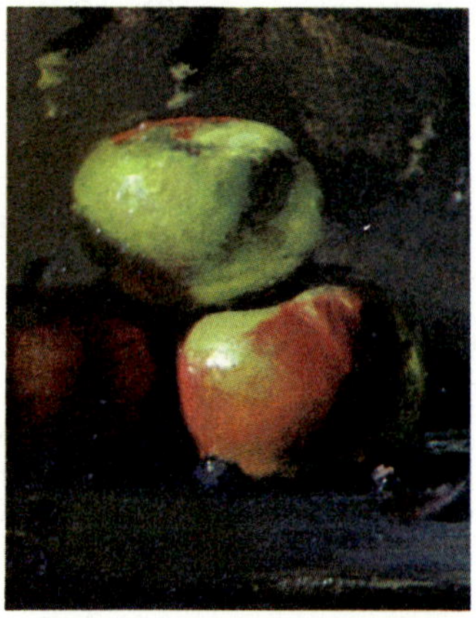

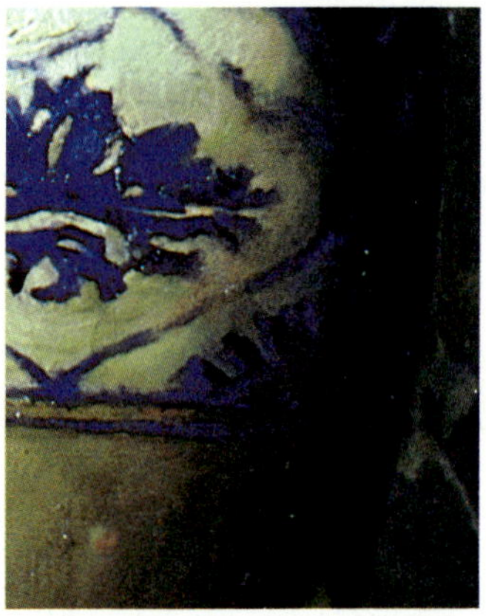

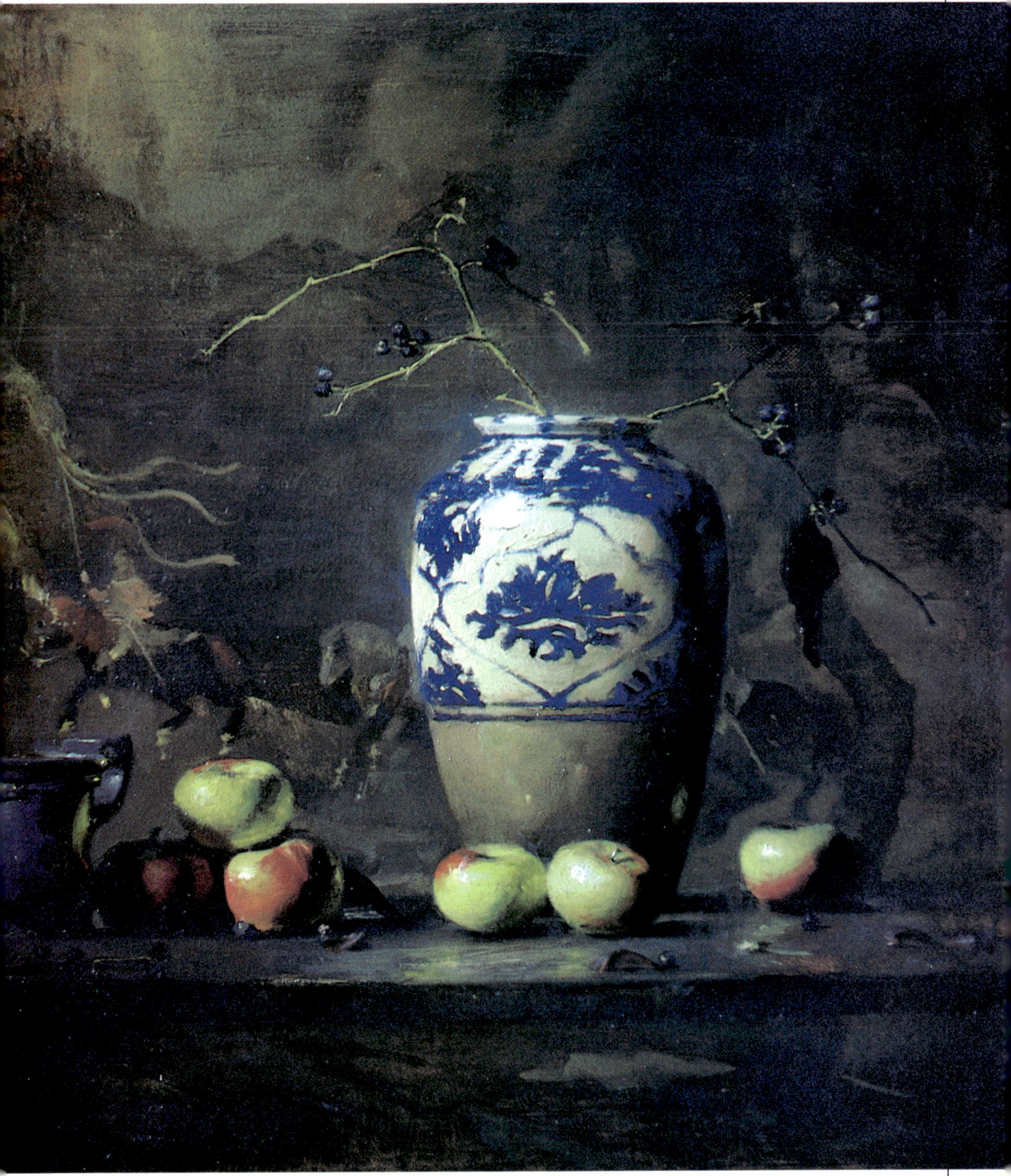

Composition in Umber, Red, and Green, oil, 18″ × 22″ (46 × 56 cm), by David Leffel. Private Collection.

Same Subject, Different Backgrounds

Mr. Leffel loved this ancient Persian vase, and so he painted it twice in oil, using two different color settings: one orange and umber, and the other in greenish hues. He wanted to explore how these background colors would affect the color of the vase. Both the warm orange and the cool blue-greens emphasized different colors in the vase, as well as different textural effects in the background.

An Afghanistan carpet formed a deep, warm background for the vase, which stands out dramatically against it. Light and texture were used to make the vase the most dominating object in the second painting. The basic overall color is green, enhanced by smaller amounts of red and black-purples.

The artist suggests that you make your colors as light and bright as you can the first day of your oil painting. You can't work too light when you first apply your bright colors. Once that first day's paint dries, it will look much darker. But when a color dries, you can make it more brilliant by reapplying the same light colors of the first day. They will look much brighter, and this time, they will remain bright.

We impute color to things according to our conditioning. As children we learn

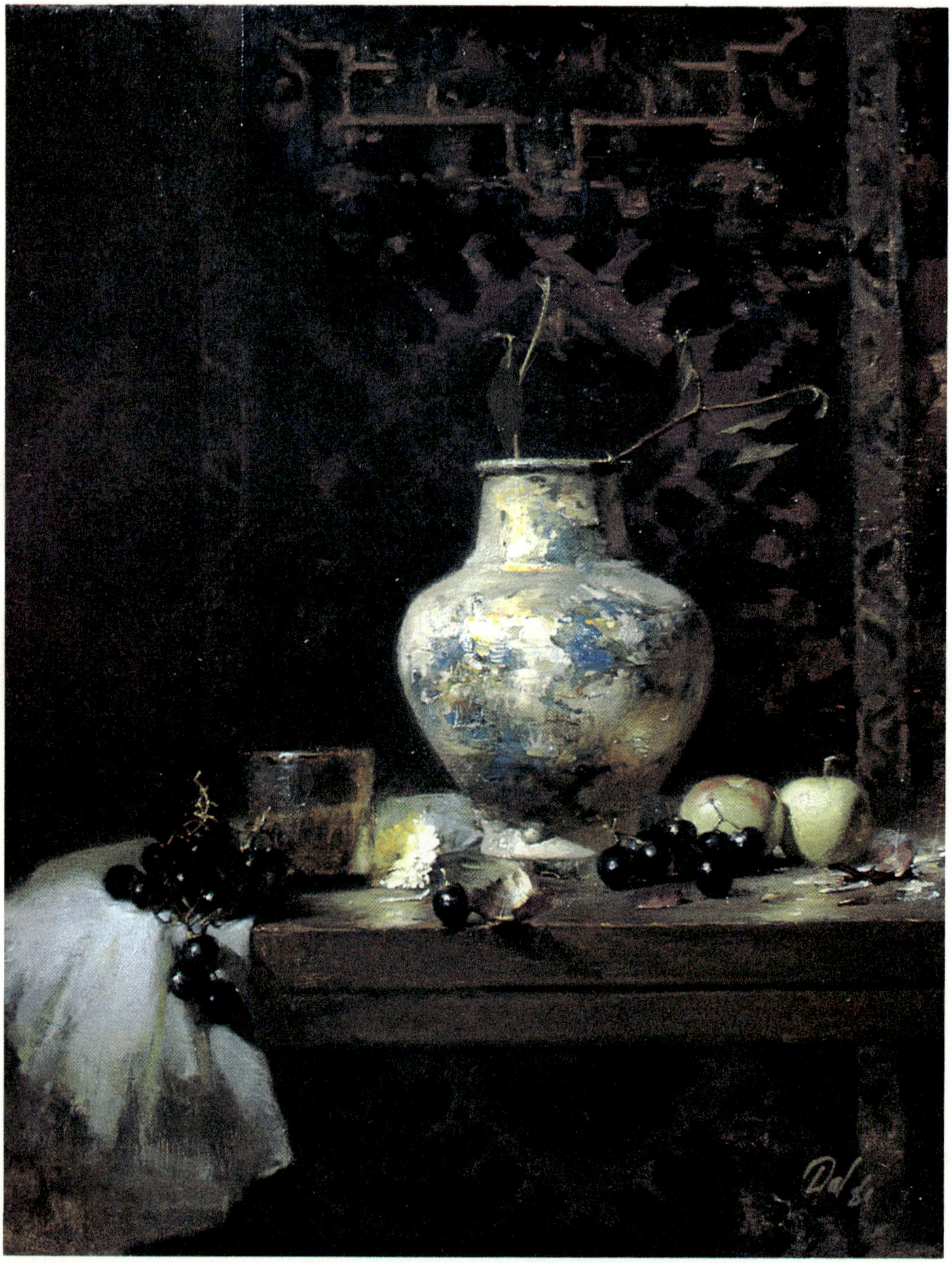

***Persian Vase with Apples and Rug*, oil, 28″ × 23″ (71 × 58 cm), by David Leffel. Private Collection.**

that grass is green, plums are purple. Mr. Leffel believes we should test our eyes and minds more and learn to see things as they actually are.

He also offers some further tips on color for the still life painter: Try to decide on the colors of your painting before you make your first brush stroke. You can either put color in one place or de-emphasize color in another place. Remember, it's color against colorlessness. For local color, which is the color of the object itself, use the richest colors you can find. Generally, think in terms of more, brighter color for your areas in the light. If your background is too warm, he suggests trying a touch of Naples yellow to give it an opaque, airy look or to make it recede so the subject comes forward.

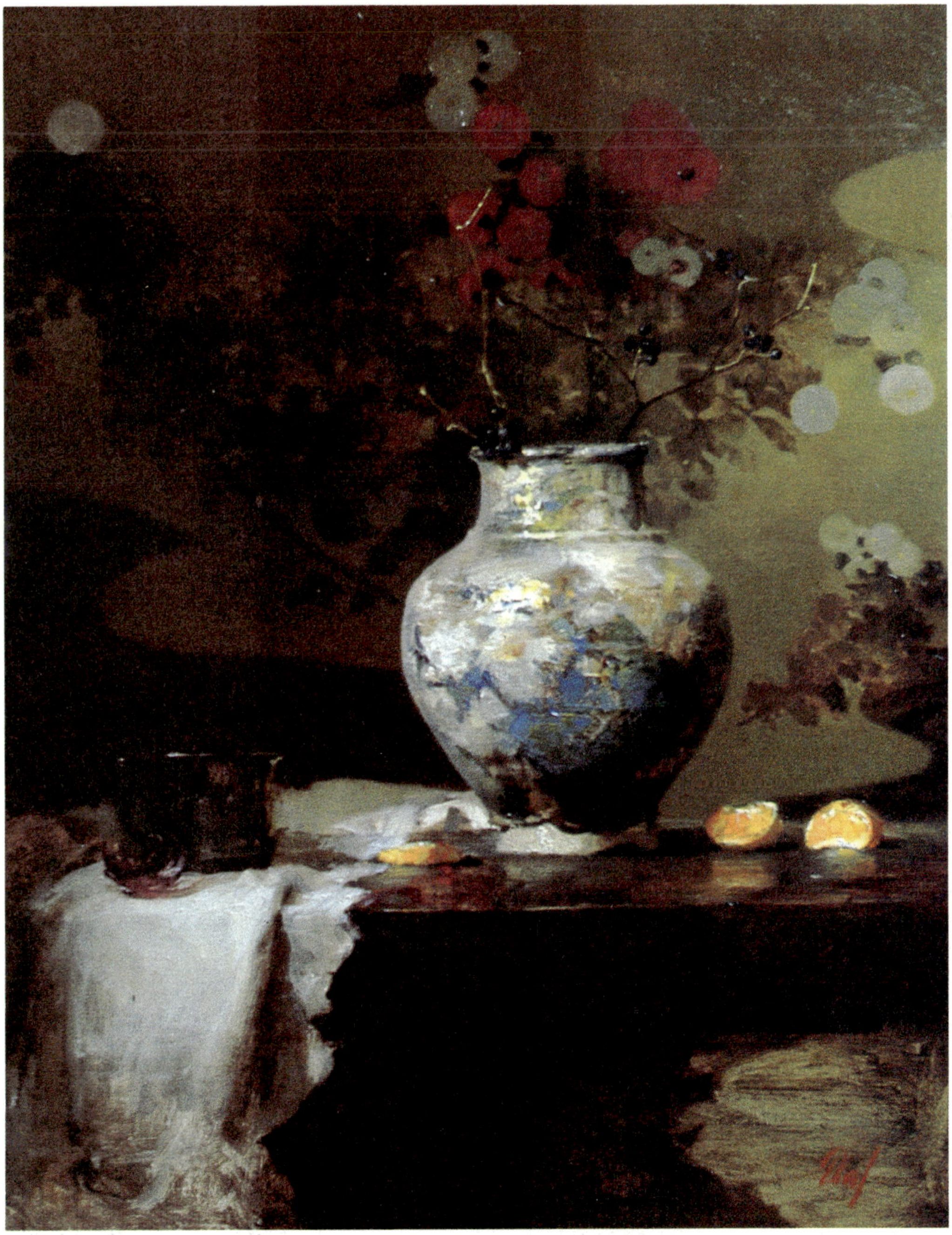

***Persian Vase with Orange and Screen*, oil, 28" × 23" (71 × 58 cm), by David Leffel. Collection of Mr. and Mrs. William Spencer.**

Working from Your Mind's Eye

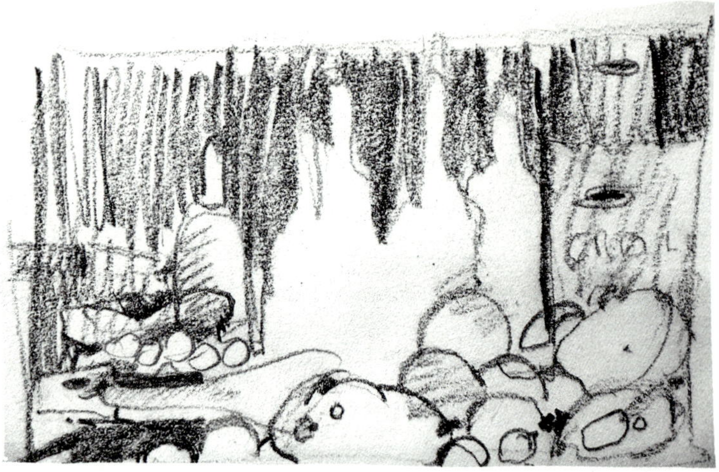

Working from Memory. You can be inspired by the essence of a scene without being a slave to reality. And you can make your own poetry from what you see in the first flash just by remembering it. Watercolorist David Millard observed a collection of marbi bottles (marbi is a Caribbean soft drink), fruit, and vegetables, at the St. Thomas marketplace but could not do a sketch on the scene. Afterward, however, he did this black-and-white memory sketch, which became the basis for a series of paintings. They came from his mind, not from objects set up in a still life. Look at what working in a series can do.

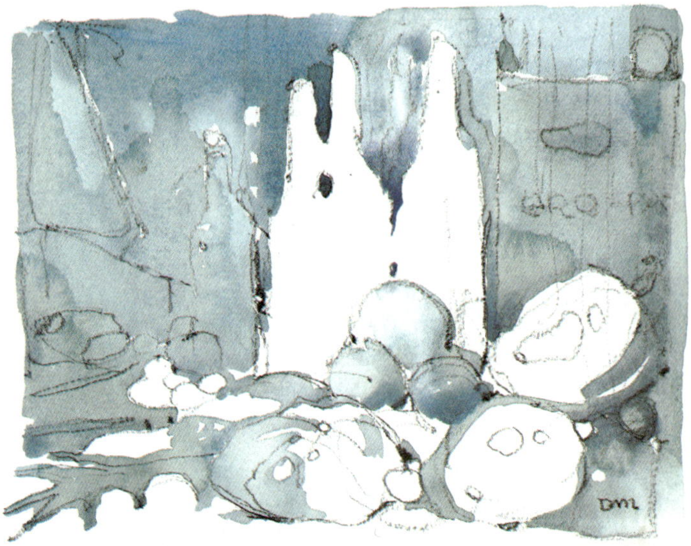

Shapes and Light. Mr. Millard used monochrome washes to do a value study of shapes and light from his memory pencil sketch. He mixed a large puddle of raw umber, cerulean blue, and Davy's gray. Then he trailed this puddle over and around the white shapes he had delineated in his fast, spirited freehand carbon sketch—but which he had seen in his mind first. He dropped touches of mauve and burnt sienna into this wash. His goal was to create an interesting abstract white shape in this monochrome.

Probing for Color. The artist drew a new arrangement (below) from memory, but he tried to maintain the essence of the first two sketches. For his background, he made a mixture of mauve, Davy's gray, burnt sienna, and cobalt violet. He colored the pink bottle rose doré and laid in a weak wash of the background mixture over most of the fruit and vegetables. Then he dropped in a pale wash of Naples yellow and Davy's gray, wet-in-wet, and also some cobalt violet wet-in-wet. He made the lime with cadmium yellow light, Davy's gray, and a touch of sap green color. He used raw umber and Chinese orange for the guavas.

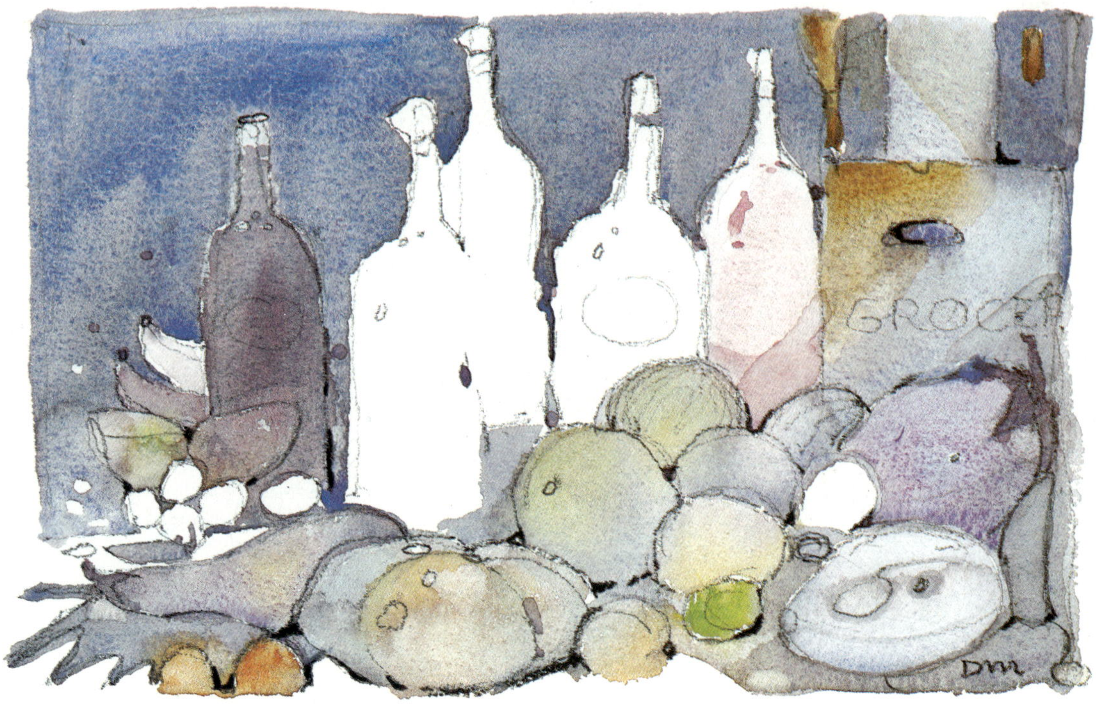

Designing with Color. In this sketch Mr. Millard explored pattern and depth. He was sketching from memory again, using a single weight line.

Adding water to the mixture left over from his previous study, he used this for his background wash. He used brown madder alizarin and Davy's gray for the three peppers and the slim stick shape. These colors are also on the base of the far right-hand bottle and a few odd fruits. To the top right side he added mauve, burnt sienna, and ultramarine blue over his first wash after it had dried. He carried spirited mixtures of these colors over to the dark background accents, plus the foreground vegetables.

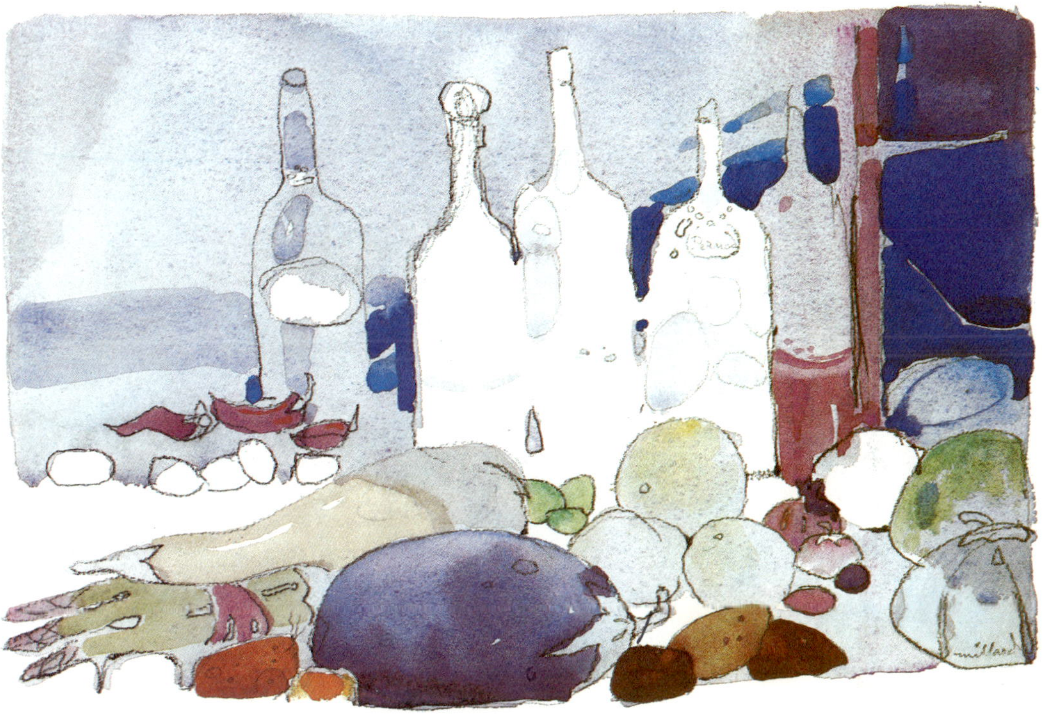

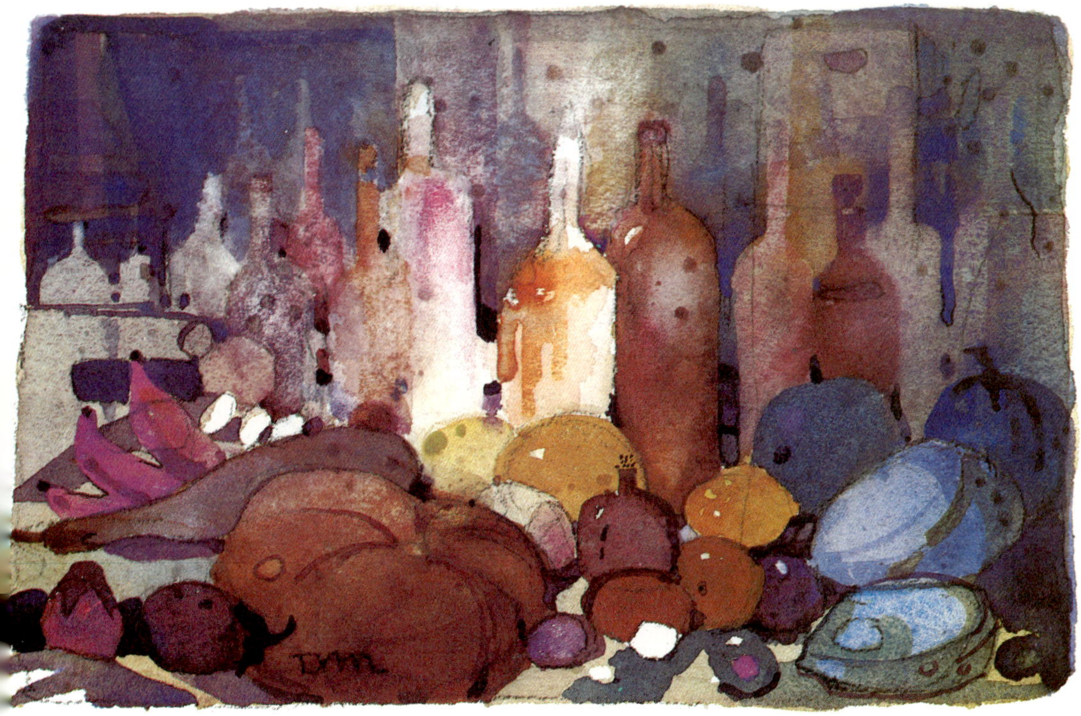

A Range of Analogous Colors. Here the artist created the spotlight effect of late-afternoon sun. Starting with white, he went to gray-lemon, and then to Indian yellow, yellow ochre, and Chinese orange, enriched by burnt sienna on the pumpkin. Then he used a burnt sienna–mauve mixture. Adding ultramarine blue to it, he made the stem and tiny dark accents around the small fruit on the bottom left, to which he had already added permanent rose. The bananas were painted with burnt sienna, mauve, and some permanent rose. The artist carried pinkish violets and reddish purples across the background.

Working in a Series

Improving Your Technique. Painting a series of "bottlescapes" is a valuable way to practice capturing form and light in a transparent and sparkling manner. It is also a good way to practice observing how and where light passes through transparent materials. It gives you an opportunity to study color mixtures that portray the tonal nuances of translucency, as when you are looking at background light or color changes through one or more bottles. You can also learn where highlights should be placed on vitreous objects to denote form.

Mr. Millard offers the following tips for painting bottlescapes in watercolor: Play with the endless variety of forms and arrangements. Build up your sequence of washes—wet over dry, wet over dry. To achieve transparency, let your background wash run right through your bottles. Keep your highlights as the white paper by painting around them and any other special light-struck planes and edges.

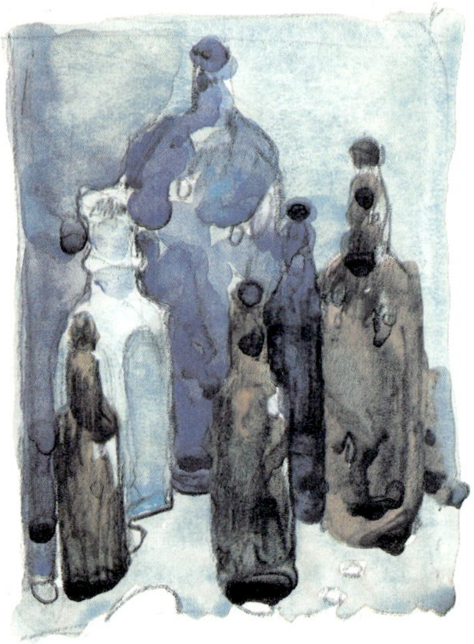

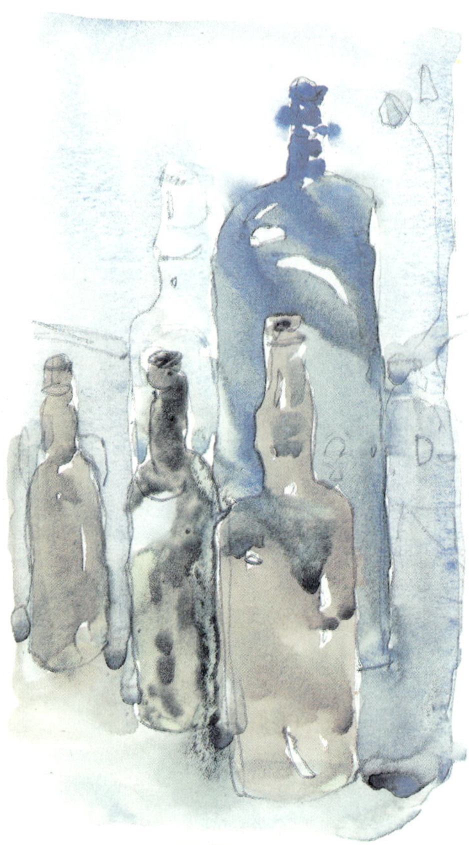

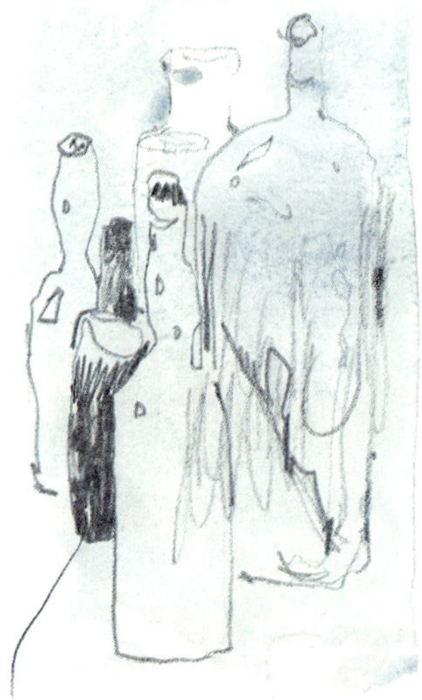

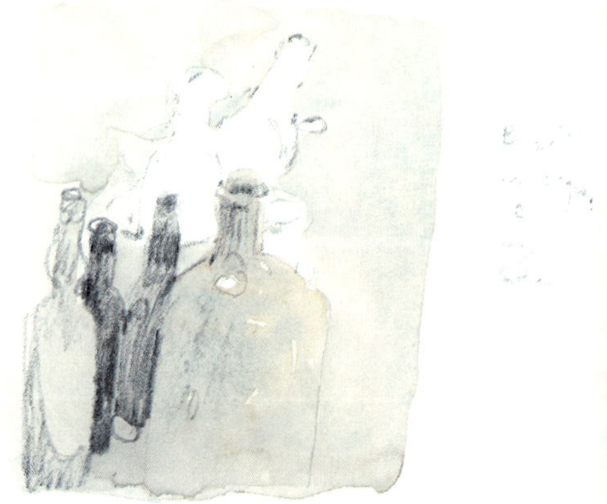

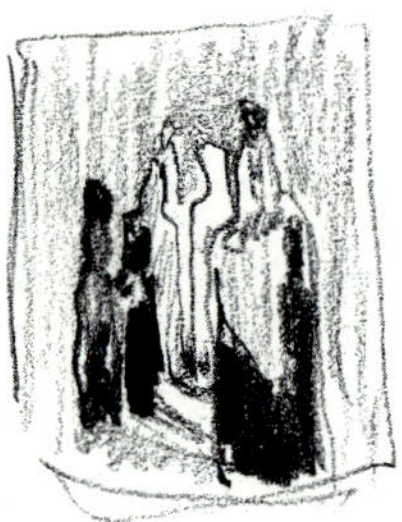

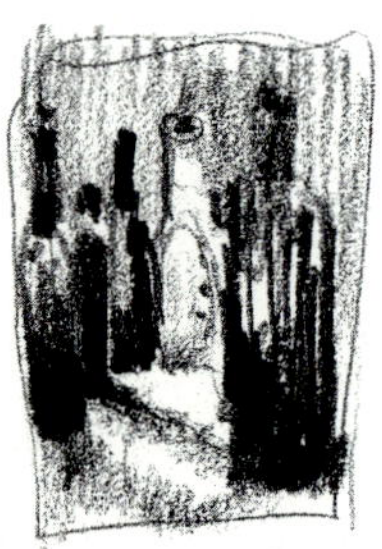

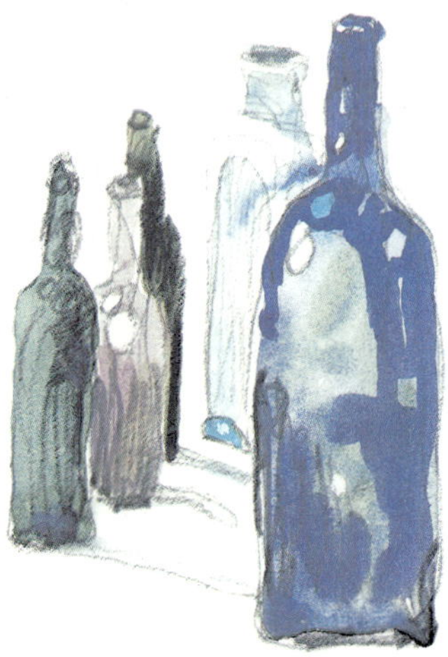

Adding Bottles to Your Still Lifes. Adding a wine bottle to a still life can perk up solid objects such as bread and apples with the sparkle and transparency of glass. Studying bottlescapes will definitely improve the quality of light in your still lifes.

Exploring Design, Value, and Color. The studies on these pages are the result of the artist's quiet, intuitive search into seven old sea bottles from the harbor bottom. He considers them preliminary sketches for future paintings. Notice how they differ in the use of wash techniques and design elements.

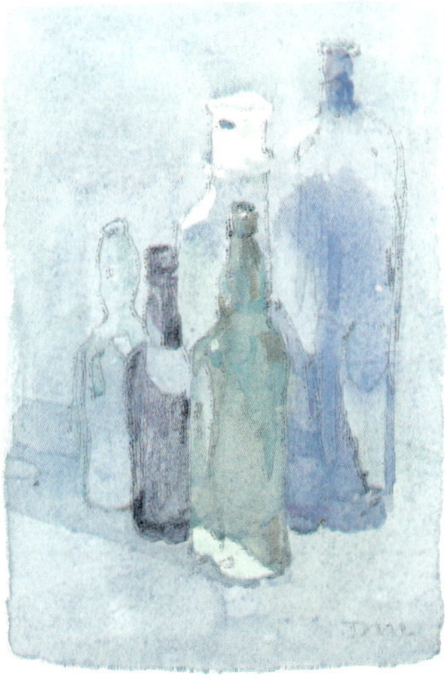

Sea Bottles 1. (Above) The artist laid in a background wash of cerulean blue and light red, adding a touch of cobalt violet as he moved to the right, and then let it dry. He painted each of the bottles here differently. The largest bottle is ultramarine blue with cobalt violet added wet-into-damp-wet in the center. In the dark green bottle, he left a provocative pattern of light, using cobalt green, sap green, raw umber, and some manganese blue at the base. The second bottle from left was painted with cobalt violet. He let the color pick up some of the carbon from his drawing. The bottle at left is manganese blue with a slight touch of cobalt green.

Sea Bottles 2. (Below) Mr. Millard laid diluted raw umber and Davy's gray over all but the white areas. For his second wash, he used the background mixture from his previous bottlescape. At top left, he dropped a mixture of cobalt violet, cobalt blue, and ivory black into the wet background and coaxed it down onto the shoulder of the largest bottle. Adding touches of manganese blue, cerulean blue, and raw umber to the background at right, he then ran this mixture onto the base of the square bottle. The darkest bottle is sap green and burnt sienna, and the one at far left is a mixture of Winsor violet and ultramarine blue.

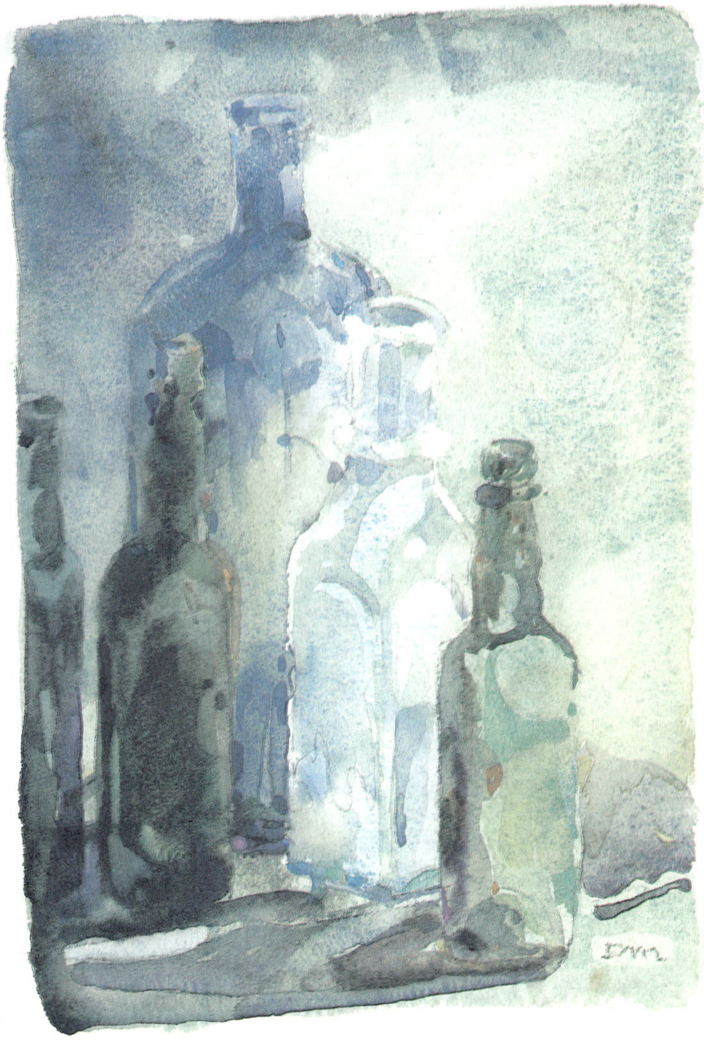

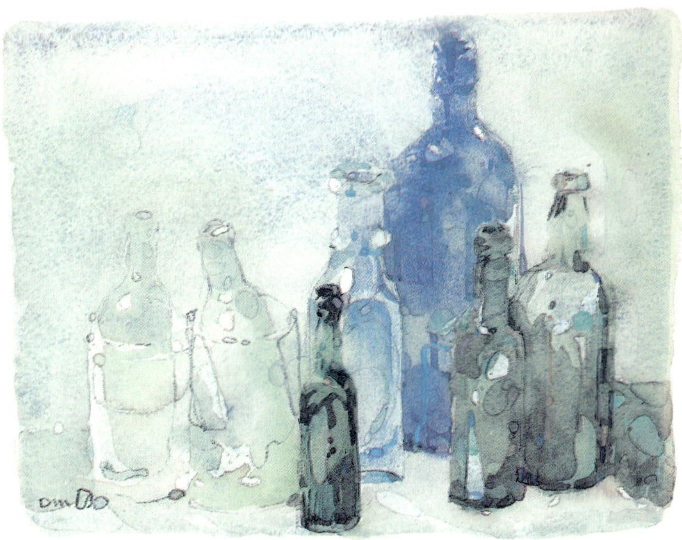

Sea Bottles 3. (Left) The background wash on the left is cerulean blue and light red, with emerald green tint added in the left-hand bottles. The background tint on the extreme right is sap green and burnt sienna. Deeper glazes of this mixture are on bottles 3, 6, and 7. Bottle 5 is based on ultramarine blue with touches of mauve, lamp black, and cerulean blue. The artist used some pure cerulean blue and a spot or two of cobalt violet. Bottles 3, 6, and 7, as well as the side shadow at right, are cobalt green with raw umber in the cool dark grayish patterns of glass.

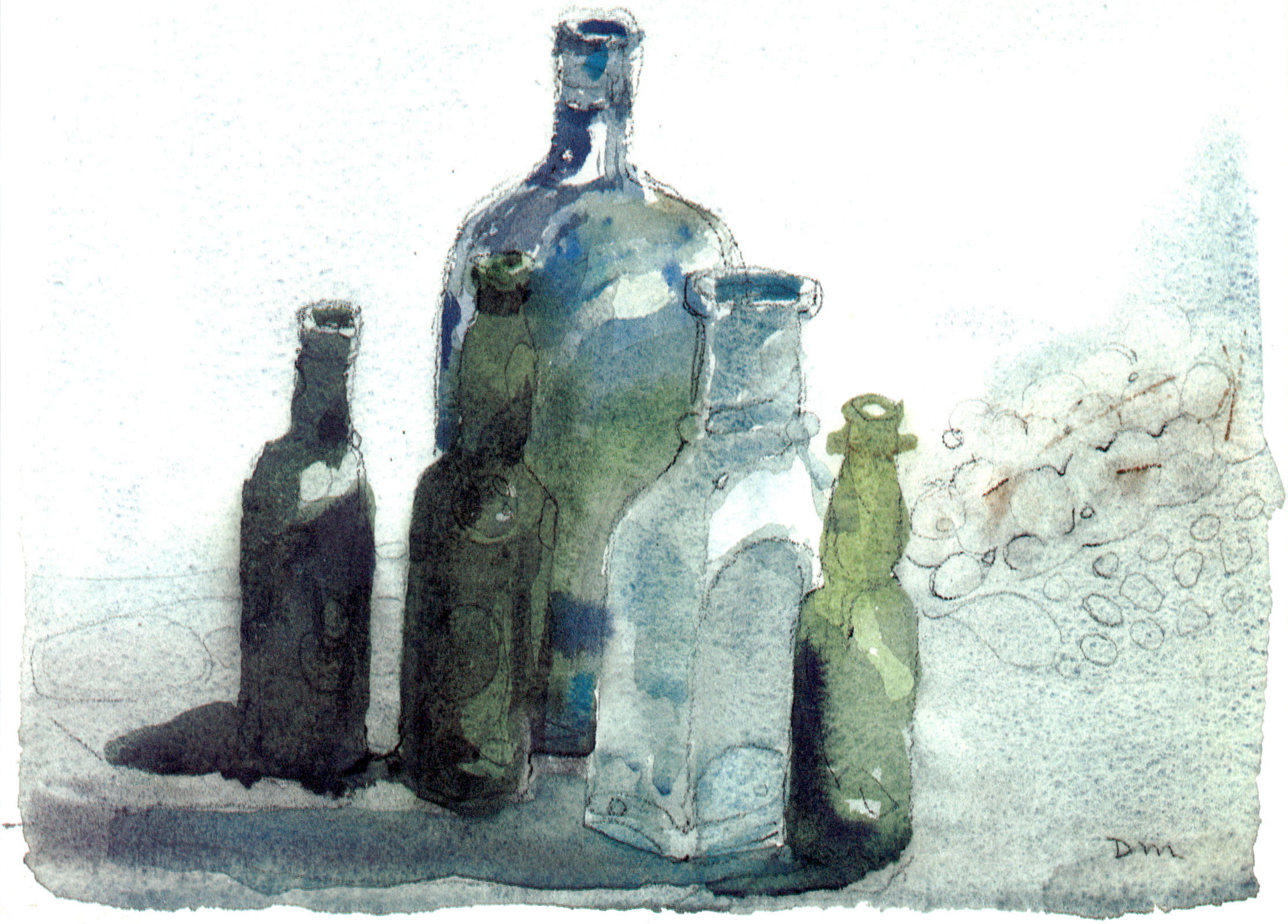

Sea Bottles 4. (Above) For this study, the artist mixed a background wash of cerulean blue and light red. He laid in subsequent washes of ultramarine blue, cobalt blue, and cendre blue, using bits of the first wash and keeping it very very pale. These same blues went into the bottles in deeper tones, which were toned down further with a touch of raw umber. The darkest bottles are sap green, burnt sienna, and ivory black. He used the same combination in the lighter green bottle. He put two touches of Antwerp blue (or he could have used phthalo) in the big bottle—one on the center shoulder, and the second near the base.

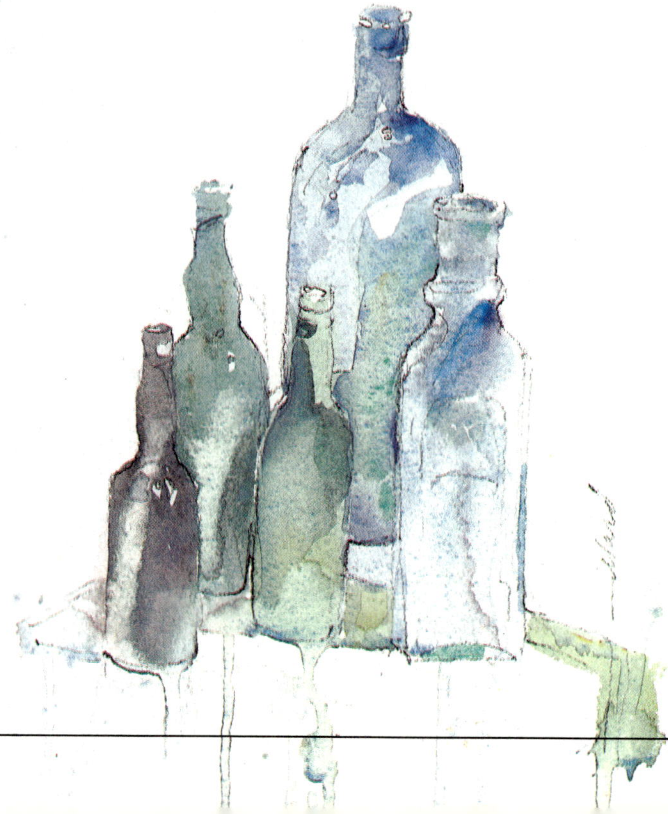

Sea Bottles 5. (Left) Mr. Millard began with a very pale background wash and then laid a second wash over all the bottles except where he wanted highlights. He made the bottle at left a deeper-toned mixture of mauve, burnt sienna, and lamp black. He used a mixture of cobalt blue, raw umber, and cobalt green for the next two bottles and to color segments of the two bottles at right, where he also added some mauve and ultramarine blue on the neck and shoulders. The right-hand bottle got some ultramarine blue and a swipe of manganese blue.

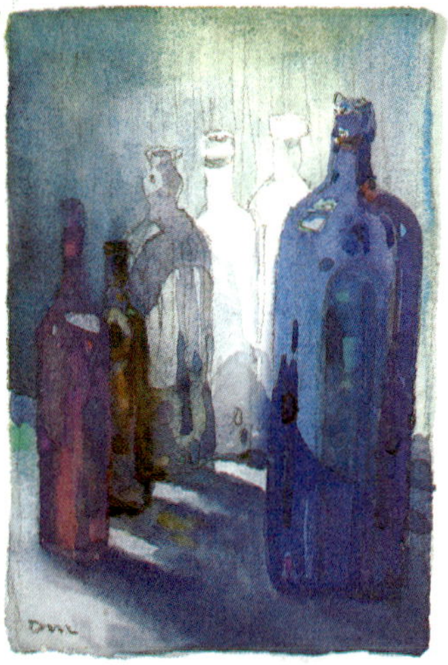

Sea Bottles 6. (Above) Here Mr. Millard mixed a background wash of cerulean blue and light red (mixing before each brushful was added). He laid it in over all but the white areas and then quickly added some manganese blue on the extreme right (but not over the big bottle) and ultramarine blue, mauve, and ivory black on the left. Some of this wash went over parts of bottle 3 after the previous washes were dry. Note that the first wash is still evident on parts of bottles 3, 4, and 5.

The red bottle was painted with mauve and permanent rose. The artist started near the bottom with ivory black and then added cobalt violet wet. He used Winsor violet and ultramarine blue to create deeper accents here. Bottle 2 is burnt umber with wet touches of sap green, and mauve. Note the touches of yellow ochre in the shadow near this bottle. Bottle 6 is a buildup of cobalt blue, Winsor violet, and mauve, with some ultramarine blue plus violet on the left and cobalt violet and rose madder toward the right. The artist was careful to save highlights between the bottle bases.

Sea Bottles 7. (Below) The artist mixed a large puddle of cobalt violet and cadmium orange with a touch of Davy's gray. He washed a spoonful of this mixture over all the bottles except the white ones. He went over the entire paper with this mixture except the white shapes, the rear jar, and the highlights on the second bottle. He used mauve and cobalt violet to paint the tones in the red bottle, and used lamp black for the deepest touches. Then, he brought washes and touches of burnt sienna into play. Finally, he used a lavender mixture of Winsor violet and lamp black to overglaze the biggest bottle, adding ultramarine blue for the deeper touches at the base. Using a razor blade, he scraped out some texture and the broken light pattern.

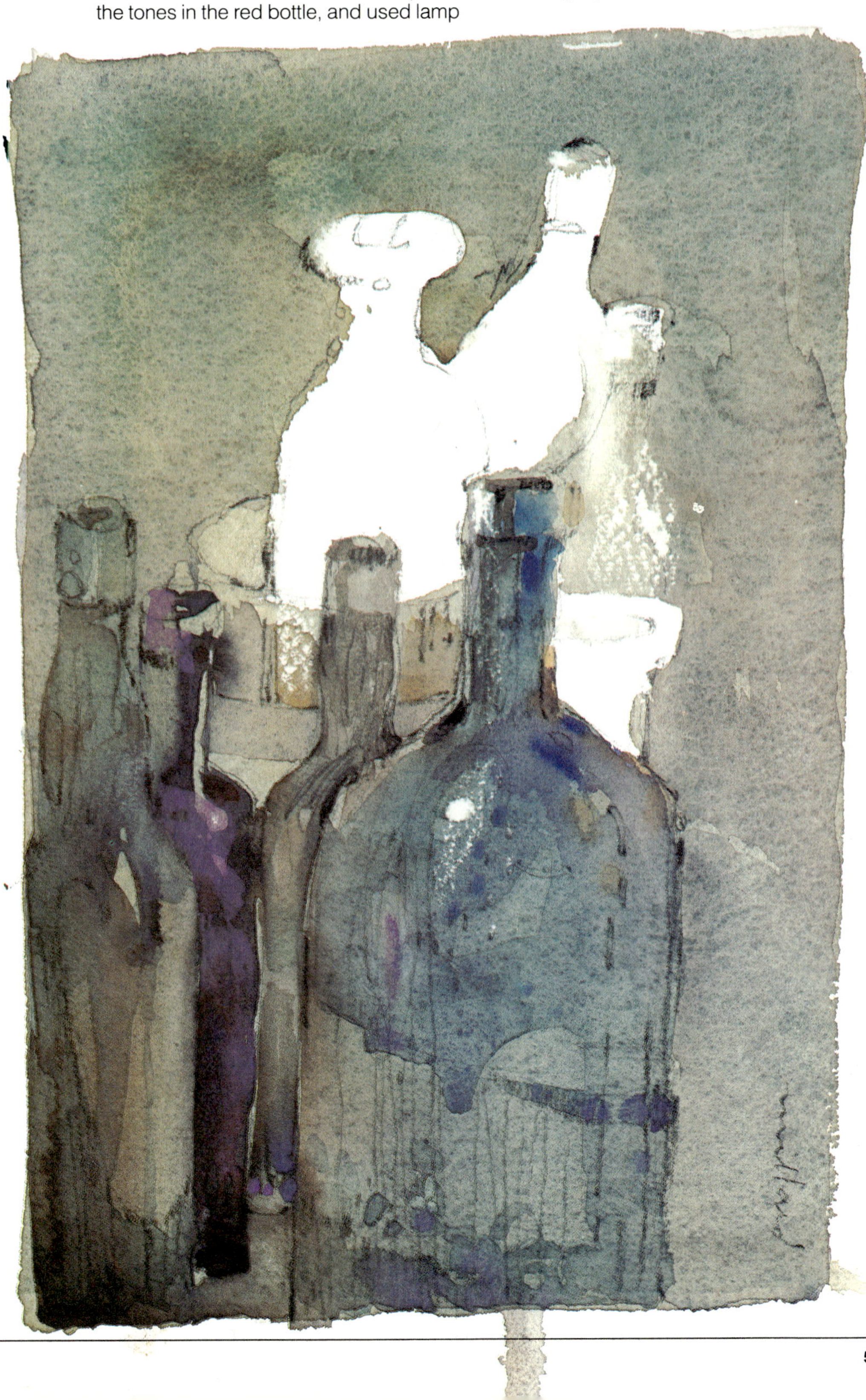

Working with Photographs

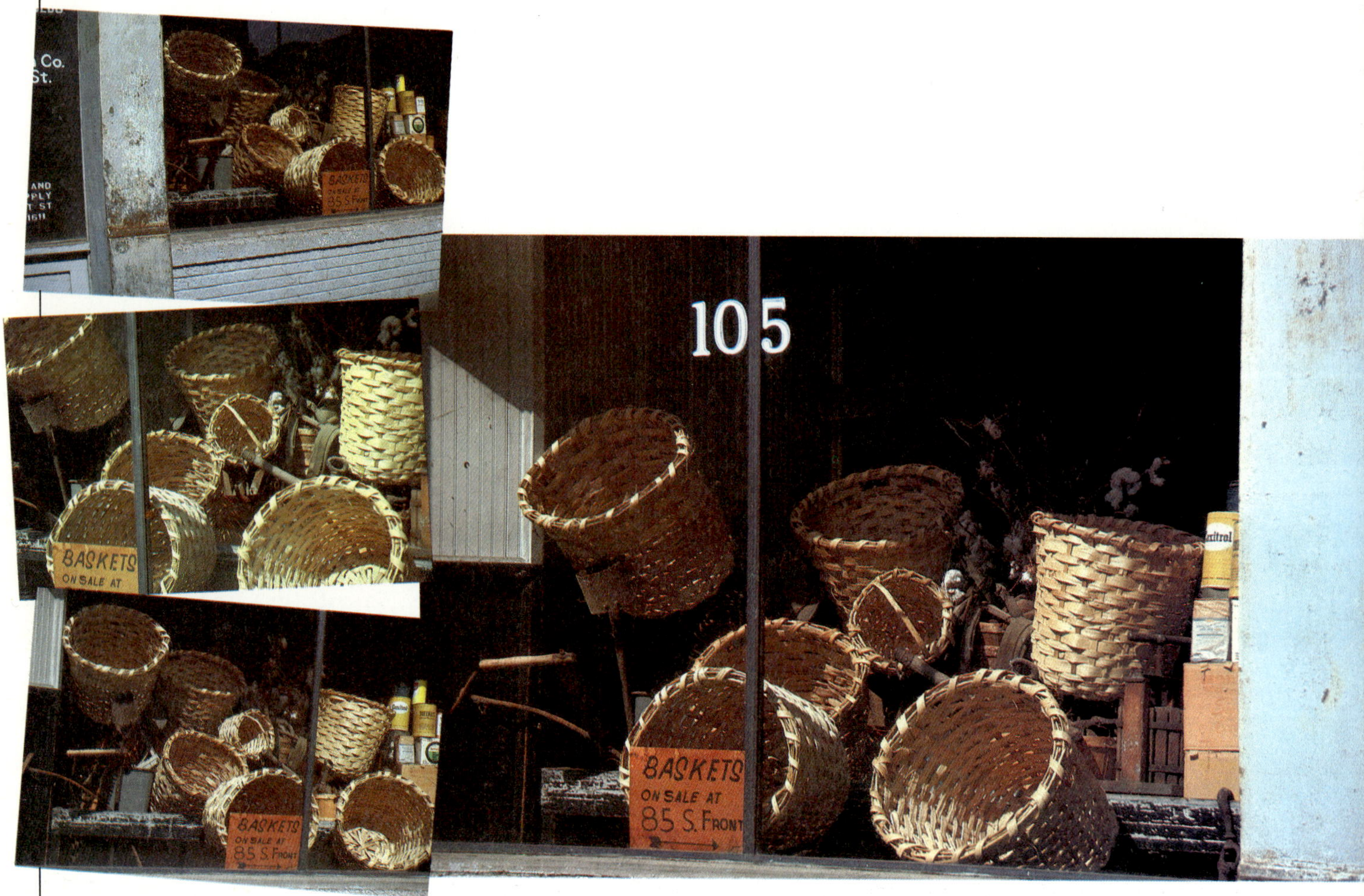

Reference Photos. Georg Shook thinks of his camera as a means of creating a space-age "sketchbook," offering him a quick and easy way to record his visual impressions. But it is really much more. It is also a way of capturing detail and qualities of light that are elusive to the eye. Since photos yield so much information, he has found them to be a richer source of reference material for his paintings than sketches.

The painting *Window Baskets* is a case in point: He came across the scene while strolling among some abandoned buildings in downtown Memphis and was intrigued by the way the sun illuminated the baskets. He knew that the light and shadows would change rapidly, and so he shot several slides from different angles to capture the shifting tones and textures. Because he photographed the scene instead of sketching it, he was able to record it from four different angles in the space of a few seconds.

After some deliberation, he decided to paint the closeup scene—but not too literally. To avoid being influenced by the overly saturated colors of the slide, he had a black-and-white print made from it. Then he had another print made in the reverse, or "flopped," position—he does this sometimes to create a more "comfortable" composition or to allow himself to get that much further from a literal interpretation of a photograph.

Early Stage. (Top right) Mr. Shook did a fairly detailed drawing on Strathmore Hi-Plate Illustration Board No. 240-4. This surface had the advantage of allowing him to develop a single area to completion rather than work on the overall painting all at once. He used new gamboge, raw umber, and raw sienna as underwashes for the baskets, and then used burnt umber, burnt sienna, Prussian blue, and Van Dyke brown for the detail and shadows. Some of the lighter shadows were done with Winsor blue and burnt sienna. Also, cadmium red medium was used to intensify the shadow area.

Finished Painting. Mr. Shook's finished interpretation of the scene is detailed, yet there are value changes and areas of soft detail that evoke the mood he wanted. Rather than being a slavish imitation of the reference photograph, this painting is the artist's interpretation of the subject—done with the *aid* of photography.

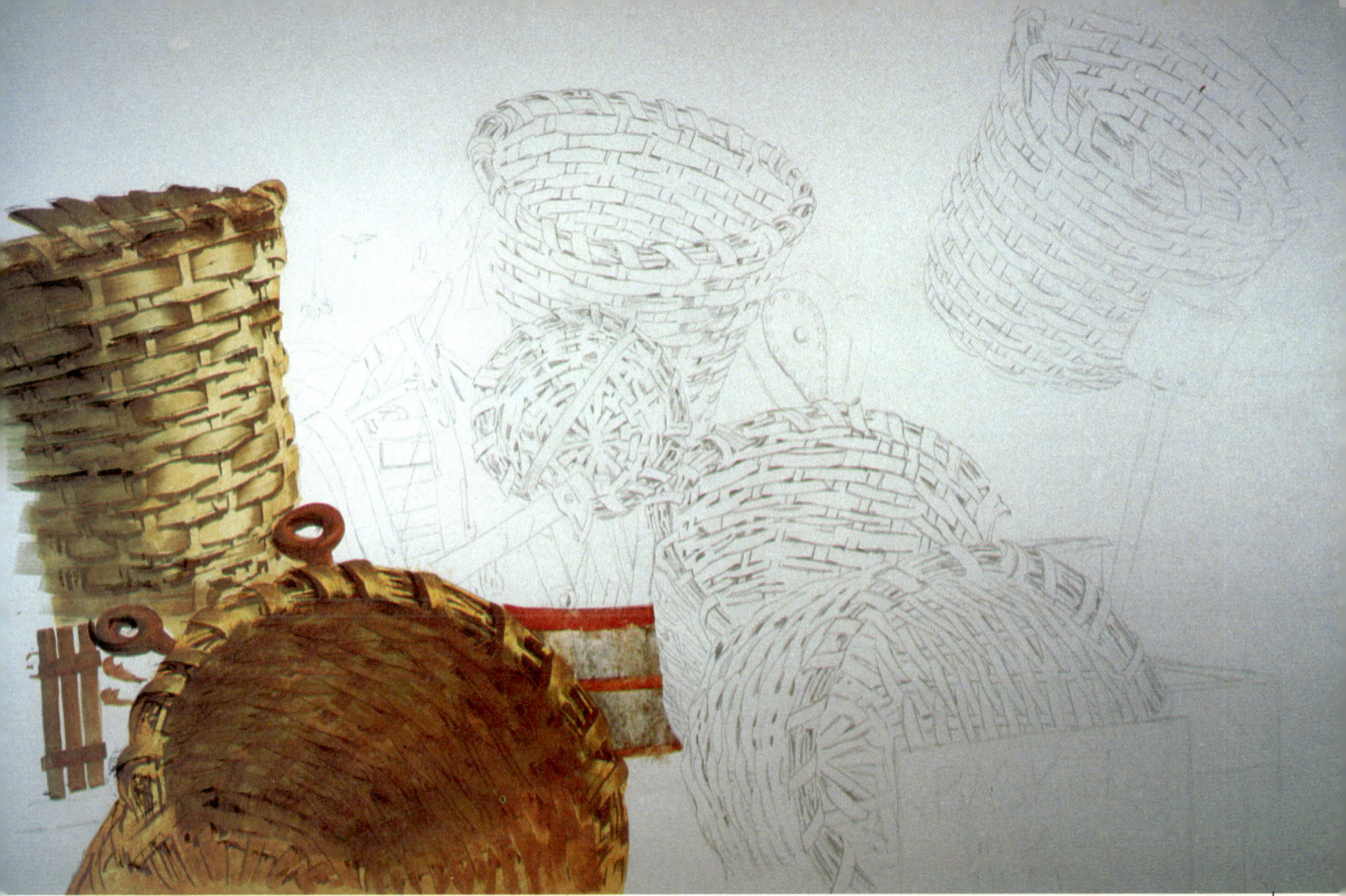

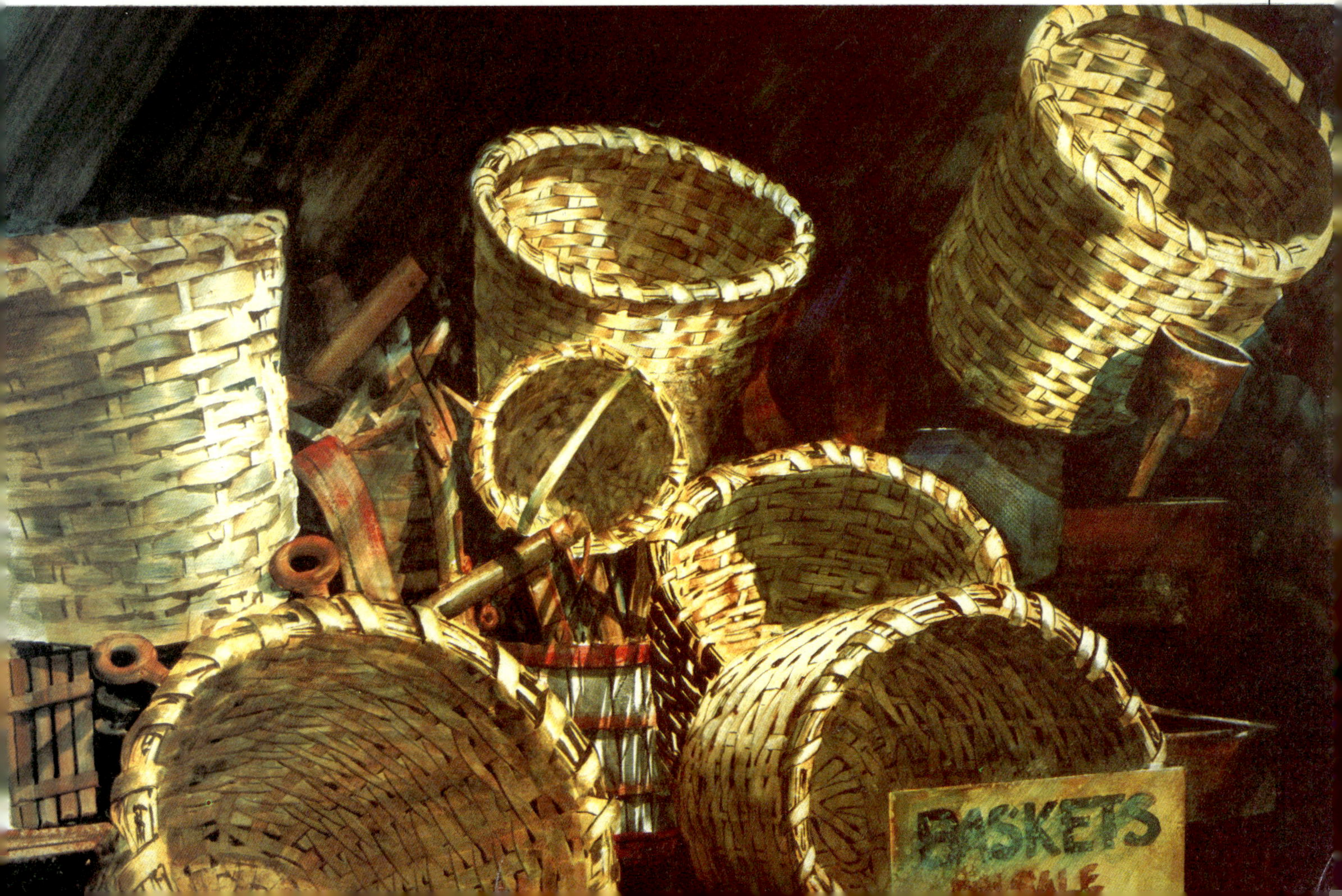
BASKETS

Two Photos, One Painting

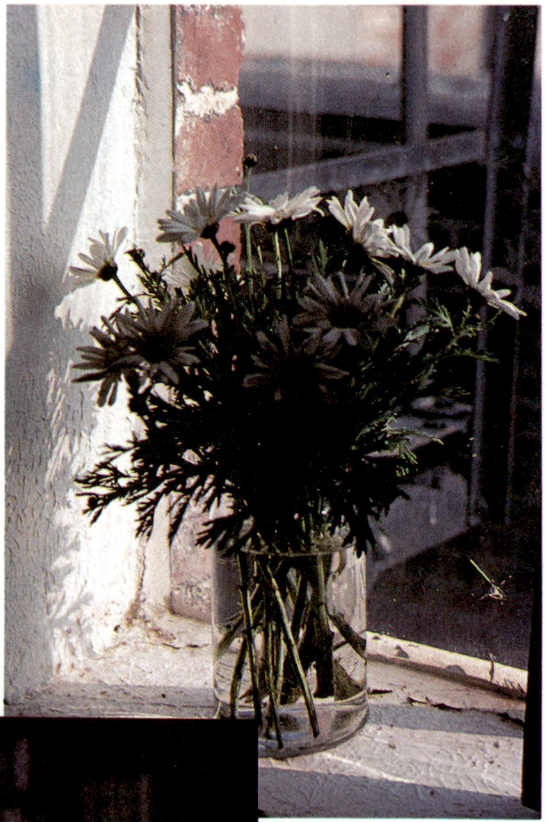

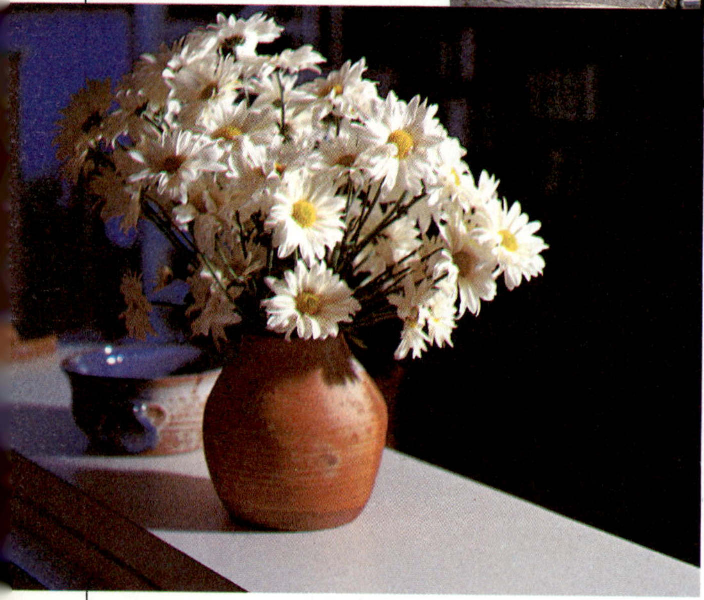

Reference Photos. Here the artist wanted to create a floral painting from photographic reference material. By consulting his slide reference library, he located two photographs that he felt would be useful. The first slide was of daisies in a terracotta vase. The fullness of the blossoms offered good possibilities. The other image was also of daisies, in a clear glass vase this time, and Mr. Shook especially liked the way the sunlight silhouetted the flowers and cast shadows across the edge of the window frame.

Sketches. (Opposite page, top) The artist began by making separate sketches, since his original intention was to do two different paintings. But he began to realize that a single strong painting could be done from this reference material, and so he combined the images into one sketch.

The Painting. (Opposite page) The sketch on the watercolor papr was left simple because Mr. Shook intended to do most of his drawing with the paintbrush. First he wet the window area, especially the panes, and floated in a mixture of Prussian blue and Van Dyke brown to get a dark background. The brick was painted with brown madder and burnt sienna, while the shadow detailing was done with Prussian blue and Van Dyke brown. At this point he used Maskoid, a resist material to block out the white daisies. He planned to wipe away this rubbery substance later and let the whiteness of the board itself show through as daisy shapes.

Returning to the sill area, the artist underpainted a mixture of Prussian blue and Van Dyke brown for the shadow; then he pulled a brush loaded with burnt sienna across the sill's edge to give a bit of color to that dark area. The final stages included applying burnt sienna as an underpainting for the pottery vase, dragging some raw sienna into it, and creating a shadow mixture from Prussian blue and Van Dyke brown. He used the same mix, but heavier on the Prussian blue, for the flower stems, and added some olive green to it for highlights.

Turning to the flowers themselves, Mr. Shook worked into the white design left by the Maskoid, using opaque white for the petals and then yellow ochre and burnt sienna for the flower centers. For the shadows he used a little Davy's gray mixed with white paint or, in some case, glazed over the white underpainting instead. Finally, he used ultramarine blue for some of the final shadow details.

In this painting the artist used photos creatively for information about shadow details, lighting, and other design elements. The final product, however, is not a copied photograph, but an original painting, a product of the artist's emotional response to the subject.

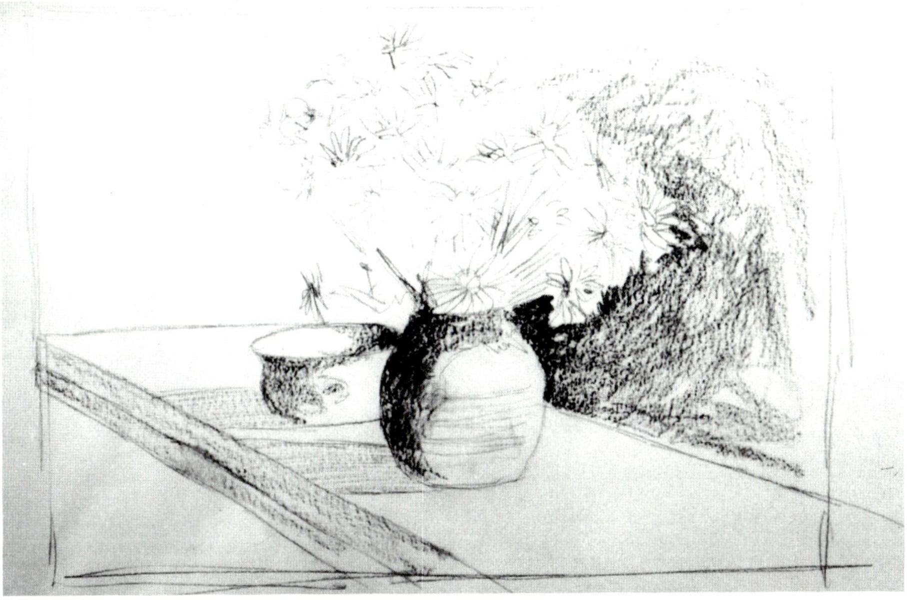

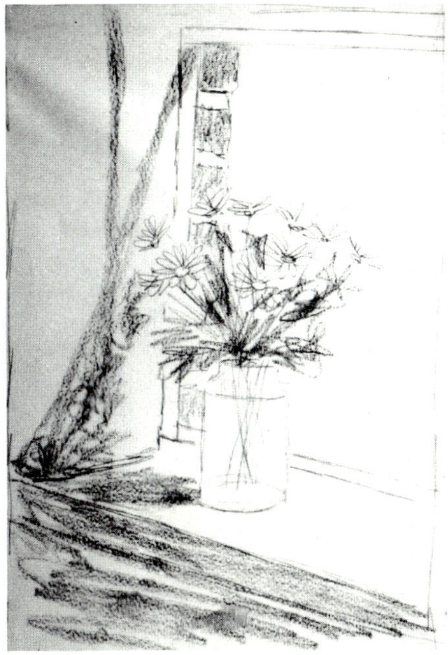

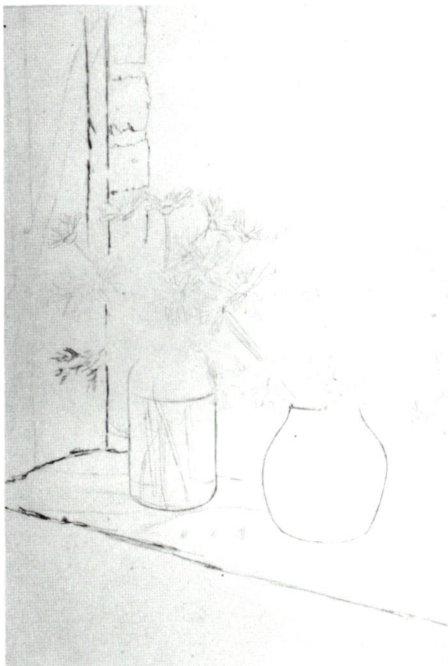

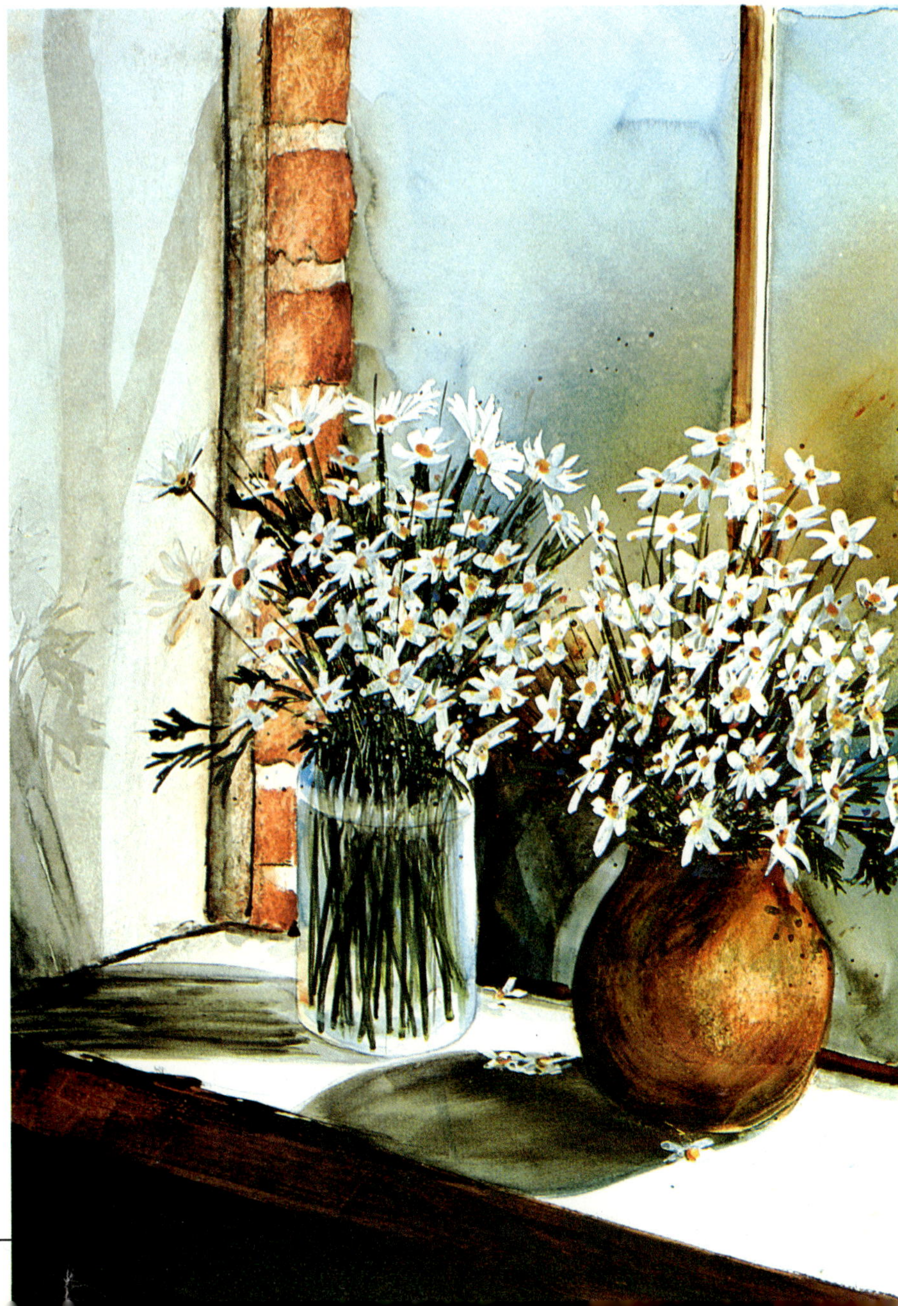

FRUIT AND VEGETABLES

Fruit and vegetables are quintessential still life subjects. Joseph Dawley, Arthur Stern, David Leffel, and David Lyle Millard show you how to paint some of the fruit and vegetables most often included in still life painting. You'll see that we've also included a loaf of bread and a fish. Neither fruit nor vegetable, these items nevertheless also present the problem of working with perishable still life objects.

Here's just a sampling of what follows in this section. You'll find invaluable tips on using shapes to effectively unify your paintings, as well as advice on adding highlights and enhancing your subjects with color. Learn how to find fascinating patterns, colors, and shapes in a simple arrangement of potatoes and turnips. Learn how to create an illusion of the "leafiness" of lettuce and how to capture the pitted, shiny quality of the outer peel of an orange.

Bread

1. A good, old-fashioned loaf of bread can be a beautiful prop for a still life painting. If you don't want to work with the whole loaf, it can be broken or sliced. The texture of bread can be difficult to paint well, and so don't be discouraged if you don't achieve stunning success with your first attempt—keep trying. Joseph Dawley used the same basic oil painting techniques on both loaves, but only his work on the rye bread on the right is described here. He began with a monochrome underpainting, using mixtures of underpainting white and raw umber. To outline the loaf and the inside portion of the bread, he used a mixture of about ninety-five percent white and five percent raw umber. The crust was filled in with a mixture containing slightly more raw umber. Returning to his lighter mixture, he painted the top of the crust on the right side, where the light hits it. He added more white to this tone to paint the white portion of the bread, as well as the board on which the bread is sitting. With a third tone, a mixture of about seventy-five percent white and twenty-five percent raw umber, he painted the background and the cast shadow on the left, which falls onto the other loaf.

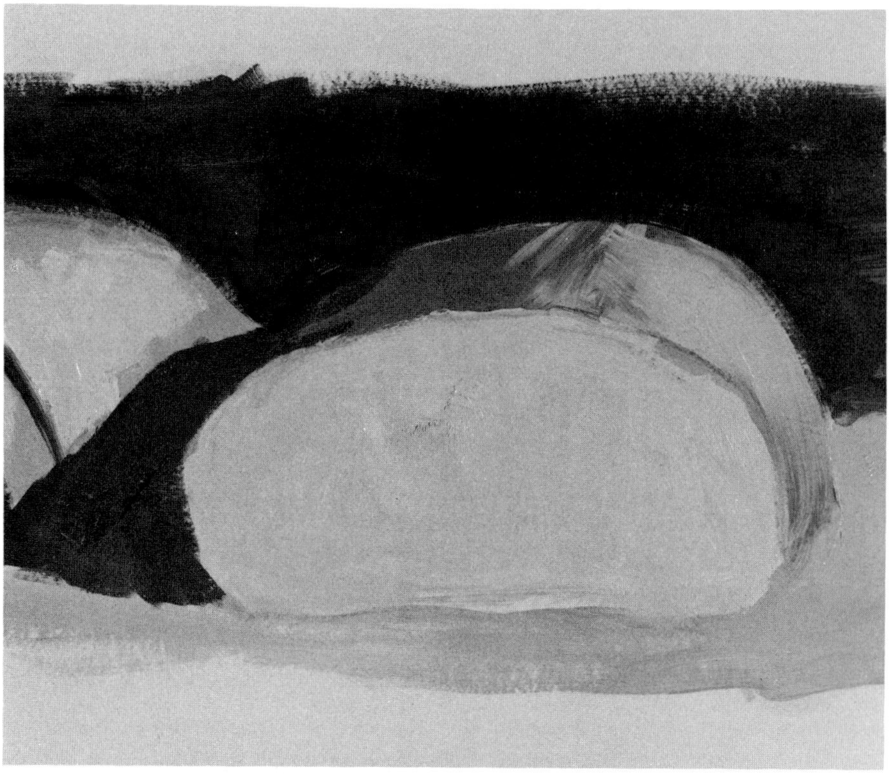

2. There is a shadow between the board and the bottom of the bread, and the artist used a stroke of his deeper tone to represent this. To begin creating texture in the crust, he scumbled white over the entire crust. Now he began some basic work on the inside of the bread. First he studied the general pattern created by the holes in the bread. These followed a somewhat circular design, and so he picked out some strategic holes to indicate this pattern and placed them in the bread. He painted a hole by first laying in his third tone for the shadow portion, then using white underneath for the highlighted area, and finally outlining the bottom of the hole with his middle tone. He then blended this tone down into the regular bread color to define the lower edge of the hole. For texture, he scumbled white and then his lightest tone in a random manner over the surface of the bread portion.

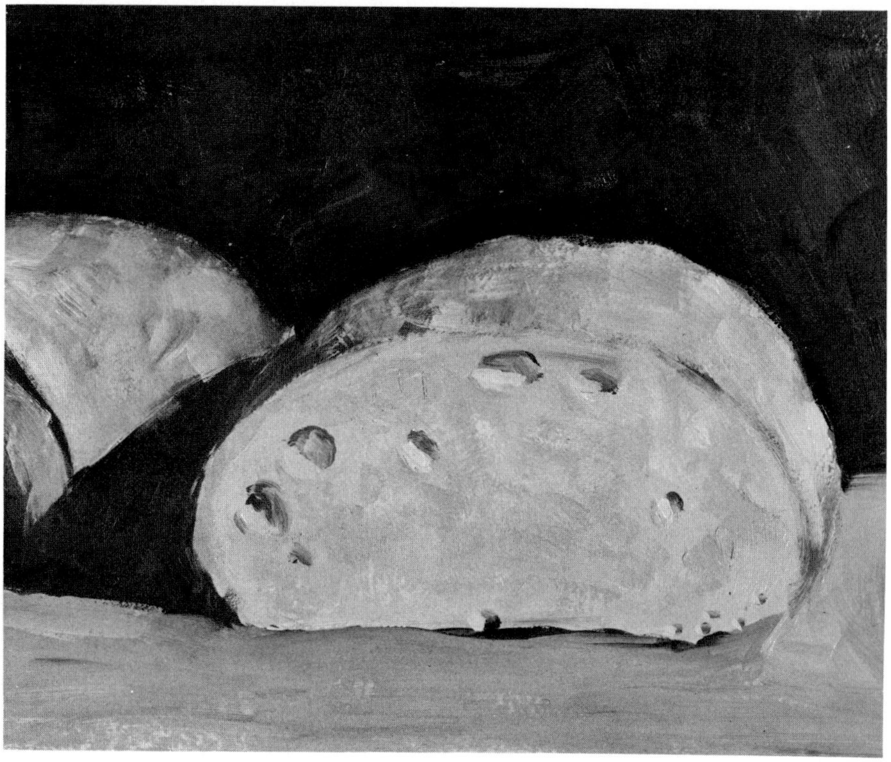

3. Next the artist added yellow ochre, burnt sienna, and phthalo blue to his palette and premixed these colors to get a light brown. Then he mixed them in different proportions to achieve a second, darker brown. Now he added more holes to the white portion of the bread. Next he mixed both tones of brown together and brushed this around in various spots between the holes, still allowing a great deal of the original bread color to remain.

For the crust, he applied the darker brown to the far left side of the loaf and extended this lightly toward the center area. This same color continues as a thin strip down the right side of the sliced edge of the crust. To create the lighter edge on the left side of this sliced section, he used his lighter brown tone mixed with white. He used his original brown for the highlighted middle of the crust. He avoided blending the two colors, instead letting them drag into each other where they meet. For the whole light area on the right side of the crust, he dabbed in a combination of underpainting white and yellow ochre.

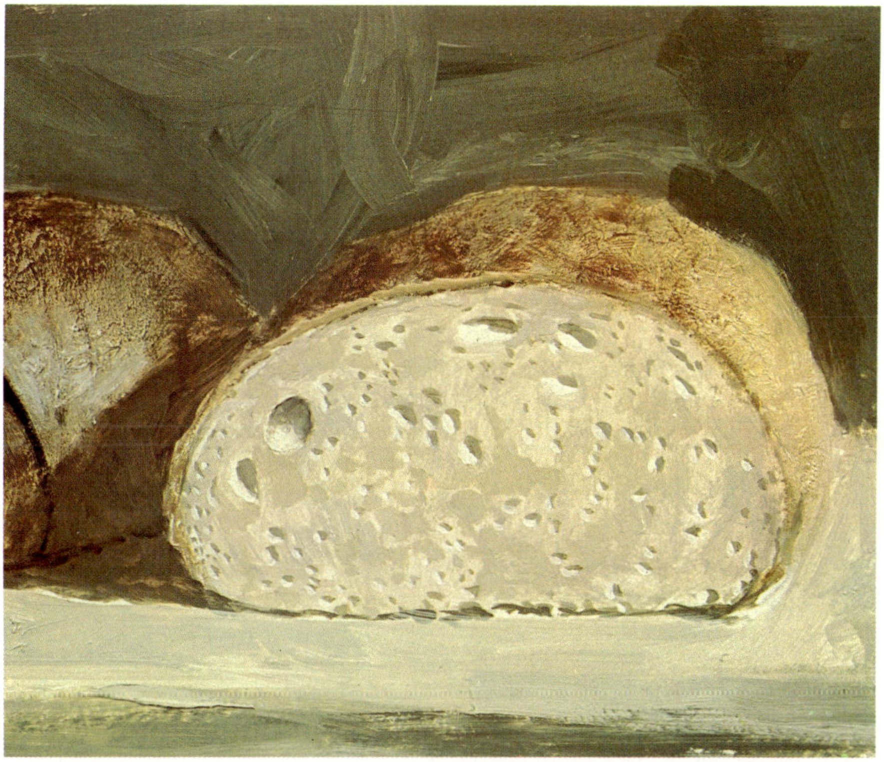

4. The artist added cobalt yellow, raw sienna, and ultramarine blue to his palette. Then he dragged a light brown mixture over the *entire* bread area, toning down the holes and highlights, and dabbed it into the bread for texture.

He blended raw sienna from the lower right of the crust up toward the highlight, which he emphasized with white and cobalt yellow. For texture he dabbed a mixture of phthalo blue, cobalt yellow, and white all over the crust. When the background was dry he painted over it with raw umber—and *let the entire painting dry completely*. Then he brushed painting medium over the surface. He lightly glazed raw umber over the far left side of the crust, and ultramarine blue was glazed into the breadboard and the shadow on the far left. To finish, he mixed his darkest tone (seventy-five percent white, twenty-five percent raw umber) with painting medium until it had a semiliquid consistency and then dabbed this over much of the bread with a small sponge, working around the holes. Finally, he mixed white with tiny amounts of cobalt yellow and burnt sienna and scumbled this into the bread at random, flicking it into various spots for highlights.

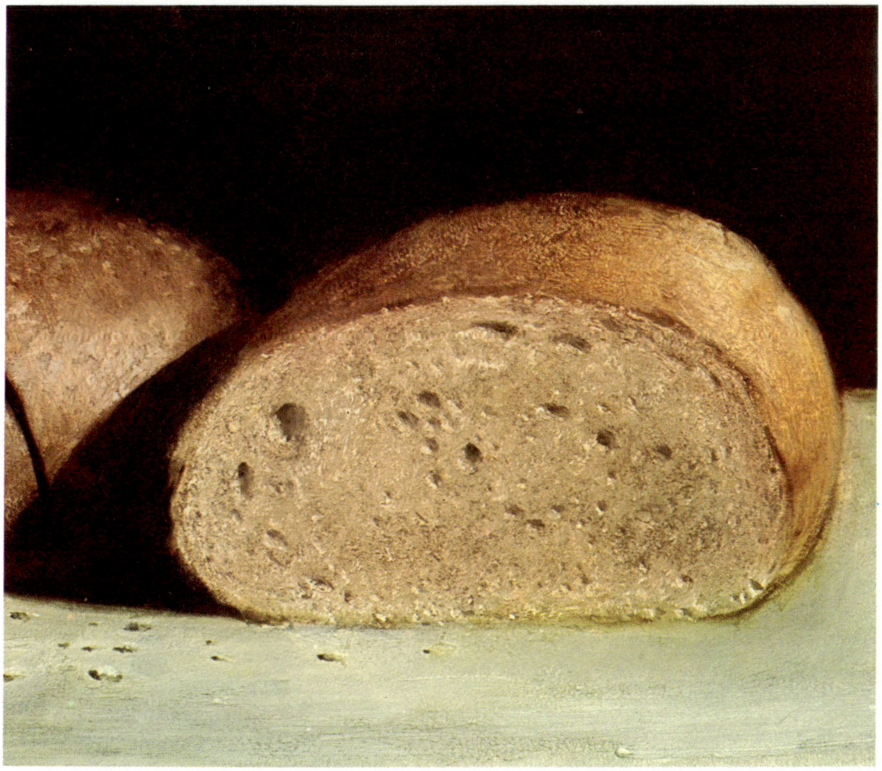

Fish

First Statement, Striped Bass. It can be good experience to paint a still life subject that rushes you—that teaches you the danger of dawdling over your painting too long. A fish is ideal for that purpose. Buy one in the morning and plan to cook it that same day. Knowing that you've got to eat the fish, you'll race to paint it before it becomes inedible. The elegant simplicity of this first statement by Don Stern, in fact, is partly due to his haste.

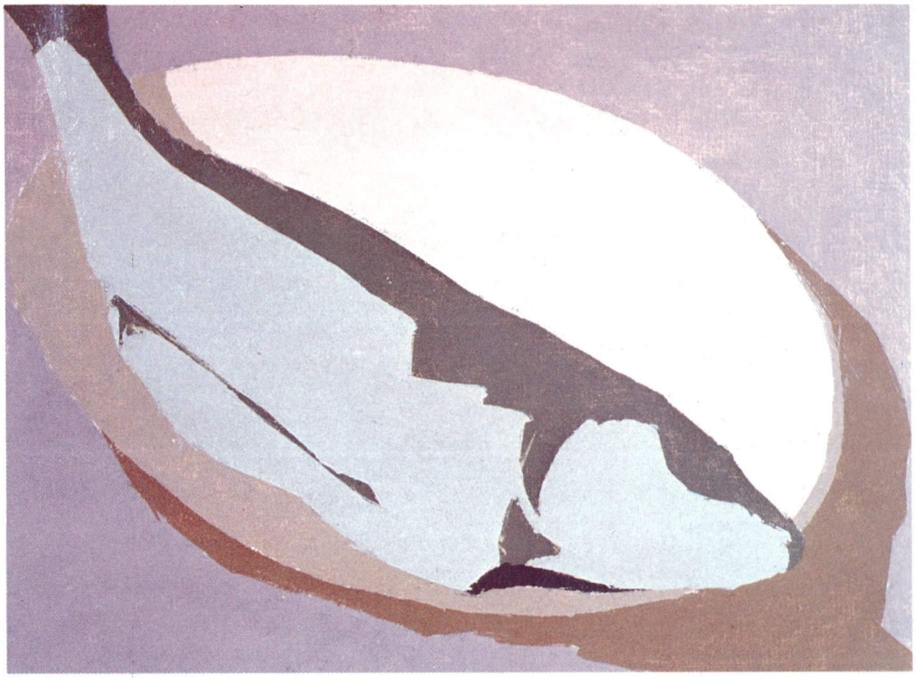

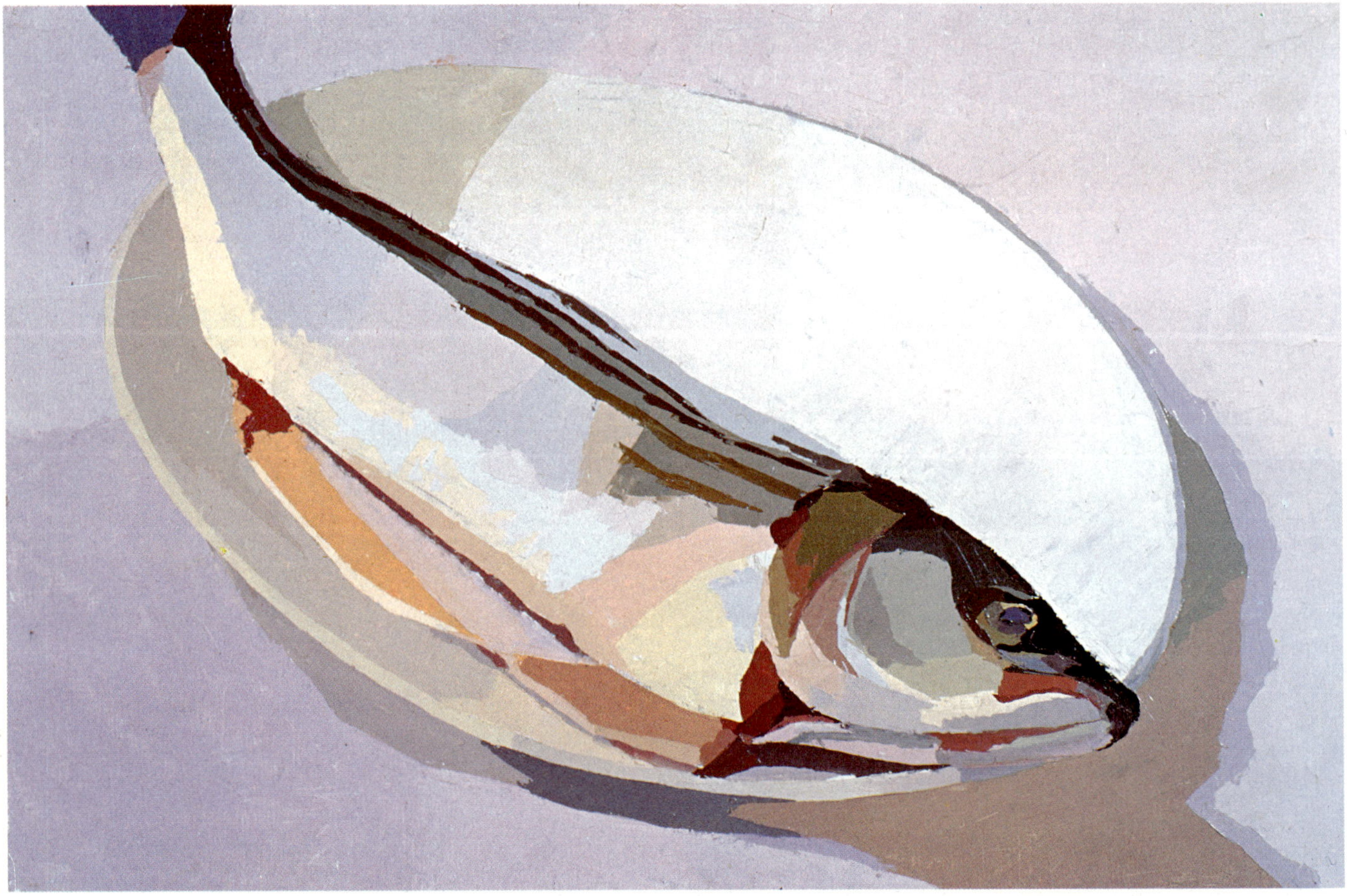

Second Statement, Striped Bass. The shiny surface of a fish provides beautiful colors to paint. But don't be put off by its shine and translucency. A fish is no more difficult to paint than a translucent plastic jug, a metal saucepan, or a glass plate. Just look for the big color spots, and don't get lost in details like fish scales. You'll probably find that a second statement is all you'll have time to do—and perhaps says all you'll want to say. (This painting is in the collection of William Fotaides.)

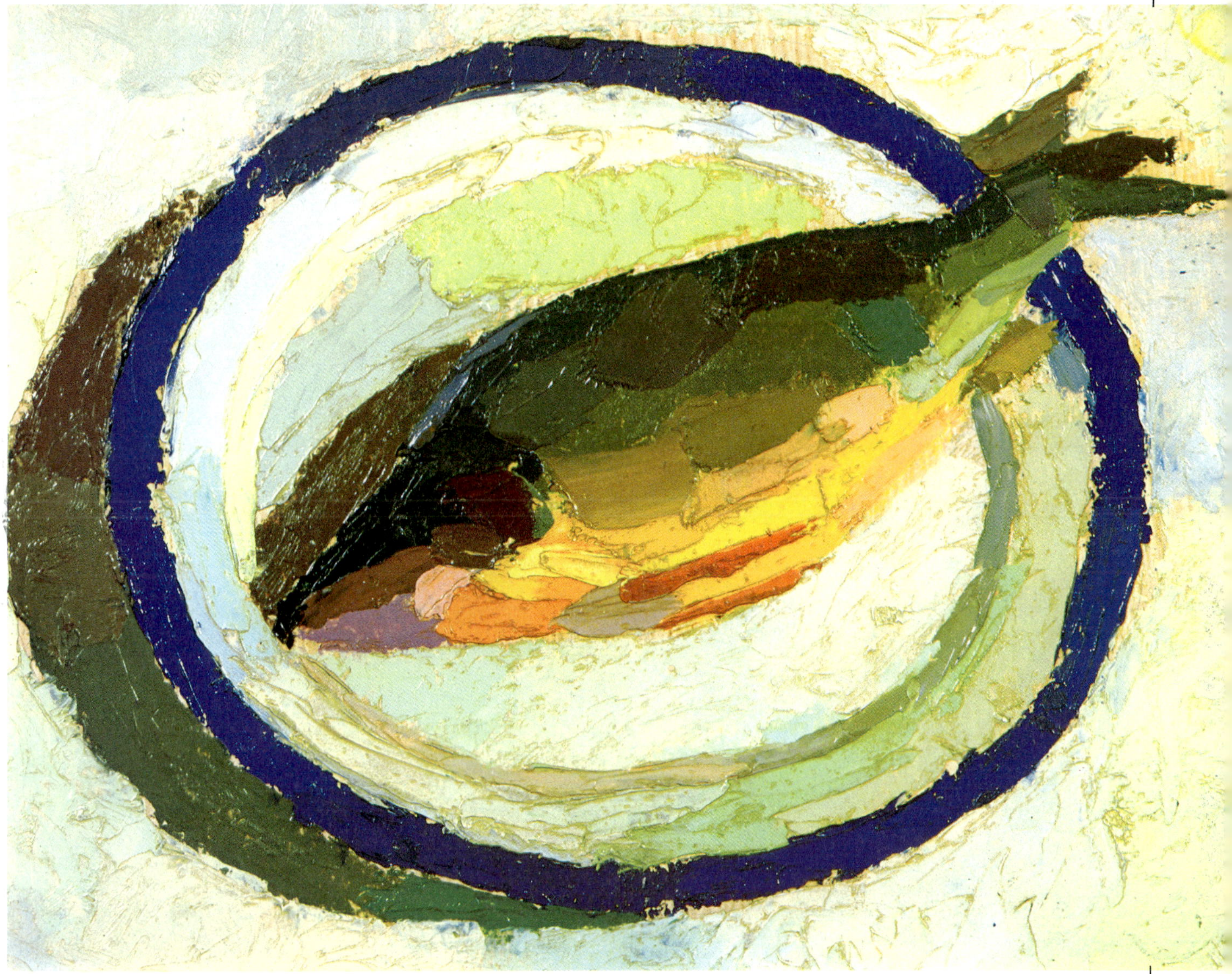

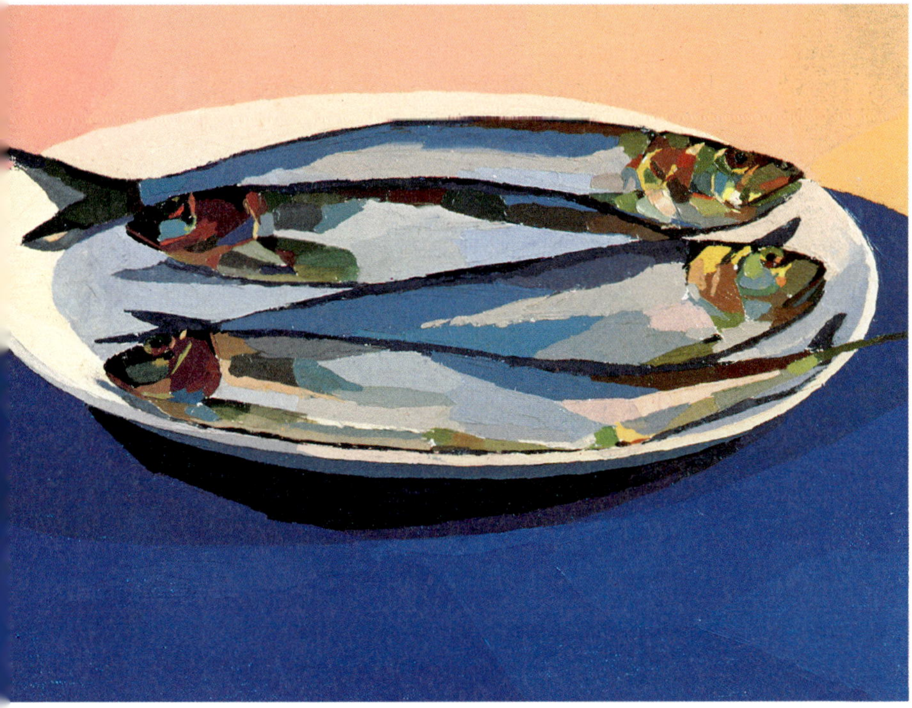

Rainbow Trout. (Above) The body of this fish is painted with large, simple, bold color spots—as are the dish and its shadow. The painter, Alexander J. Yow, has paid no attention to details, focusing his attention primarily on color variations in the tail and its shadow, subtle color changes in the dark rim of the dish, and the succession of colors in the dish's shadow. He has captured the almost unearthly glow of the fish's body, making it clear why it is called *rainbow* trout.

Four Sardines. Certainly four fish can be harder to paint than one—because you have to paint four times as fast before they spoil! You have to work quickly and decisively, identifying each color spot and mixing it swiftly, and placing it on the painting surface with a few economical strokes. The brilliant surface of the fish was a delight for Don Stern to paint.

Smooth Vegetables

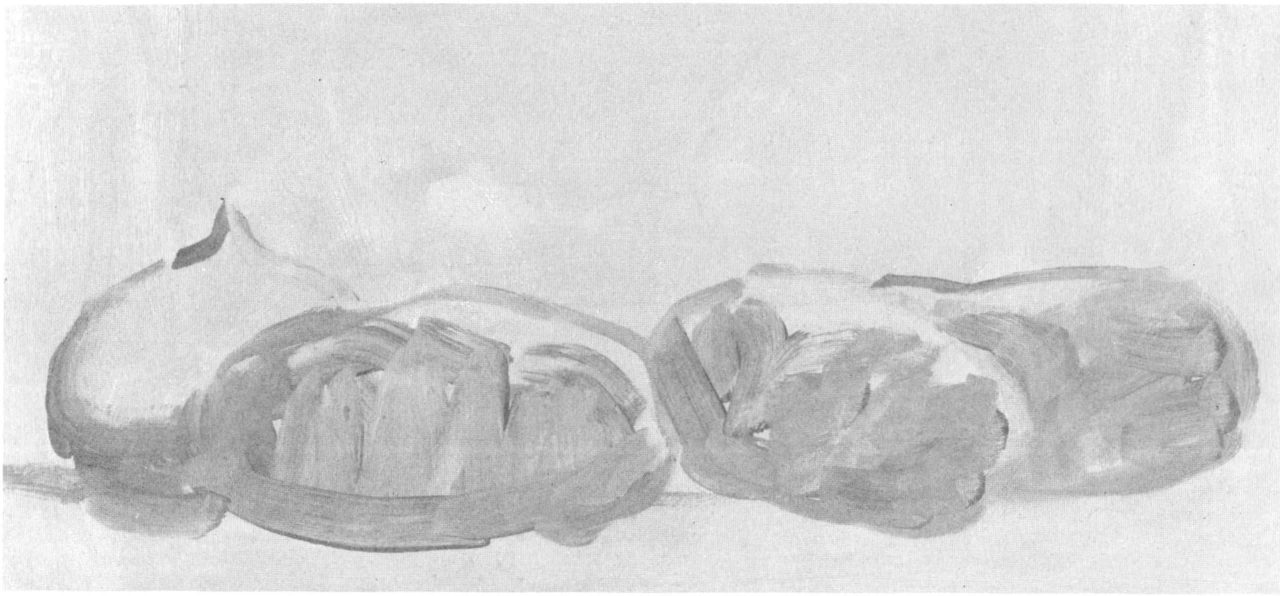

1. Smooth vegetables, like any other painting subject, must be rendered convincingly. If you decide to arrange your own vegetables, you'll discover a variety of fascinating patterns, colors, and shapes that make smooth vegetables lovely and unique still life subjects. Here oil painter Joseph Dawley has limited his composition to a turnip and three potatoes. Each vegetable has its own characteristics. In the case of the turnip, there is the uneven blending of the purple into the white, as well as the variations of color within the white and the dark pitted markings. The potatoes have interesting variations in size, shape, and surface indentations.

The artist started by painting the entire working surface with white paint, which would affect both the texture and the color of the paint applied over it. After this he brushed in the outline of each vegetable with a light mixture of white tinted with raw umber and used this same color to block in the strongest color areas and indicate the shadow underneath the turnip.

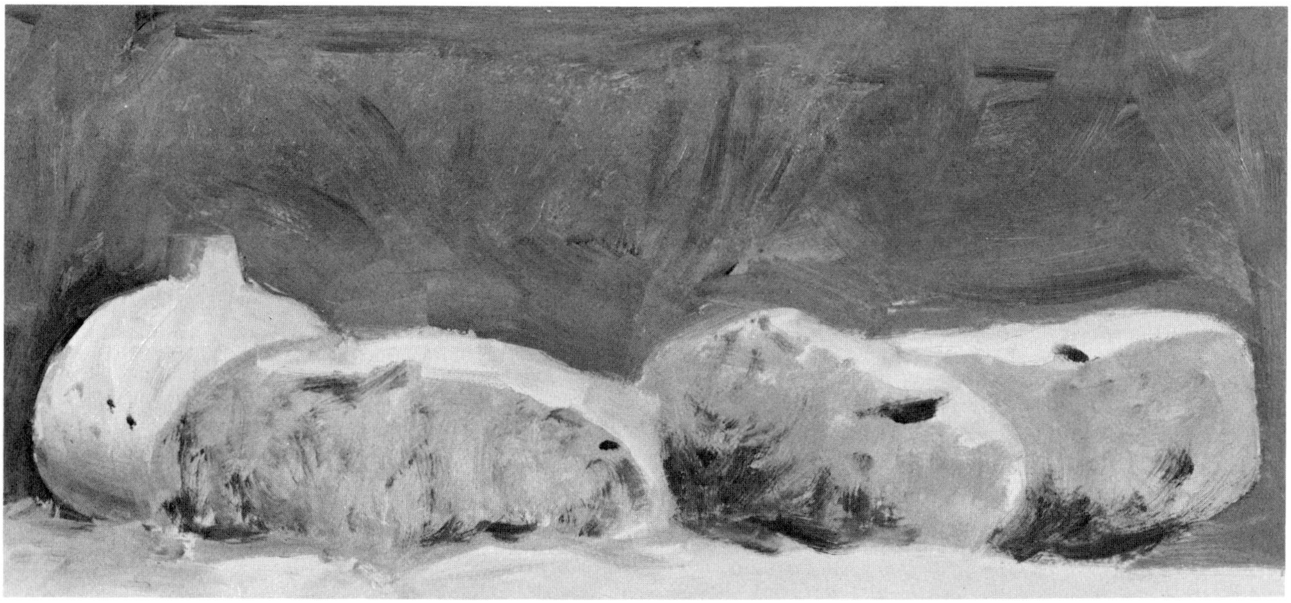

2. The artist brushed a slightly darker tone, consisting of about ninety percent white and ten percent raw umber, into the top portion of the background, but he kept the area below the vegetables white to represent the tablecloth. The light tone he had applied at the beginning was now smoothed out just enough to refine the brush strokes. To further refine the shape of the turnip, he applied his middle tone along its lower edge and then blended this upward into the white, fading it off toward the center. The two dots of a deeper tone, seen near the center, completed the work on the turnip for now.

Next he stroked large, sweeping areas of white across the top of each potato. To begin the texture of the potatoes, he roughly brushed in his middle tone almost in a scumbling manner. Then he scumbled in the deeper tone where the color looked darkest, and also in the shadow areas on the lower parts of each potato. He dabbed in this tone for the indentations—such as those in the white portion of the potato on the right.

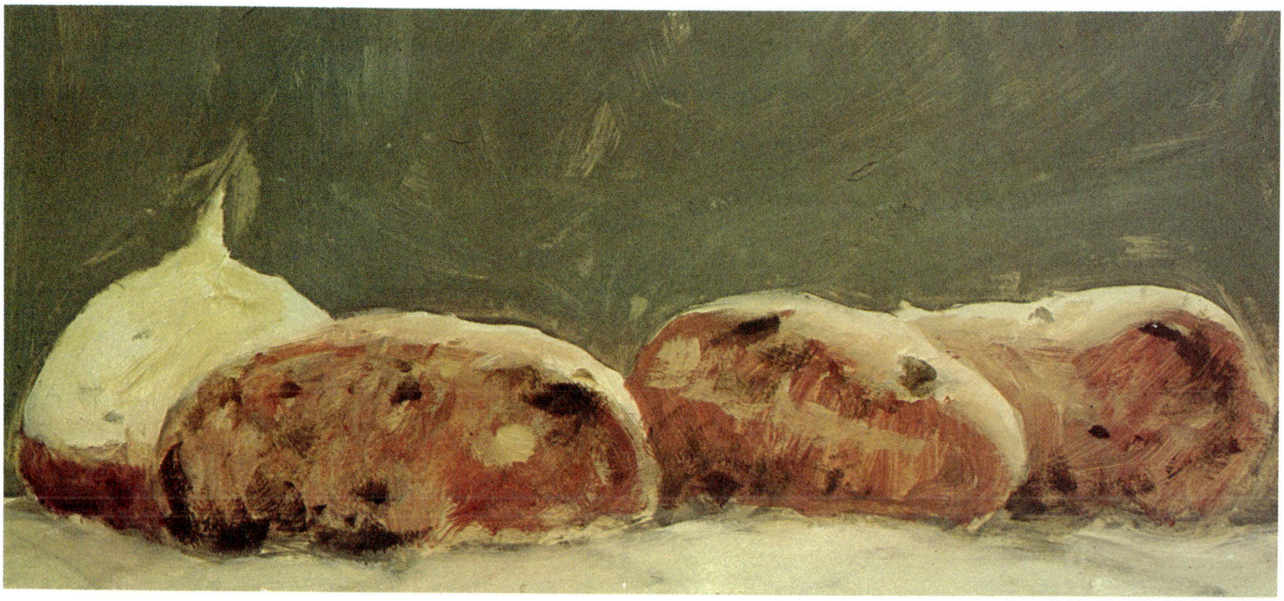

3. Having established the composition in monochromatic tones, the artist added yellow ochre, cobalt violet, Venetian red, and ivory black to his palette. He began with the turnip and brushed yellow ochre into the upper portion of the white area, especially in the center section just below the peaked root. He added cobalt violet to the lower portion of the turnip. Dabs of his second white–raw umber mixture replaced the deeper dots he had added to the white portion in the previous step.

The artist used Venetian red for the color of the potatoes and brushed it on over the whole surface, with the exception of the top white highlight. Only a slight amount was blended into the highlights to suggest a pinkish coloring. Next the dark spots and shadows, a combination of yellow ochre and ivory black, were brushed in where needed. Mr. Dawley used white with a touch of yellow ochre for the light areas in the red parts of the potatoes—for example, the light streak in the middle of the center potato and the brighter highlight on the right side of the potato nearest the turnip.

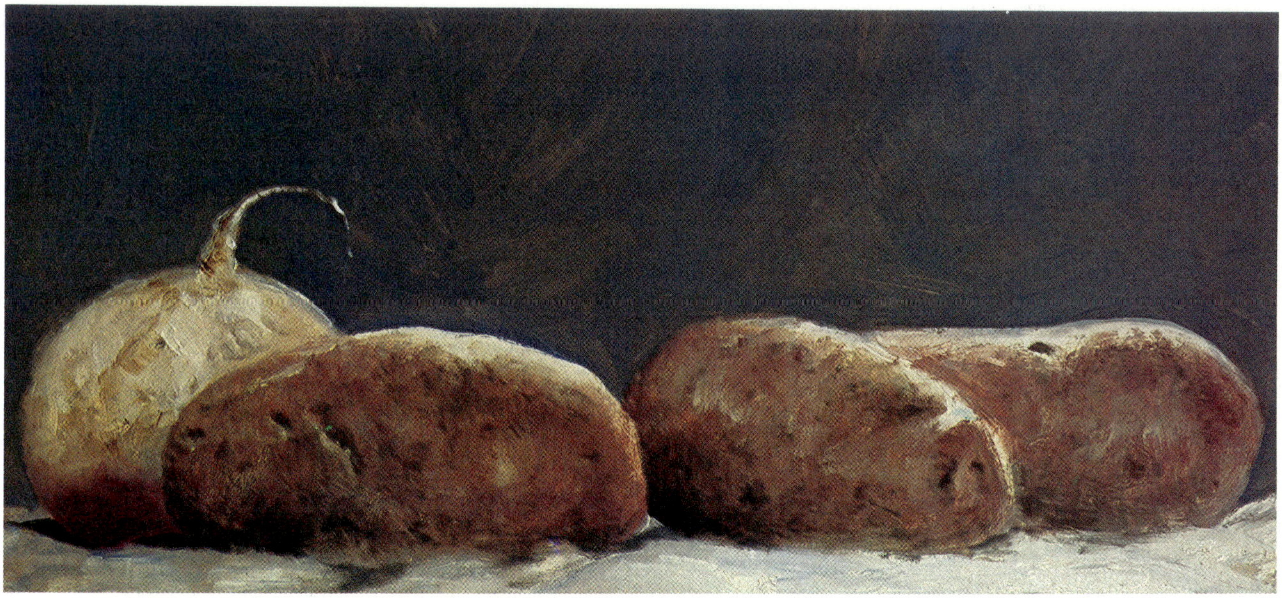

4. When all the elements had basically been laid in, what remained to be done was blending and refining. The additions the artist made here were to illustrate the dents and rough areas in the vegetables.

He added ultramarine blue to his palette and brushed this into his background for color. He added a curl to the end of the turnip root for design. He continued to blend yellow ochre into the white and also brushed in a bit of raw sienna in the left center portion. The lower purple color was gradually smoothed upward into the white portion.

The lights and darks previously painted into the potatoes were now blended into the red areas. Mr. Dawley used a combination of yellow ochre and black for major dents and shadows. He carefully blended the lower shadows upward into the potatoes to accentuate their form. The highlight color along the tops of the potatoes, individual highlights on the skins, and reflections from the dents were painted with yellow ochre and a tiny bit of black mixed into a great deal of white. Ultramarine blue and raw umber were used for the cast shadows and finishing touches on the tablecloth.

Leafy Vegetables

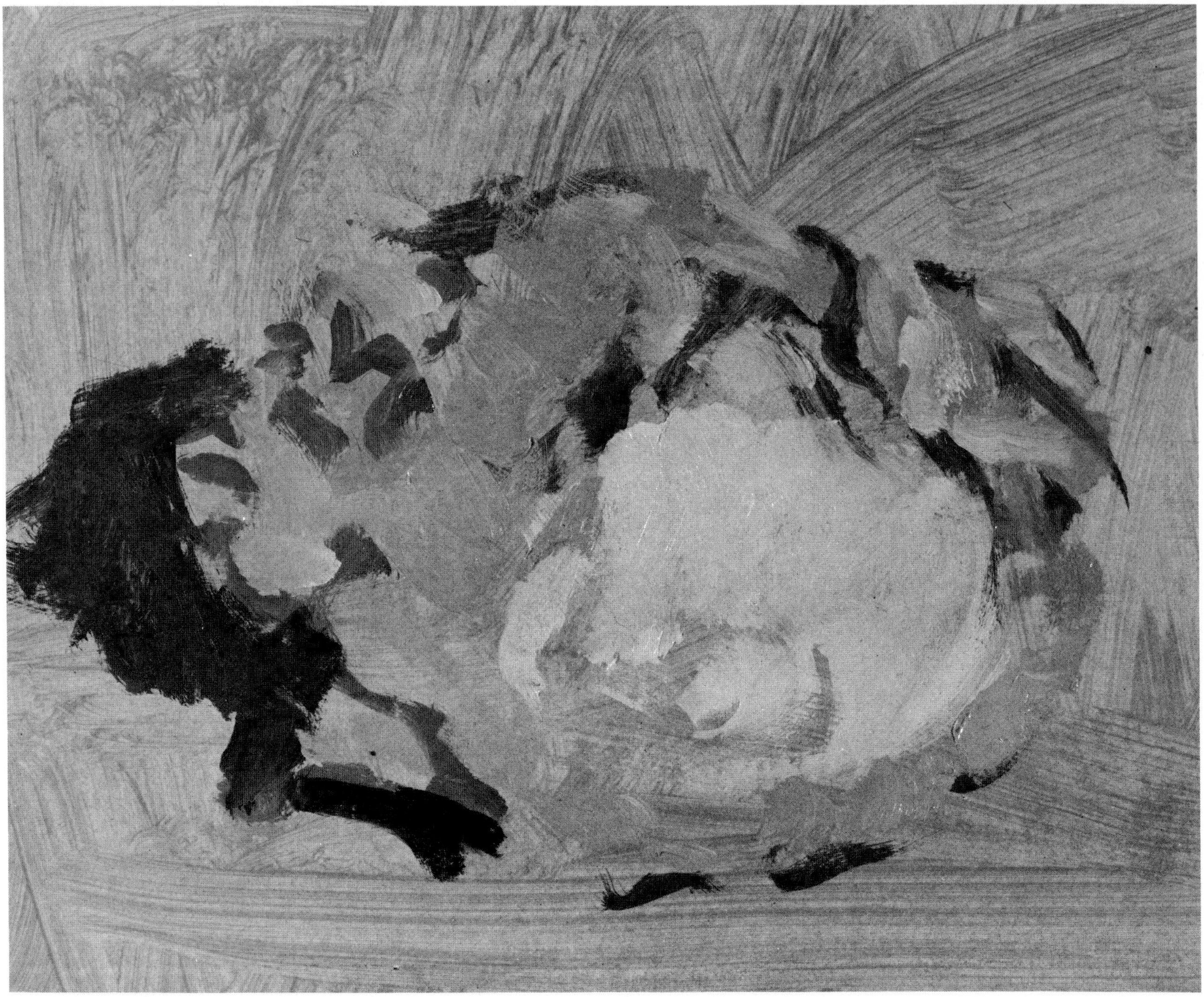

1. Leafy vegetables can present problems in still life painting, but the main things you should concentrate on are the position of the object and its areas of light and dark. What you're actually trying to create is an *illusion* of the leafiness of the leaves of lettuce surrounding and fanning outward from a solid core. Joseph Dawley used a somewhat impressionistic oil painting technique here to create this illusion.

The artist began by blocking in the general tonal areas in a very loose manner, using monochromatic mixtures of white and raw umber. First he thinned his lightest tone, which was mostly white with only about five percent raw umber, with turpentine and brushed it over the entire painting surface. He used white to represent the core of the lettuce, which would provide a reference point from which to paint in the leaves. He then dabbed in a slightly darker value of his monochrome undertone to represent the major shadows among the leaves. Returning to his lighter tone, he used it to represent the actual leaves; he also dabbed it in as a filler between the areas of shadow. The large shadow to the left of the lettuce was done with a mixture of about seventy-five white and twenty-five percent raw umber.

2. Now Mr. Dawley began to define his subject more precisely, using his lightest tone to paint in the wavy outline of the lettuce and to tone down the white of the core. To provide contrast, and to see exactly what was happening in the lettuce, he filled in the background with his middle tone, which he also used for the dark accent lines within the core.

The leafy portion was enhanced by adding some middle tones to supplement the colors already there. White was brushed around at random and allowed to mix with the lighter tone to create some light areas. The artist then worked around and refined the darker shadow areas of his middle tone in the leaves. He used his deepest tone for the large shadow on the lower left.

3. Now the artist added cadmium yellow light, raw sienna, phthalo blue, and burnt sienna to his palette. He mixed his blue and yellow together for the light green in the major portions of the lettuce leaves and made a darker green by adding more blue and a dab of raw umber. The darkest green in the shadow areas was made with the same combination, but with more raw umber added.

These three greens were brushed in with no attempt to blend them. The artist swirled, dabbed, and stroked his brush to achieve a loose, fluffy impression. Where he needed lighter areas—such as on the top or on the right side of the lettuce head—he added a stroke of white. A little of his lightest green was brushed into the upper portion of the core. The rust color in the core was made with burnt sienna, and Mr. Dawley blocked in the background with raw sienna and used raw umber for the cast shadow.

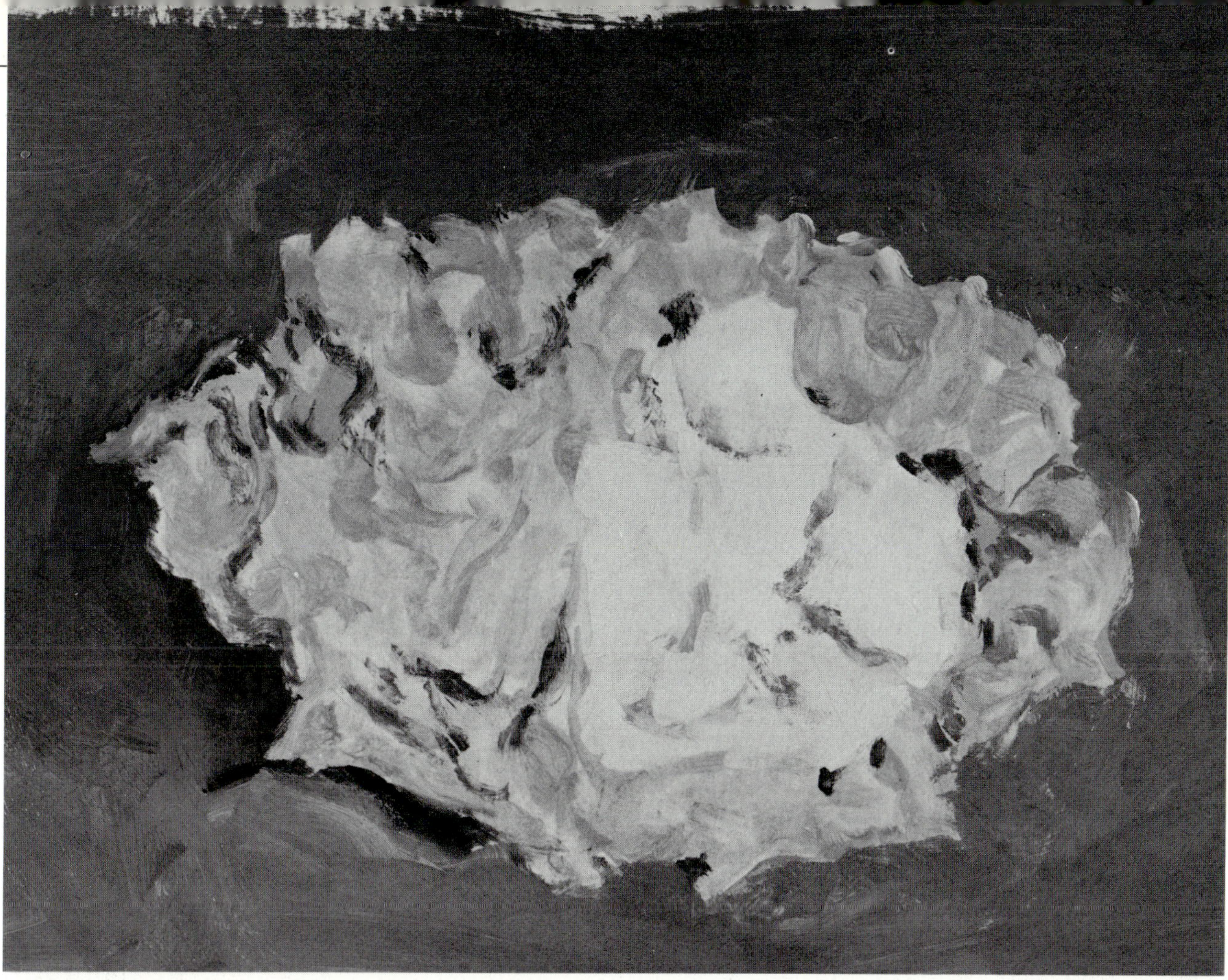

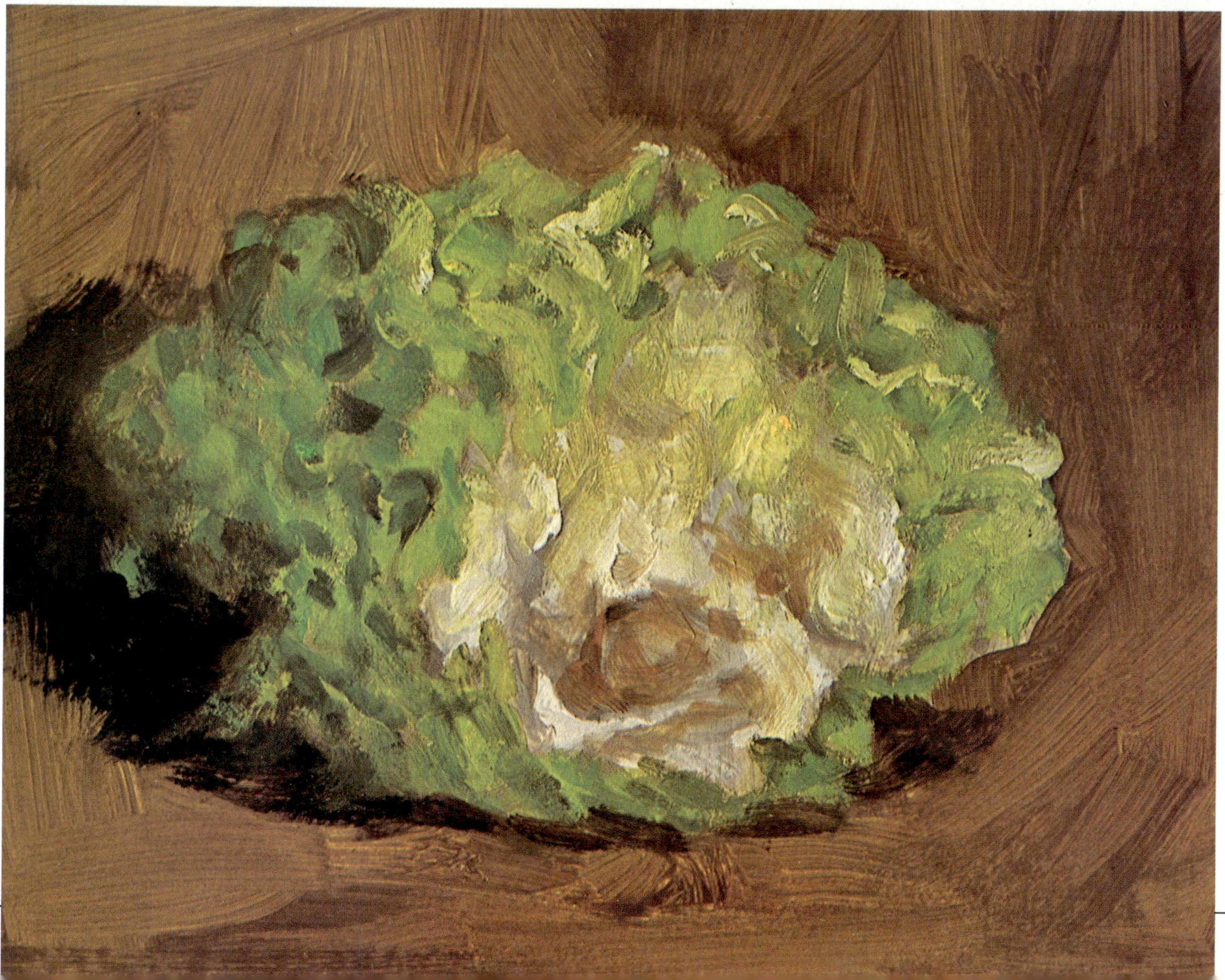

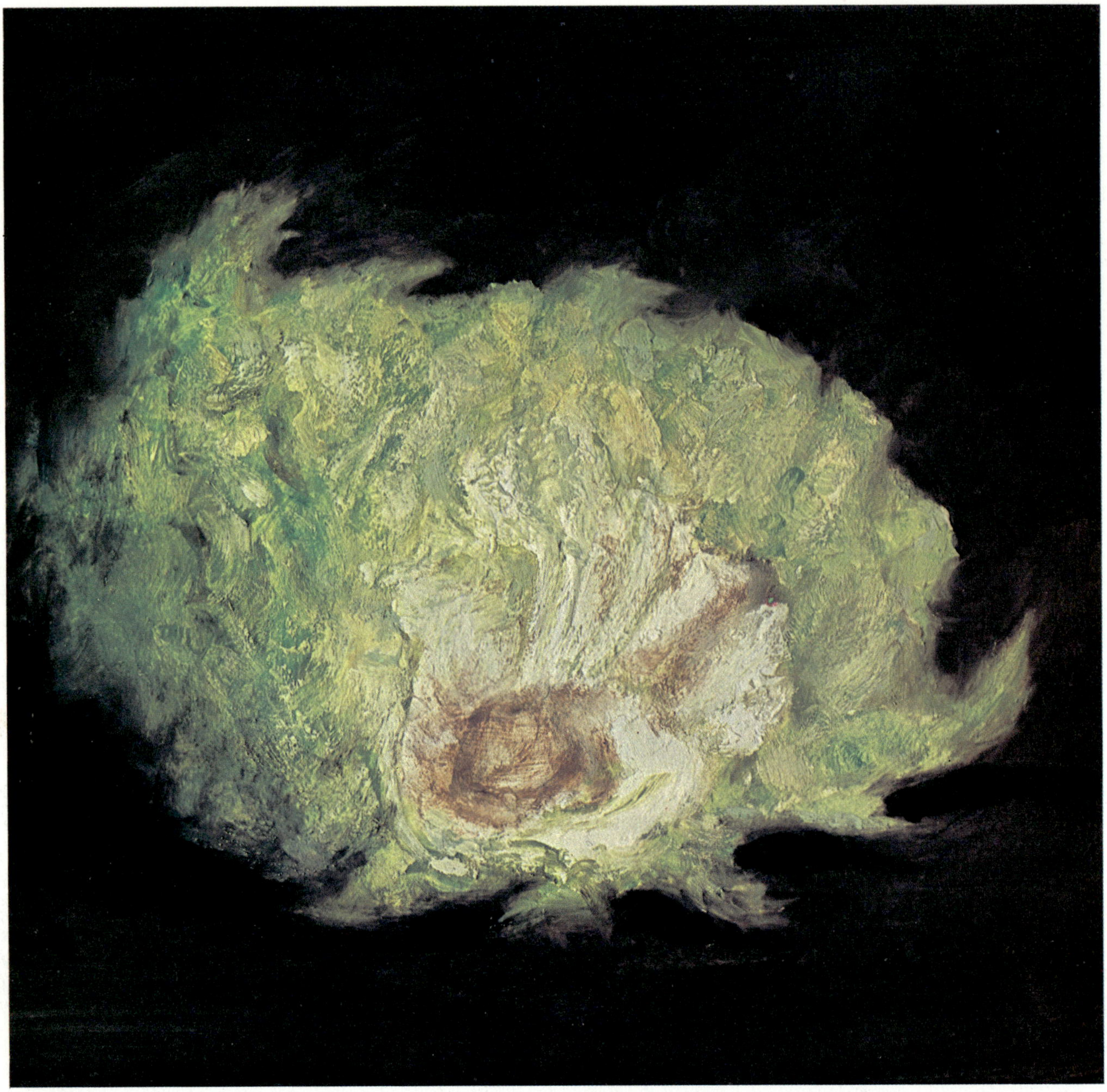

4. The artist decided to add some leaves in the lower right and upper left areas that would stand away from the lettuce. He also expanded his palette with underpainting white, cobalt yellow, and viridian green. He brushed underpainting white into the leafy portions, covering the leafy area in a random manner and frequently allowing the underpainting to be exposed. He left a large area exposed on the left side, where many important crevices are located. When the underpainting white had become sticky, he mixed viridian green and cobalt yellow and scumbled this light green into the white. The entire painting was allowed to dry before being brushed over with painting medium. He finished the background with a combination of black and raw sienna, accentuating the cast shadow with raw umber and the rusty areas of the core with burnt sienna. He softened the outer edges of the head by brushing out into the background with a combination of cobalt yellow and viridian green. He also flicked bright touches of viridian green into the leaves.

Citrus Fruit

1. The techniques shown here can be used to paint an orange or any other citrus fruit. The outer peel is bumpy, pitted and shiny. A dabbing technique can be used to create this texture. The white skin is slightly rough, dry, and dull in luster. The artist's prime concern here is to produce a dull white and keep it toned down in relation to brighter highlights elsewhere. The pulp is composed of many moist, semitransparent little pieces massed together to form the sections of the orange. As with the peel, a dabbing technique is particularly suited for capturing their glossy, uneven surface.

Beginning with a monochrome underpainting in mixtures of white and raw umber, the artist used a middle-value tone thinned with turpentine to outline the orange, the peel on the right, and the outer edges of the white inner skin. He also filled in the entire pulp area lightly. Still using this tone, he defined the perimeter of the plate, and then he filled in its interior with a very light tone. Returning to his middle-value tone, he painted the cast shadow to the left of the orange.

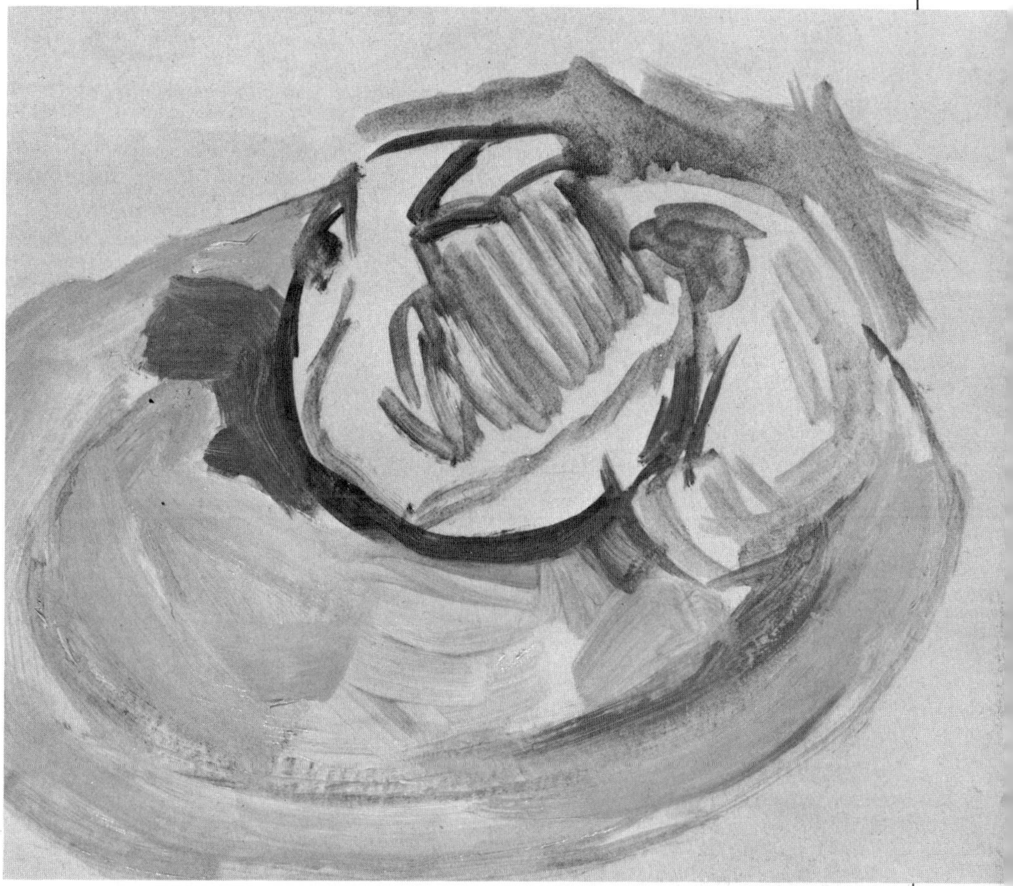

2. Now the artist filled in all areas with paint, using his middle-value tone for the peel, the lightest tone for the pulp, and white with a tiny bit of tone mixed in for the white skin. For the shadow inside the right peel, he used his deepest tone for the first time, shading it slightly with his middle tone. He didn't apply any of this paint too thickly, since he would be working over it.

He began to create texture in the orange-peel area. With a ¼-inch brush, he painted in separate little dabs of his light tone on top of his middle tone. On the right peel only, he dabbed in white and the lightest tone to indicate the highlighted areas. On the white skin areas, he added a few dabs of light tone where the skin might have bumps in it, such as the lower left portion. He needed smaller spots on the pulp, and so he used the edge of his brush to dab his middle tone on the sides and edges of each pulp section. He dabbed white into the middle of the sections to represent their sparkling highlights. Then he filled in the background with his darkest tone.

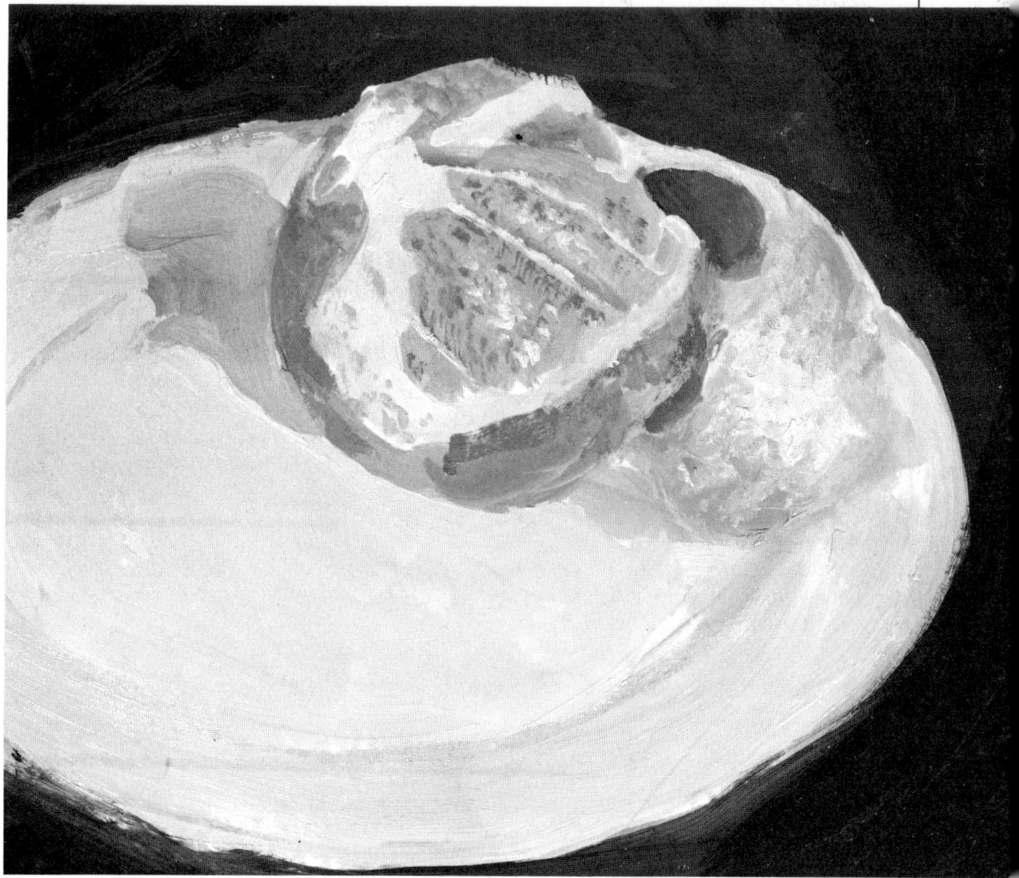

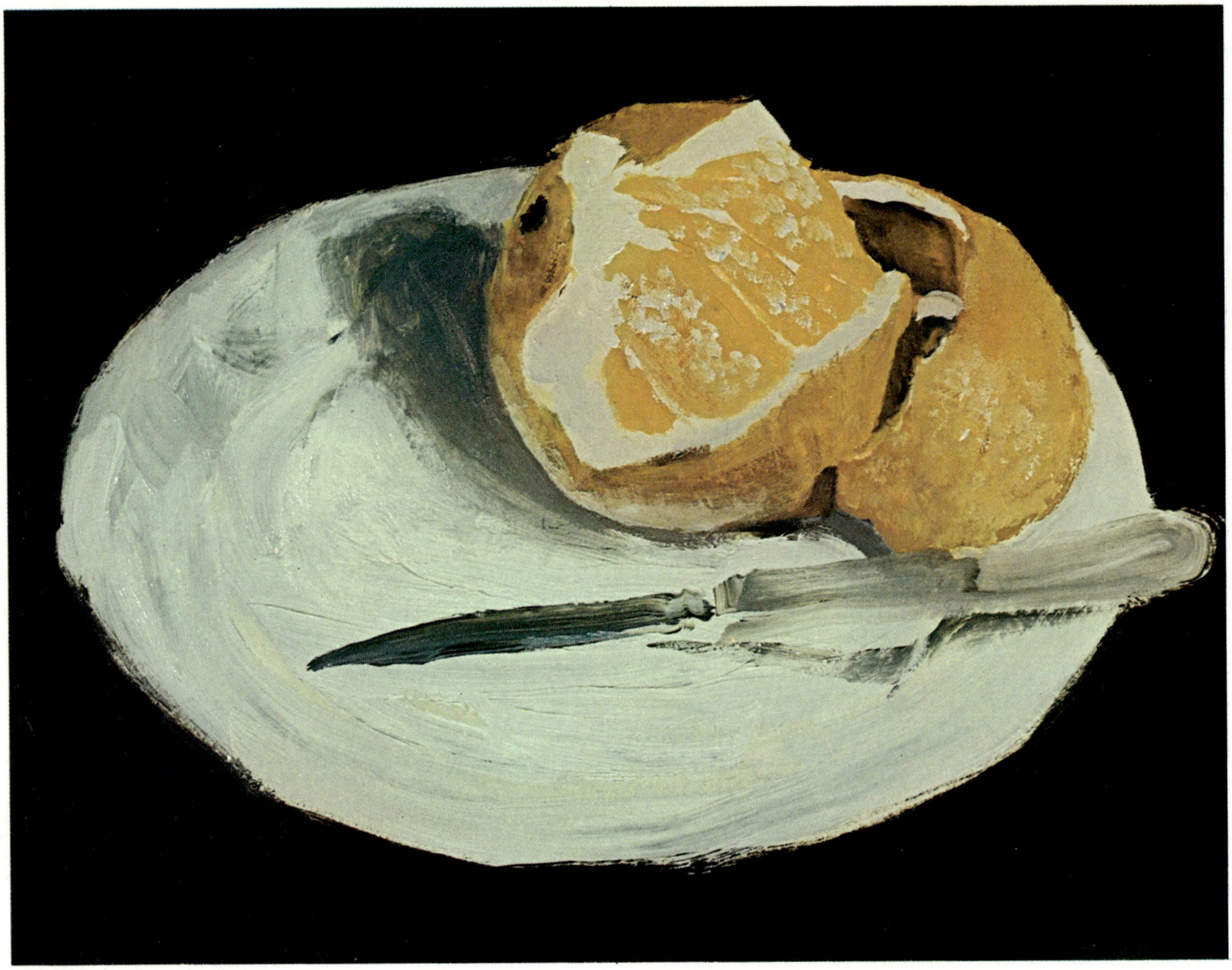

3. Mr. Dawley added cadmium yellow light, cadmium orange, ultramarine blue, and underpainting white to his palette. He mixed the orange and yellow together in equal proportions and spread this color smoothly and thinly over all the orange-peel areas. The resulting color appeared slightly dull, as he was working over the raw umber tones already there.

Adding a very small amount of ultramarine blue and his lightest monochrome tone to white, he painted over the white skin portions. Then he mixed orange and yellow, with more yellow than before, to paint into the pulp. He dabbed underpainting white into the pulp sections for the small, sparkling highlights. He combined underpainting white and the pulp color and dabbed this into the highlighted section of the peel on the right. Then he dabbed a small amount of white into the center of the peel's highlight.

He added a small amount of blue to his middle tone for the shadows on the plate. He also blended in white at the bottom of the orange for the reflected white from the plate. A bit of blue was added to white for the plate, and he added a knife to strengthen the composition.

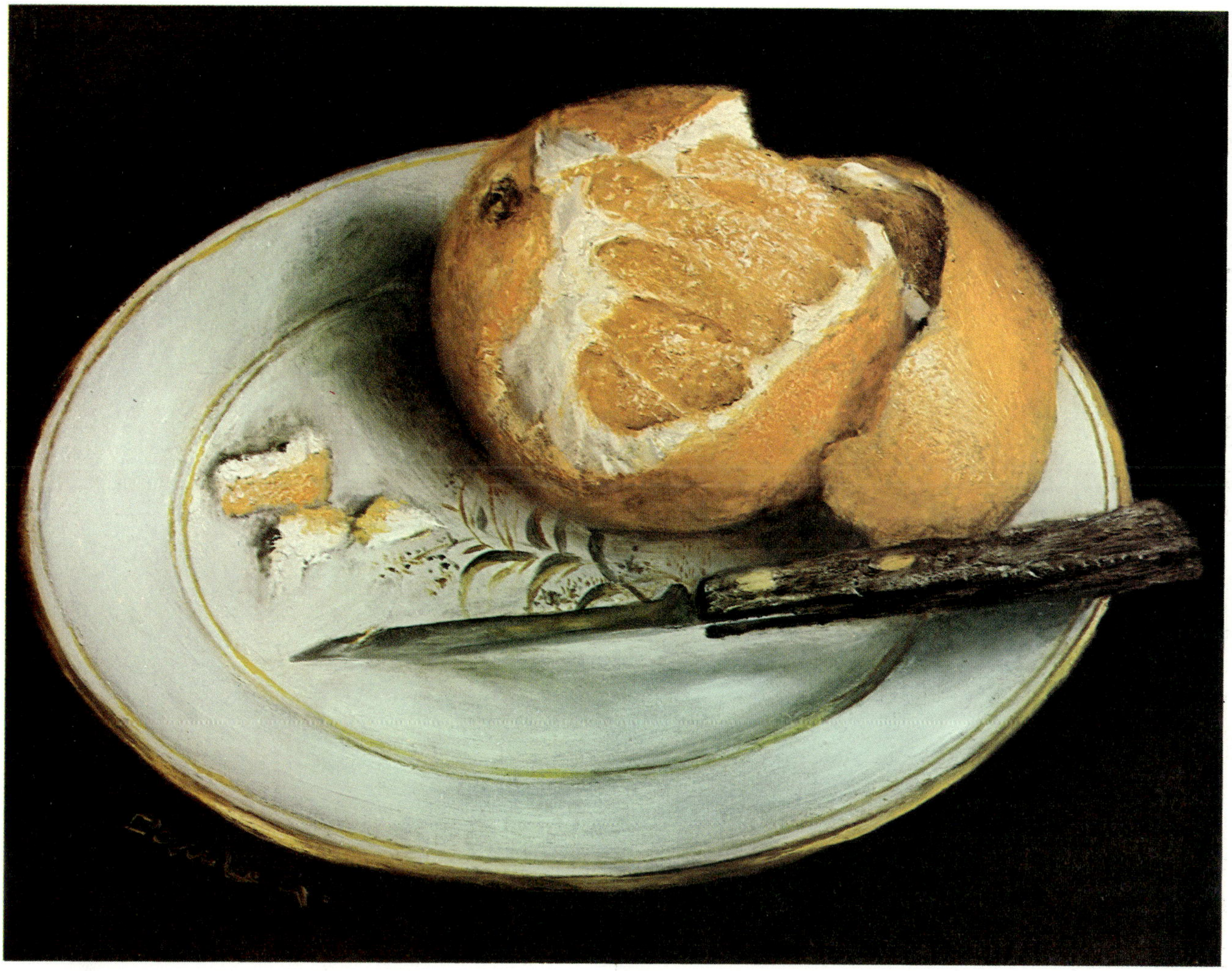

4. Yellow ochre was added to the palette. Then the artist combined cadmium orange, cadmium yellow, and underpainting white—with a predominance of yellow—and painted this over each pulp section. Then he combined raw umber and ultramarine blue and painted this into the darker portions—such as on either side and on the lower part—of each section, blending this well into the orange color. Now he dabbed underpainting white over a large portion of each section. For the lightest portions of the white skin, the artist combined underpainting white with slight amounts of his lightest tone and blue. For the shadowed parts of the skin, such as on the lower left, he used a combination of blue and his middle tone.

Mr. Dawley began the peel by thickly dabbing on a mixture of underpainting white, cadmium yellow, and cadmium orange. Underpainting white and yellow were used to accentuate highlights on the separate peel. He brushed a combination of raw umber and blue into this where shadows occur, such as around the bottom and to the far left. Note that this was blended in on the left side but breaks off sharply for the cast shadow on the right. The peel was now allowed to dry to a sticky texture. The artist scumbled raw umber and blue lightly over the peel, and after this became sticky, he scumbled again with a yellow and orange mixture. This covered most of the peel, but bits of the raw umber and blue mixture showed through to create a realistic bumpy effect. The artist used blue and raw umber for the dark shadow on the plate, extending this under the orange and blending it upward slightly. Raw umber, blue, and yellow ochre were used to paint the navel.

Grapes and Oranges

Unifying with Shapes. Artist David Leffel paid careful attention to relationships between objects in this oil painting, and their shapes hold together beautifully. The group of oranges makes one unit, the grapes hold together, and the vase does too. It is important to spend time at the beginning of your painting getting the placement of your objects right in terms of mass and shape. Draw shapes and "cut" into things, thinking sculpturally. Be loose. You can make the shapes more specific later.

If a white tablecloth is painted stark white, he cautions, it may look unrelated to the rest of the picture. To soften it, introduce brush strokes of color from the light section of the picture. This will also help unify the painting.

Adding Highlights. If you're painting an object that looks somewhat shapeless, add a highlight and it will look better. When you place a highlight on a bottle, place it and then let it trail off. Don't play around with it. Mr. Leffel has put three highlights on the dark bottle: one at the top rim where it turns into the neck, another at the bottom of the neck where it turns into the body, and the third where the body of the bottle turns at the side. Highlights on a bottle are crisp because glass refracts more light. Highlights on a peach, on the other hand, are diffused and fuzzier because the surface is softer.

Mr. Leffel suggests that you avoid putting all your light in the middle of an object with nothing going to the edge. Light should start at an edge; it should continue. *You* may have to decide how it is to continue. If you have one fruit with a bit of framed light and another fruit with a bit of light they will lack cohesion.

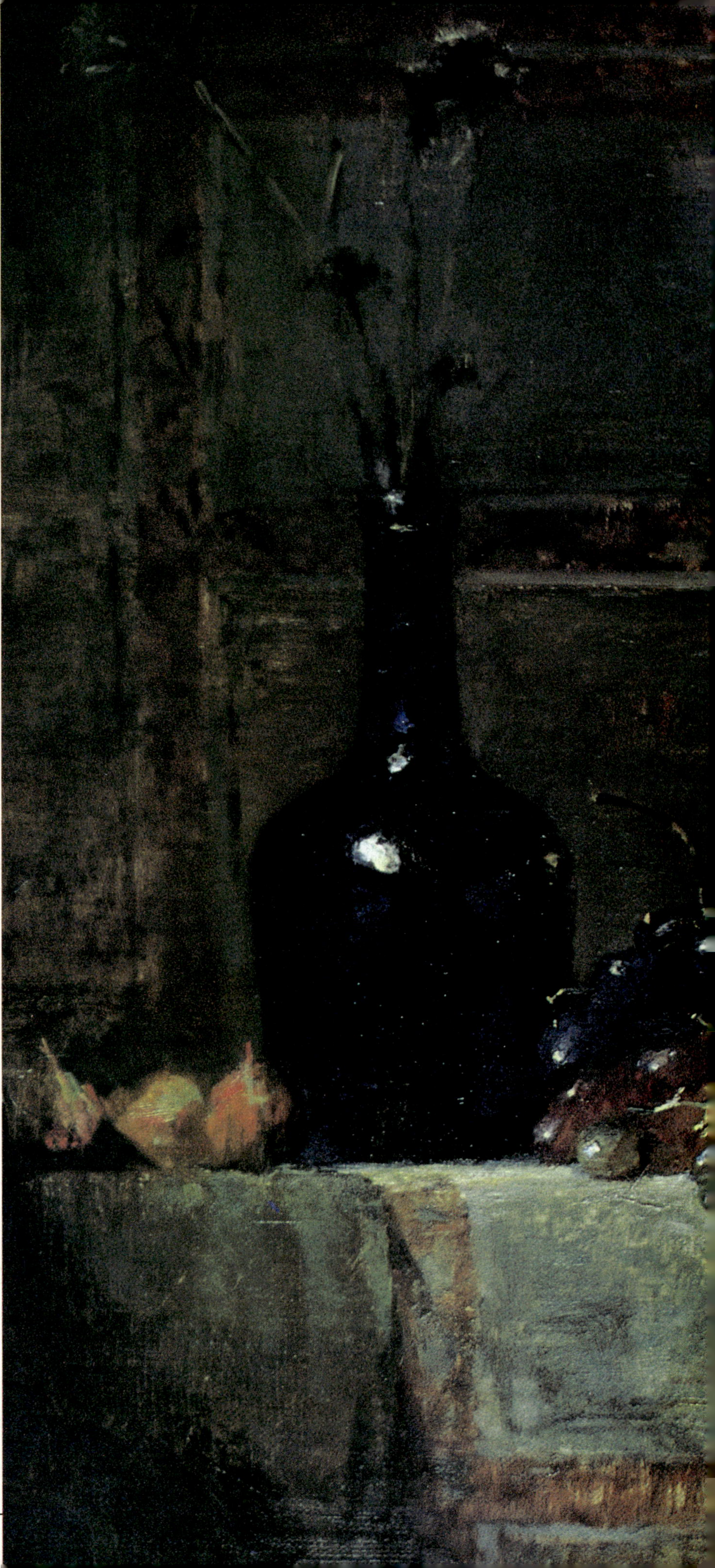

***Still Life with Prayer Rug*, oil, 20″ × 24″ (51 × 61 cm), by David Leffel. Collection of Mr. and Mrs. Peter Stremmel.**

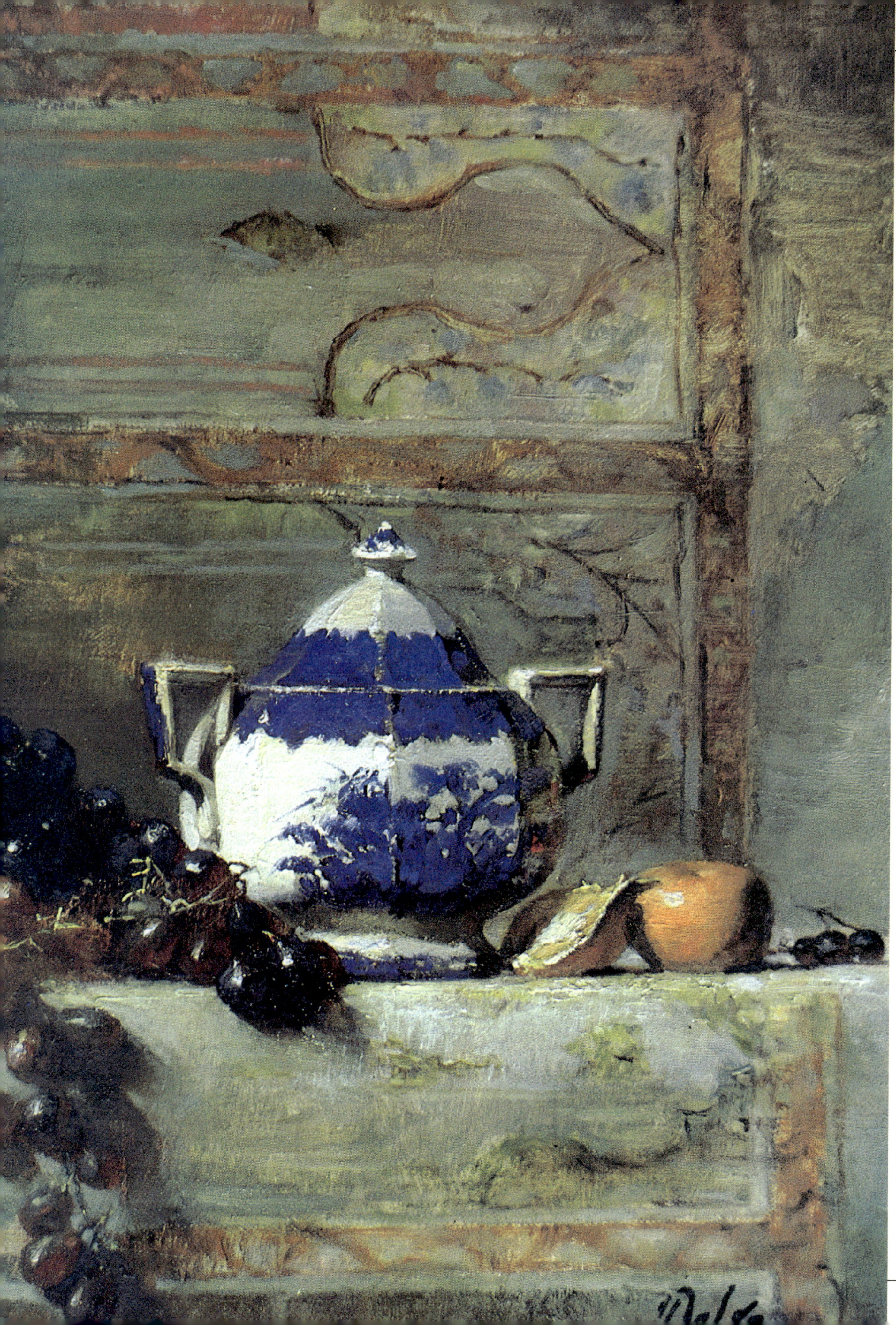

Pear and Grapes

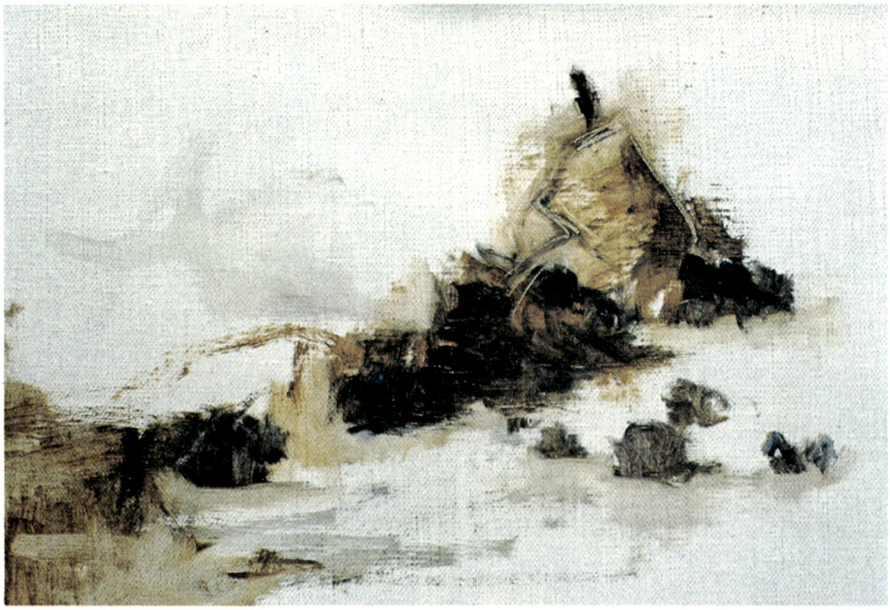

1. The four stages of this oil painting by David Leffel illustrate how he realized his original concept. In the final painting nothing in the composition has been changed; it merely has been embellished and elaborated upon. Mr. Leffel's idea for the painting was to create a sense of movement through space. He tried to arrange the fruit so that it would lead the eye from one space to another in the still life. He wanted a diagonal movement and arranged his objects accordingly, starting from the lower left-hand edge of the canvas and leading to the upper right-hand portion, always remaining conscious of the size and placement of the objects. Notice here that the grapes have been treated broadly, as a mass.

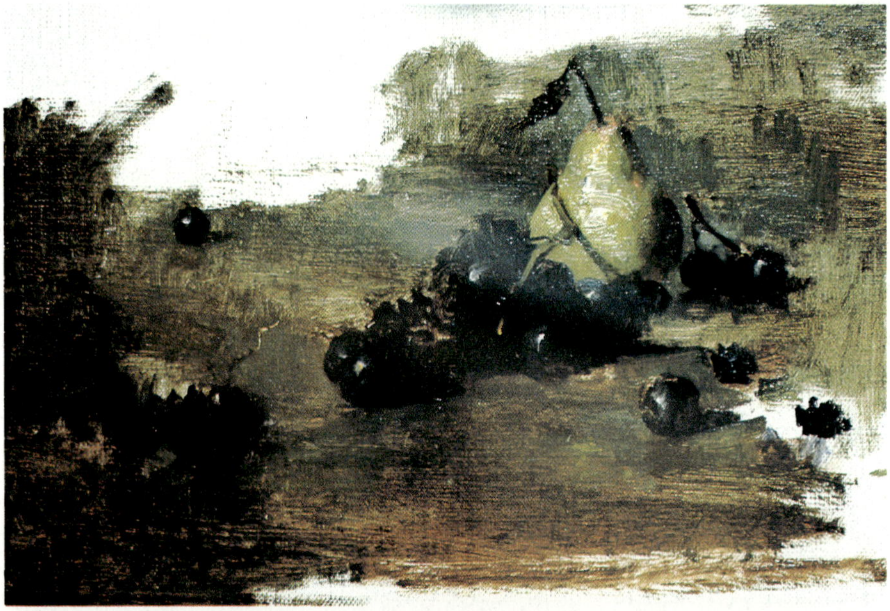

2. From his general conceptual idea, the artist now made the objects more specific. He introduced some counterpoint—the use of contrast and interplay of elements—by means of two grapes, one large one toward the lower right and the other at the upper left. The pear, as the strongest element, would hold its own as the actual center of interest.

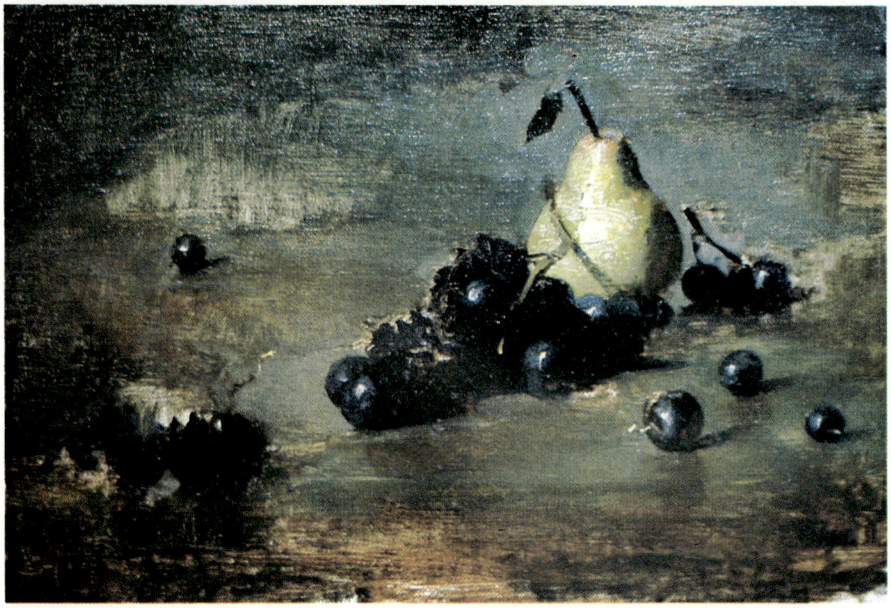

3. The artist elaborated, transforming the dark mass into more specific grapes. He also arranged highlights on the grapes to form a "melodic" line, being selective about the brightness and dullness of the highlights to evoke this feeling. Note that some grapes remain as a mass.

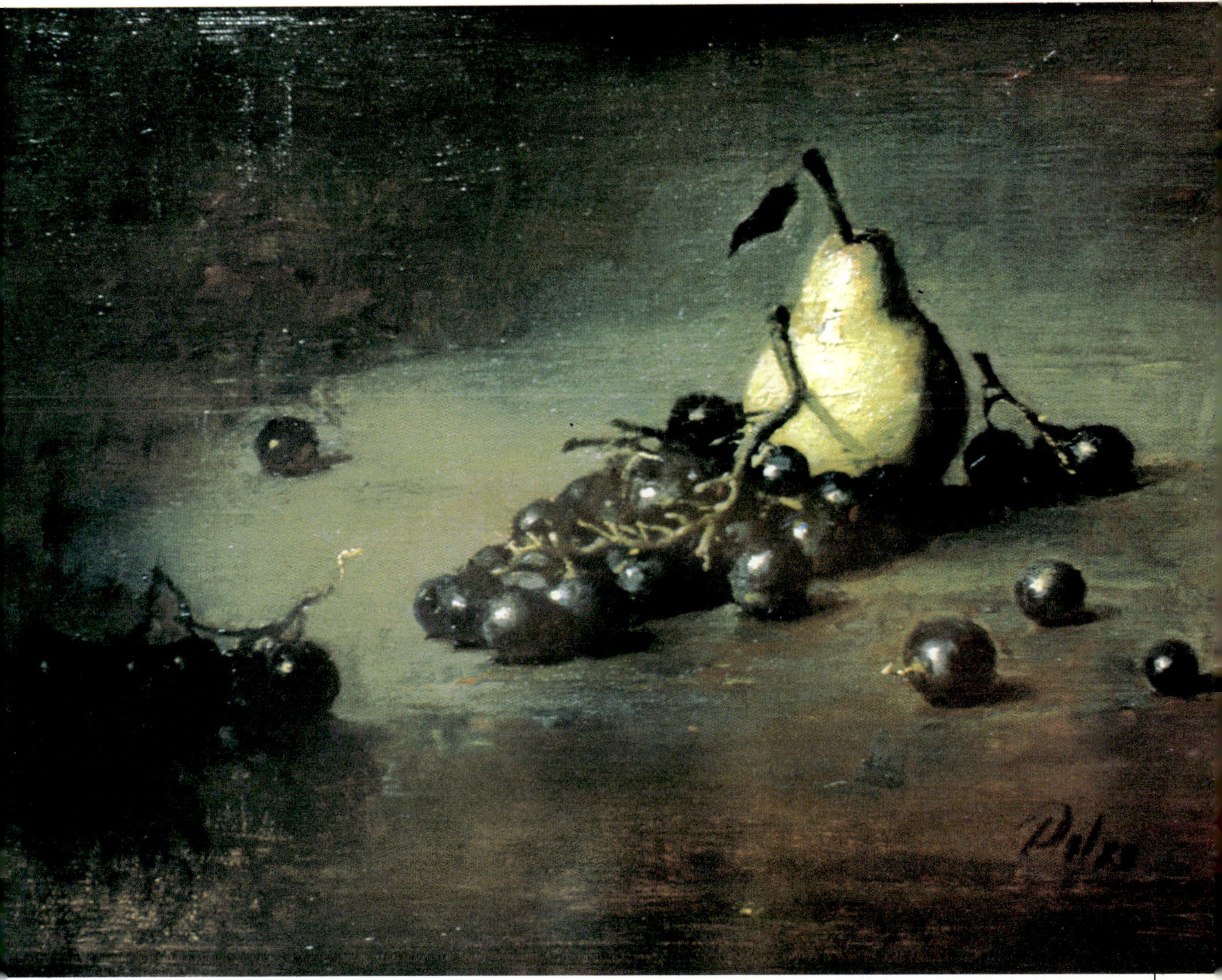

Pear and Grapes, oil, 11″ × 14″ (28 × 36 cm), by David Leffel. Collection of Lois McCune.

4. In the finished painting, the grapes in the foreground, where the diagonal movement begins, are still fairly generalized; the remaining grapes have been built up more specifically. The light on the pear, which is the center of interest, is raised in value, and a grape stem leads your eye to it.

Geometric Shapes in Fruit and Vegetables

The Initial Sketch. Working from the center outward, artist David Millard used the design technique of encircling areas of light in his carbon sketch of a piece of pumpkin, detailing the labyrinthian complexities of seeds, flesh, and rind.

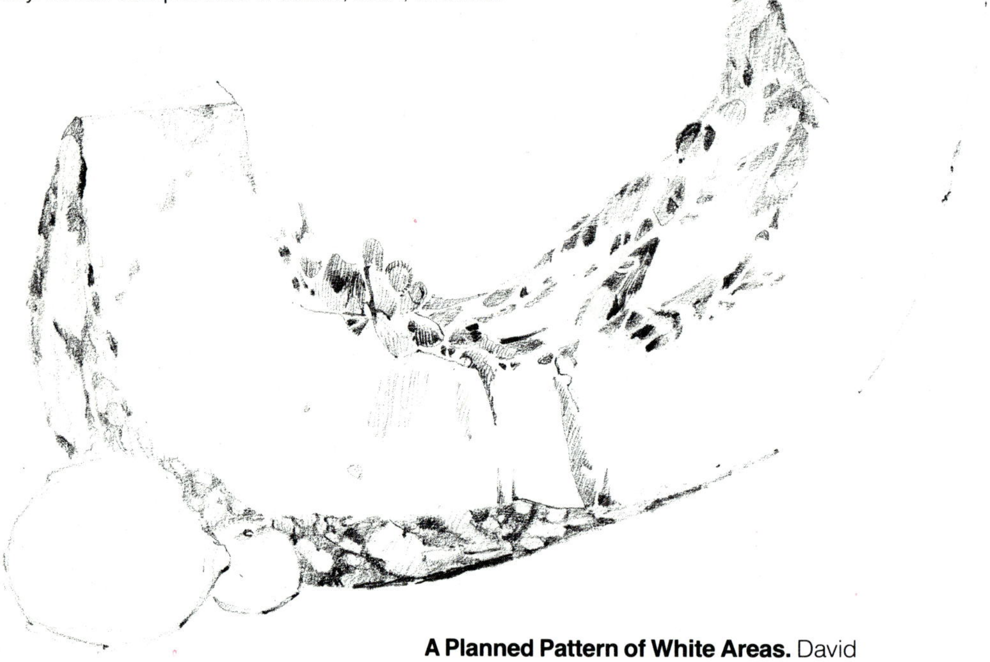

A Planned Pattern of White Areas. David Millard believes in trying creative techniques and color combinations. To him, it is important to think, invent, and then paint color. In the watercolor sketch below, he substituted the white of the paper for the pumpkin's orange color, developing a filigree design around the seed area, which created an effect of brilliance.

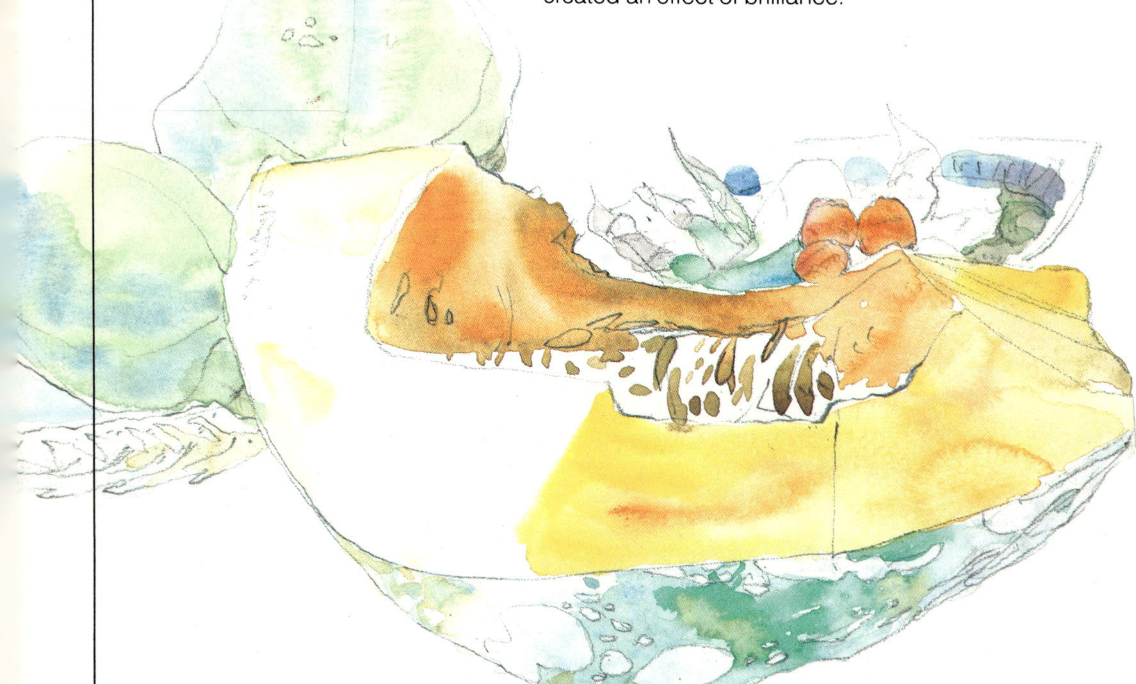

Changing the Planes. (Opposite, top) The rough facets of the crudely chopped pumpkin inspired the hand-carved Japanese wood-block effect in this watercolor. The fragmentation was carried out not only in the pumpkin but also in the overall picture. The artist chose colors reminiscent of vegetable and root dyes, and because he was painting on a rainy day, he used some Davy's gray in all the paint mixtures. He mixed a big puddle of cobalt violet and raw umber (with, as mentioned, Davy's gray) and flooded a broad wash over everything except the garlic buds and glass rim of the bowl. When this was dry, he flooded a second wash of cendre blue (with Davy's gray) over the shadow patterns and designed the background fabric effect. He made his reds using Venetian, Indian, and light reds, plus brown madder alizarin. Similarly, the earthy blues and greens were made up of multiple combinations.

Faceted Planes. (Opposite, bottom) One idea led to another, and Mr. Millard found even more design possibilities in the placid piece of pumpkin. This time he hacked it with a hatchet to give himself a fresh, unconventional set of shapes and planes to color. Notice how the design controls the rhythm here. Look at the understated secondary colors—orange, green, and lavender—and see how the artist has worked to keep the harmony between the colors.

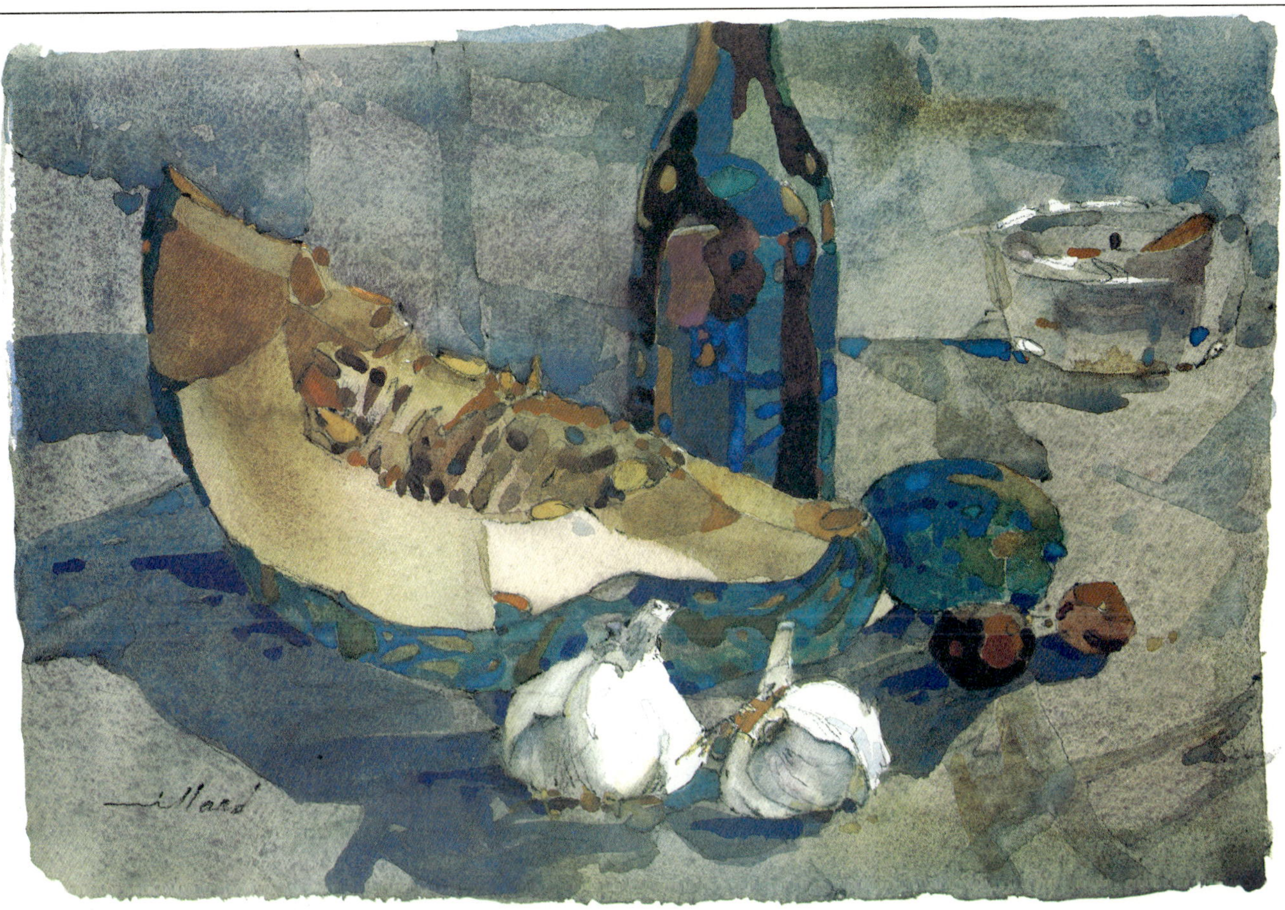

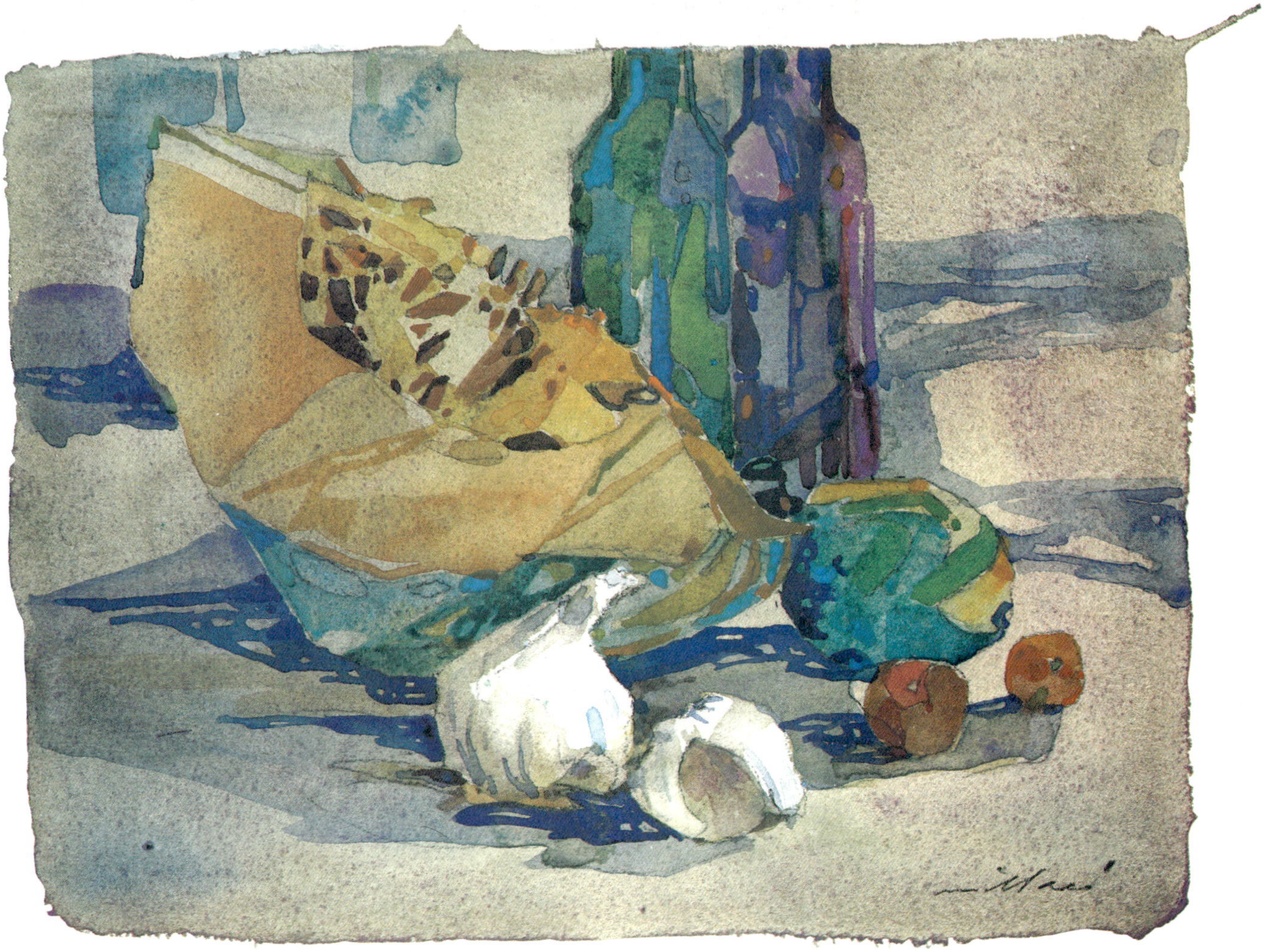

Enhancing the Subject with Color

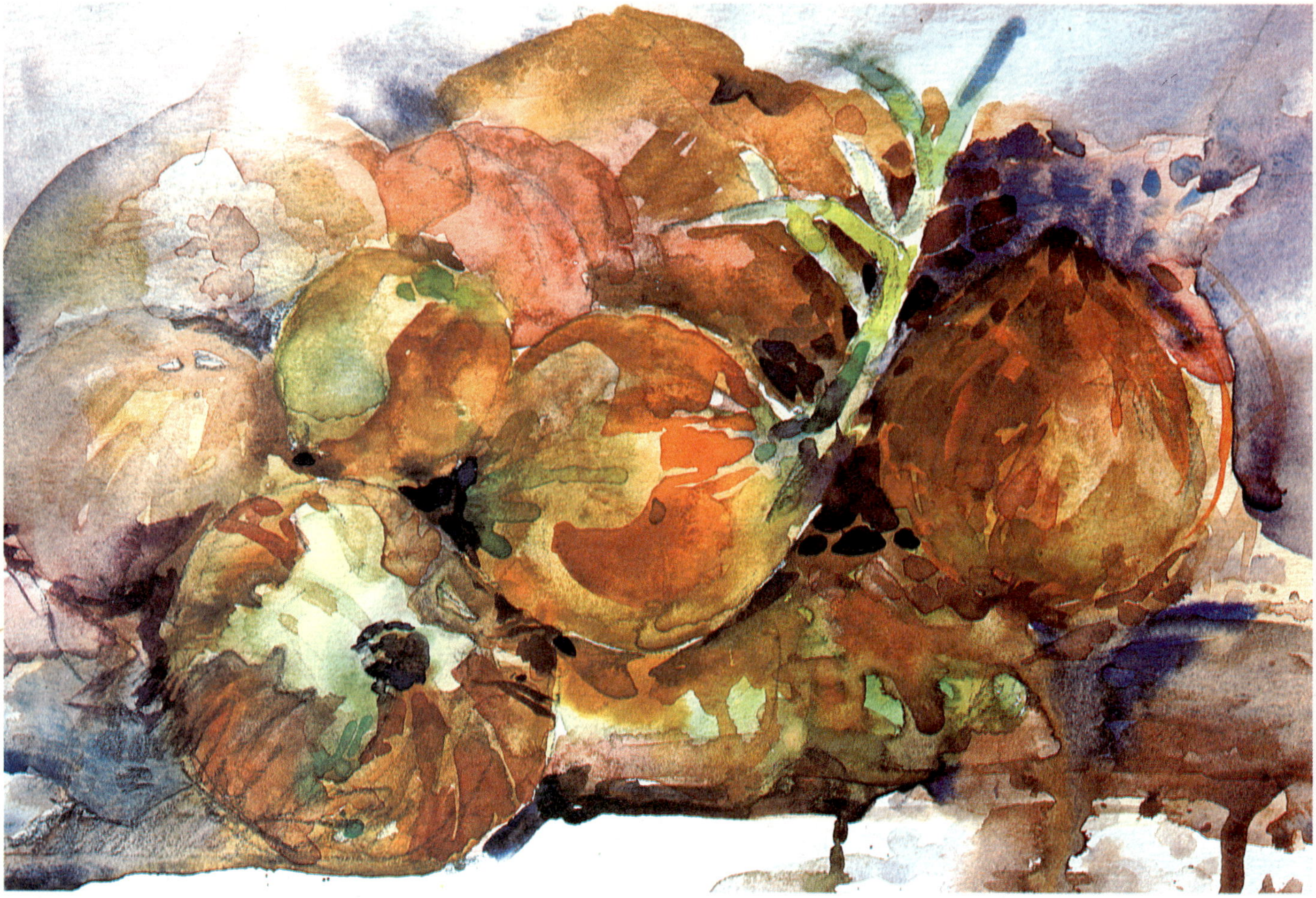

Unusual Colors. David Millard was attracted by the orange color and round shapes of a cluster of onions. He decided to see what he could learn by trying different colors in his painting. He stopped to study and absorb the visual pattern, looking for a basic abstract design. There was a small major circle surrounded by an outer ring of onions. He shifted the onion with the green sprout from a flat position to an interesting diagonal. Now the sprout would catch the viewer's eye and lead attention to the small circle of three onions.

Starting with a black-and-white sketch, the artist planned his composition and design; then he planned his color. He kept turning the onion at the lower left until he found the broken skin. Likewise, the smaller one above it. He decided to concentrate his center of interest in this area. He noted that all of the onions appeared to be of equal tonal value and color. He concentrated his strongest color on the opaque skins of these three onions after laying in his palest washes for the exposed surfaces under the skins—pale green, pale orange, and raw umber. Next he put in the stronger-colored outer skins and finished these three onions, including the green sprout.

Next, in palest tones, Mr. Millard applied the under-skin colors of the outer ring of onions—green, pink, lavender. He let this dry and then put slightly stronger tints of pink, lavender, umber, and greens on the outer skins. He knew this would visually "push back" these onions into the background. Now he placed his dark accents around the sprout and put in the shadows. He left the strip of white tablecloth for contrast with the pale tones.

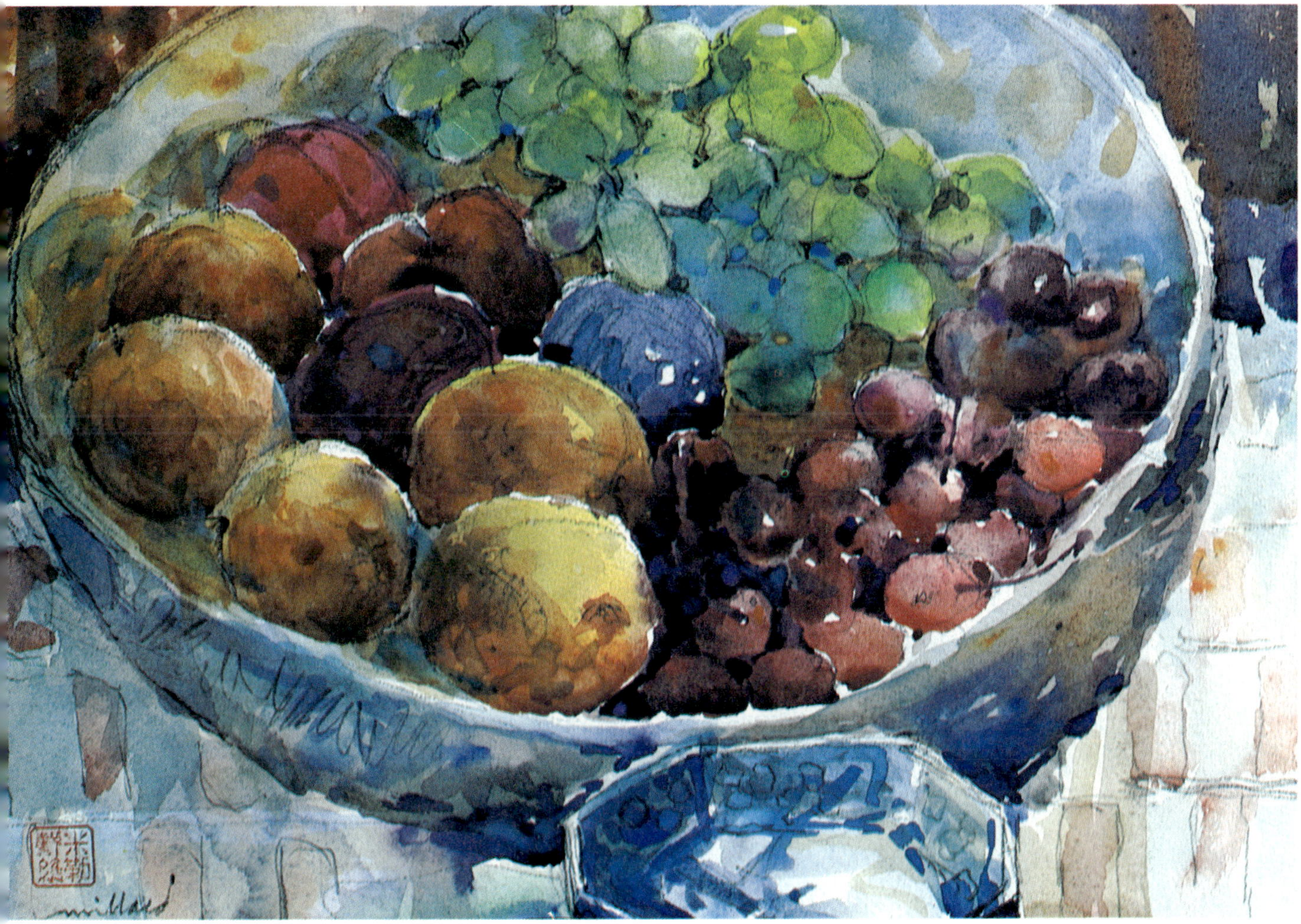

Realistic Color. The difficulty the artist encountered here was the need to model form as he applied color. He also had to work out some other problems: How could he make the light travel across the bowl and then into it? How could he keep the plums and deep burgundy cherries a luscious dark, and yet maintain a luminous quality? You can never make your painting equal what you see in your mind's eye, but the more you try, the better you get. Here are a few of Mr. Millard's suggestions.

First, take considerable care with your drawing—but draw as fast as you can push yourself. Keep a spirited line. It will be reflected in your finished painting.

Use your imagination. Notice how Mr. Millard has achieved a luminous quality in this painting through color. Look at the dark upper right-hand corner next to the light-colored back of the bowl. Do you see how the "path of light" moves diagonally from the angled green grapes to the pinkish cherries, then down along the rim of the bowl into the brightly illumined inside of the many-sided small dish, and finally, off to the right onto the "faded" checkered cloth? This path of light is an imagined thing—it existed only in the mind of the artist. It was not painted with a lift-out technique, but by the discipline of painting lighter tones in this imaginary path.

Finally, notice how the artist has kept all the little sparkly bits and specks of flickering white paper (he did not allow himself to do any masking) and handled the edges in a painterly "lost and found" manner, making some hard and some soft.

FLOWERS

Flowers are synonymous with still life painting. Here is an opportunity to study with Charles Reid, a masterful painter of flowers in both watercolor and oil.

You will learn to paint flowers with slender petals, solid petals, radiating petal forms, and compact forms. You will learn to paint flowers as diverse as daisies, anemones, and orchids, as well as mixed bouquets and dried flowers.

Reid's insightful teaching helps you master elements of color and composition, and you will be inspired to experiment in bold new ways.

Painting Flowers with Slender Petals

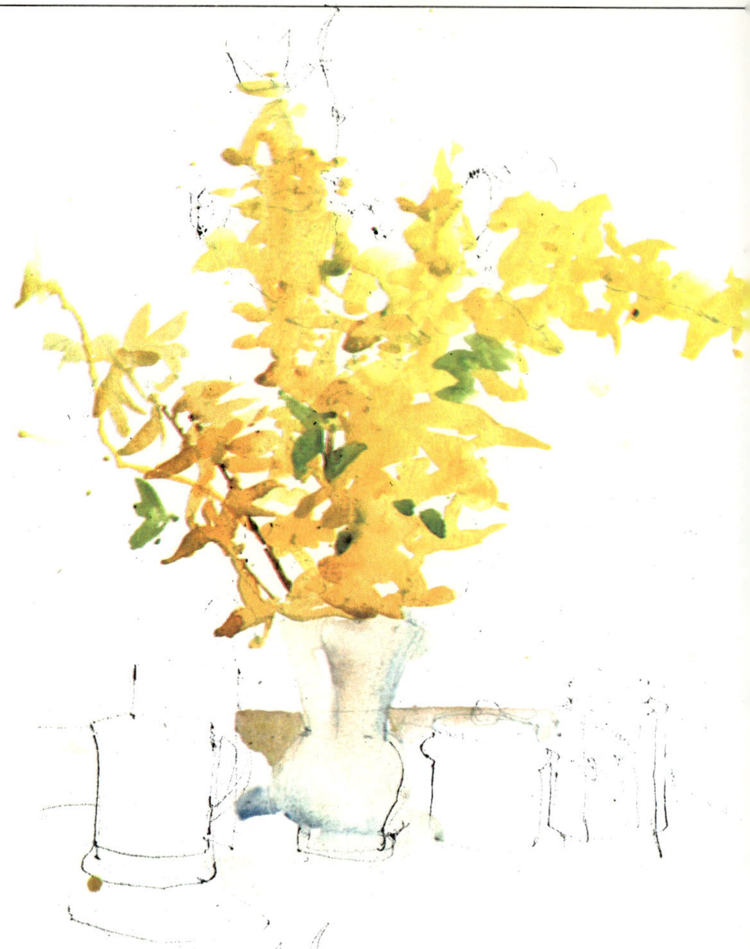

1. To paint flowers which have very slender individual petals, you must also determine how the overall shape of the bouquet works in terms of design. On 140-lb. cold-pressed paper, Charles Reid used cadmium yellow and cadmium yellow pale to establish both the characteristically slender forsythia petals and the flower mass as a whole. Some raw sienna crept into the left-hand section of the flowers because he put the stems in while the flower areas were still wet. He developed almost the whole bouquet with these colors, using more raw sienna to indicate some of the darker sections. After the yellows were dry, he added cerulean blue and cadmium yellow for the darker leaf accents. He added the vase, using alizarin crimson and cerulean blue with a little cadmium yellow, and got a fairly hard edge, since the flowers had now dried. He tried very hard to get a specific shape. Since the vase was still wet, he got a blend without completely losing the boundaries.

2. Next the artist painted the wall behind the flowers and several of the foreground objects. He also added more green leaves—some fairly dark, and some in the middle-value range—with ultramarine blue and cerulean blue mixed with cadmium yellow and cadmium yellow pale. Note the variation in colors on the tabletop, which he painted after the three objects and their cast shadows had dried. The foreground ink bottle was painted with burnt sienna and alizarin crimson, and the top is ivory black with ultramarine blue. The herb container is alizarin crimson, ultramarine blue, and cadmium yellow—the same colors that were used in the bottle to the right, but with less blue and more yellow for more warmth.

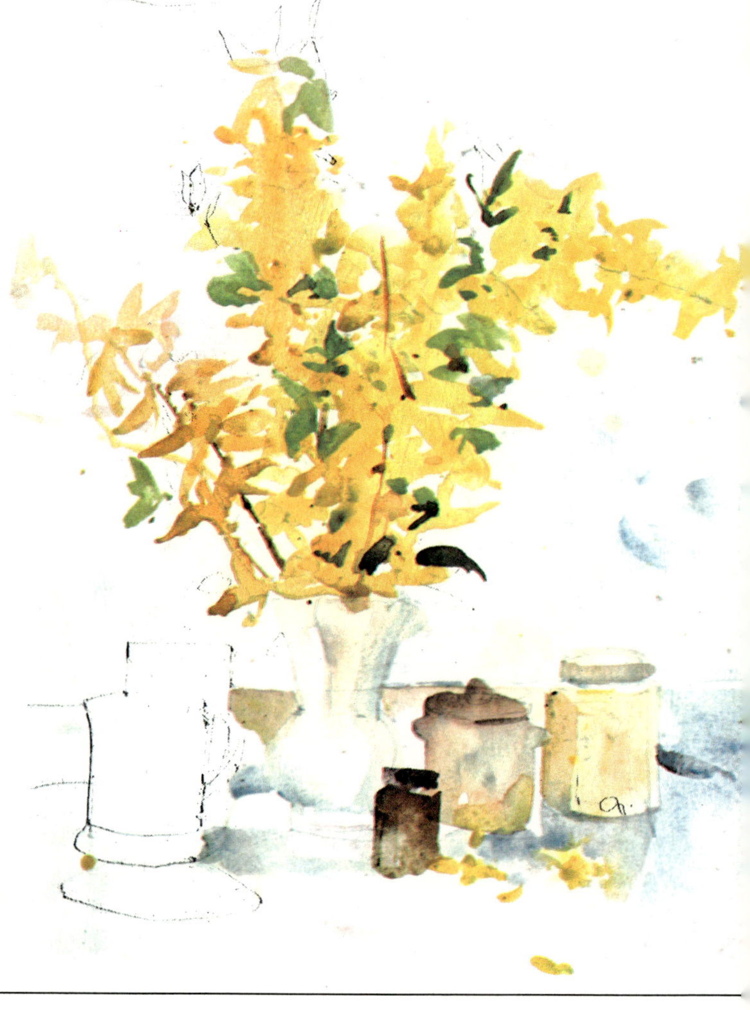

3. Now Mr. Reid worked all over the picture (opposite page). He mixed the colors in the cigarette lighter right on the paper, starting with cerulean blue at the top and adding cadmium yellow as he worked to the right and down. As he worked, he left a white strip of paper down the middle for a highlight. He added cadmium red light wet-in-wet and put in a cast shadow with alizarin crimson, ultramarine blue, and cadmium yellow. The cup to the left of the vase was painted with the same colors, with white paper left for the light-struck section. The mustard container above it was painted with cadmium yellow pale and cerulean blue, with the darkest part where the container meets the light.

Now the artist darkened the values in the vase and added a black ink bottle to the left of the coffee cup to strengthen the lower section. He added another sprig of forsythia in the hole to the right, where he also put in an additional postcard. He didn't want too much weight on this side of the painting, and so the postcard is much lighter in value than the one on the left. At this point there was a mixture of very generalized masses of color, but in other areas the artist had shown the actual shapes of individual petals—and so he had achieved a mixture of the specific and the general.

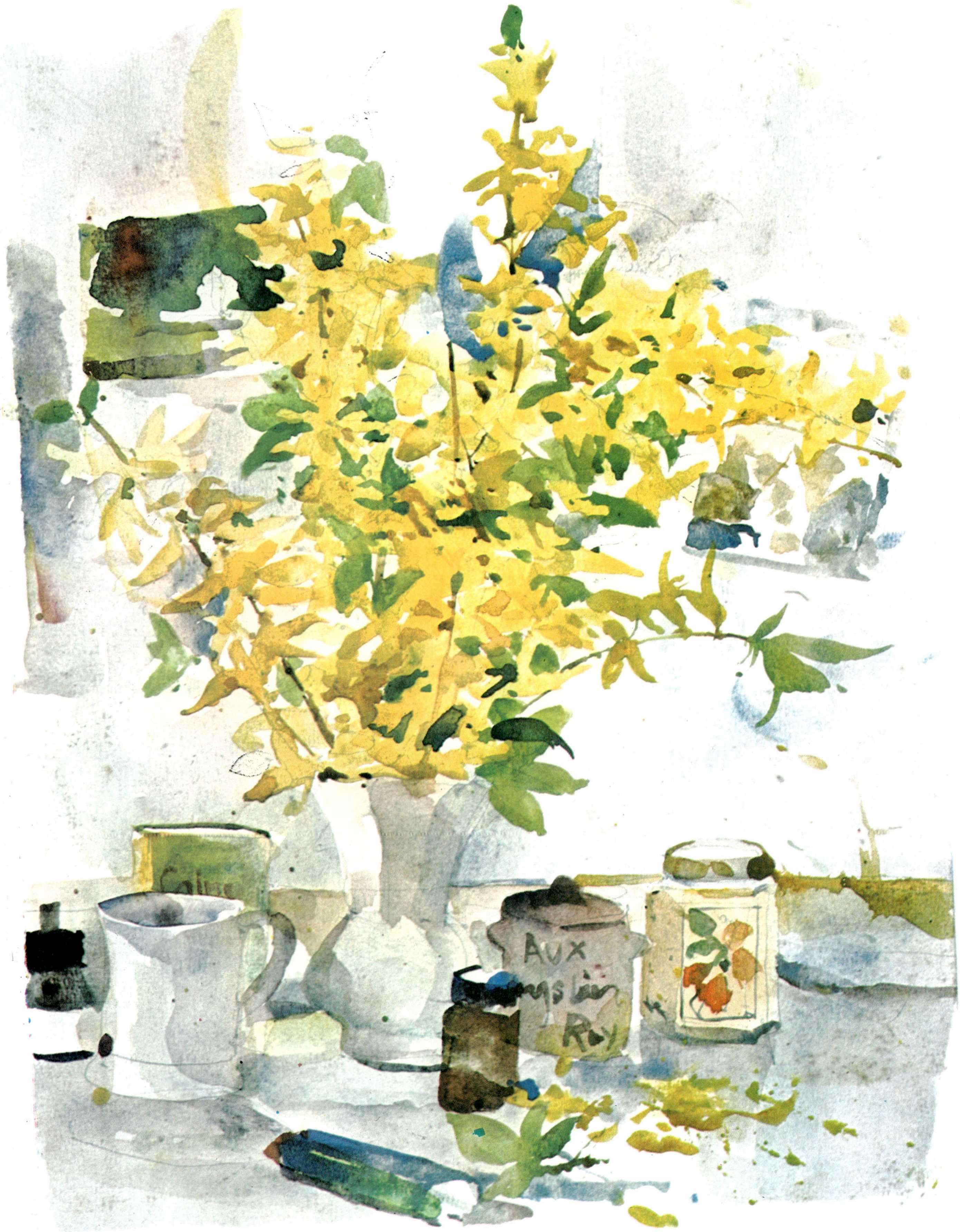

Painting Flowers with Broad Petals

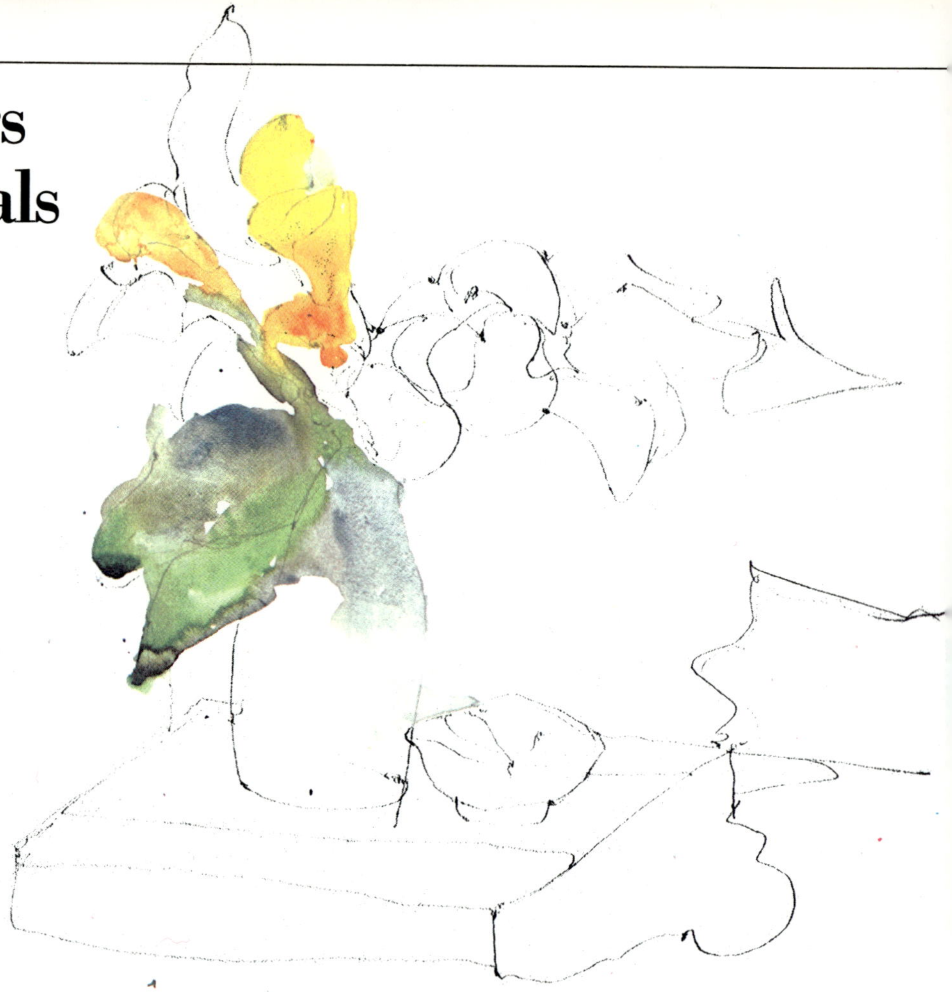

1. In this painting Charles Reid concentrated mostly on the calla lilies. Almost all his color mixing for the large leaves and flowers was done on the paper, wet-in-wet. Working in relatively small areas kept his colors from drying too quickly.

Using 140-lb. cold-pressed paper, the artist started at the broad tip of the lily on the left, with cadmium yellow on his no. 10 brush. He pressed the brush down to make a nice broad stroke, leaving it on the paper until he had painted the whole flower. Putting less pressure on the brush, he approached the narrower part of the flower. While it was still wet, he added a stem of cerulean blue and cadmium yellow, continuing it down and out into the large leaf formation. He worked over into the shadow side of the vase, switching to cerulean blue and alizarin crimson with just a touch of cadmium yellow. He painted the other lily the same way and added cadmium orange wet-in-wet as he worked toward the narrow section. Then his wash flaired out, and he worked to the left, connecting the wash with the stem of the first flower.

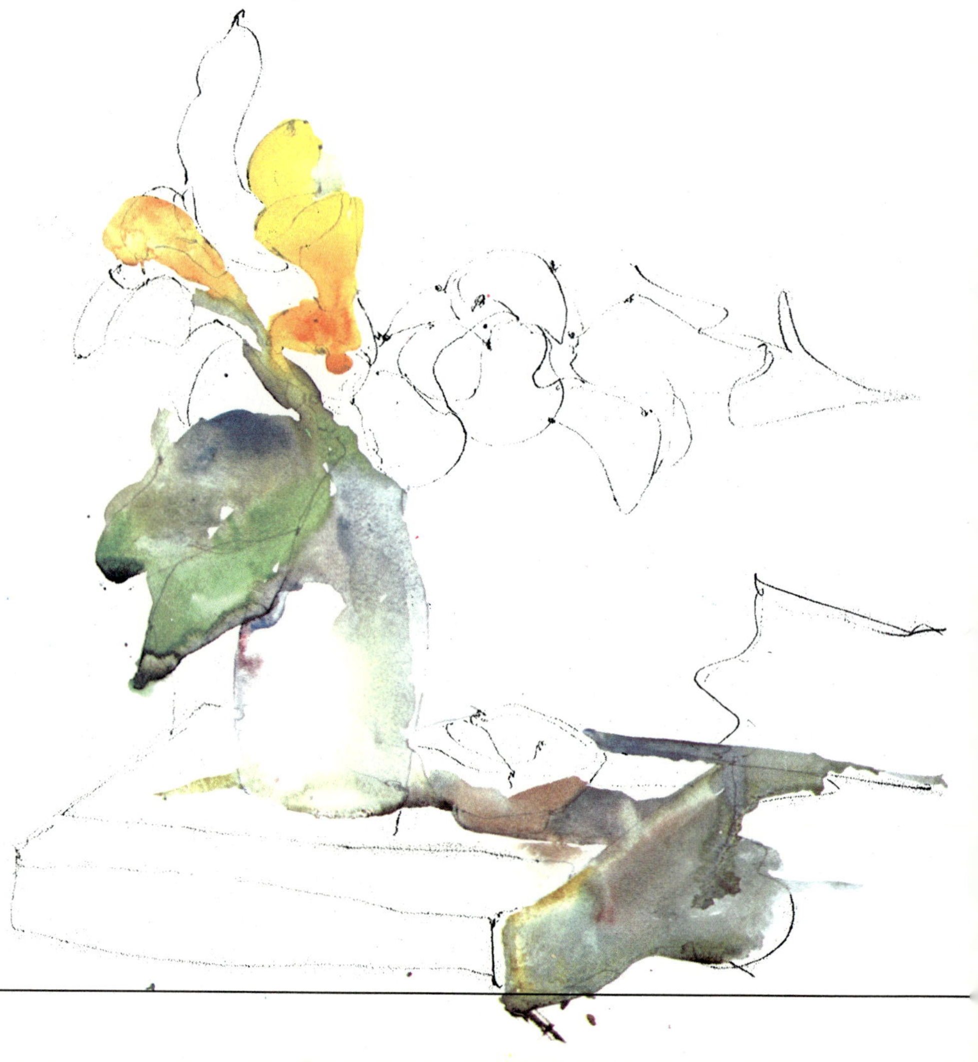

2. He continued down the vase, using the same colors, and then suggested the shape of the ashtray. On the left side of the vase he used ultramarine blue for the dark cast shadow under the leaves. The ashtray was still damp, and so he got a nice blur when he added a touch of cadmium red light and ultramarine blue mixed with cadmium yellow. The shadow to the right of the vase was cooler and darker, and so he added some of his blue mixture. He worked to the right and down to show the shadow on the side of the block, adding alizarin crimson, cerulean blue, ultramarine blue, yellow ochre, and cadmium yellow wet-in-wet. For the cool stripe above the block he started at the ashtray, using his fairly dark blue mixture, and worked to the left until he hit the shadow on the block.

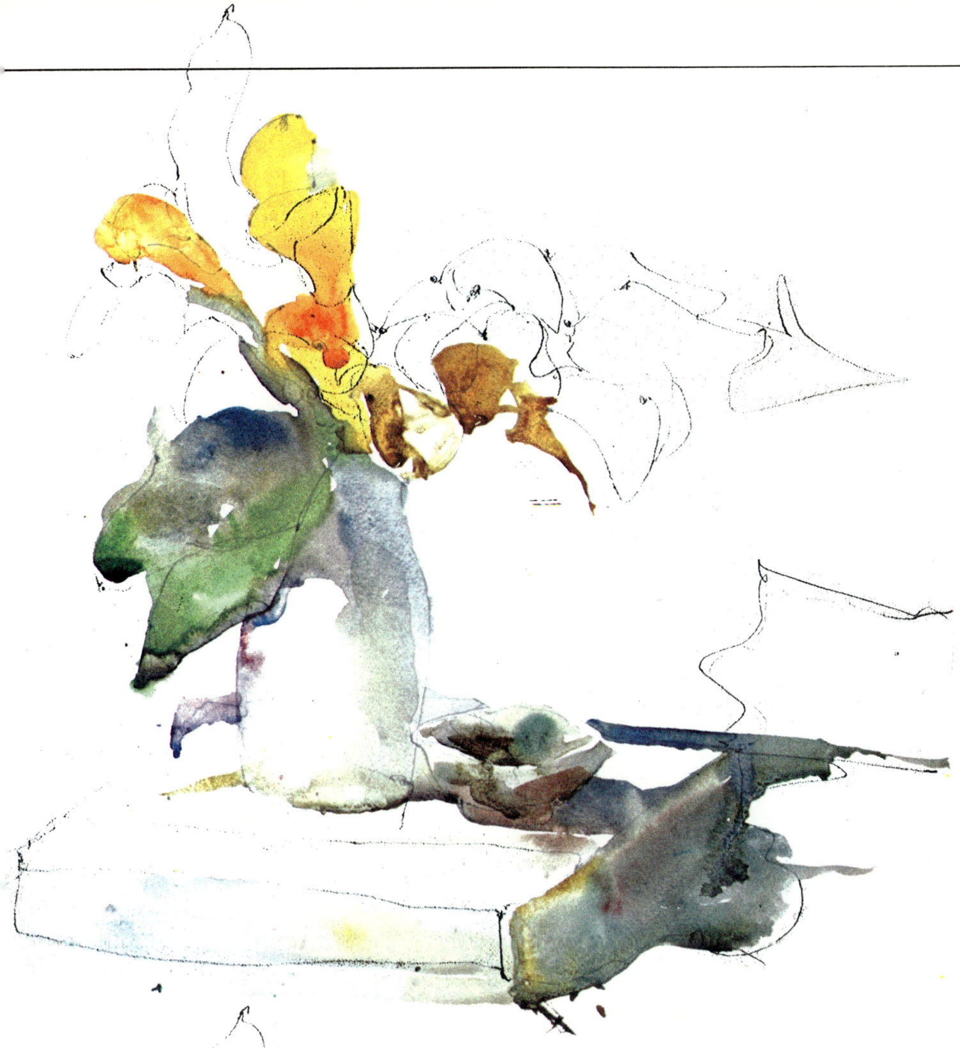

3. Now the artist worked a bit more in the lower section of the painting. He added an overwash to the base of the ashtray, leaving white paper for the rim, and painted the inside with cadmium red light mixed with yellow ochre, ultramarine blue, and a little alizarin crimson. He didn't let the white rim go all the way around, however, since this would make the ashtray look too static. Starting at the bottom of the lily that overlaps the right rim of the vase, he painted a specific shadow shape of a third lily, using raw sienna and cadmium yellow. Switching now to cadmium yellow with very little water, he washed in around the shadow he had just painted. Look closely, and you'll see a white paper rim running on the left of the shadow. This was left to keep the shadow from blending with the light wash Mr. Reid had just painted. He then took his raw sienna–cadmium yellow mixture and painted the shadow shape of two additional lilies.

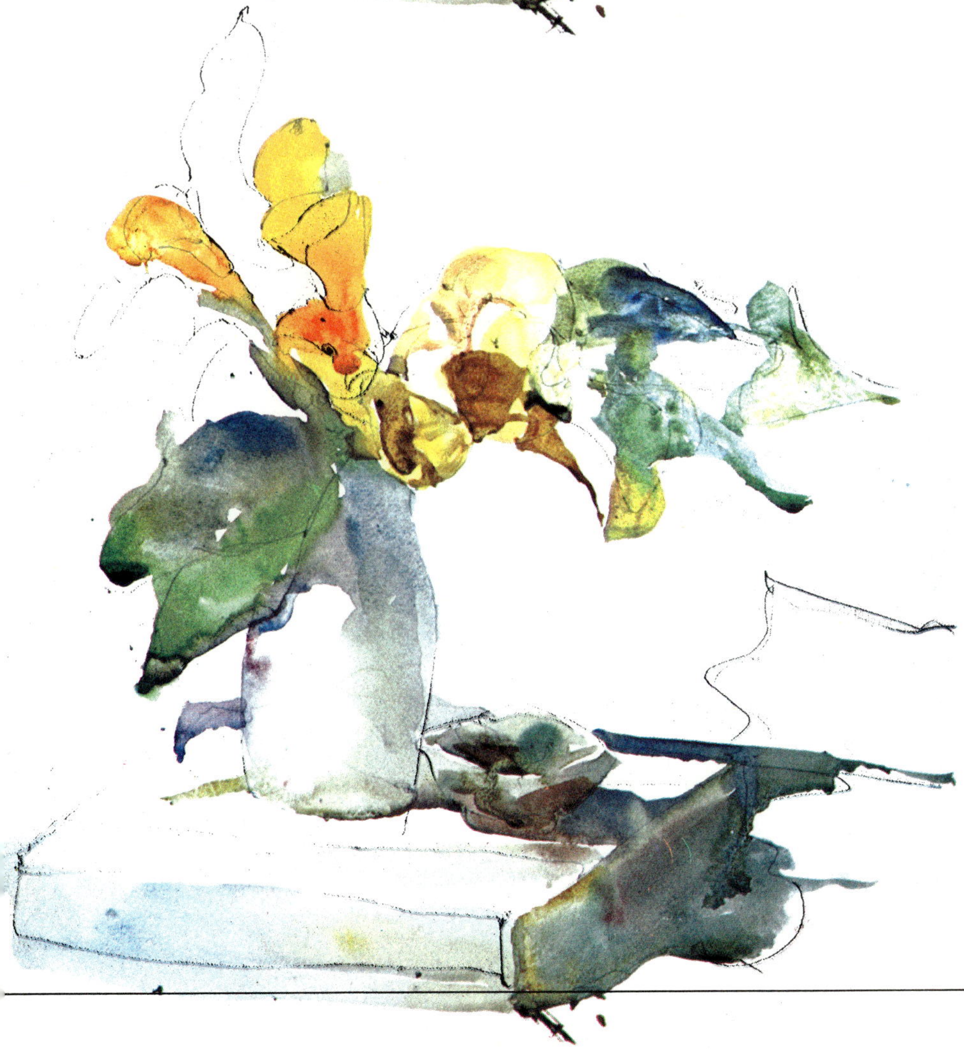

4. Mr. Reid added an overwash of pure cadmium yellow, mixed on the palette, to a section at the right of the shadow he had just painted. With this yellow he went on to the flowers to the right. Having just suggested the shadow sections with raw sienna and cadmium yellow, he waited a moment for the shadows to dry. Then he put in some leaves with cadmium yellow, cerulean blue, and ultramarine blue. Their greens blended with the still-wet shadow on the lily in the lower right side of the arrangement. He blotted some of the leaf areas with a tissue when they seemed too dark; when the leaves were dry, he added a darker green shadow value, which was in fact a darker version of the green combination he had already used.

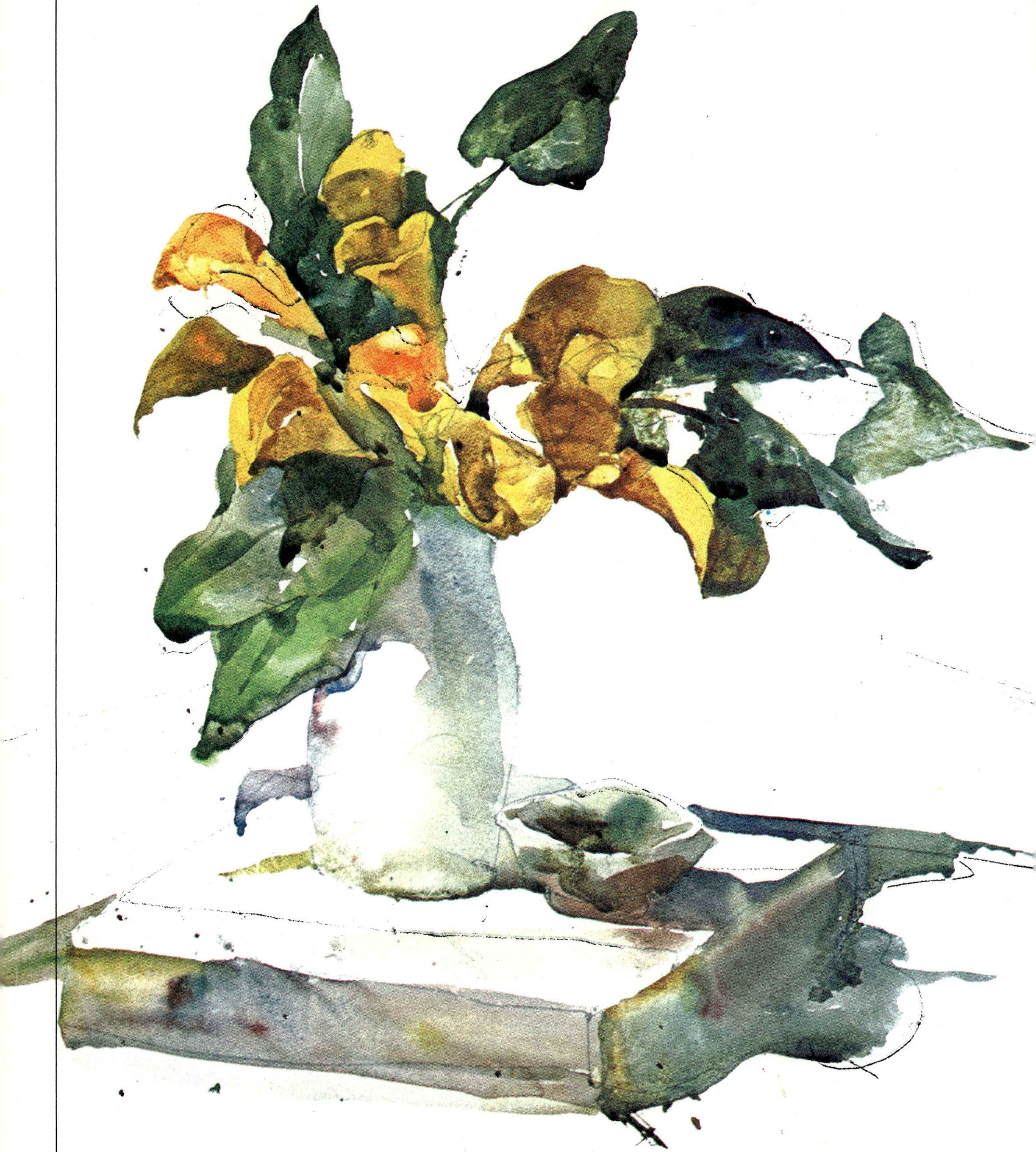

5. The artist added more flowers, starting with their leaves, using cerulean blue, ultramarine blue, a touch of alizarin crimson, and cadmium yellow. He began the top left-hand leaf at its tip, working down the left side to the lower boundary. He then worked his way down the leaf again, with a lighter green wash, leaving a strip of white paper in the middle. He painted the other leaf in the same way, but without leaving any white showing. When the wash had dried, he defined the conformation of the leaf with a darker overwash. He painted the dark flower on the left with one wash of cadmium yellow, raw sienna, and cadmium orange. The cadmium yellow flower just below was allowed to dry before the artist added shadows, plus some darker accents in the upper flowers, with cadmium yellow, cadmium orange, and raw sienna.

Solid Flower Forms

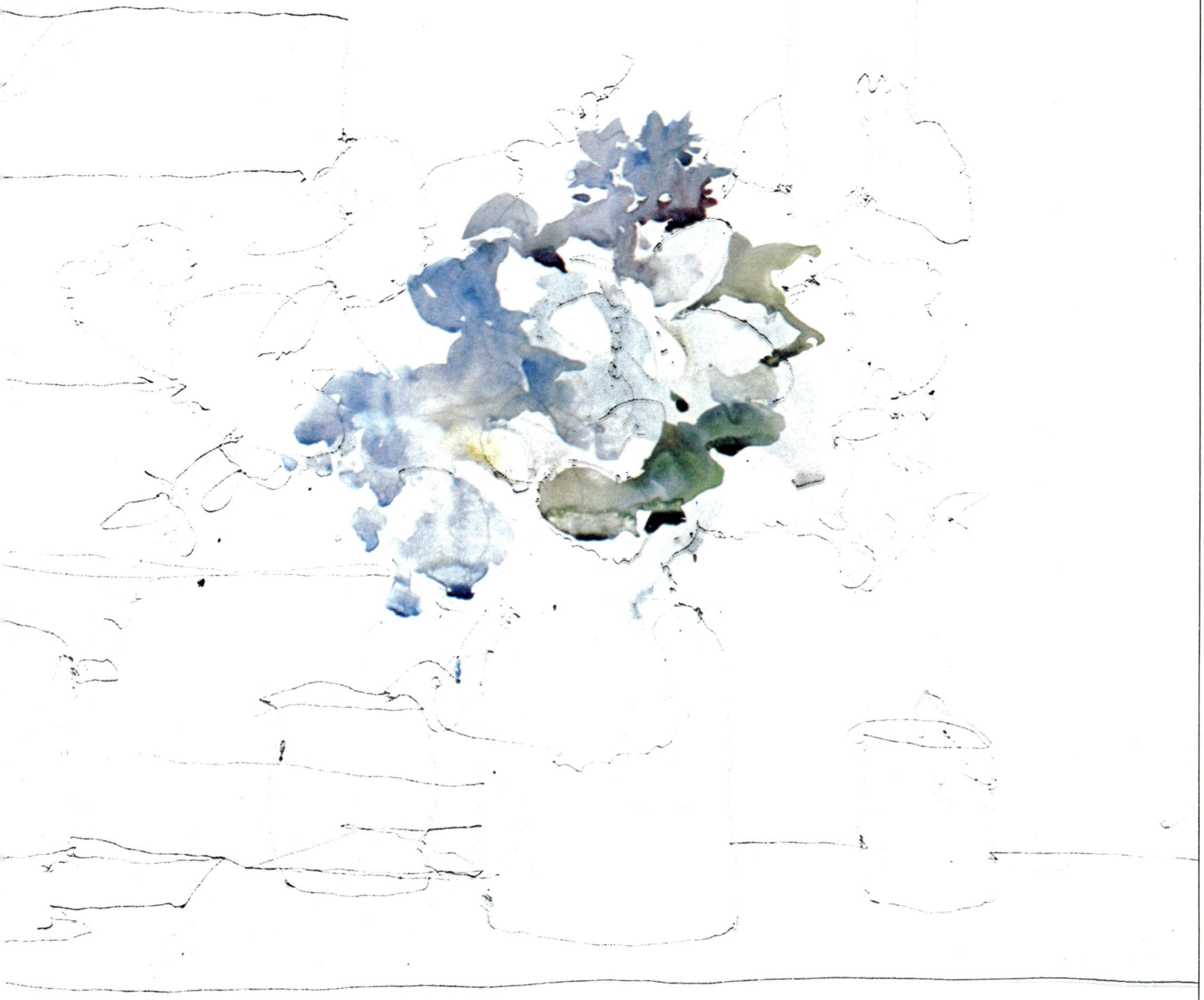

1. If real flowers are not available for a still life, artificial ones will do—and the bouquet will not wilt! In this painting Charles Reid used colors and values to define the solid forms of some silk flowers. Working on 140-lb. cold-pressed paper, the artist sketched with his usual no. 2 pencil. Then he started the painting with a light wash of alizarin crimson, ultramarine blue, and cerulean blue mixed on the palette. Darker puddles of color gathered in the lower section of petals. He worked carefully around the shapes that would become white flowers. He allowed some darker purples to bleed into the shadow of the white flower to keep a connection between the two areas. Next, using a mixture of ultramarine blue and cadmium yellow, he painted a small section of light leaves. He continued to work around the white flowers, but his purple wash had become too weak, and he knew he would have to restate this area later. But he was trying to keep some edges soft without completely losing the shape of the white flowers. Notice the combination of hard and soft edges, and the values, especially in the greens where intentionally made some sections of the leaves darker than the others.

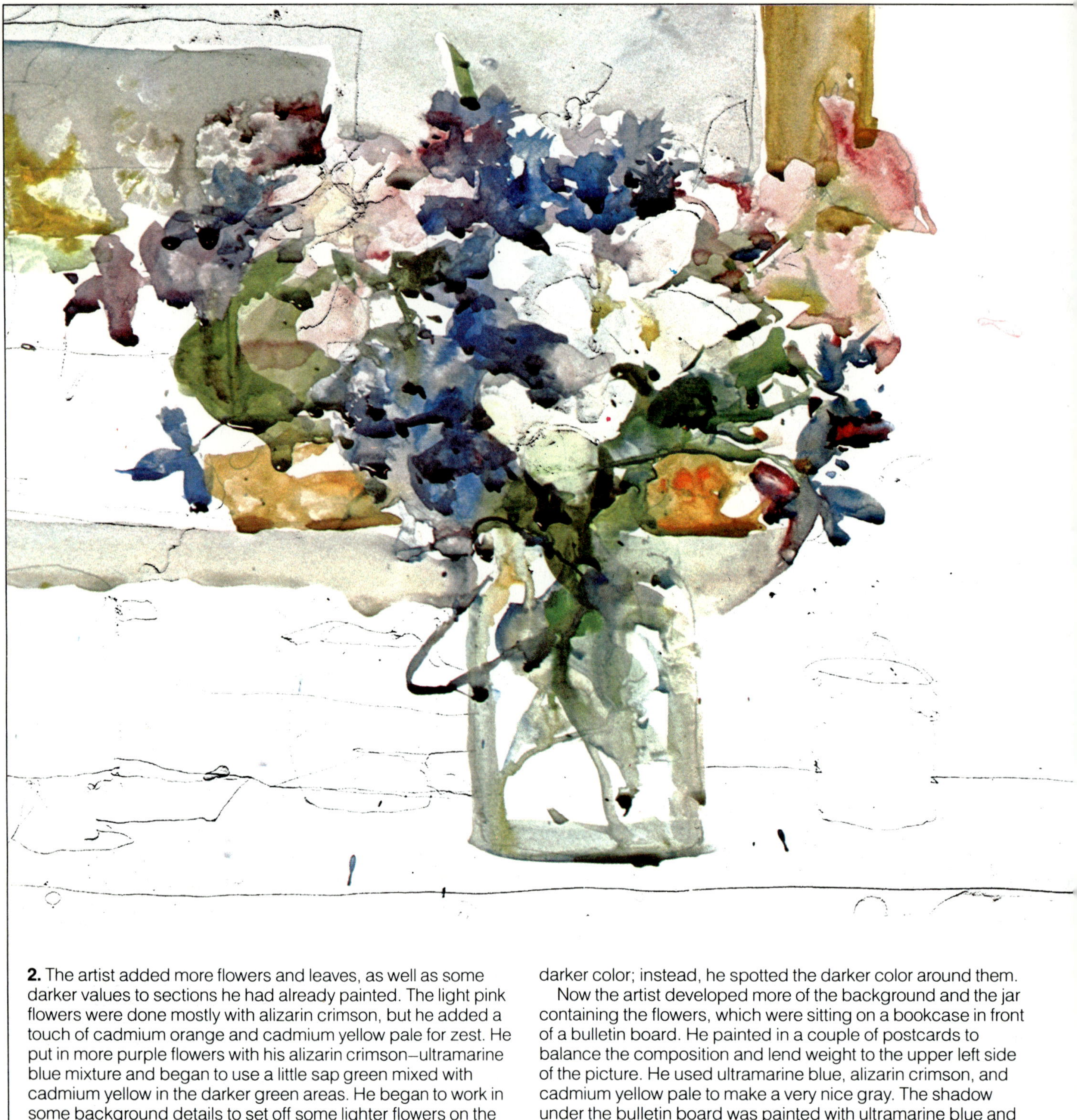

2. The artist added more flowers and leaves, as well as some darker values to sections he had already painted. The light pink flowers were done mostly with alizarin crimson, but he added a touch of cadmium orange and cadmium yellow pale for zest. He put in more purple flowers with his alizarin crimson–ultramarine blue mixture and began to use a little sap green mixed with cadmium yellow in the darker green areas. He began to work in some background details to set off some lighter flowers on the upper right. The warm browns were painted with a mixture of cadmium orange, raw sienna, and cadmium yellow. He added darker purple overwashes to the washed-out purple flowers. In the flowers to the left, he made only a few darker accents, allowing some of the original washes to show through next to the white flowers. The artist didn't outline the white flowers with darker color; instead, he spotted the darker color around them.

Now the artist developed more of the background and the jar containing the flowers, which were sitting on a bookcase in front of a bulletin board. He painted in a couple of postcards to balance the composition and lend weight to the upper left side of the picture. He used ultramarine blue, alizarin crimson, and cadmium yellow pale to make a very nice gray. The shadow under the bulletin board was painted with ultramarine blue and cadmium orange. He continued it into the jar but switched to cerulean blue mixed with cadmium orange for most of the rest of the jar. He also used some ultramarine blue and cadmium yellow mixed with alizarin crimson. He added the bale of the canning jar with ultramarine blue, alizarin crimson, and cadmium yellow.

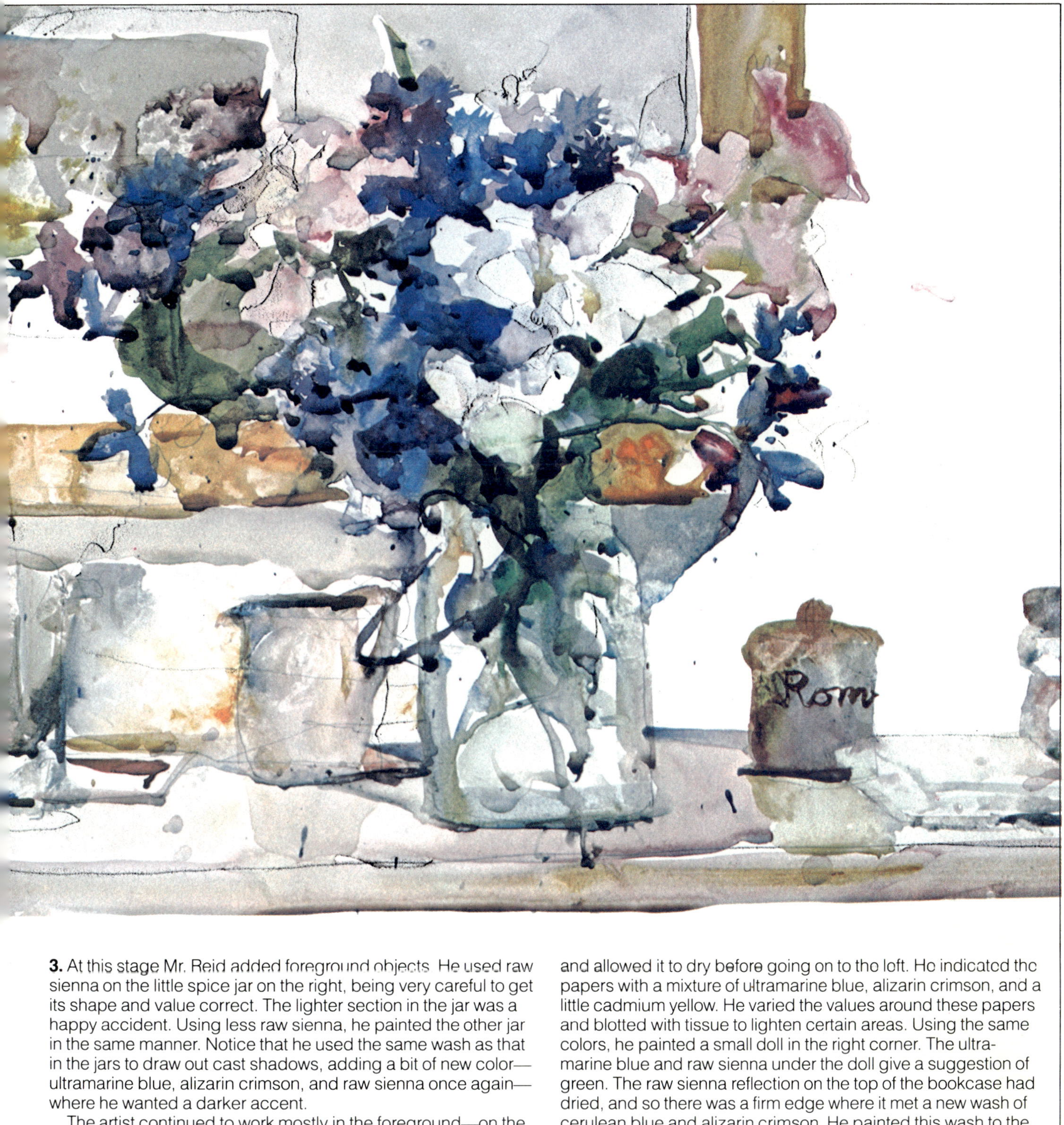

3. At this stage Mr. Reid added foreground objects. He used raw sienna on the little spice jar on the right, being very careful to get its shape and value correct. The lighter section in the jar was a happy accident. Using less raw sienna, he painted the other jar in the same manner. Notice that he used the same wash as that in the jars to draw out cast shadows, adding a bit of new color—ultramarine blue, alizarin crimson, and raw sienna once again—where he wanted a darker accent.

The artist continued to work mostly in the foreground—on the top of the bookcase, some papers, and one or two other objects. The top of the bookcase was somewhat glossy and picked up suggestions of color from the objects. Working mostly with raw sienna, he painted this reflection below the spice jar and allowed it to dry before going on to the left. He indicated the papers with a mixture of ultramarine blue, alizarin crimson, and a little cadmium yellow. He varied the values around these papers and blotted with tissue to lighten certain areas. Using the same colors, he painted a small doll in the right corner. The ultramarine blue and raw sienna under the doll give a suggestion of green. The raw sienna reflection on the top of the bookcase had dried, and so there was a firm edge where it met a new wash of cerulean blue and alizarin crimson. He painted this wash to the left and used it to show the front of the bookcase where he added some raw sienna wet-in-wet. He worked rather splashily here and left quite a bit of white paper.

Radiating Petal Forms

1. When painting flowers such as daisies, squint your eyes and think of the overall mass of the flower, not the individual petals. Charles Reid began this painting by spotting hard-edged dark greens around the daisy in the top center, starting with sap green and then adding a little cadmium yellow and cadmium red light. He deliberately blurred the soft edge on the left side of the petal, blotting with a tissue to control it. He continued to paint around the flower, using cerulean blue, sap green, cadmium yellow pale, and, on the right side of the flower, alizarin crimson and cerulean blue.

2. For the heather-colored area behind the top daisy the artist used alizarin crimson with sap green and cadmium yellow pale. Notice the spatter work and short jabbing strokes here. The cast shadow from the flowers was painted with cerulean blue, alizarin crimson, and some cadmium yellow. To add background, Mr. Reid dampened the paper and then painted in cerulean blue. He added a dark green-yellow center to the daisy on the left, which bled into the wet background. Dampening sections of the flowers with clear water, he painted light shadows into them. He painted the vase, part of the background, and the cast shadow with ultramarine blue, alizarin crimson, and yellow ochre, wet-in-wet. Then he painted the carton of cream and the jar at the left with the same colors and values, reserving white paper for light-struck areas.

3. Still using ultramarine blue, yellow ochre, and alizarin crimson, he did a very light background wash (opposite page). Next he painted the top on the jar in the left foreground, using Hooker's green dark and cadmium red light. The yellow bowl on the right is cadmium yellow on the right side and yellow ochre on the left. The artist also picked up a bit of ultramarine blue, alizarin crimson, and yellow ochre.

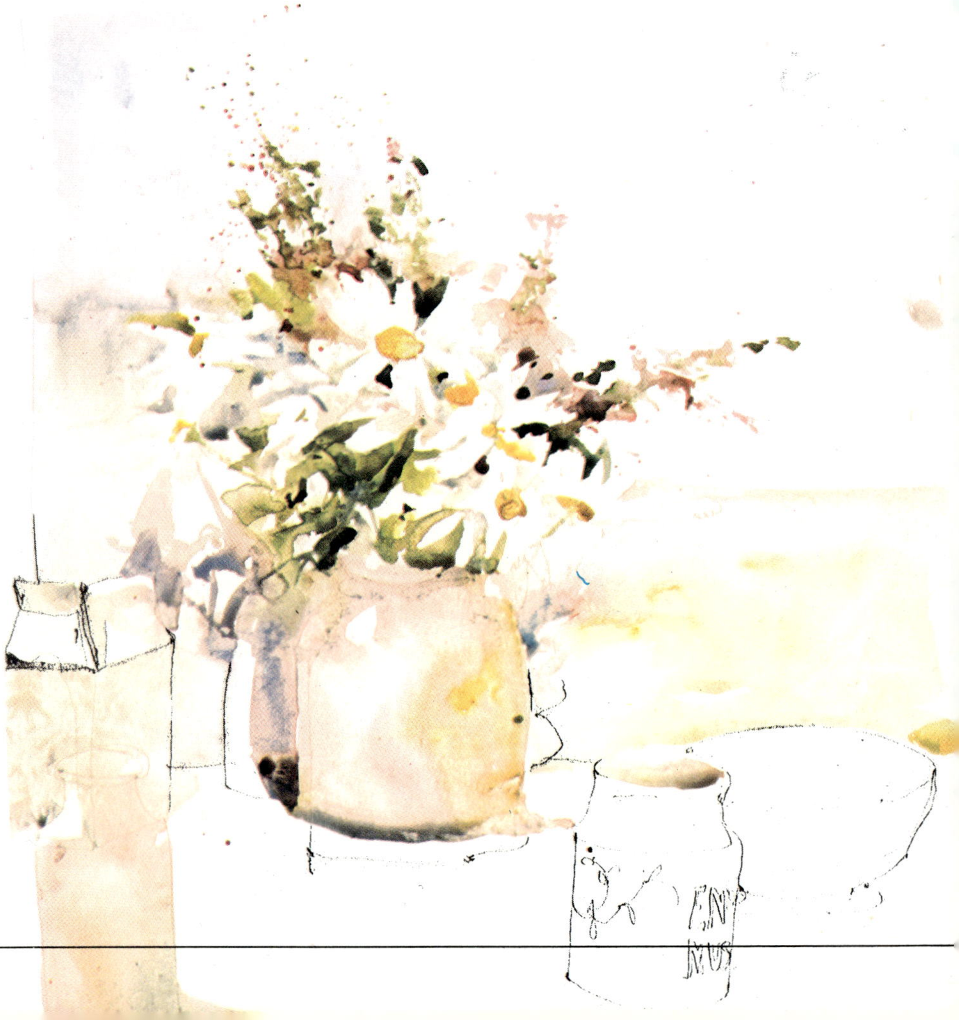

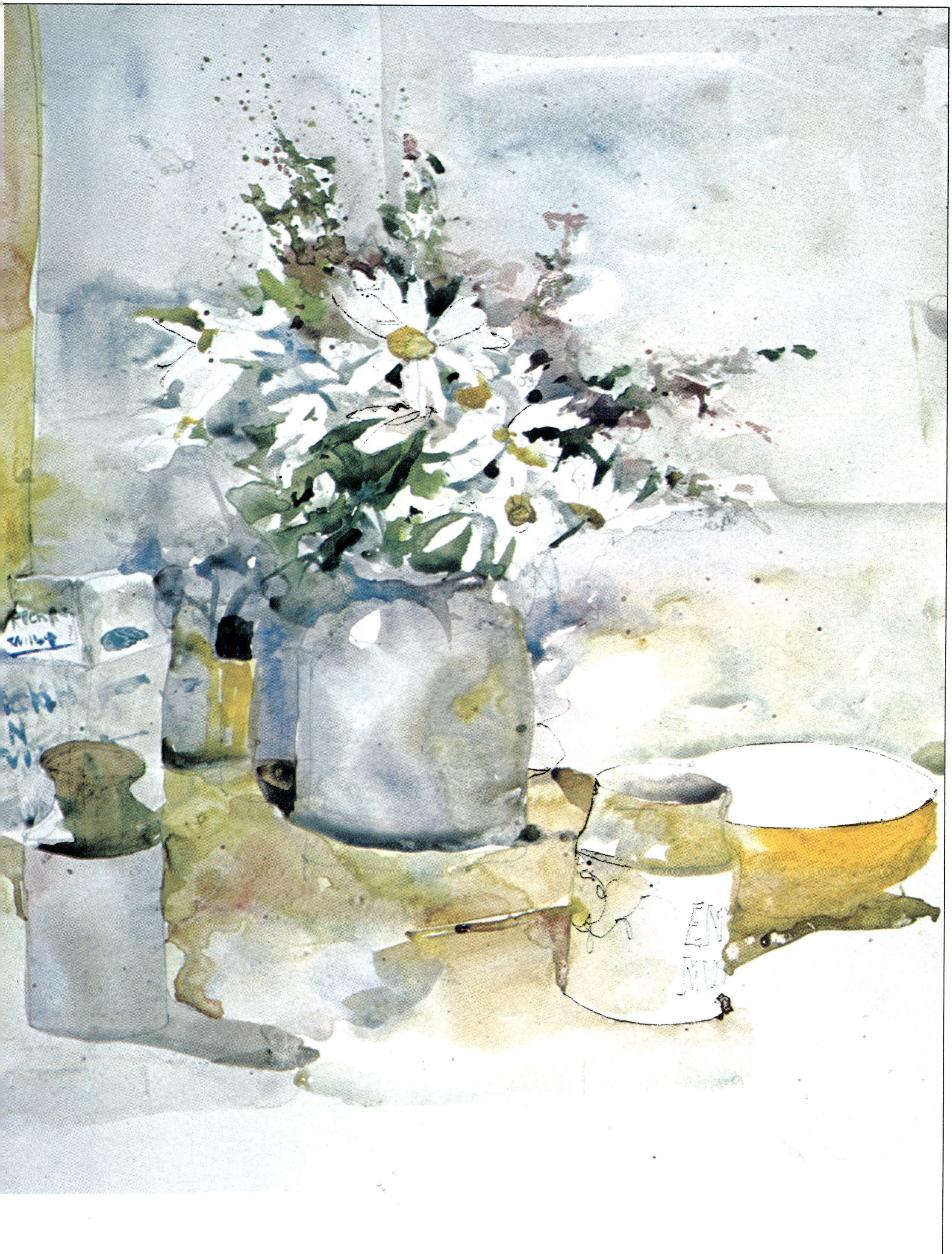

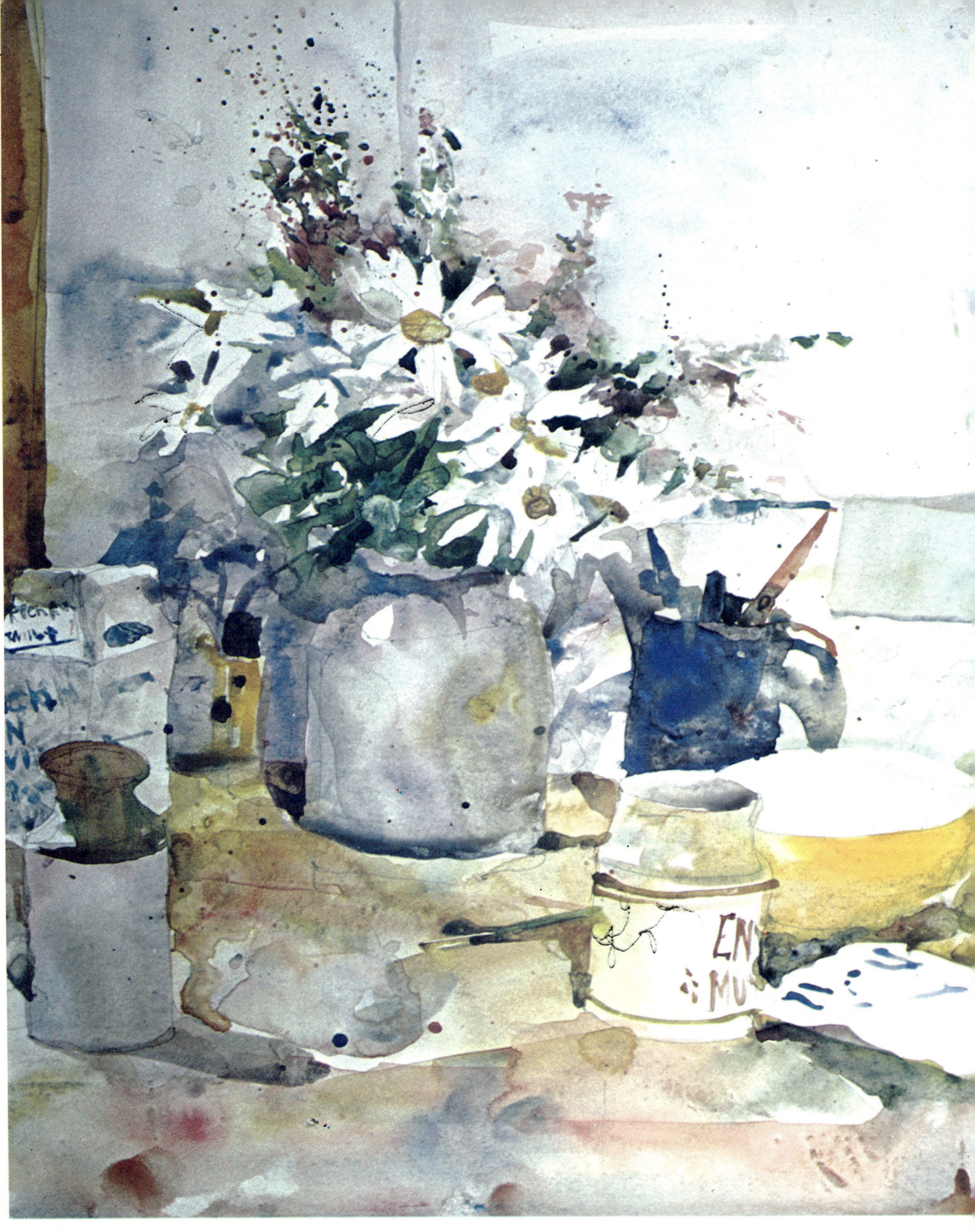

4. In this final step the artist added a dark blue mug containing some pens and a pencil. He painted the mug with ultramarine blue, alizarin crimson, and yellow ochre, and while it was still wet, he added the pencil, using cadmium orange and a little yellow ochre. The pens were painted with ivory black. He continued painting the tabletop with a mixture of ultramarine blue, yellow ochre, and alizarin crimson. Then, using a no. 6 round sable brush, he rendered the lettering on the mustard jar. As you can see, he used a limited palette throughout this painting. It was not necessary to work with a lot of colors. Mr. Reid was able to get the effect of lots of colors by using just a few colors in a variety of ways.

Compact Forms

1. Charles Reid tried an unusual approach to this composition, which has a blue iris sticking out of an otherwise compact bouquet. He did not include the bottom of the vase in the composition because he wanted to concentrate more on the flowers. He completed his drawing on 140 lb. cold-pressed paper and then started right out with his no. 8 round sable brush to paint the purple iris. He made a purple mixture of ultramarine blue and alizarin crimson, hoping to complete the top iris as much as possible with his first wash. He worked down and to the left without lifting his brush, then around and into the lower petal at the center and the two petals on the right, adding cadmium yellow pale. The green was painted with sap green and cadmium yellow light, and he painted the stem while the petals were still damp to blend the colors where the two areas meet. The light blue at the bottom of the stem is cerulean. Mr. Reid suggested another iris and began massing in a fairly large section of yellow flowers with cadmium yellow, showing some of the petal shapes around the borders. While these were still wet, he painted the stems with sap green and cadmium yellow, adding a touch of cadmium red in the lower sections to warm the green. He drew in more delicate stems with the same combination and then went back into some of the yellow flowers to darken and blend certain areas.

2. Now the artist added more yellow flowers and another iris, darkening his colors here and there, as well as lifting out color to create lighter values. He left small bits of white paper to prevent his colors from blending completely. He added dark purple to the iris in the center and then drew the purple down and began the stem. Using sap green and cadmium yellow, he showed the delicate shape of the stem. He painted in more of the yellow flowers with cadmium yellow, and then he did the other stem, near the top of the vase, with his green combination which now had an added touch of red.

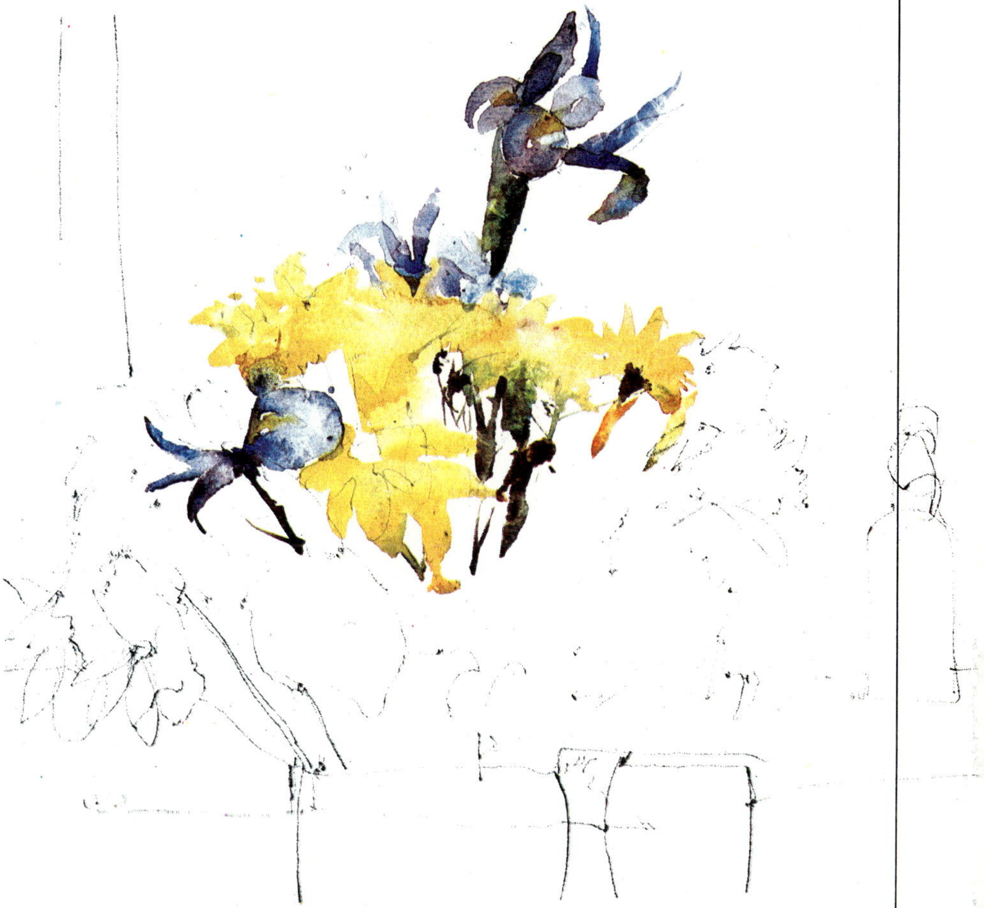

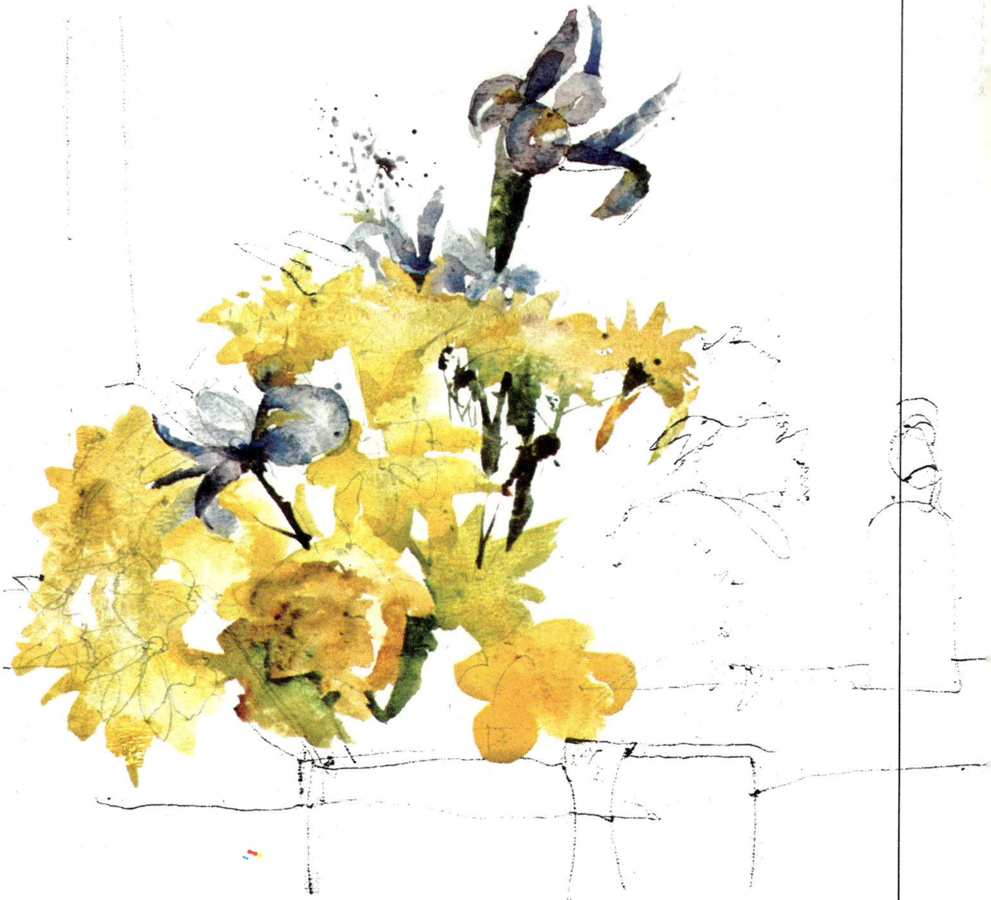

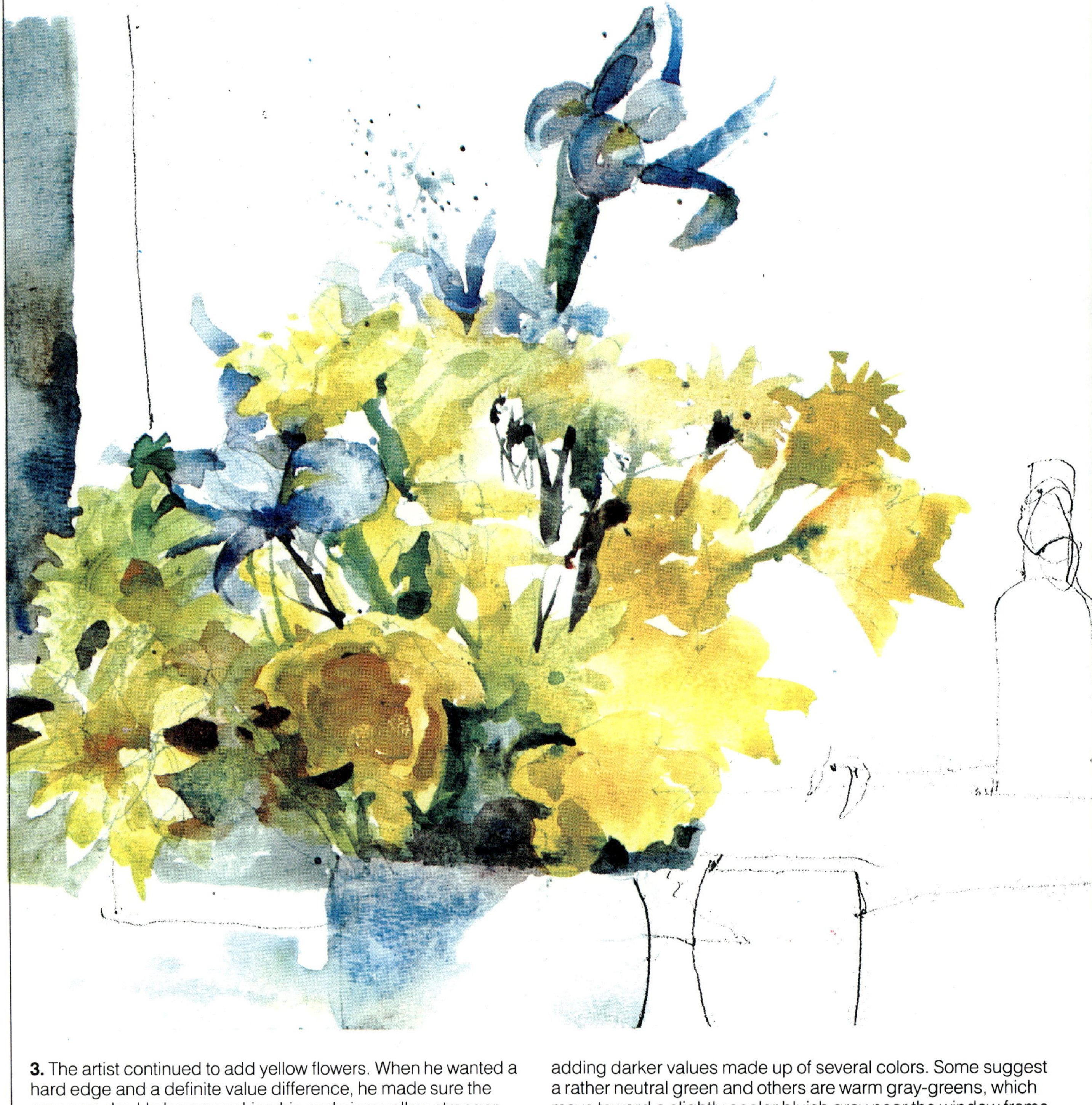

3. The artist continued to add yellow flowers. When he wanted a hard edge and a definite value difference, he made sure the area was dry. He began making his cadmium yellow stronger, using very little water, and he used raw sienna wet-in-wet in places to describe the construction of the flowers. Then he added a green made up of ultramarine blue and cadmium yellow to the flower in the lower section that was in shadow, and he painted more flowers at the right. Notice the difference in values and colors within the total flower mass. The top section has picked up color from damp stems, and the lower section has become much richer with a good charge of strong cadmium yellow. The artist kept other yellow areas light, since it was important to work for variety in both value and color. Now it was time to get on with the background. The artist had started the painting with a fairly dark value in the form of the iris, later adding darker values made up of several colors. Some suggest a rather neutral green and others are warm gray-greens, which move toward a slightly cooler bluish gray near the window frame. He kept these darks from getting too deep because he wanted a dark that was *relatively* darker than the flowers, but no darker than that. The accents around the flowers are also not really dark. As he put in the vase, he began with the shadow side, instead of starting with an overall light wash and then adding overwashes to develop his shadow. He let this dry for a few moments and then drew the shadow out into the light. He followed this with a very light wash of alizarin crimson and cerulean blue for the light side of the vase, leaving white paper along the upper border to retain a hard edge. He then allowed everything to dry.

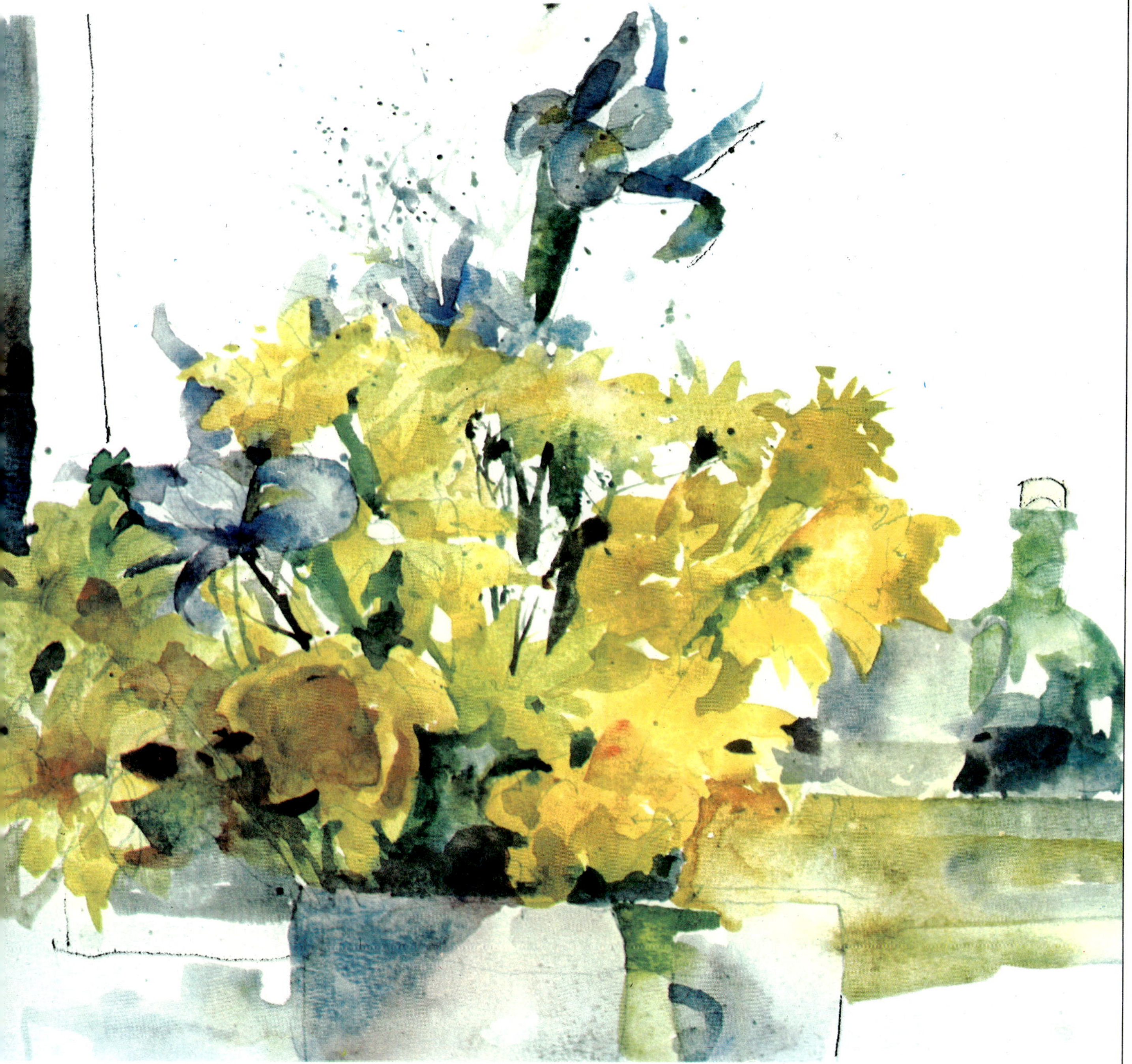

4. To finish the painting, Mr. Reid started with the lower section of the window frame. He painted the whole thing, including areas that would be covered later by darker overwashes. He used alizarin crimson and cerulean blue with a bit of raw sienna, starting at the right and working to the left, adding more raw sienna as he went. He painted around the cup to the right of the vase. Next he added a light wash of alizarin crimson and cerulean blue to the cup, leaving a white rim along the top. A darker version of the same colors was painted to show the cup's shadow. Next he painted the shadow section of the window frame, using the same colors he had used in the light section, and then the remaining objects. The cooler grays were painted with alizarin crimson and cerulean blue, and the greens were mixed from cerulean blue and cadmium yellow pale.

Anemones

1. The white anemone in this still life arrangement really stood out—and Charles Reid started his painting with the hope that he would be able to put its shape in the right place. However, he started off with his darks first, keeping them fairly thin. Never try to paint a light value against a light tone on a white canvas or panel. Always place some darks first.

Notice the shadow shape on the vase. There were also reflected lights and textures on this vase, but the artist ignored them and painted only this simple, one-value shadow. It's vital to see only the obvious at this early stage. Notice the lines that connect the flowers with the border on one side and the vase with the border on the other side. Always think of the whole picture. At this stage, Mr. Reid was thinking of what he would try to do with all that white emptiness around his vase of anemones.

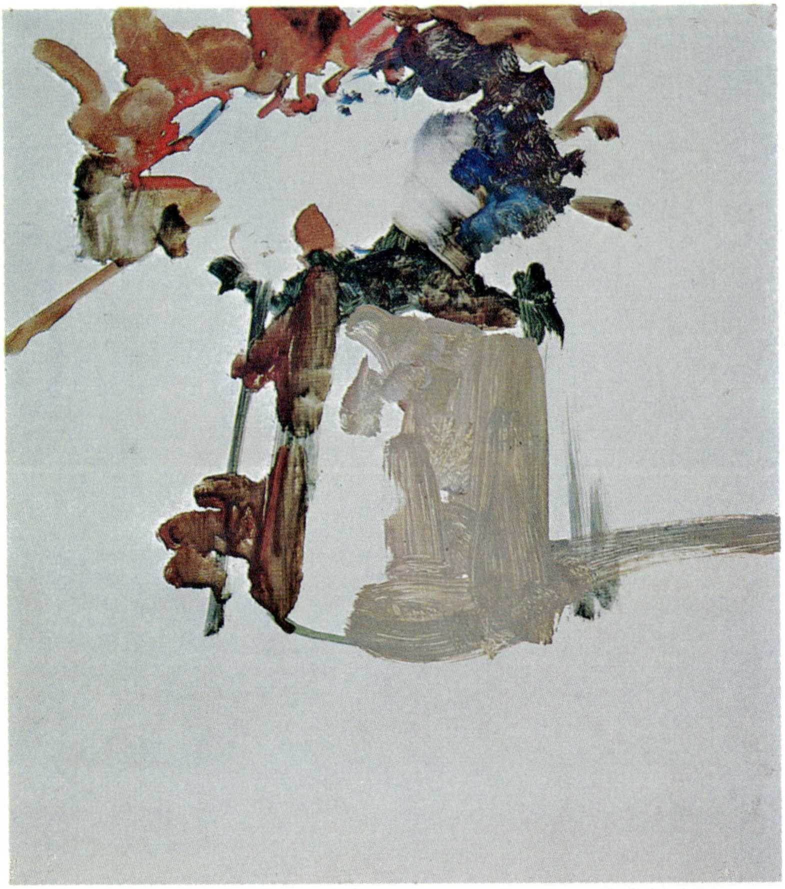

2. The artist was painting very thinly on a Masonite panel primed with Liquitex gesso. (Masonite presents a slippery surface to work on. You might like it or hate it.) He was using a gel medium that comes from a tube called Win-Gel (manufactured by Winsor & Newton). Mr. Reid feels the gel works better than an oil medium on Masonite because it gives a bit more control.

As Mr. Reid worked on his palette, some of the burnt sienna, raw umber, and burnt umber tended to get into the purples and greens of the flowers, but it didn't worry him. It's important to develop color themes in your pictures. The easiest way to do this is to have some of the same colors in adjoining areas.

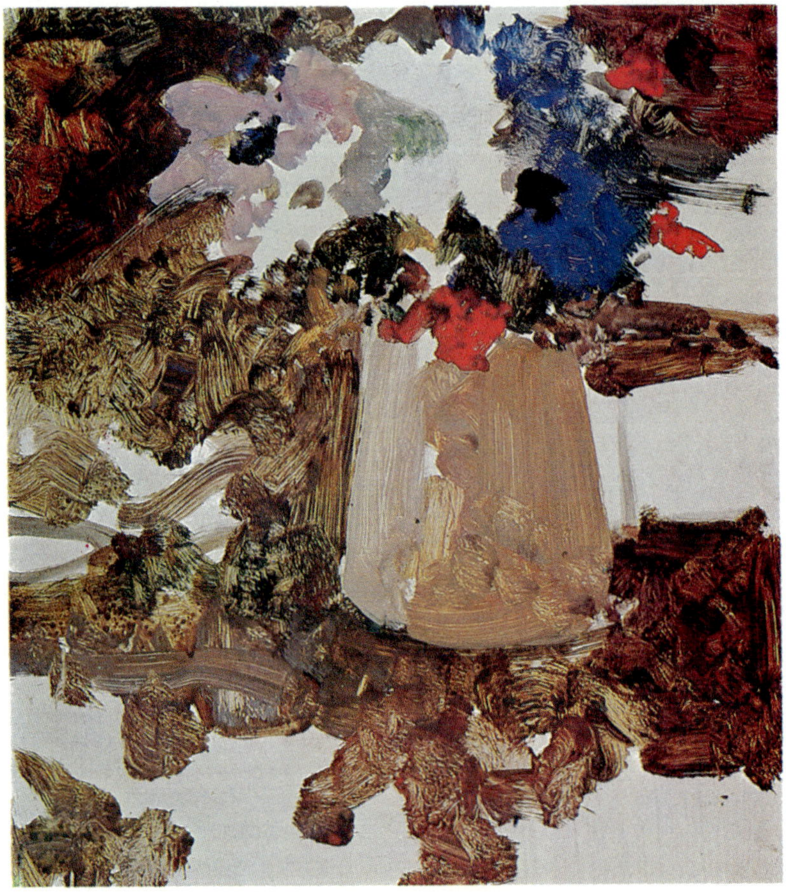

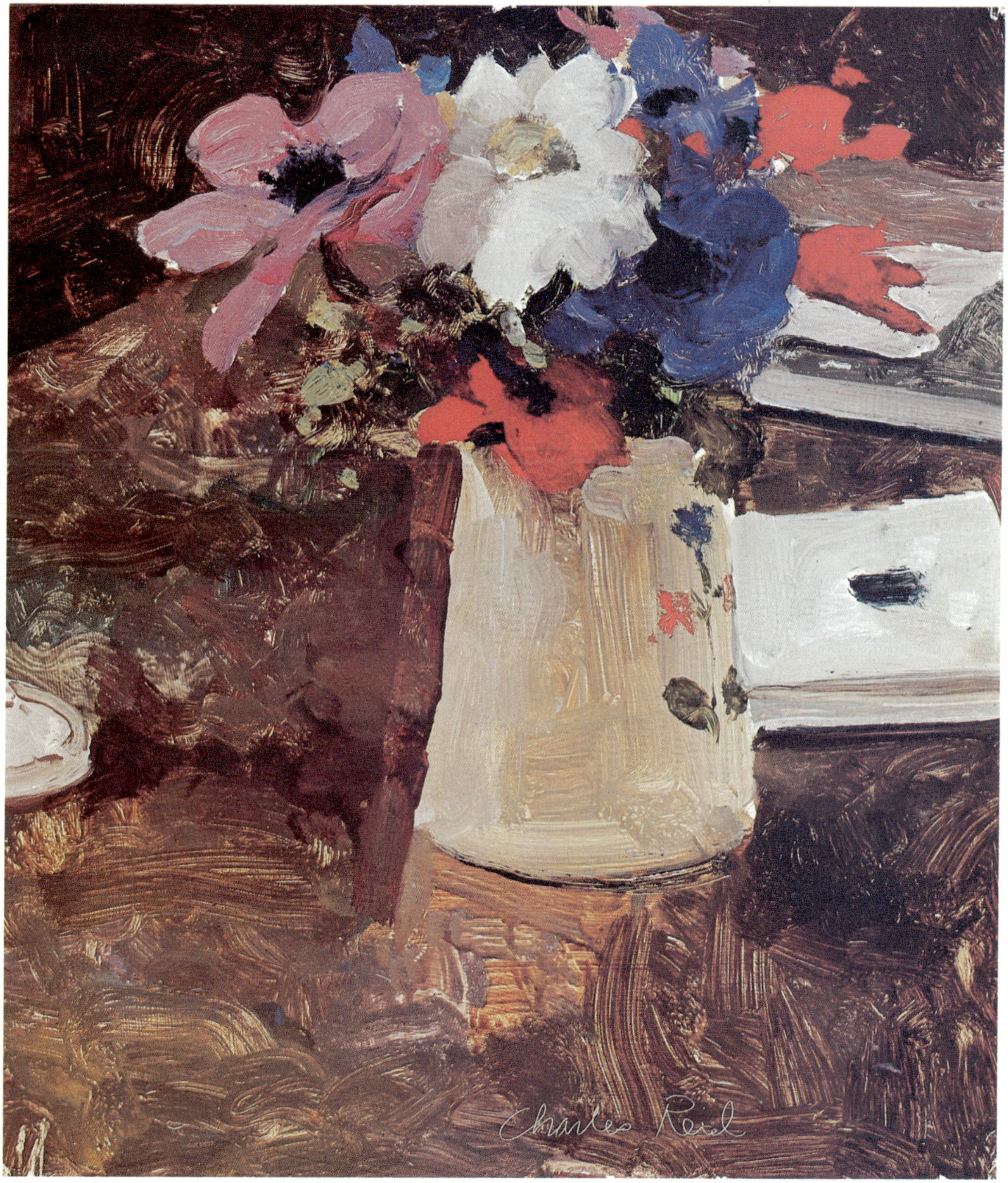

3. Now all areas were covered. The artist added reflected light to the vase carefully, making certain that this area never got as light as the main light on the vase. Notice that the table recedes and the brown goes toward purple in some areas, toward green in other areas. The value also changes slightly. But don't overdo such color and value changes or you'll break up the overall tone.

Mr. Reid was not too pleased with the white book, but he decided not to fuss with the painting anymore. Like many artists, he is never completely happy with what he paints; there's always something he'd like to change.

Simplifying a Still Life

1. To paint a little clutch of Star of Bethlehem flowers, Charles Reid concentrated on simplicity, handling most areas broadly with only a few colors. Working on 140 lb. cold-pressed paper, he did a contour drawing with a no. 2 office pencil. For a cool green he mixed cadmium yellow and cerulean blue and made a single downward stroke with his no. 8 brush to show the leaf. He then worked around what would become one of the flowers. He painted around the lettering of the blue can with ultramarine blue and allowed it to dry before painting the label with raw sienna and cadmium yellow. He defined the flowers with a very light, mixture of alizarin crimson, cerulean blue, and yellow ochre.

With sap green and cadmium red light, he put dark green under the flowers and worked down into the top of the vase, adding more red. He painted the round vase top, leaving a little white highlight on the lower left and adding cerulean blue on the right to suggest a cool reflected light. He painted the pitcher with a cool gray mixture of alizarin crimson, ultramarine blue, and yellow ochre. He let this dry before painting the rim and the darker inside section at the top. Then he added a slightly darker overwash on the left side of the pitcher, leaving a bit of the original wash untouched to suggest reflected light. The L-shaped section of the tabletop is cadmium orange and raw sienna.

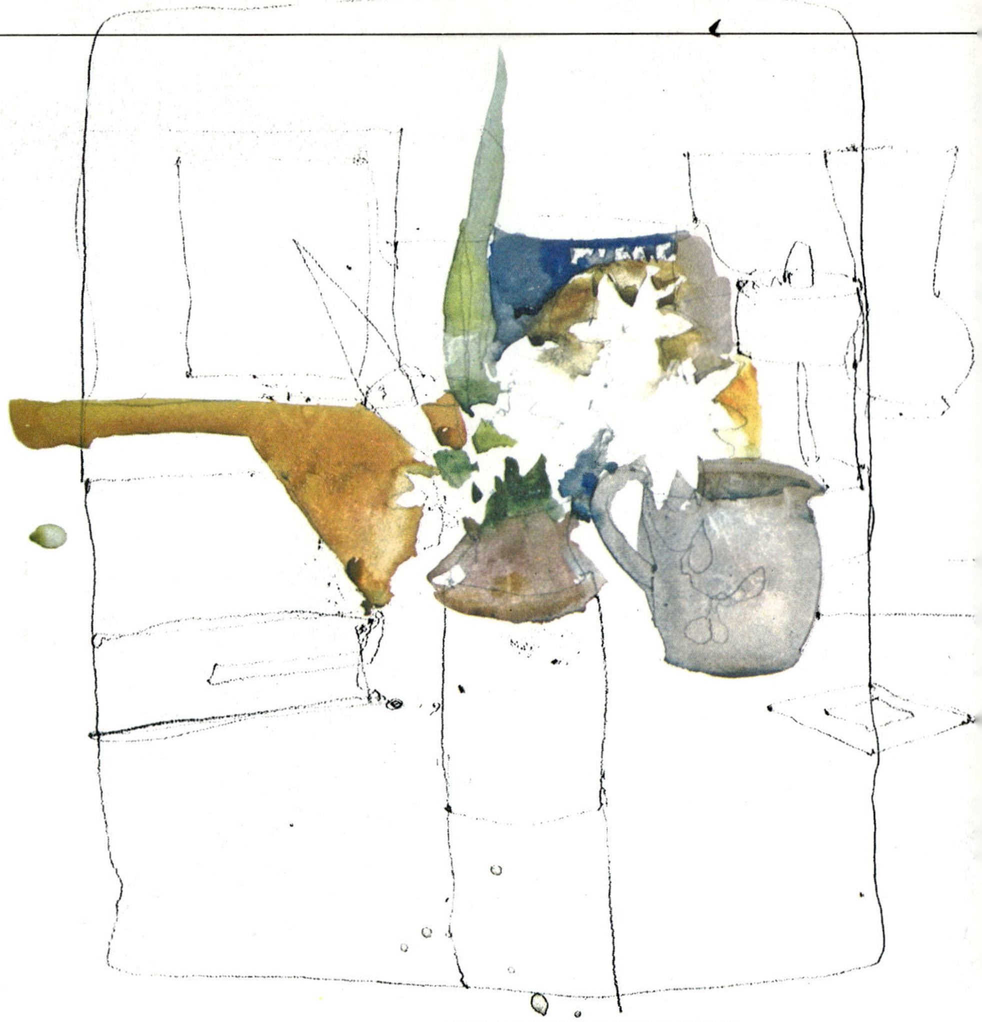

2. Next he added the table section to the right of the vase. Starting with raw sienna, he put in a touch of cadmium red light at the top and then worked his way down, adding some cerulean blue. Still working quite wet and applying his colors directly, he added alizarin crimson to the table, painting around the slide. Instead of continuing into the vase and its cast shadow, he left hard edges on the washes.

The artist finished painting the table, adding colors wet-in-wet. He painted right up around the book, leaving a hard edge and using more raw sienna with a touch of cadmium orange. He also painted the vase and its cast shadow with these colors and values. He didn't like the hard edge together with the extreme color and value contrast between the upper and lower sections of the vase, and so he introduced some cadmium red light and a little sap green along the upper back section. The grays in the book cover were mixed from cadmium red light and sap green. The artist combined cerulean blue and cadmium yellow for the second leaf and the transparent salt grinder behind the pitcher.

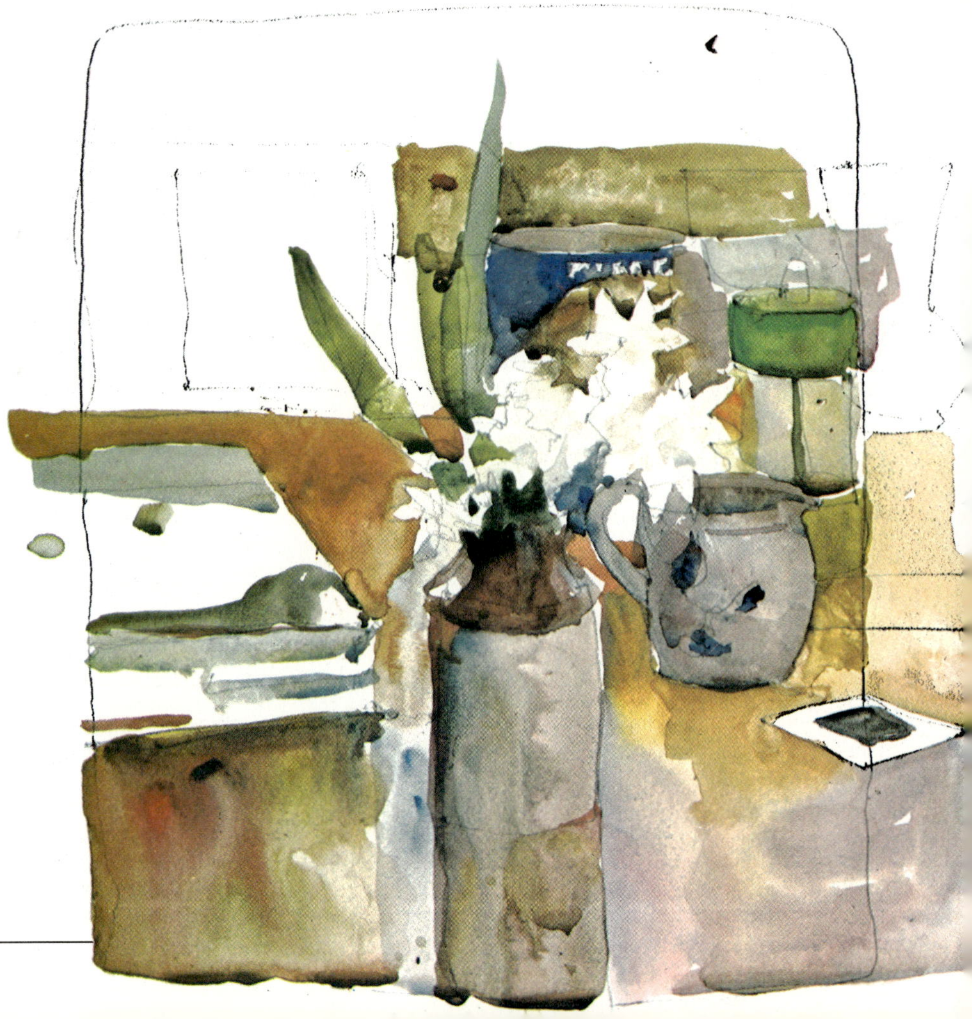

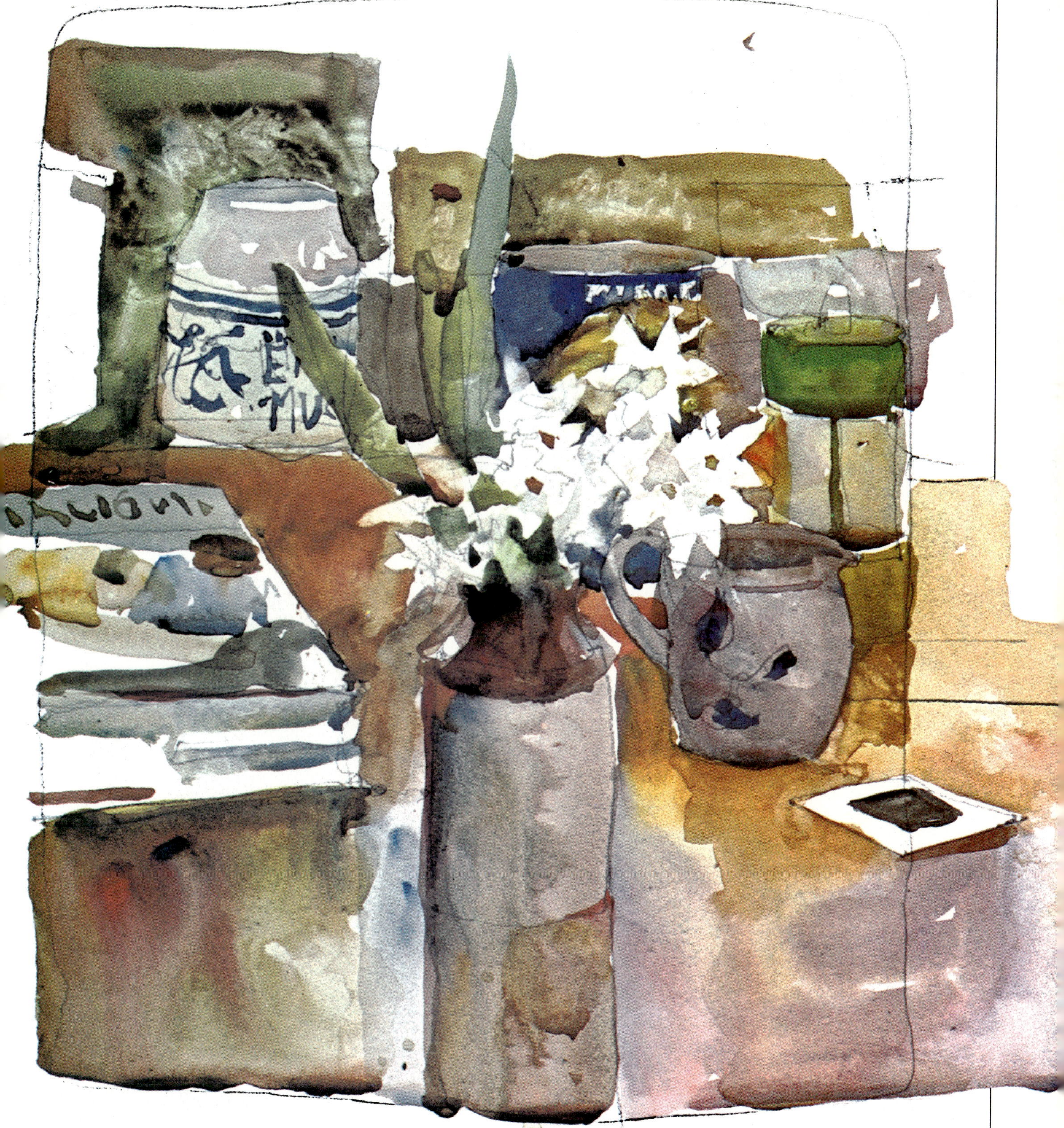

3. Here the artist "lifted out" several flower petals by scrubbing them lightly with a clean, damp brush. Then he cleaned the brush, blotted the brush with a tissue until it was only damp, and then worked at the area until it was light enough. Now he turned to the book cover, which he painted with a very watery wash of yellow ochre and cadmium orange, adding a pale wash of cobalt blue when the first wash had dried. The book lettering was done with a combination of sap green and cadmium red light. The mustard jar behind the flowers in the upper left area was painted with cerulean blue and alizarin crimson with a little yellow ochre at the cooler top section. When this was dry, he added the lettering and the stripes. Finally he went back to the flowers, adding cast shadows (cerulean blue, alizarin crimson, and cadmium yellow pale), some color in the centers (cadmium orange and yellow ochre), and lifting out and softening many of the edges.

Dried Flowers

1. Charles Reid made only a few lines to indicate the relative positions of objects in this oil painting, and then he started laying in large masses of color. He was using only turpentine as a medium here; the oil paint was practically the consistency of watercolor. He made color changes as he went but kept the values pretty much the same. He concentrated on putting in the middle values, not lights or darks. These middle values would dominate the painting.

Because he was working on white canvas, the artist tried to get as much of the white covered as soon as possible. All areas looked practically the same in terms of finish; the artist didn't develop any one area but tried to keep the whole painting going at the same pace. If he had been painting flowers that might fade quickly, he probably would have concentrated on them—but only after massing in a good part of the surrounding areas.

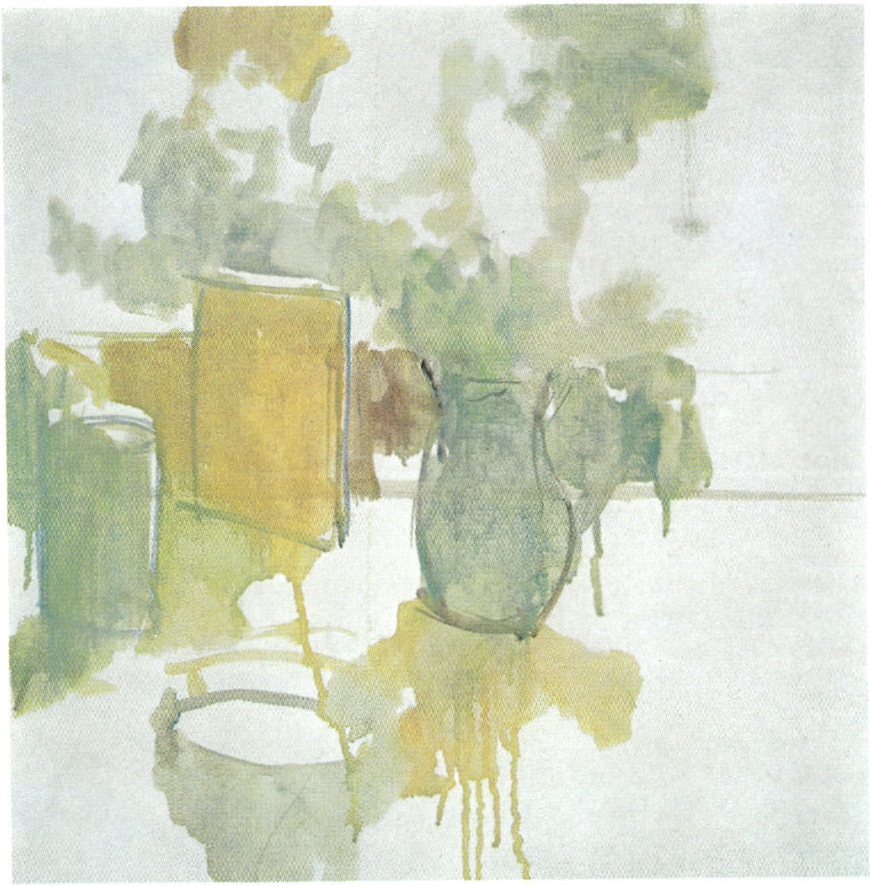

2. Almost all the canvas was covered now. It was time to develop individual areas. The artist switched to his regular painting medium because he wanted the paint to have a heavier, more buttery consistency. (Be sure not to let your oil paint get too thick. The more paint you have, the harder it is to handle.) At this stage, Mr. Reid usually exaggerates his color. Notice how much yellow he has used here for the countertop. The white pitcher, which is in shadow, has been painted a very cool gray. It's best not to use black and white to mix gray. Get in the habit of using complementary colors instead. Notice that Mr. Reid has kept areas of similar value connected and massed, without hard divisions. The bouquet and the background, as well as the cast shadow below the pitcher and the pitcher itself, have been painted in practically the same color and value.

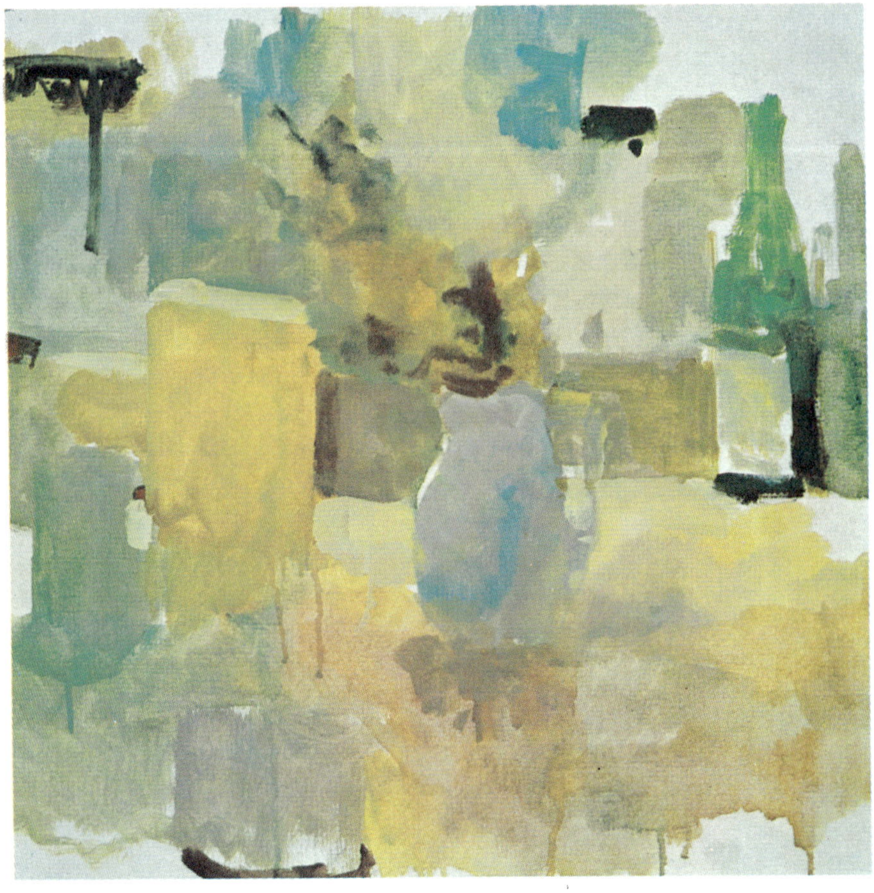

3. Now Mr. Reid began to bring objects into focus. He started to separate individual areas, but he tried to "lose" edges in areas where the value was the same. For example, notice how the flowers flow into the background to the left of the base, and the yellow cereal box and its cast shadow have been painted with almost the same value and color. Mr. Reid started massing in the hundreds of complicated stems and buds as two or three large areas. It's much easier to see larger areas of lights and darks if you have a single light shining on your flowers. In this case, the main light was coming from above and behind the flowers, and so most of the flowers were actually in shadow. The artist could see that the lightest area was in the goldenrod at the top of the bouquet. The dried flowers to the left of the goldenrod were also affected by the single light source, but they had a darker local value than the goldenrod.

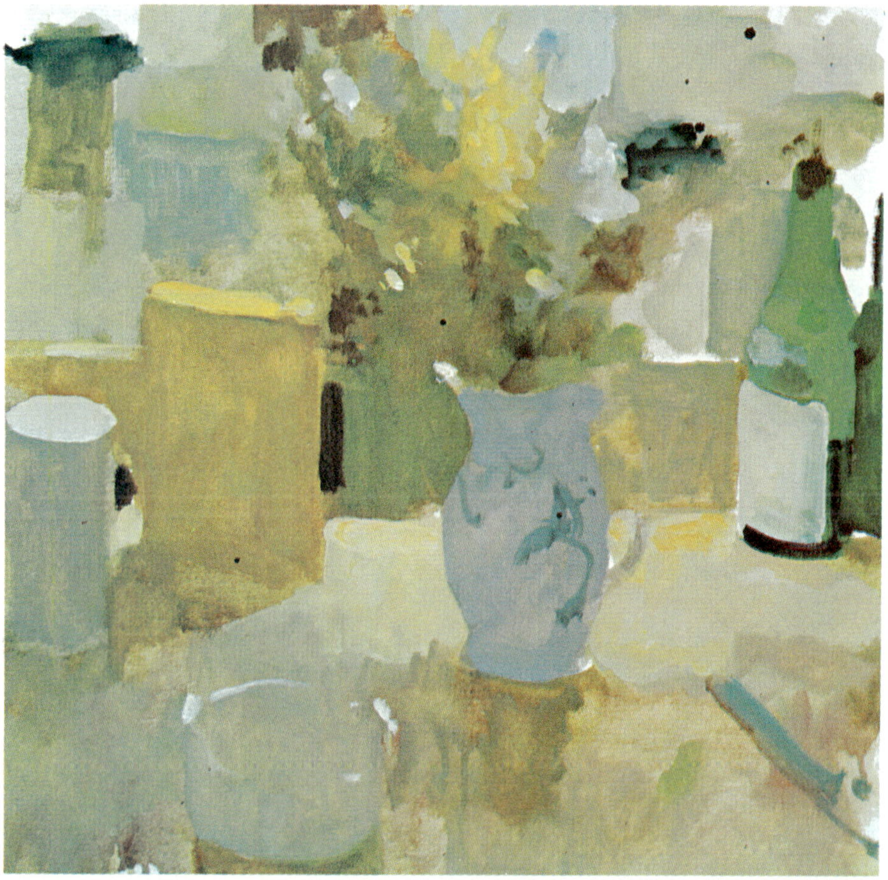

4. Mr. Reid did some more tightening up here. He added more details, deepened contrasts between areas, and suggested sections for further work where he would be placing highlights, reflected lights, and additional detail. He worked more color and shapes into the background and into the objects on the table. He added more lights and darks to the flowers, as well as a hard edge where the base meets the dark leaves—the center of interest of the painting. However, despite the addition of small forms, the basic value areas have remained relative to each other.

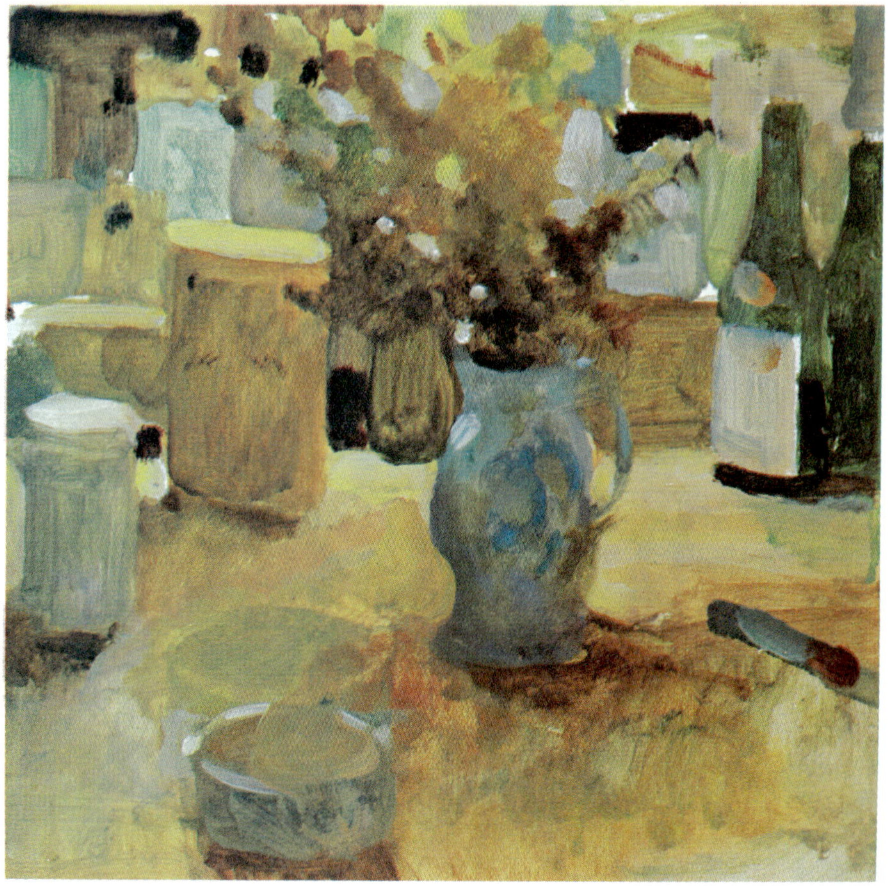

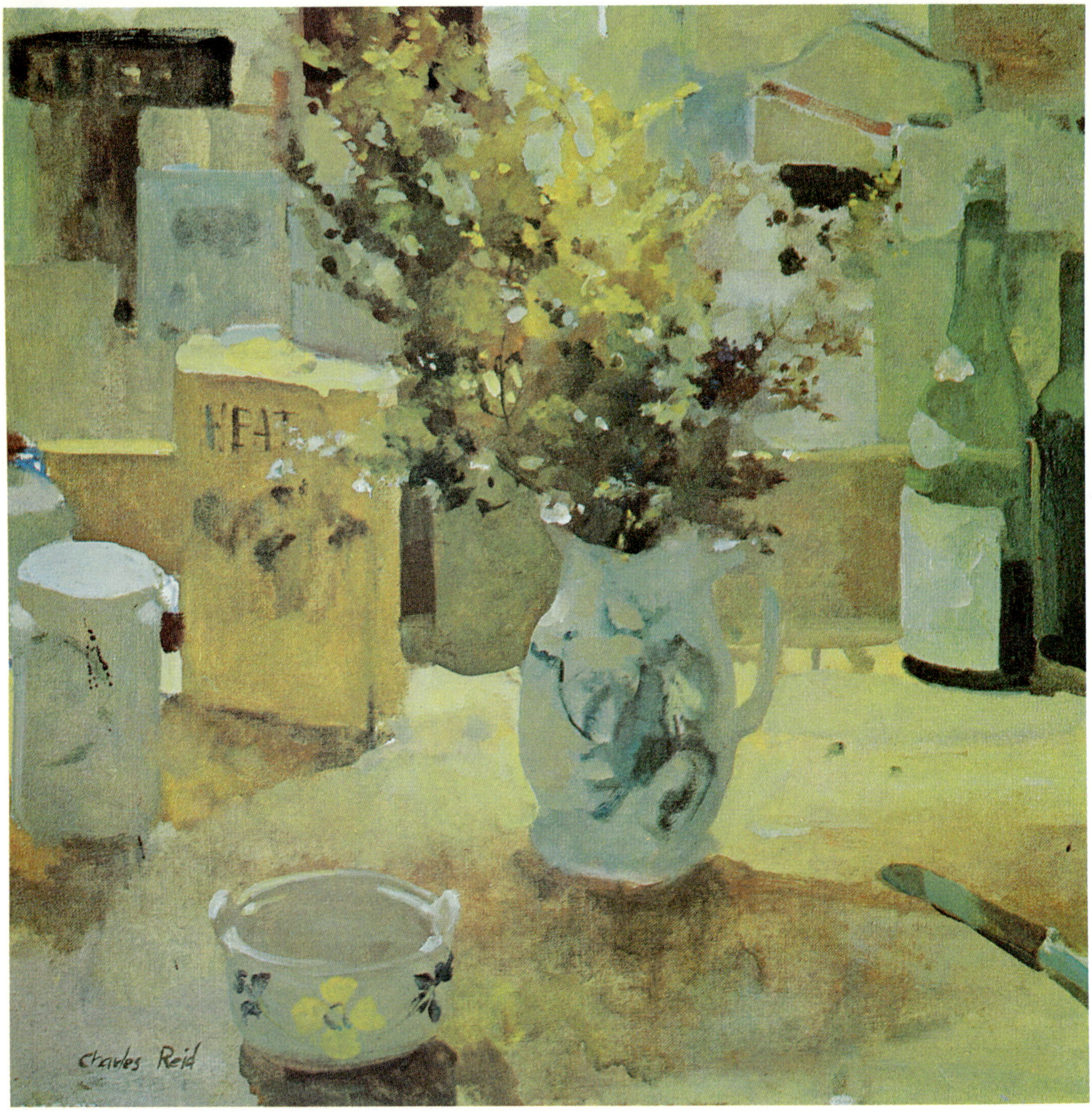

5. To finish the painting the artist carefully placed his darkest darks where they would give the painting depth and emphasis and would direct the eye through the picture. For example, the black label above and to the right of the flowers helps to make the white flowers stand out and also strengthens this area. More darks are found at the top left and in the bottles. This helps the eye move on to the vase and its design, and then on to the small container in the foreground. Mr. Reid concentrated primarily on the structure of this picture, dealing with shapes, color, and value rather than painting individual objects. Some artists may prefer to carry their paintings to a highly finished state, while others might want only a spontaneous, "loose" impression of a still life. This is the stage where each artist's individual style should take over.

Orchids

1. Normally Charles Reid sketches in his oil paintings with a brush (usually a long-handled no. 4 or no. 6 flat bristle brush). Here, however, he used a 2B pencil. (You can also try using charcoal to establish your drawing, but if you do, dust your painting with a chamois or cloth to get rid of excess charcoal. Leave just the vague drawing as your guide.) Then Mr. Reid immediately started blocking in his big dark shapes. (Don't be afraid to lose your drawing.) He squinted his eyes so that all the big dark shapes seemed to merge into a large, simple mass. This was what he painted.

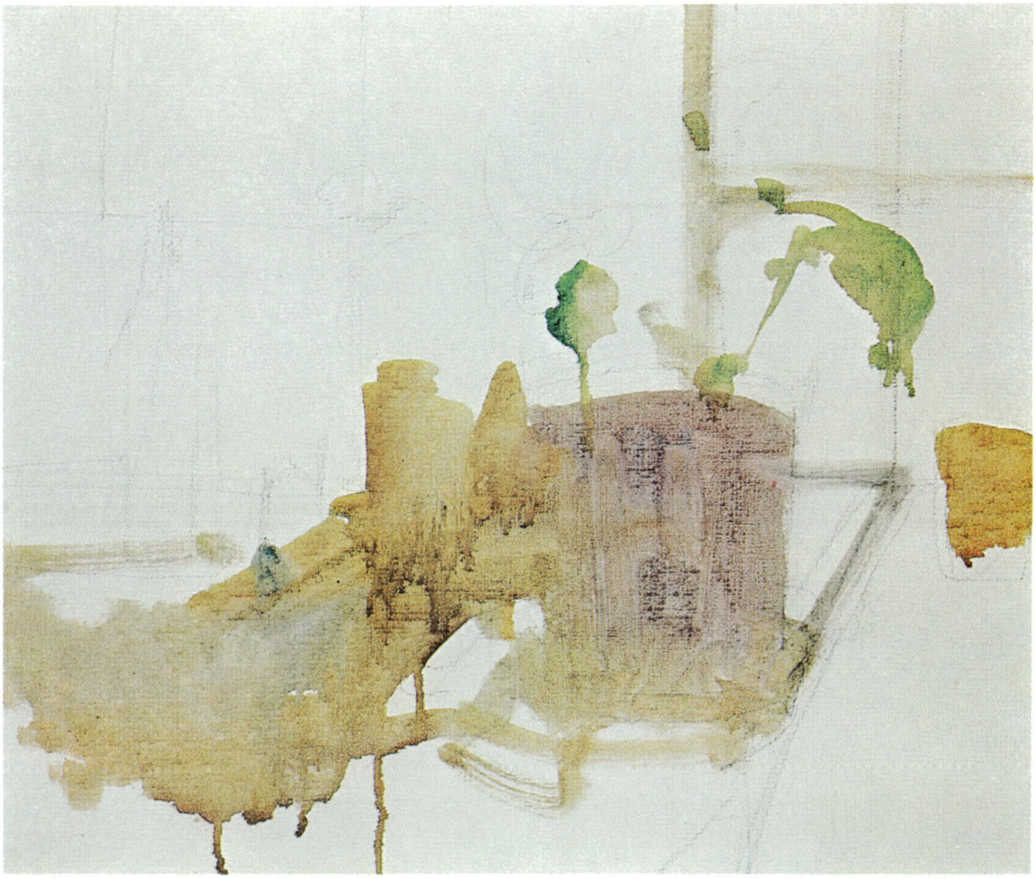

2. Next the artist tried to connect his darks with adjoining darks; his lights, with adjoining lights. Notice, for example, that the flowers have been painted the same value and color as the window. As the painting developed, the artist would make some separations, but for now, he tried to avoid all small differences and minor value changes. Notice, too, how thinly he applied the paint.

In massing his values, he allowed adjoining colors of similar value to mix. Here, some of the earthy reds of the clay saucer mix with the cooler colors of the flowerpot. The artist's main concern was to merge adjoining color areas, such as the cool bluish pot and the warm reddish saucer, without making a value change.

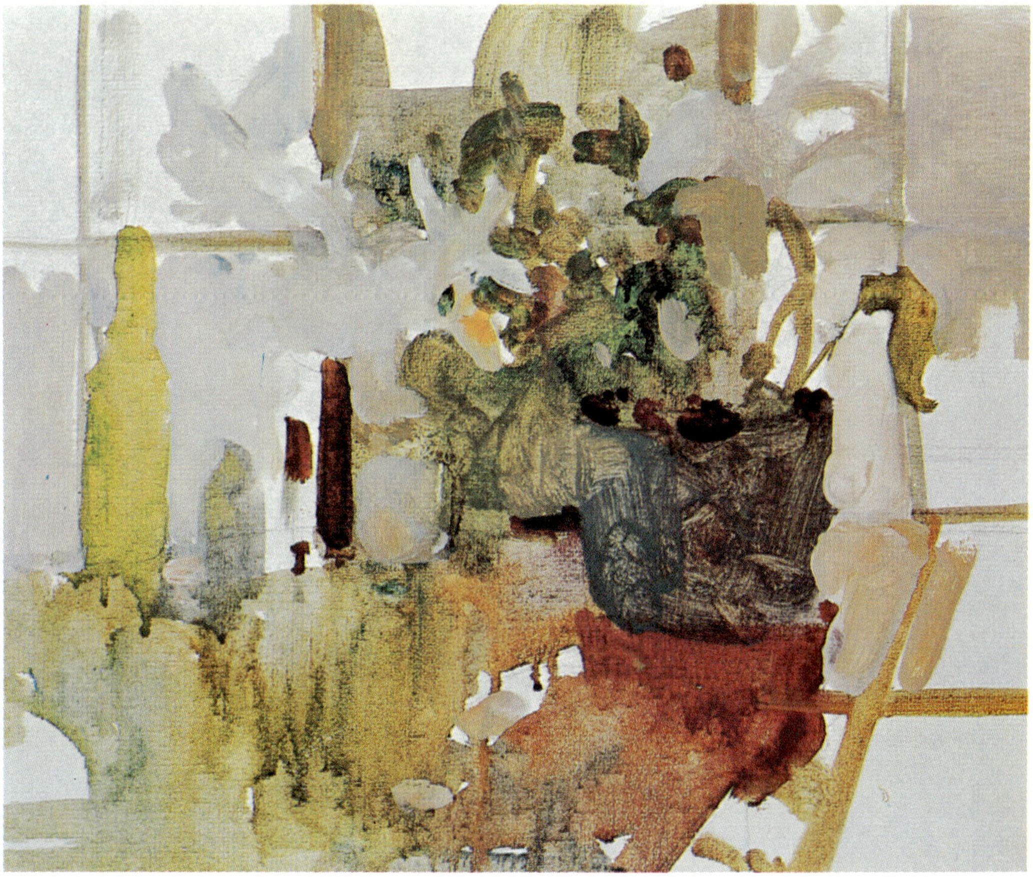

3. Now the artist made many changes in his painting. For Charles Reid, painting is a growing process and he constantly adjusts and modifies. For example, the flowerpot has been made much lighter than it was before, and the cool greens in the table have become darker, warmer browns. As you paint, always keep several areas in mind. As you make color and value changes in one area, you must constantly adjust colors and values in other areas. For example, if you change the color or value in a flowerpot, you must check the other areas—especially the surrounding ones—to see if they need adjustment.

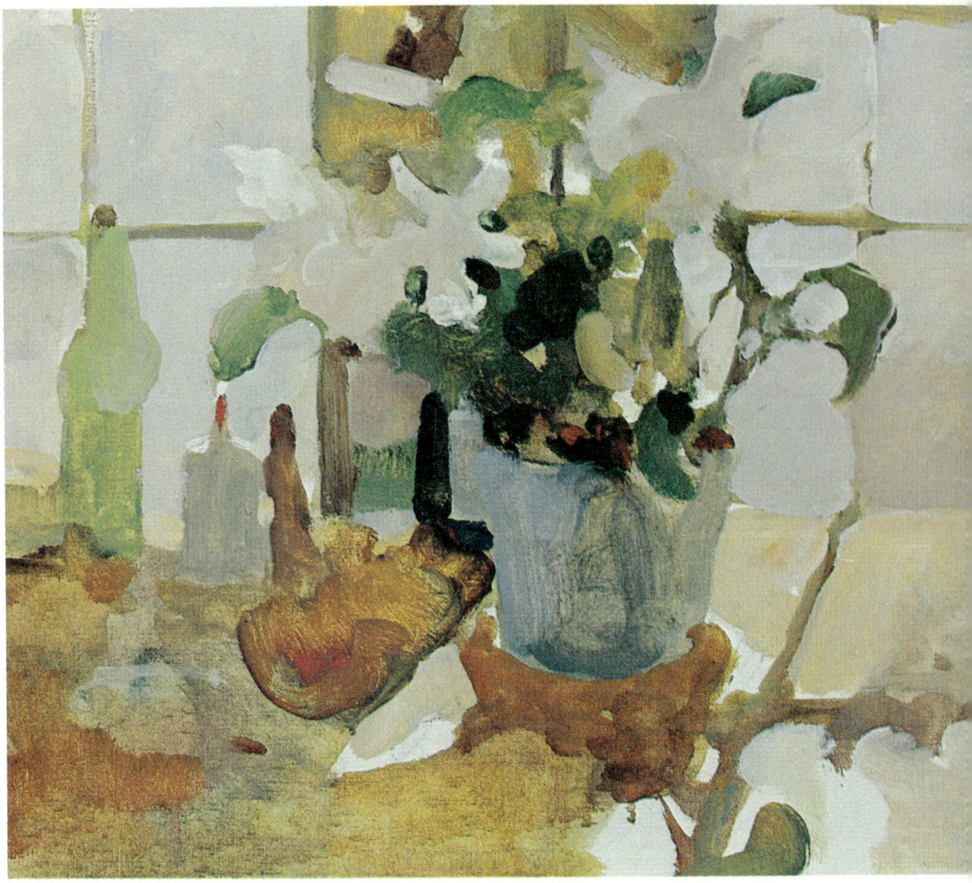

4. What you see here is a "color diagram" the artist made to show the color combinations he would use to reach his final painting. The point is that he has used the same colors over and over. He varied the ratio of one color with another, but the same colors can be found throughout. The color swatch in the lower right-hand corner shows his basic color combinations.

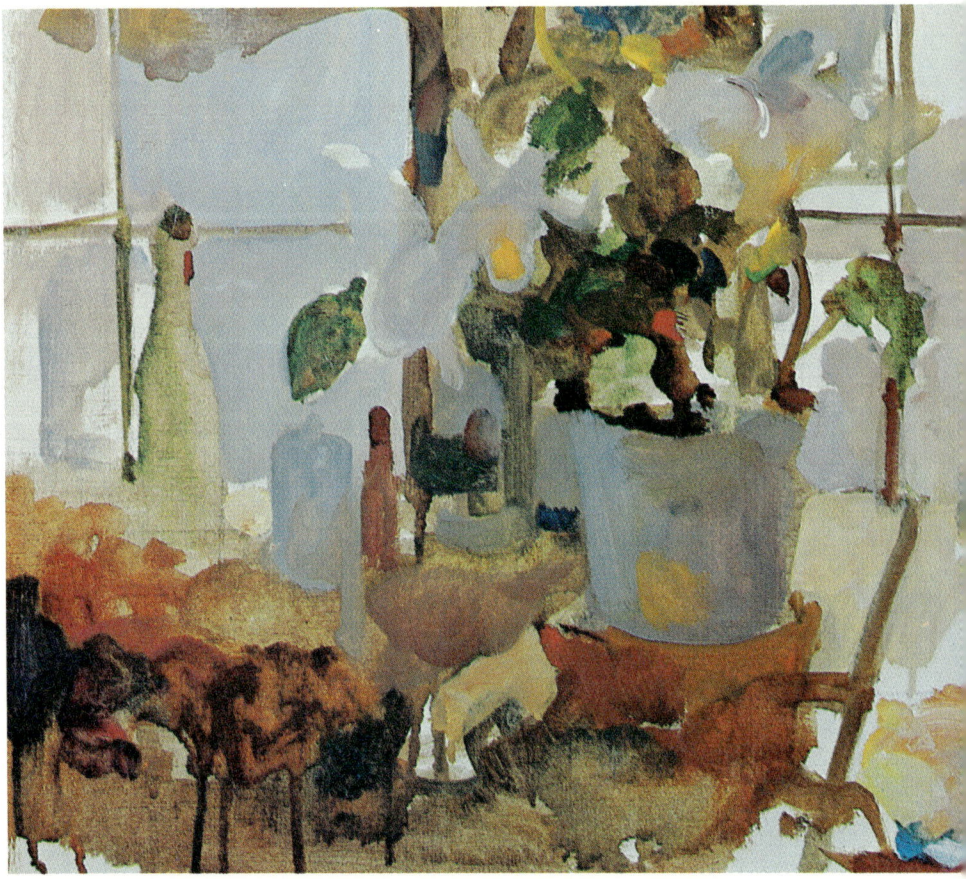

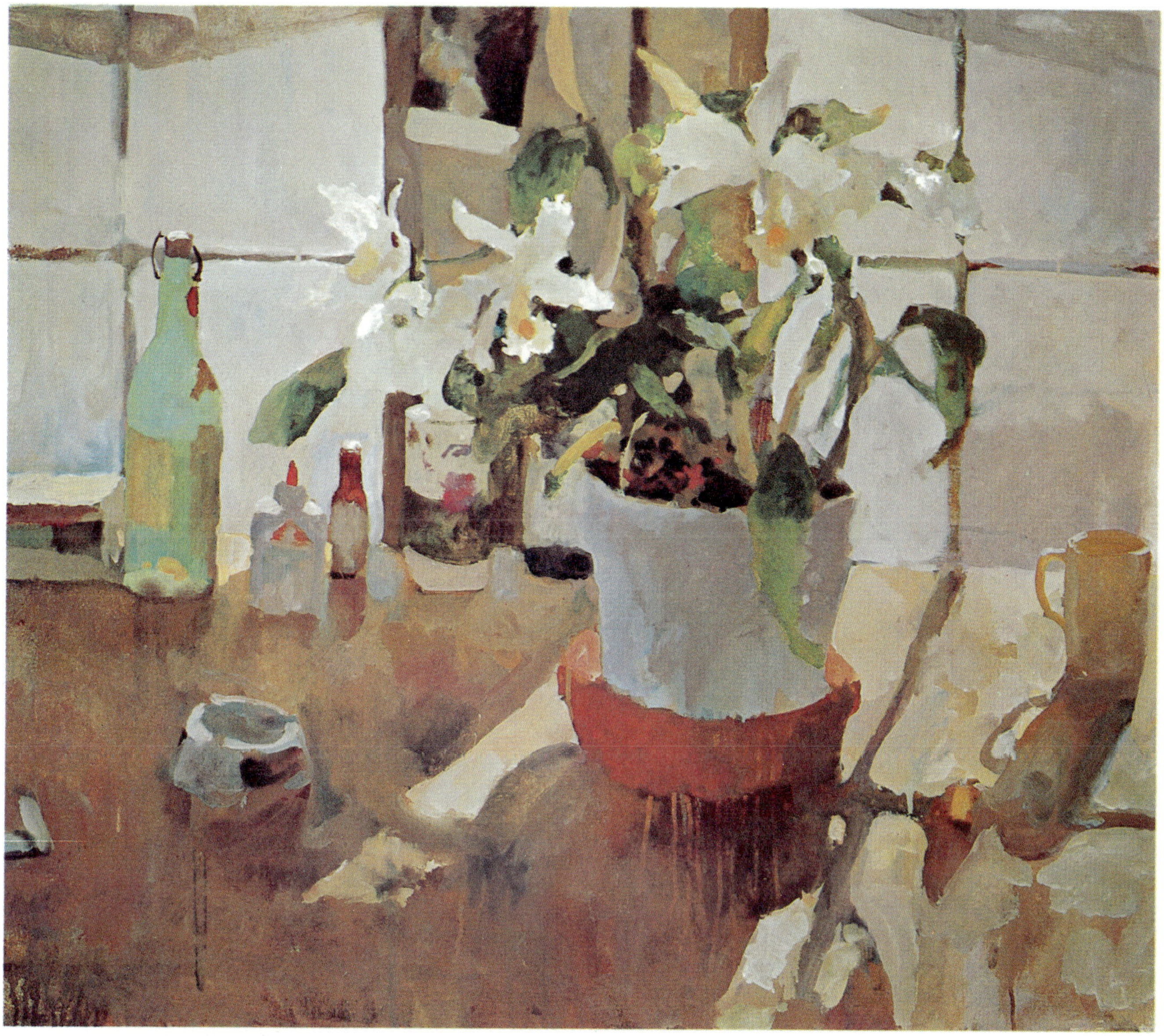

5. As you compare the finished painting to the preceding stage, you can see that quite a bit has been done to tighten it up. The artist tried to keep his painting fluid as long as possible, although by this stage most of his big color and value relationships had been established, and only minor adjustments remained to be made. In making his final changes, Mr. Reid fixed boundaries and hardened edges as he brought various objects into focus.

Again, comparing this painting with the preceding color diagram, study individual areas to see where the artist used the warmer side of his basic color combination. Note where he went cooler. Observe that he placed a coffee cup on the right-hand side, since he found the area to the right of the flowers too empty. He also added an ashtray. The window divider behind the bottle was moved in order to break up the window area more.

One of the hardest things to do is maintaining a balance between defining the flowers enough and not too much. If you define too much, you'll lose the soft texture that's so necessary in flower painting. You might want to refine flowers more than Mr. Reid has here, but be careful not to go overboard. Too many hard, defined edges will make the blossoms and leaves look like metal.

Kitchen Flowers

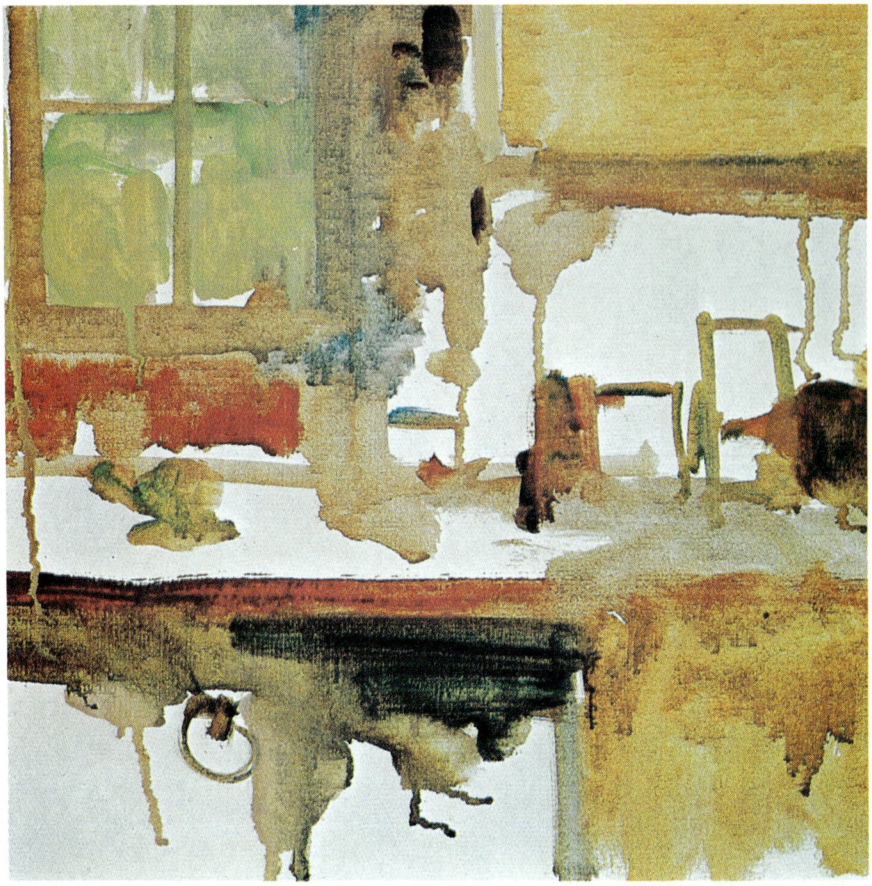

1. Charles Reid looks at still life subjects in a purely abstract way: how to make large masses of lights and darks balance each other. This is what makes a composition. Where you place individual objects is not as important as the placement of your big masses of lights and darks.

Notice how everything is connected at the beginning stages of this oil painting. The window on the upper left ties in with the cupboard over the counter. They form a large middle dark along the top of the picture. Diagonally across and below the window is another area of dark: the cupboard under the counter. The artist left his lights untouched, concentrating on blocking in the darker areas.

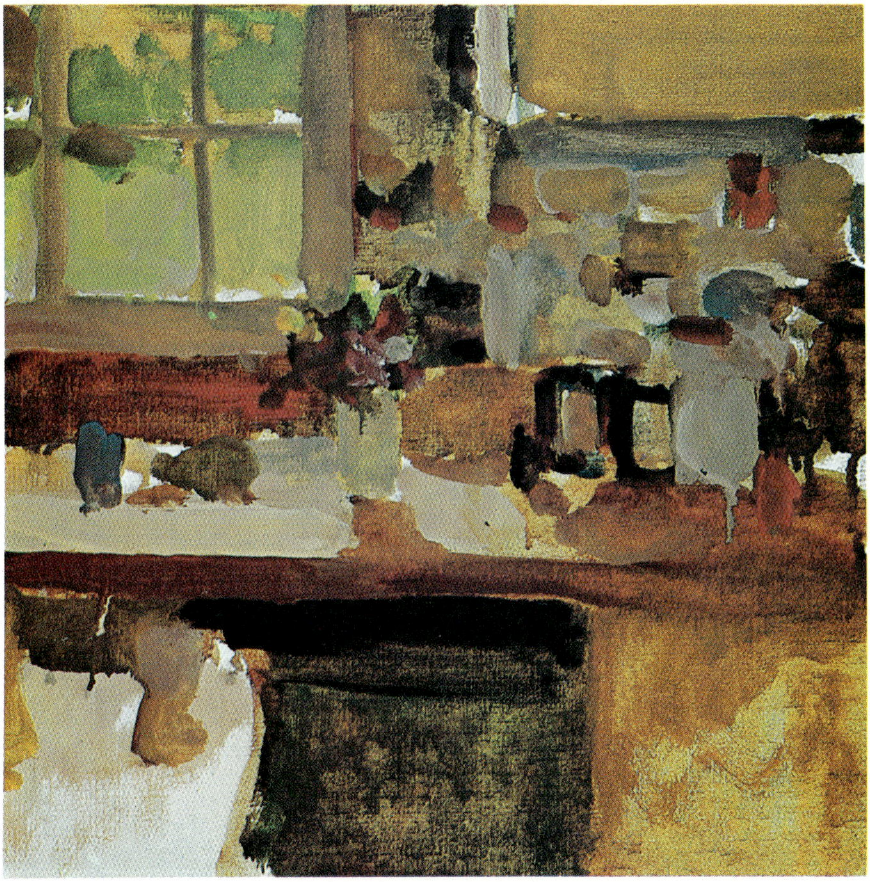

2. Now that the canvas was covered, the artist made some big changes from the previous stage of the painting. As you probably know, it is almost impossible to judge your values correctly in the beginning. In this case, in addition, the artist had the tricky problem of painting the window and the landscape outside as well as the interior. The window area was very light, but the light-struck counter was even lighter.

It's vital to squint most of the time at this stage, and to compare one section with another to find that area's color or value. You can't just look at the wall of wine labels to come up with the correct value or color. You must compare it to the window.

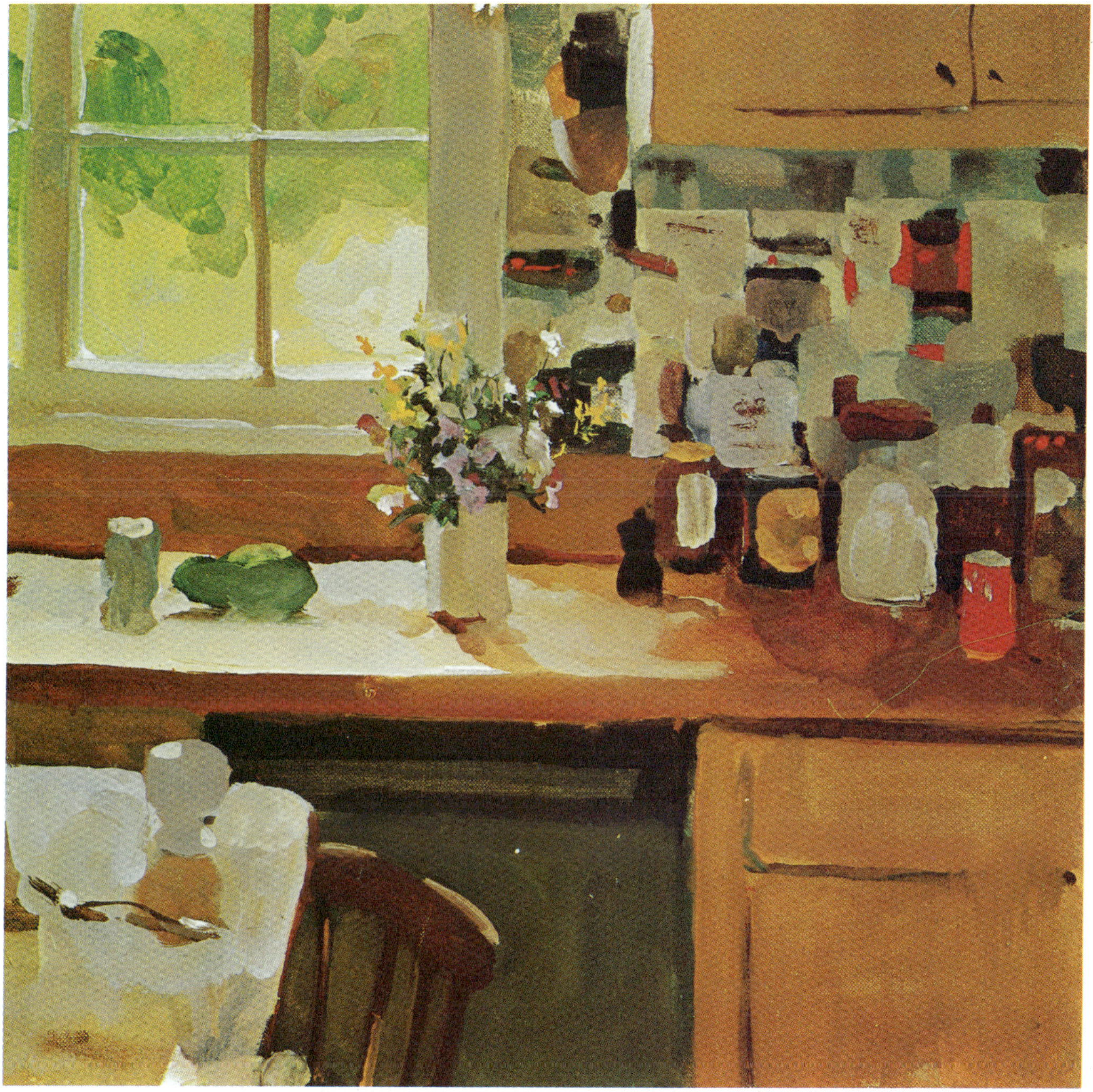

3. Looking at his painting again, the artist began to feel the darkness invading the composition. This is the stage when coming back to your picture after a trip to the supermarket can be a real eye-opener.

It's important to realize that to show light, you must also show dark. In this case, Mr. Reid lightened the window and the counter in front of the window. This fairly limited amount of very light area seems to suggest that the whole painting is "light." (Be aware, however, that too much light in a picture often succeeds only in making it look washed out or weak.)

To finish the rest of the picture, the artist merely firmed certain edges, especially those out in the light. Notice how generally he has painted the wine labels. He wanted the wall to look like a whole wall, not a bunch of labels. Keep yourself from getting too hard-edge, too specific. Try to see the wall out of focus (squint). Also, try painting the wall while you're actually looking at the flowers next to it.

Mixed Bouquet

1. This busy bouquet had many small blooms of various colors and shapes. Charles Reid put them against a window so that the back lighting would help simplify the darker colors, making a mass. The flowers were so lovely, it seemed natural to do a closeup. Since they were complicated, the artist decided not to put anything else in the picture.

The composition is very simple. The artist merged the fairly dark mass of the vase with the similar value and color of the windowsill. Next he squinted to see the large mass of dark which made up most of the bouquet. He did not want to worry about details until later.

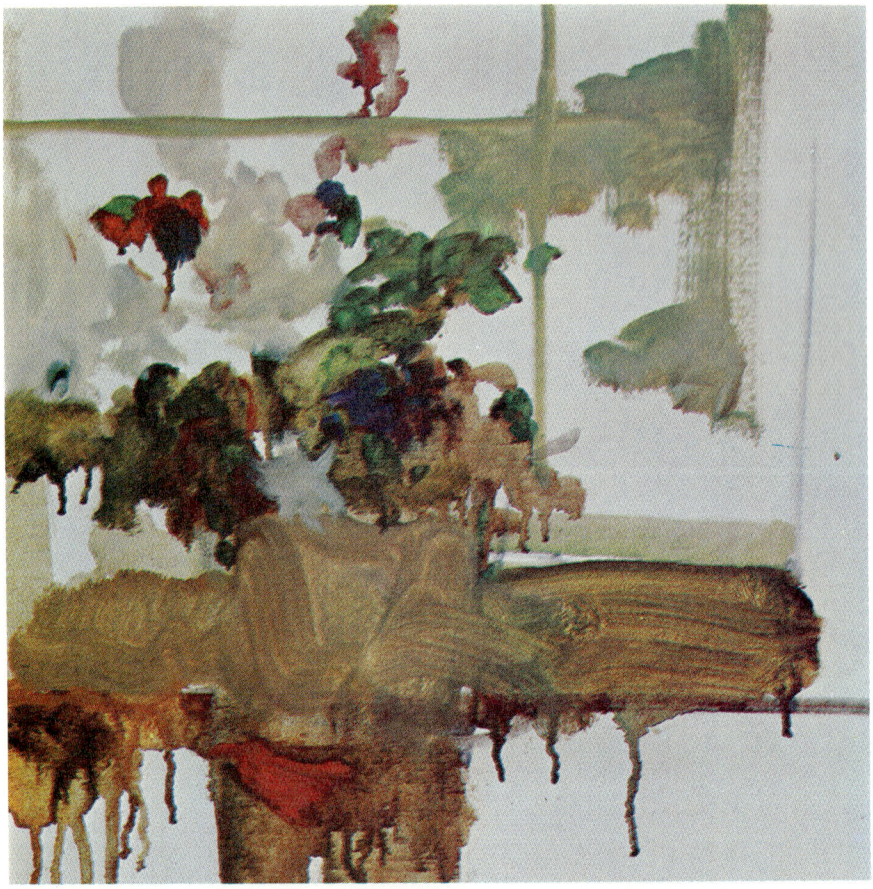

2. The background outside was very important here. The artist wanted to tie it in with the flowers. It was hard to decide how dark or light to make the trees outside. As he looked through the window, it seemed that they were fairly dark. Yet when he looked at the flowers, the window area looked light. He felt the answer lay in the composition. He must adjust the values in both the flowers and the background so the design would work well for him. At one point, he thought he might make the trees outside darker.

He connected the white flowers at the top of the bouquet to the curtain by making both curtain and flowers the same value. The vase and the wall to the left are also the same value. The windowsill has been drawn up into the window area and connected with the trees.

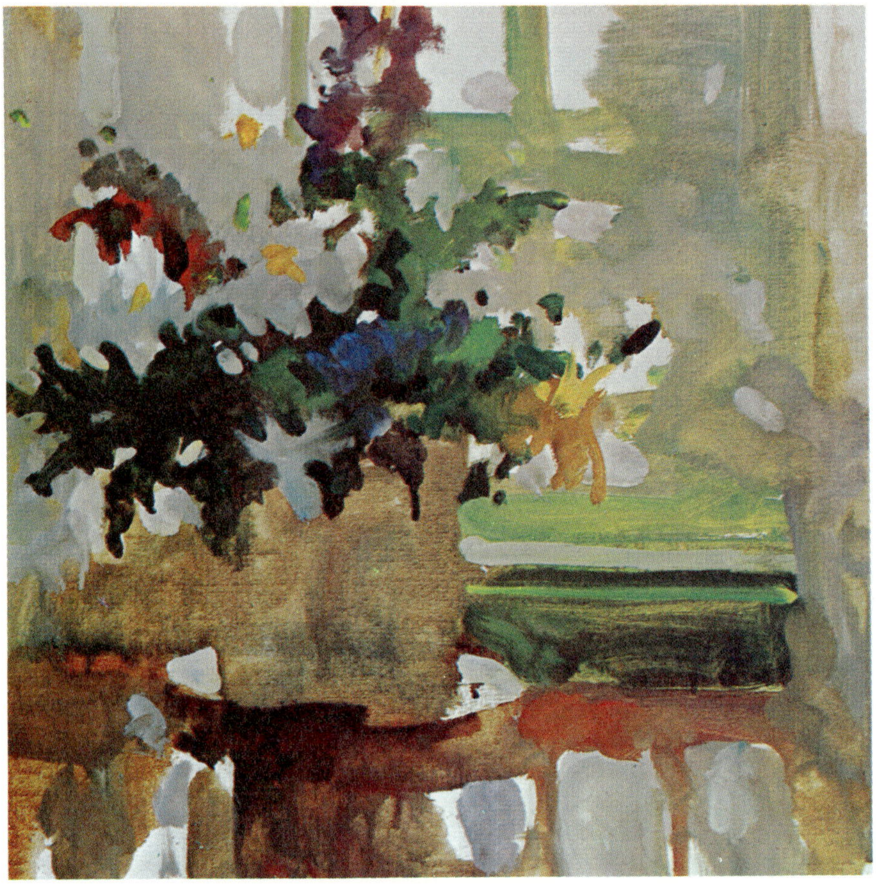

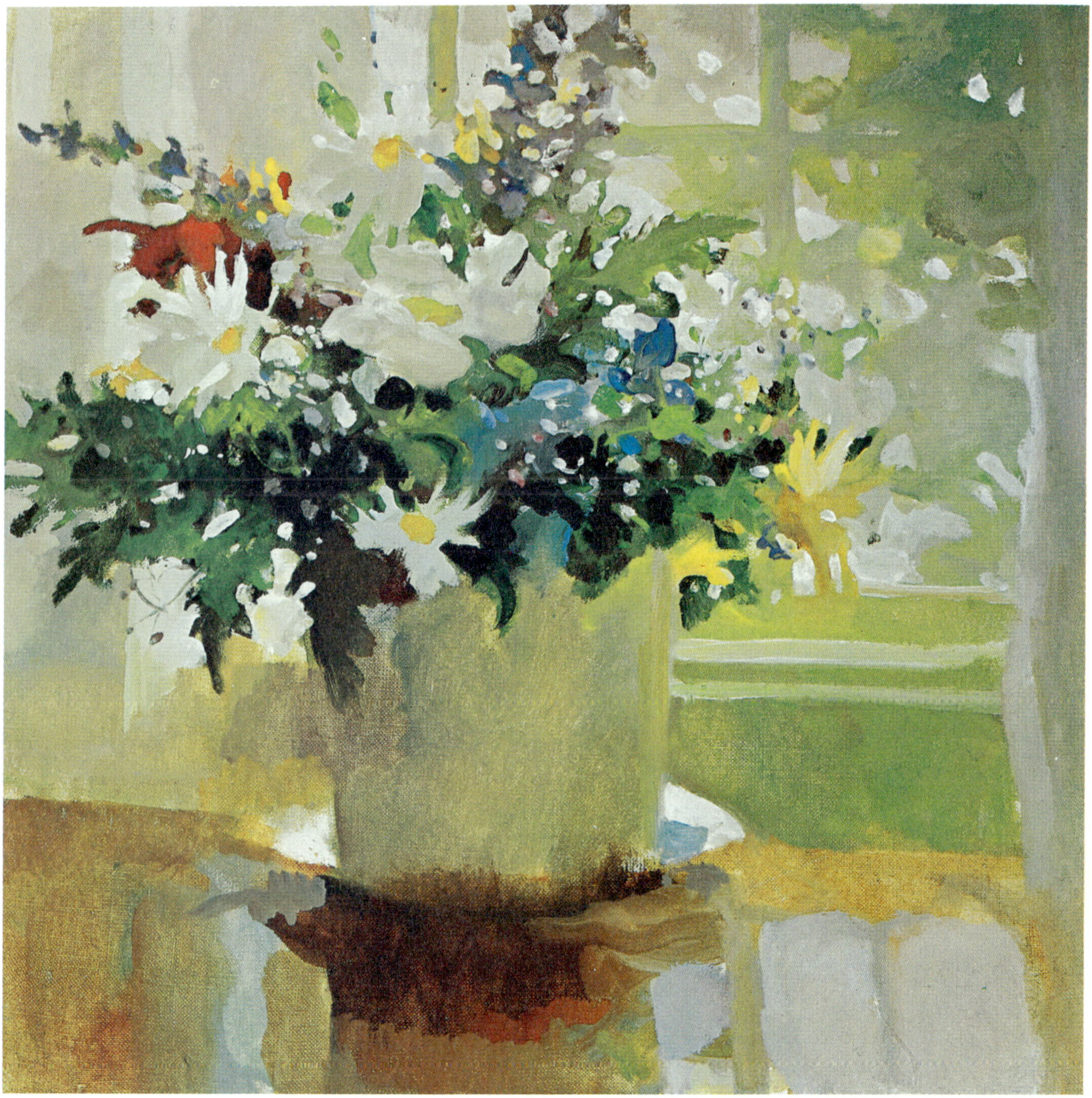

3. Now Mr. Reid refined the painting, changing many values in this final stage. The windowsill seemed too dark, and so he lightened it. He hoped it would make the picture more luminous. He added small buds—but here he was careful. One or two buds might look great, but he would have to fight a tendency to keep on adding too many little dots of color. If you can control your values well (that is, not make the dots too light), you can probably add as many as you like. However, Mr. Reid felt that the big mass of dark in the bouquet was important, and that it "carried" this busy arrangement. So he tried to control his urge to flick spots of lights all over.

MANMADE OBJECTS

Being able to effectively capture the quality and texture of manmade objects is essential to good still life painting.

Here you will learn to paint a wide variety of subjects—baskets, lanterns, buckets, plastic bottles, paper bags, glass, silver, china, fabric, and candles.

And, once again, you will have an impressive group of teachers to learn from—Georg Shook, Joseph Dawley, and Arthur Stern.

Baskets

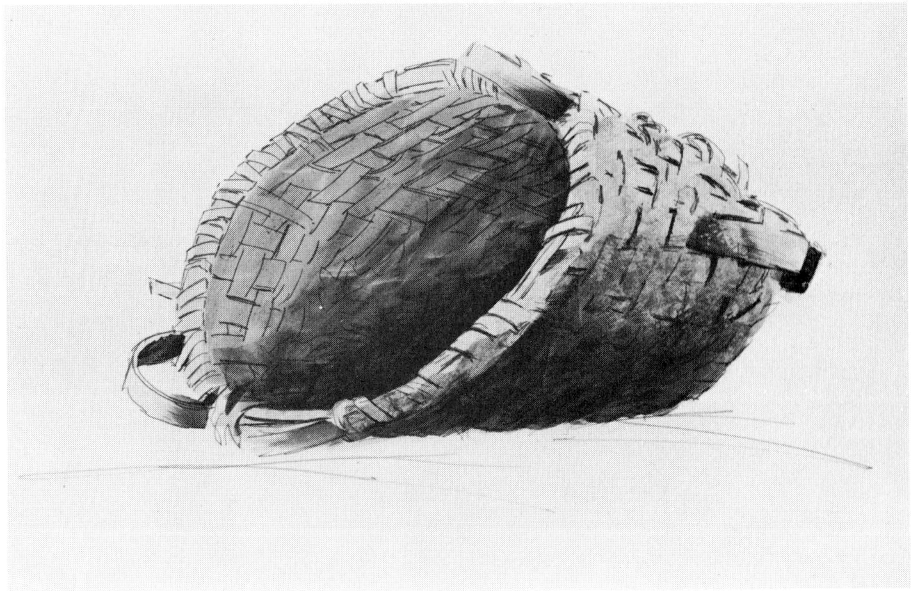

1. Georg Shook began this watercolor of a plaited basket with a thoroughly detailed drawing, using a 4B pencil. He chose a soft pencil so that after the wash was applied and much of the graphite washed away, a delicate but distinct drawing would still remain.

Now the artist applied an underwash of yellow ochre and raw sienna to the basket with a ¾″ (19 mm) chisel-edged sable brush. Then he blotted the area with a wet paper towel for texture. Having made sure the pigment was dilute enough to preserve the pencil detail underneath, he added shadows to the inside of the basket and under it, using Van Dyke brown and Prussian blue in a ¾″ chisel-edged brush. He made the shadows inside the basket a little cooler by increasing the Prussian blue in the mixture and applying a second wash.

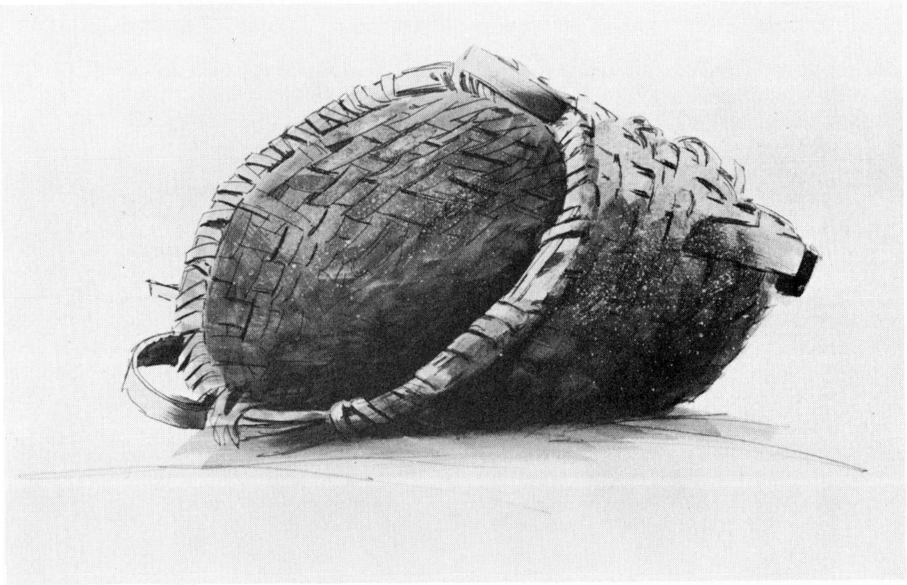

2. Next the artist added brush detailing to emphasize the contour of the rim, the handles, and the plaiting of the basket. This was done with a highly concentrated mixture of Van Dyke brown and Prussian blue in a pointed red sable brush. He then cleaned the brush and used it to highlight the basket by wetting certain areas and lifting them with a dry paper towel. He spattered portions of the basket with clear water and then lifted out the spots of color by blotting in order to lend a weatherbeaten look to the basket.

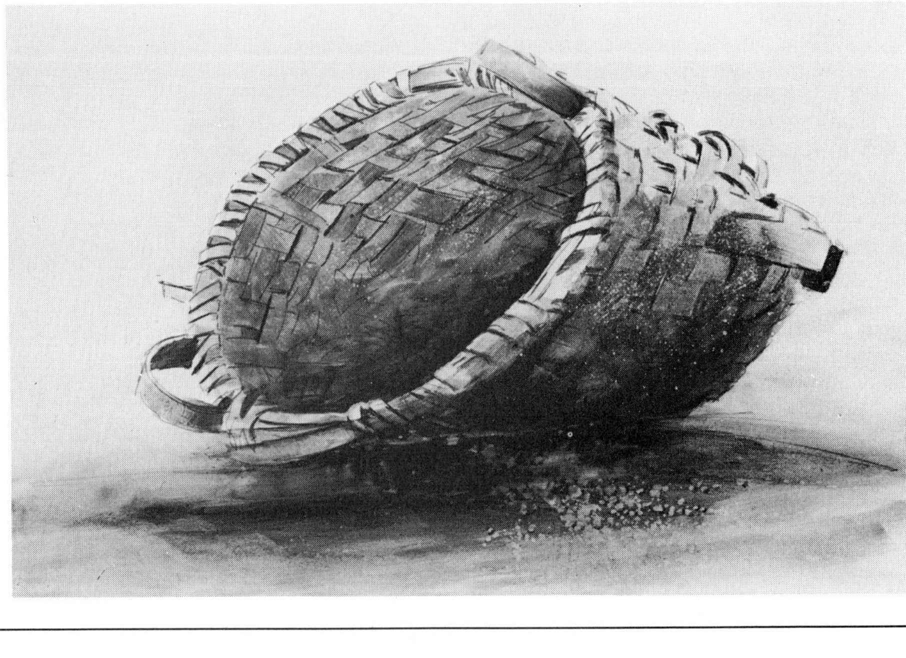

3. The artist added further detail to the plaiting of the basket with a mixture of Van Dyke brown and Prussian blue in a pointed sable brush. Then he used a ¾″ chisel-edged brush loaded with a heavy mixture of Prussian blue and Van Dyke brown to accent the shadow area beneath the basket. After allowing the shadow area to dry, he spattered it with clear water and lifted out the color as before.

1. With a 2B pencil, the artist made a detailed drawing of an apple basket and then used a ¾″ (19 mm) chisel-edged brush to apply a moderately diluted wash of olive green to the grass area. With the same brush he picked up a little pure burnt sienna and applied it over the olive green in a few spots to add some warmth. While the area was still wet, he used a clean stiff-bristle brush to mix the colors on the surface with short, choppy upward movements. Now he wet a paper towel and wrung it out slightly so that when it was used no water would drip from it. He laid the damp paper towel over the painted area and ran his hand across it to make sure that the towel was in complete contact with the painting surface. Then he lifted the towel to see what interesting textures he had created. Mr. Shook prefers to use ordinary paper towels for this procedure because they bring their own texture to the method.

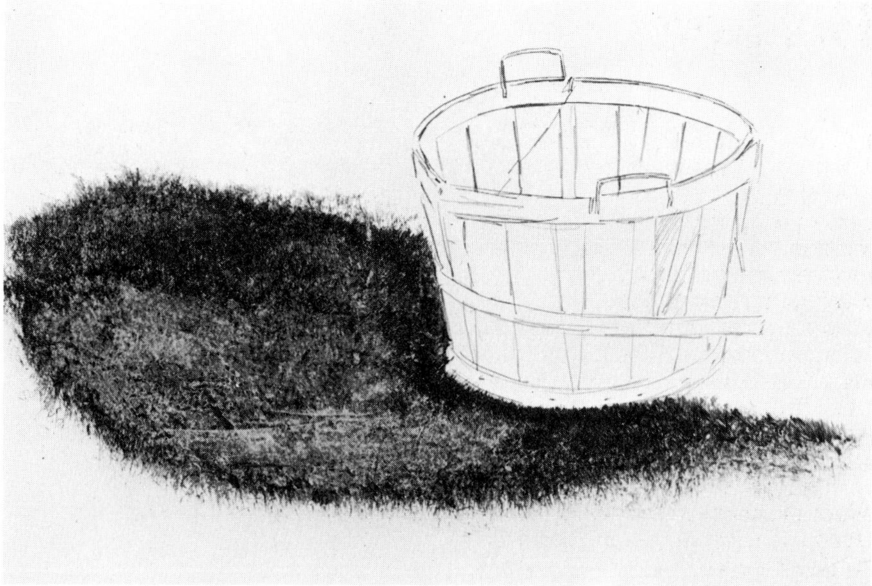

2. After the paint had dried, the artist blotted again for additional texture. As before, he squeezed water from a wetted paper towel, smoothed the towel out slightly, and laid it over the painted area. He ran his hand over the towel, pressing it into contact with the surface, and then removed it. He knew that if this final effect wasn't satisfactory, more blottings would give alternative textures.

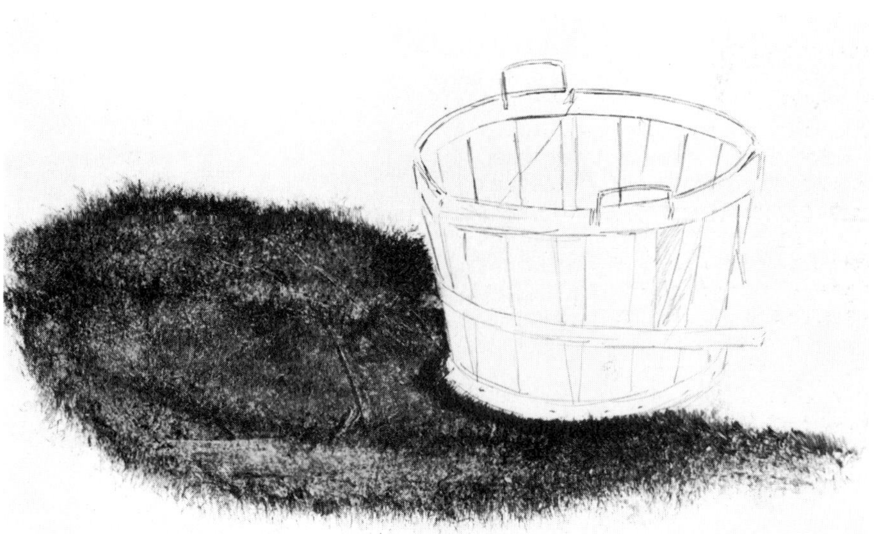

3. He began painting the basket by using a ¼″ (6 mm) chisel-edged brush and a mixture of Davy's gray and burnt sienna to lay a thin wash over the entire form. He blotted the area with a damp paper towel to create texture. Next, he used the same brush to paint the individual wood strips of the basket. He varied the mixture each time, picking up some extra burnt sienna in one stroke, adding more Davy's gray to the next, adding a little Winsor blue to the next, and blotting after each stroke with a damp paper towel. Finally, he mixed Prussian blue and Van Dyke brown and used a ¼″ chisel-edged brush to add shadow inside the basket and to the right of it, once again blotting for texture.

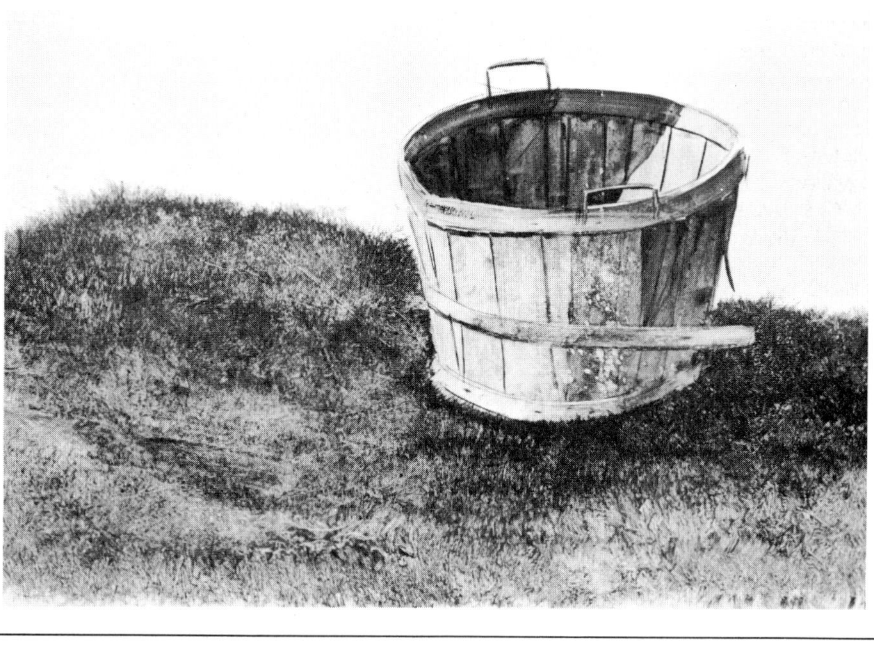

Lantern, Fence, and Barrel

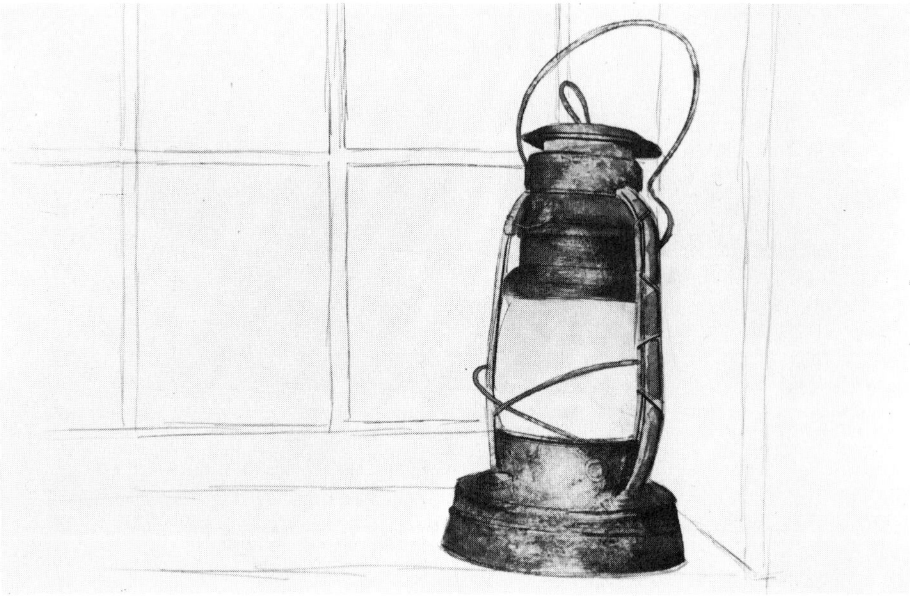

1. Mr. Shook drew a lantern in detail with a 2B pencil and then blocked in the metal areas with a thin wash of burnt sienna and a pointed sable brush. He blotted the wet surface with a dry paper towel to create texture. After the paint had dried, he added drybrush detailing to the lantern. Picking up a thin mixture of Van Dyke brown and Prussian blue with a pointed sable brush, he wiped the brush across a folded paper towel and then dragged it across the burnt sienna undertoning to give the lantern a rusty appearance. Using the same colors—this time with more pigment and less water—he added a shadow to the right side of the lantern.

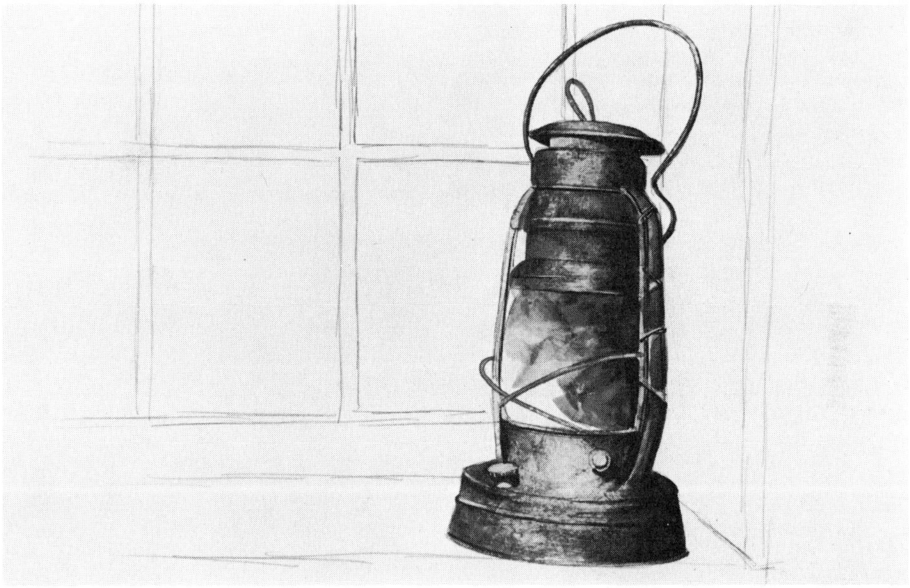

2. Now the artist used a ¾″ (19 mm) chisel-edged brush to add a graduated wash of Winsor blue and Van Dyke brown to the glass chimney, giving it depth and contour. He accented the contours of the lantern with a ¾″ chisel-edged brush dipped in clear water, lifting out highlights in the glass and on the edges of the metal sides and base. He loaded a pointed sable brush with Prussian blue and Van Dyke brown to add handles, wires, and screws to the lantern. He also added shadows beneath the screws and lantern top with a very dark mixture of these colors.

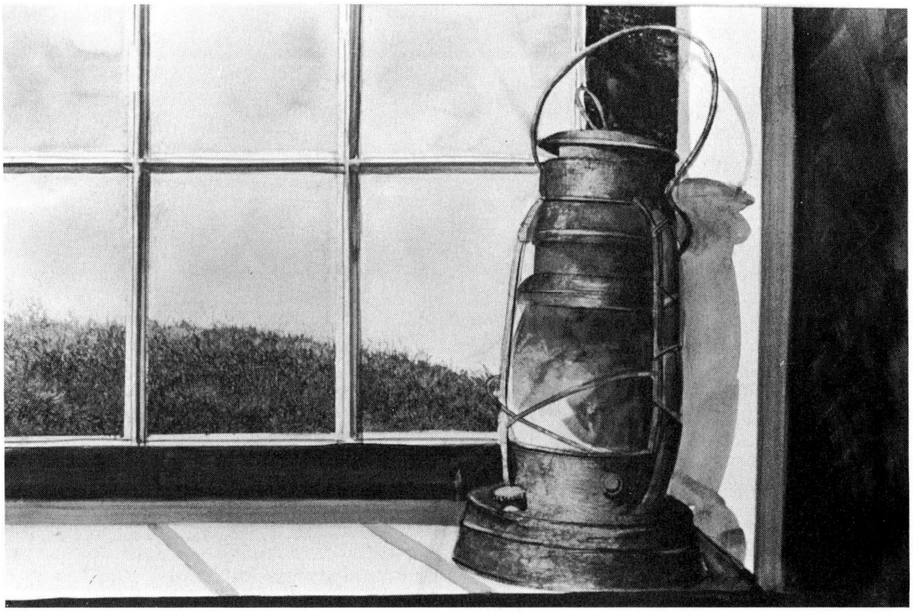

3. The artist covered the wooden dividers between the windowpanes with thin strips of masking tape. Then, using a bristle brush, he surface-mixed olive green and burnt sienna for the grass. He moistened the sky area, painted in a highly diluted wash of Winsor blue with a ¾″ chisel-edged brush, and then added Davy's gray, tilting his board slightly to float the colors around a bit. He painted the interior wood with a heavy mixture of Prussian blue and Van Dyke brown and then diluted this mixture on his palette and laid in the shadows cast by the lantern and window. He removed the masking tape and painted the exposed wood with a thin wash of Davy's gray, adding details with Van Dyke brown and a pointed sable brush.

1. The artist used a 2B pencil to draw a fence, a 55-gallon drum, and part of a collapsed roof. Then he carefully protected these parts of the drawing with masking tape. He trimmed the tape with an X-acto knife to fit the curves of the metal drum.

Now he covered most of the board, including the resist area, with a mixture of Prussian blue, olive green, and burnt sienna using a ¾″ (19 mm) chisel-edged brush. Then he made sharp upward strokes into the wet pigment with a stiff-bristle brush to create the texture of grass and weeds.

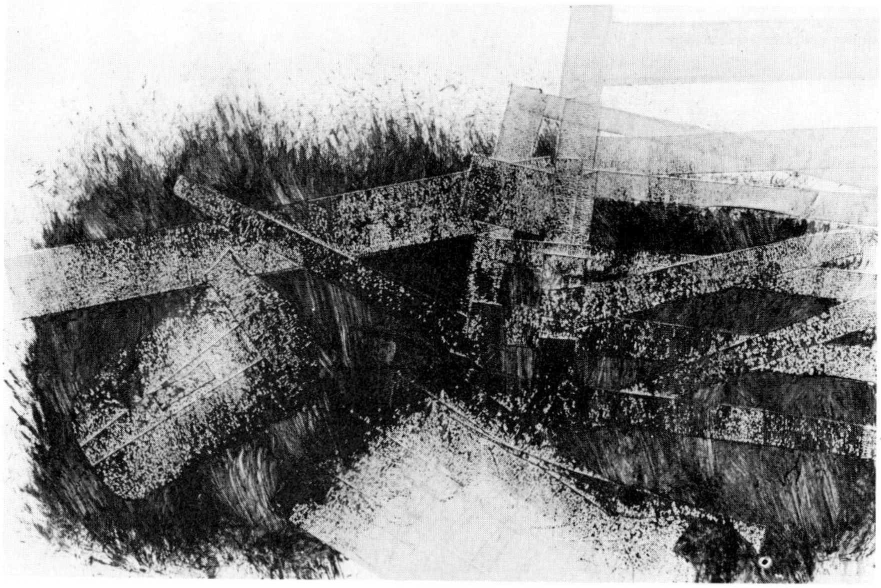

2. After making sure that the paint had dried, Mr. Shook carefully removed the tape. He softened the edges between the painted and reserved areas by dragging a wet ¾″ chisel-edged brush over them. The hard lines were softened as the pigment bled into the unpainted areas.

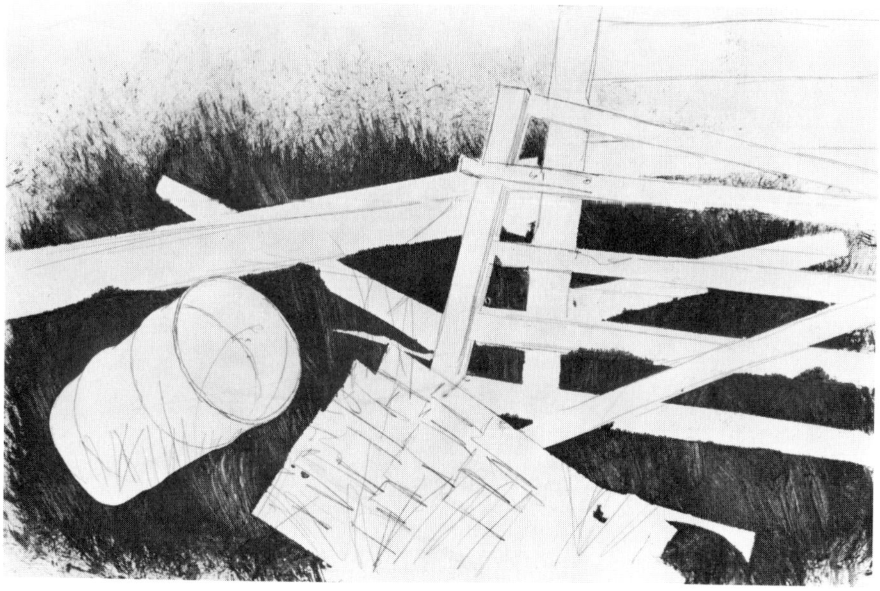

3. The artist painted the wooden fence and the broken roof with a ½″ (13 mm) chisel-edged brush loaded with a wash of Davy's gray and burnt sienna, and then he blotted the areas with a damp paper towel. Now he used the same brush to apply a mixture of burnt sienna, Winsor blue, and raw sienna to the barrel and gate hinge. Finally, he added shadows and detailing with a mixture of Van Dyke brown and Prussian blue in the same ½″ chisel-edged brush, using the edge of the brush for the finer detail work.

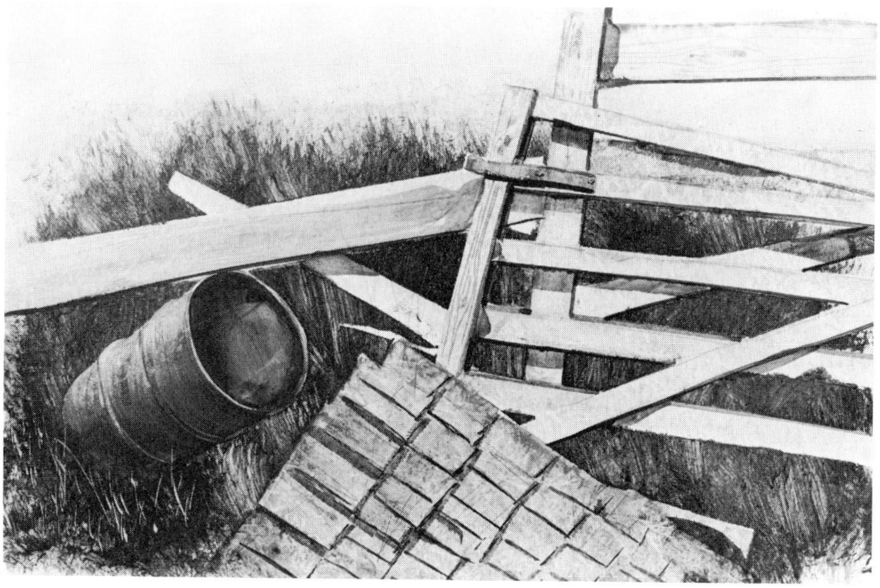

Wooden Barrel and Wheelbarrow

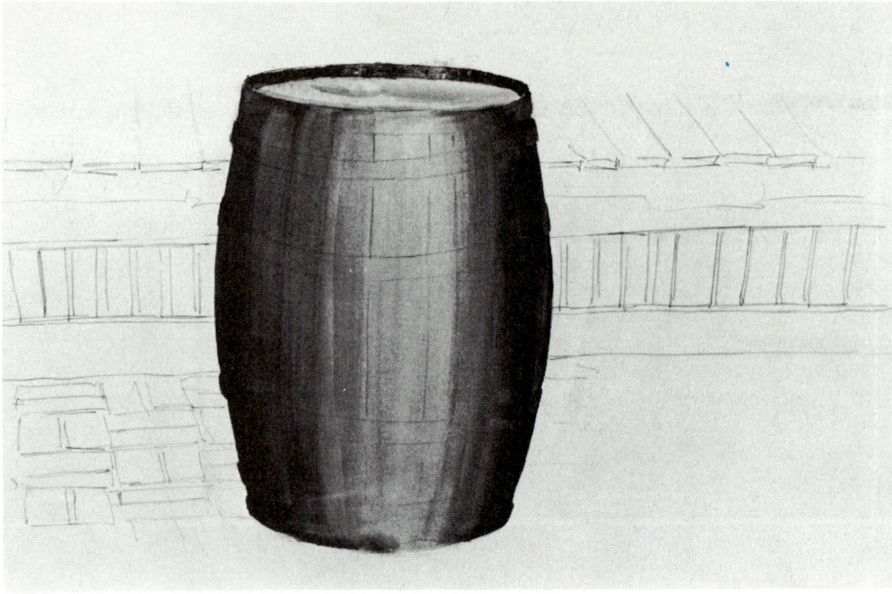

1. The artist started by drawing the barrel with a 4B pencil. Then he blocked in the tonal color over the drawing with a flat underwash of burnt sienna, using a ¾″ (19 mm) chisel-edged brush. He applied a dark blend of Van Dyke brown and Prussian blue to both sides of the barrel with a red sable lettering brush, using a single brush stroke on each side. Now he gave dimension to the shape by pulling clear water from top to bottom through the heavily pigmented areas on either side of the barrel. Each brush stroke, made with a single vertical motion, slightly overlapped the previous stroke, diluting and lightening the color. The curvature of the barrel was highlighted by lifting out some of the color with a ¾″ chisel-edged brush dipped in clear water and then blotting with a dry paper towel.

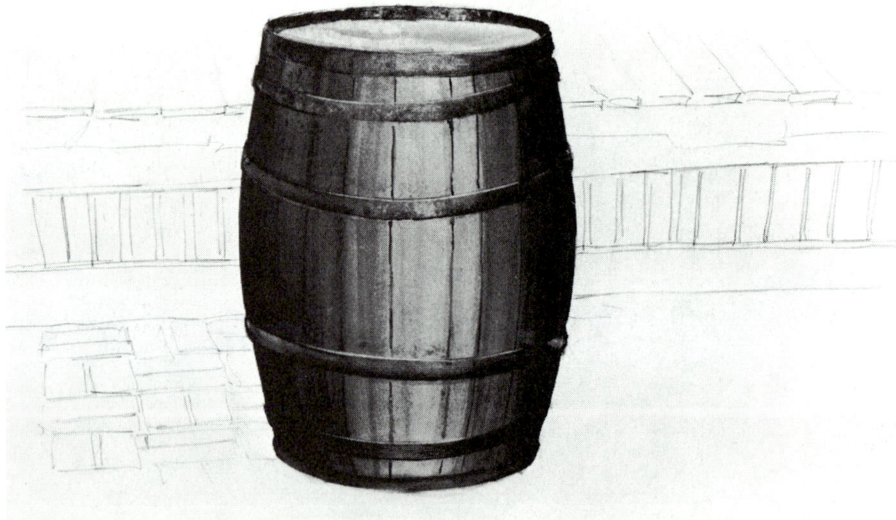

2. Mr. Shook used a no. 8 pointed sable brush, loaded with a mixture of Van Dyke brown and Prussian blue, to emphasize the rings and staves of the barrel. Then he used a clean pointed sable brush and clear water to lift a little color above the rings to suggest depth. This lifting technique was completed by blotting the area with a dry paper towel.

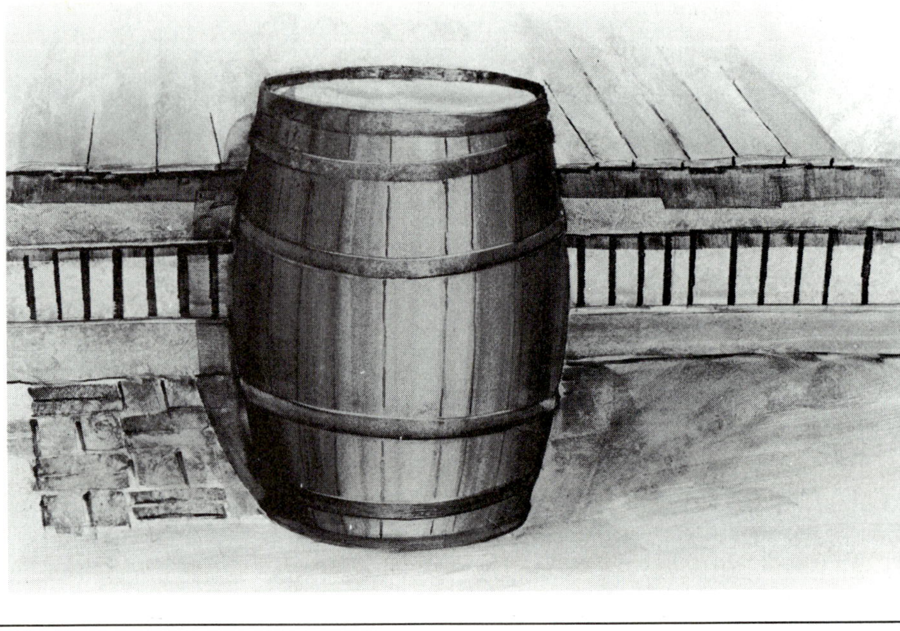

3. To complete the wooden platform, the artist mixed burnt sienna and Winsor blue and applied a flat wash to the surface with a ¾″ chisel-edged brush. He also added touches of highly diluted burnt sienna to some of the boards for warmth and variety. He made a mixture of Prussian blue and Van Dyke brown and used the sharp edge of a ¾″ chisel-edged brush to paint details and shadows on and around the platform. Now he used burnt sienna in a ¾″ chisel-edged brush to paint the bricks in the foreground individually, picking up a bit of Winsor blue occasionally to vary the tonal range. A thin wash of Prussian blue and Van Dyke brown completed the foreground.

1. A wheelbarrow, which the artist drew with a 2B pencil, was the focal point of this painting. Then he blocked in an undertoning of olive green in the background with a ¾″ (19 mm) chisel-edged brush, using broad, random strokes. Now he squeezed olive green and burnt sienna from the tubes onto his palette and mixed each with a very small amount of water. Then he picked up some of each color with a small, round sponge and dabbed the sponge onto the area above the wheelbarrow. The shape and texture of the sponge created a realistic impression of foliage. He dabbed selectively so that some of the underpainting showed through, adding depth.

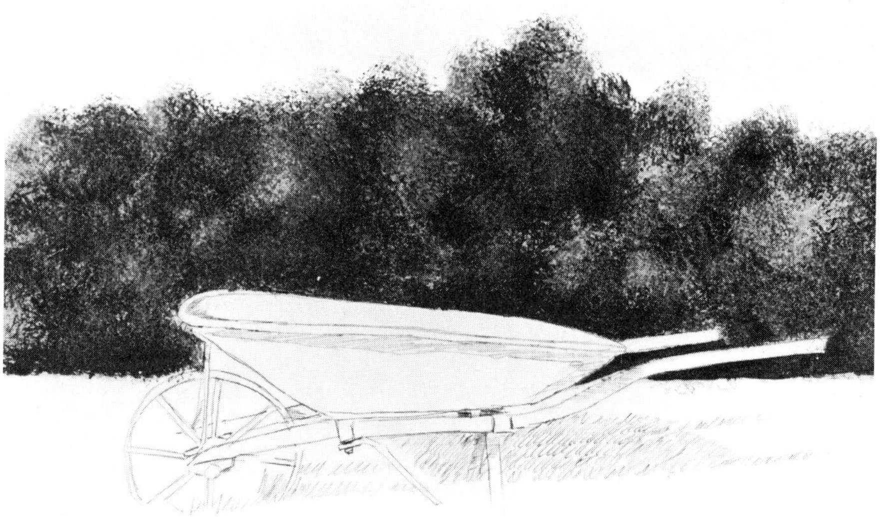

2. Now Mr. Shook added shadows to the foliage by sponging on a mixture of Prussian blue and Van Dyke brown. A sponge gives the artist very good control: you can darken areas by adding more pigment or lighten them by lifting out pigment with a clean, damp sponge.

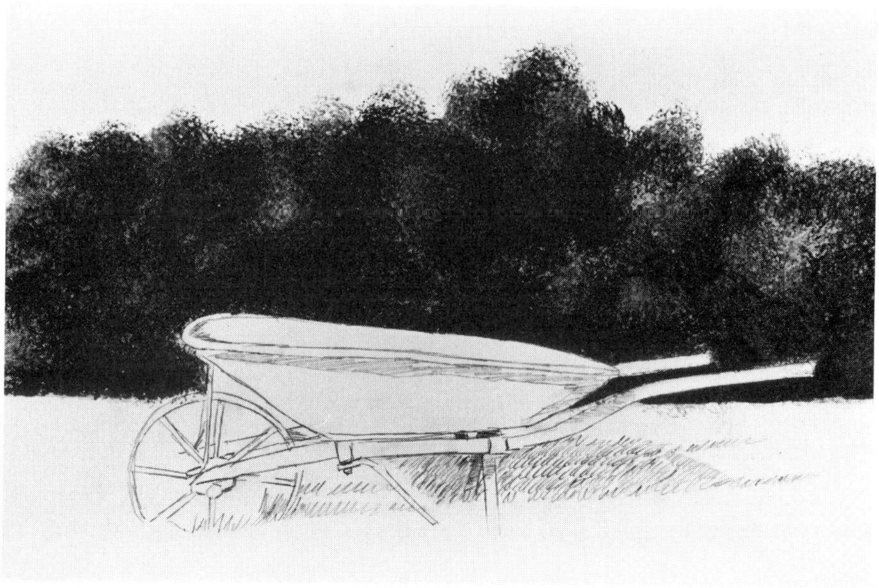

3. The artist varied the density of the hedge by dabbing a damp sponge onto selected areas to lift a little pigment. Next he used a pointed sable brush loaded with a mixture of Winsor blue and burnt sienna to paint the wheelbarrow. The grass in the middleground and foreground was added by surface-mixing olive green and burnt sienna with a stiff-bristle brush. Now the artist completed the painting by adding detail and shadow in and around the wheelbarrow with Prussian blue and Van Dyke brown. He used a pointed sable brush for detail and a ¾″ chisel-edged brush for shadow.

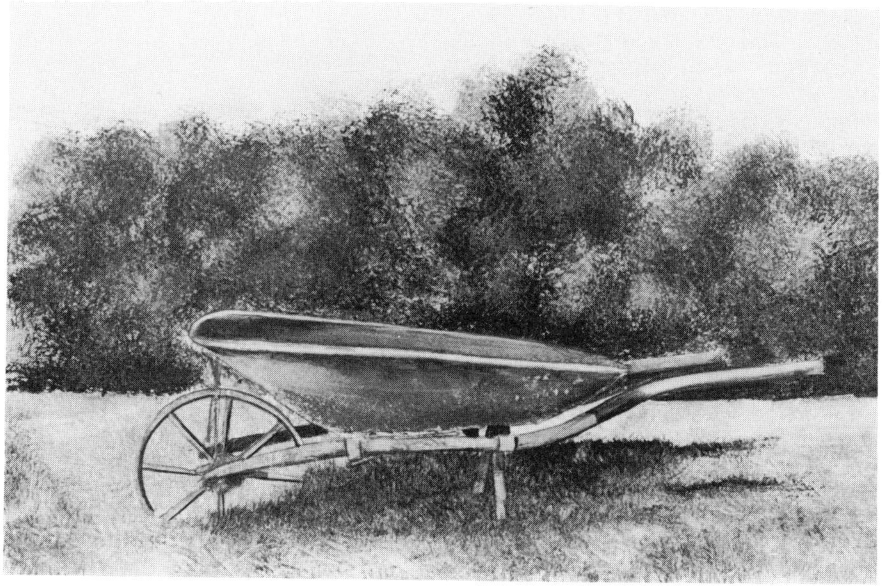

Bucket and Window

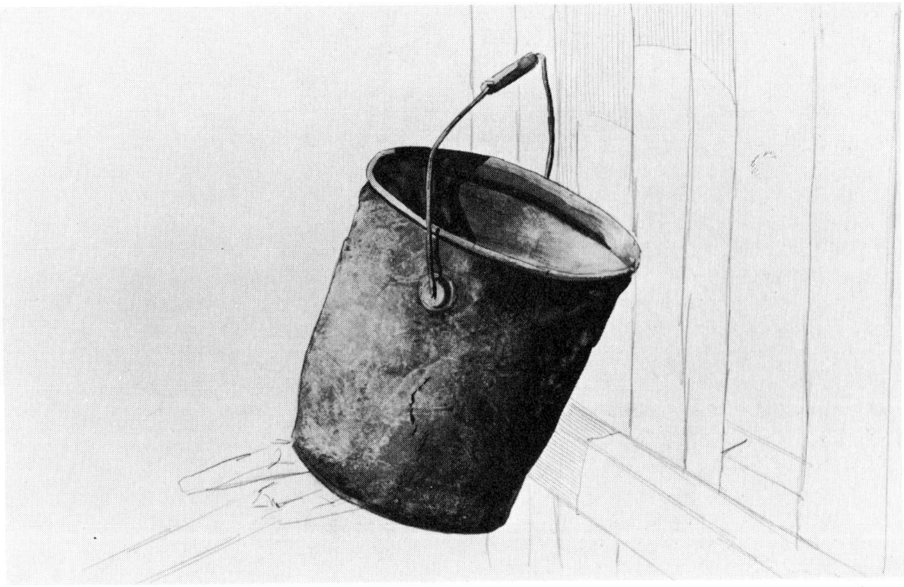

1. Georg Shook used a 2B pencil to make a detailed drawing of a bucket and the fence behind it. Then he blocked in an undertoning of burnt sienna over the entire bucket with a ¾″ (19 mm) chisel-edged brush. After the undertoning had dried, he mixed Prussian blue and Van Dyke brown for the shadow and detail. Using a ¾″ chisel-edged brush, he applied this mixture to the right side of the bucket to create a broad shadow area. Then he switched to a pointed sable brush and added the inner details to the handle.

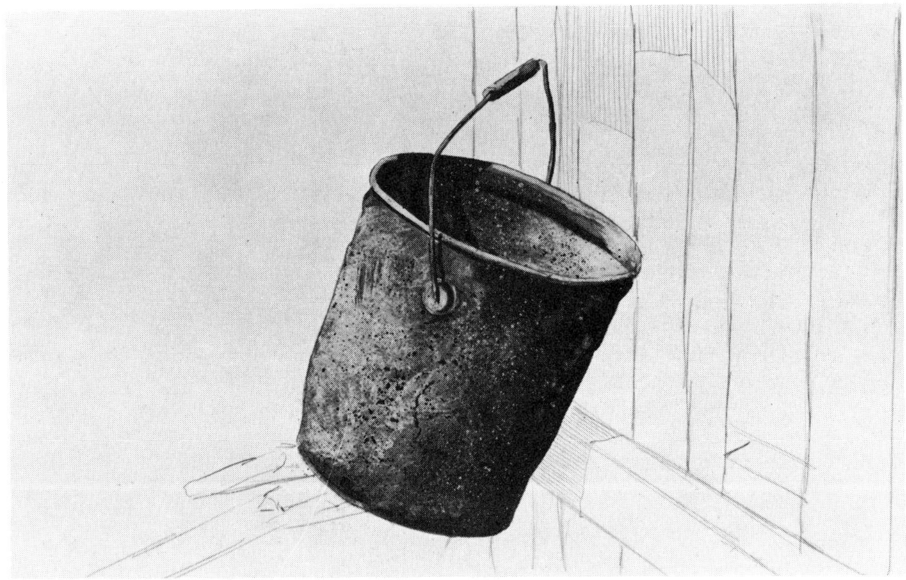

2. At this stage Mr. Shook spattered the bucket. To do this, he picked up the Prussian blue and Van Dyke brown mixture with a toothbrush, held the brush over the proper area, and dragged his thumb across the bristles. The size of spattered drops of paint depends on how far the brush is held from the surface; and in this case, it was held quite close. You can use any stiff-bristled brush for this procedure, but Mr. Shook feels he has better control over the direction of the spatter when he uses a toothbrush. Areas around the subject can be covered with a paper towel to protect them from stray drops of paint.

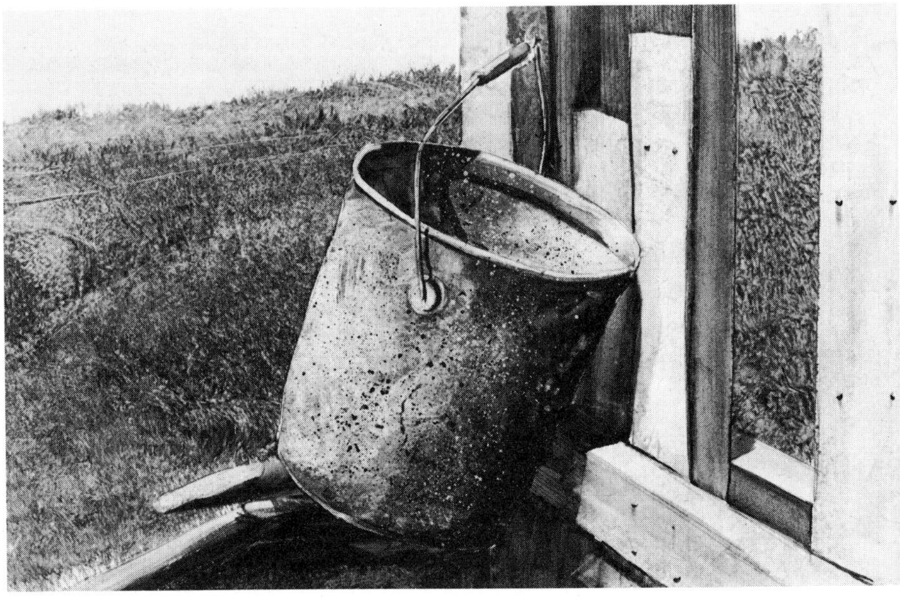

3. To complete the painting, the artist surface-mixed olive green and burnt sienna to add grass to the back, middle, and foreground areas. Then he blotted the entire area with a damp paper towel for additional texture. For the wooden fence he mixed a wash of Davy's gray and burnt sienna and applied it with a ¾″ chisel-edged brush. Now he added shadows under the bucket by loading the same brush with a mixture of Winsor blue and Van Dyke brown. Finally, he painted in some rusty nails with a pointed red sable brush and pure burnt sienna.

1. Negative spattering—flicking clear water onto the surface and then gently blotting with a dry paper towel to lift away spots of pigment—can be used to lend a weatherbeaten look to wood or metal surfaces. Georg Shook applied this technique to a painting of a weathered window. First he made a detailed drawing with a 2B pencil. Then he brushed a highly diluted undertoning of Davy's gray onto the wall area with a ¾″ (19 mm) chisel-edged brush. Next he picked up small amounts of burnt sienna, Winsor blue, and Davy's gray on his brush and painted the individual boards with single, continuous strokes. He used different proportions of the three pigments for each stroke to give the weathered boards a realistic look.

Now he used a mixture of Van Dyke brown and Prussian blue in a pointed sable brush to add shadow under each board and create the appearance of clapboard.

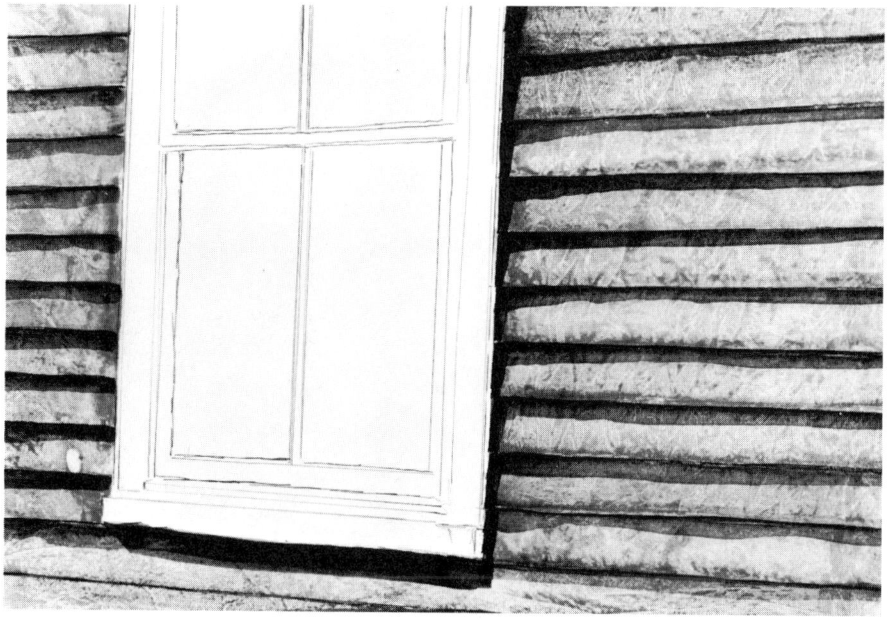

2. Now the artist "aged" the wood by dipping a clean toothbrush in clear water, holding it over the painting, and tapping the brush against his finger to flick droplets of water onto the surface. He used a clean, dry paper towel to blot away the pigment lifted by the drops of water. Now he reemphasized the shadow areas with the Van Dyke brown and Prussian blue in a pointed sable brush. While the negative spots still showed through, this restoration of the shadows was necessary for realism since shadows lie over a surface and are always continuous.

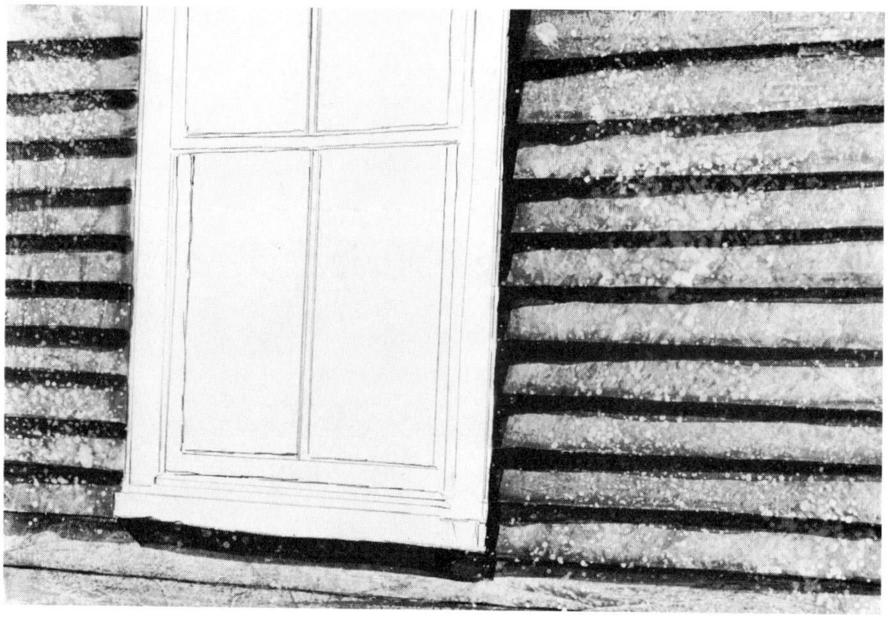

3. Finally the artist painted the window. He used a ¼″ (6 mm) chisel-edged brush to lay in a wash of Davy's gray and burnt sienna on the wooden window frame, and then he blotted this area for texture with a damp paper towel. To paint the windowpanes, he began with an underwash of Winsor blue in a ¾″ chisel-edged brush. After this had dried, he used the same brush to add another wash of Davy's gray. Then he lightly mixed the colors on the surface by pressing the palm of his hand lightly into the paint and twisting it slightly while the pigment was still wet.

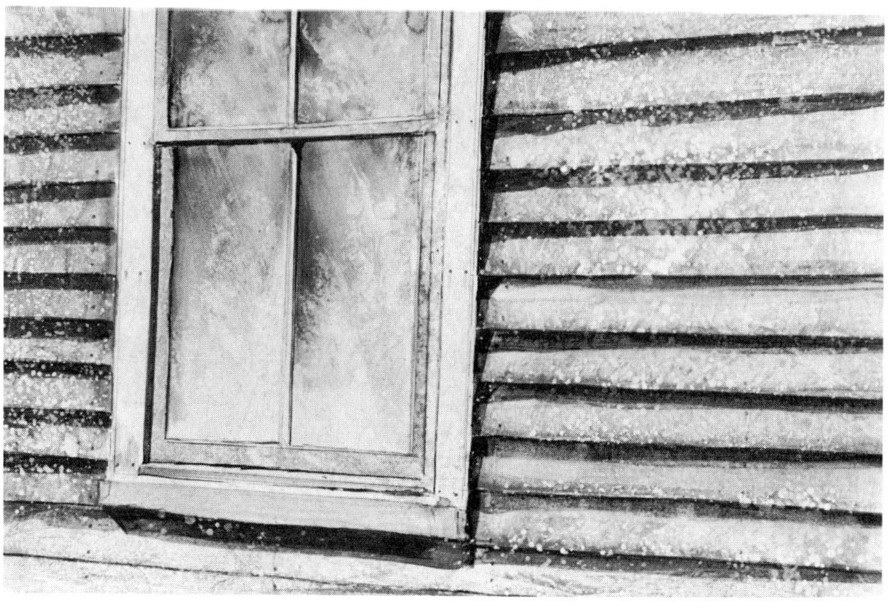

Translucent Plastic Bottle

First Statement. To help his students tackle the problems presented by translucent objects, Arthur Stern has them paint a big empty jug of colorless, cloudy plastic—the kind that's often used to package cider. To do this, soak off the paper label, rinse out the jug, pour in about a pint (or half a liter) of water, and recap. Line the left wall of a two-sided setup box with green paper, the right wall with blue, and the floor with red. Pose the jug so that it overlaps the corner of the setup box, where the two walls meet, with its handle in back and out of sight. If the jug is angular in shape, one of its corners will point toward you. Your eye level ought to be at about the midpoint of the jug. Place a lamp in front of the setup box and to the left, so that the jug casts a sizable shadow on the floor and right wall of the box.

Work on a full sheet of canvas paper, held vertically, and use a 3:4 viewfinder. (To make a viewfinder, see the instructions on page 21.) Now forget about the translucency of the bottle and just go ahead and paint the colors of the jug as you would paint any opaque object in oil. Punch a hole in a gray or black piece of cardboard and look through this "spot screen" to isolate and study the colors of the jug and its surroundings. Look for about eleven color spots: two for the walls of the setup box, one for its floor, two for the cap of the jug, two for the empty upper part of the jug, two for the water-filled lower part, and two for the cast shadow on the floor and wall.

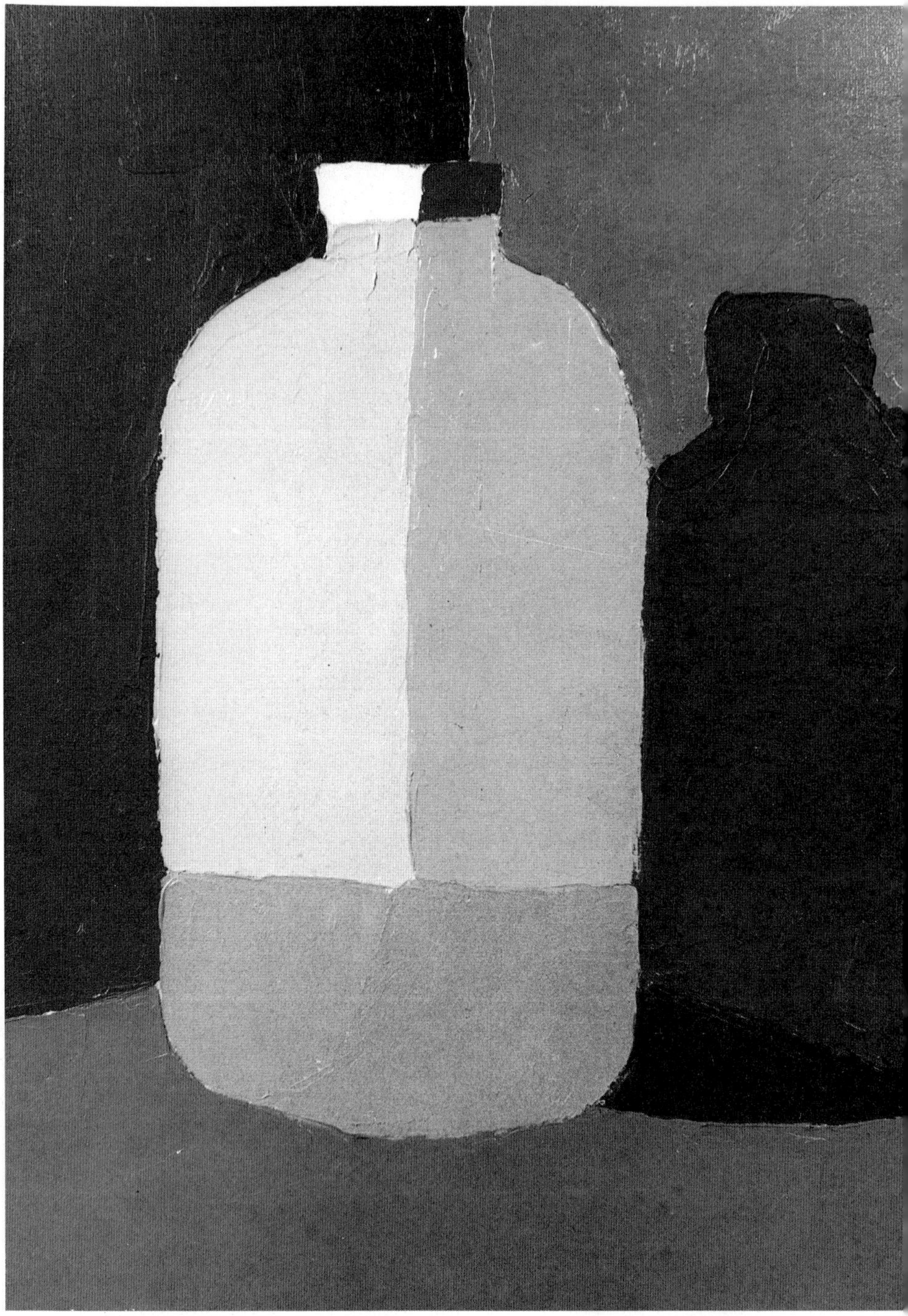

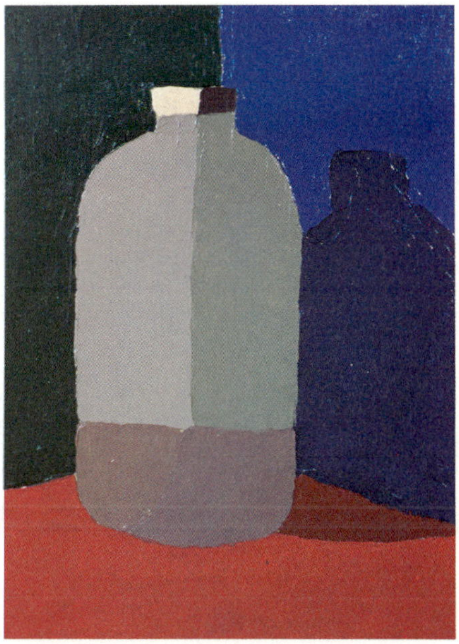

Observations. If you observe and mix all the colors of the jug with reasonable accuracy, they will begin to convey some of that mysterious, opalescent quality that you might have *thought* would be so difficult. You may find it hard to see two distinct color areas in the lower section of the jug—the part that's filled with water. If that is so, and all you see there is a single color, then paint only that color. Don't follow these instructions uncritically, inventing color spots just because you are asked to look for them. Paint only the colors you find; your observations don't have to agree exactly with Mr. Stern's suggestions, or with the student work reproduced here. In this first statement, notice that the shadow on the right wall is lower than the actual jug. That's not a mistake—the shadow is lower because the setup light was higher than the jug.

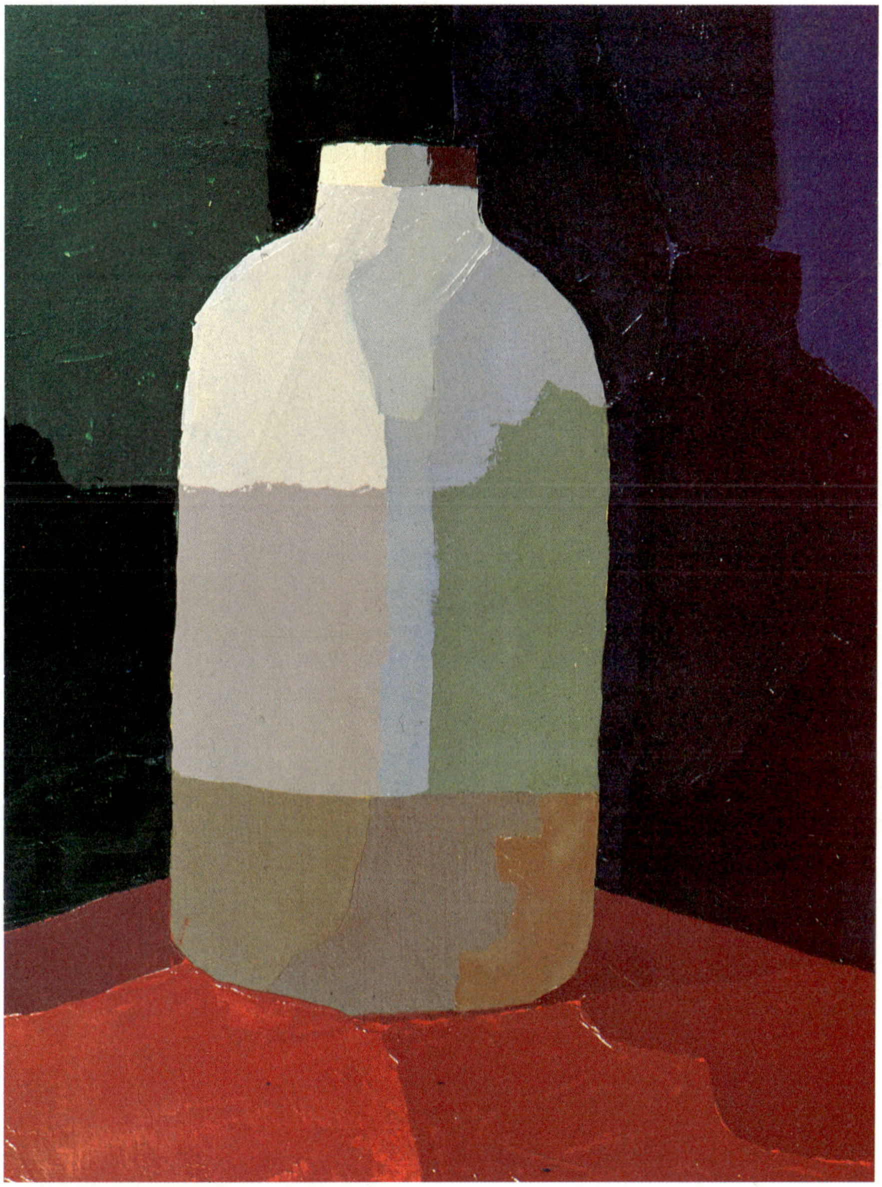

Second Statement. When you get to your second statement, you will observe that each color area of the first statement can probably be subdivided into three or four smaller color spots. (Naturally, it doesn't *always* work out that way, since some surfaces are simpler than others.) So now look again at the jug and its surroundings, and find your own color spots for your second statement. The original eleven color spots of the first statement may develop into as many as thirty or forty different colors. The precise number is up to you.

Third Statement. A second statement, like the one on the preceding page, sometimes looks slightly disjointed. Some color spots may seem to jump out at you, while others may look just wrong or somehow out of place. The contrast between colors also may be too strong, suggesting the need for transitional colors between them. A second statement rarely looks complete and decisive—that's why you go on to paint a third statement, to make corrections and insert transitions. First go over the entire second statement to determine what's awry. Double-check the hue, luminosity, and intensity of every color spot that looks dubious. Also check its size, shape, and position relative to those spots that look right. Then make these corrections as you repaint the entire surface. Now start looking for connections, or transitions. Scrutinize the setup again with your spot screen. Look especially hard at the areas *between* the color spots you've painted in your second statement. Search for contrasts that seem too harsh, and add in-between colors to make the statement look more realistic. One note of caution about these transitions: Never make an in-between color spot by blending two adjacent color spots or mixing their colors to make a third. A transitional color spot must be newly seen and freshly mixed. It is a *new* color spot.

Your third statement reinforces what you already saw in the first statement, namely that a translucent object is no harder to paint than an opaque one—if only you forget about its translucency and observe the color as you really see it. There's no problem unless you *create* the problem by imagining something especially difficult about translucent color. Having learned this lesson, you'll then be prepared to paint other supposedly difficult, translucent subjects.

Extra Project. You can try a variation on this project by pouring out the water from the jug and replacing it with some colorful liquid, such as cold tea or leftover cider—or some other fruit juice. Line the setup box with different colors of your choice. Keep the lighting the same, and proceed to paint three more statements based on your color observations of the setup.

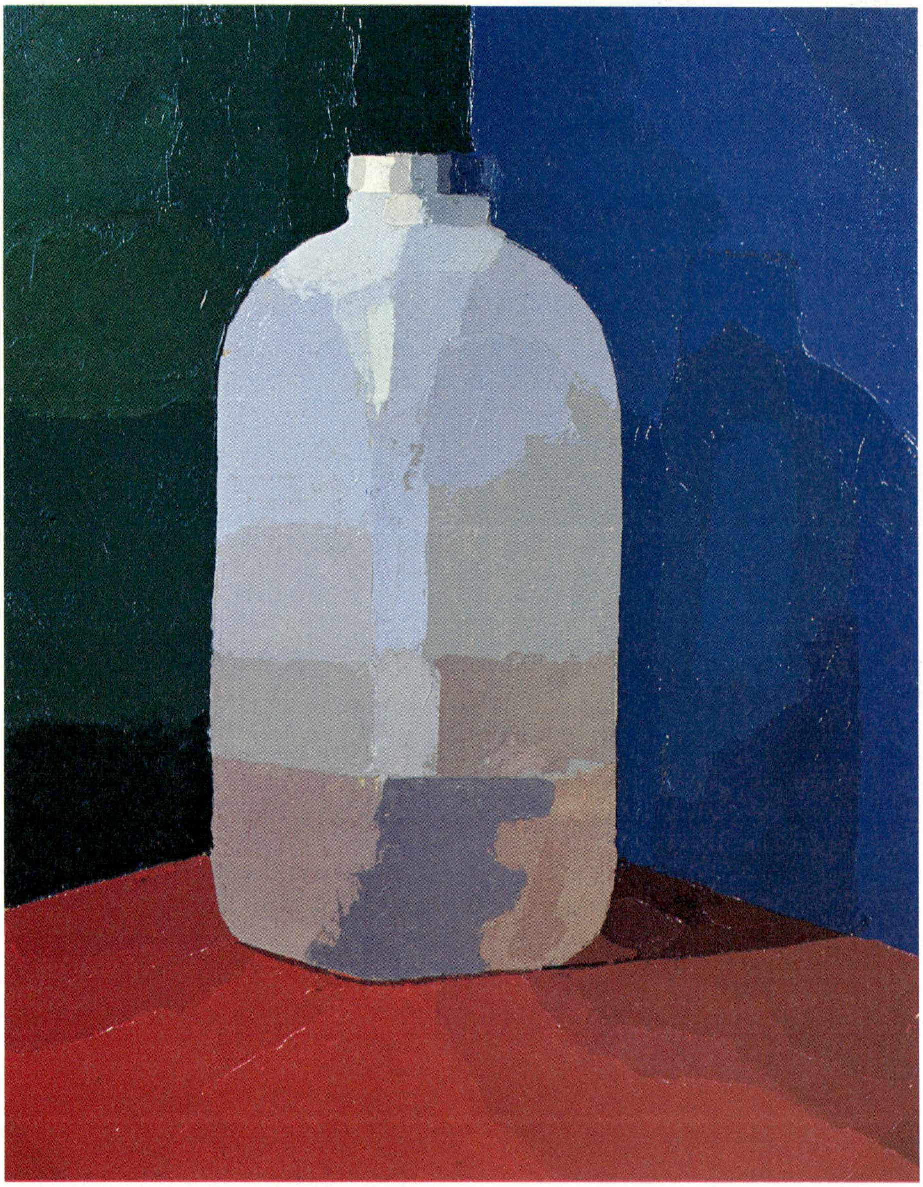

Paper Bag

The Setup. Unlike a plastic jug, a paper bag is theoretically opaque. But if the light is right, parts of the bag can become translucent. The resulting play of opacity and translucency can be a visual delight. For this project, Arthur Stern suggests obtaining an ordinary brown paper bag, slightly battered from use so it will exhibit interesting creases and folds. Line the left wall of a two-sided setup box with green paper, the right wall with red, and the floor with blue. Drop some weighty object, such as a thick paperback book, into the bottom of the paper bag to help it stand upright. Then put the bag in the center of the setup box. You should place a lamp toward the front and at the left of the setup so that some light shines through the bag to create a translucent effect, and so that the bag also casts a sizable shadow on the floor and right wall. The bag should be placed just low enough to let you see a bit of the inside. The corner of the box, where the two walls meet, should be directly in line with your eye so that you see both walls equally. The box should be just low enough so that you can see a fair amount of floor.

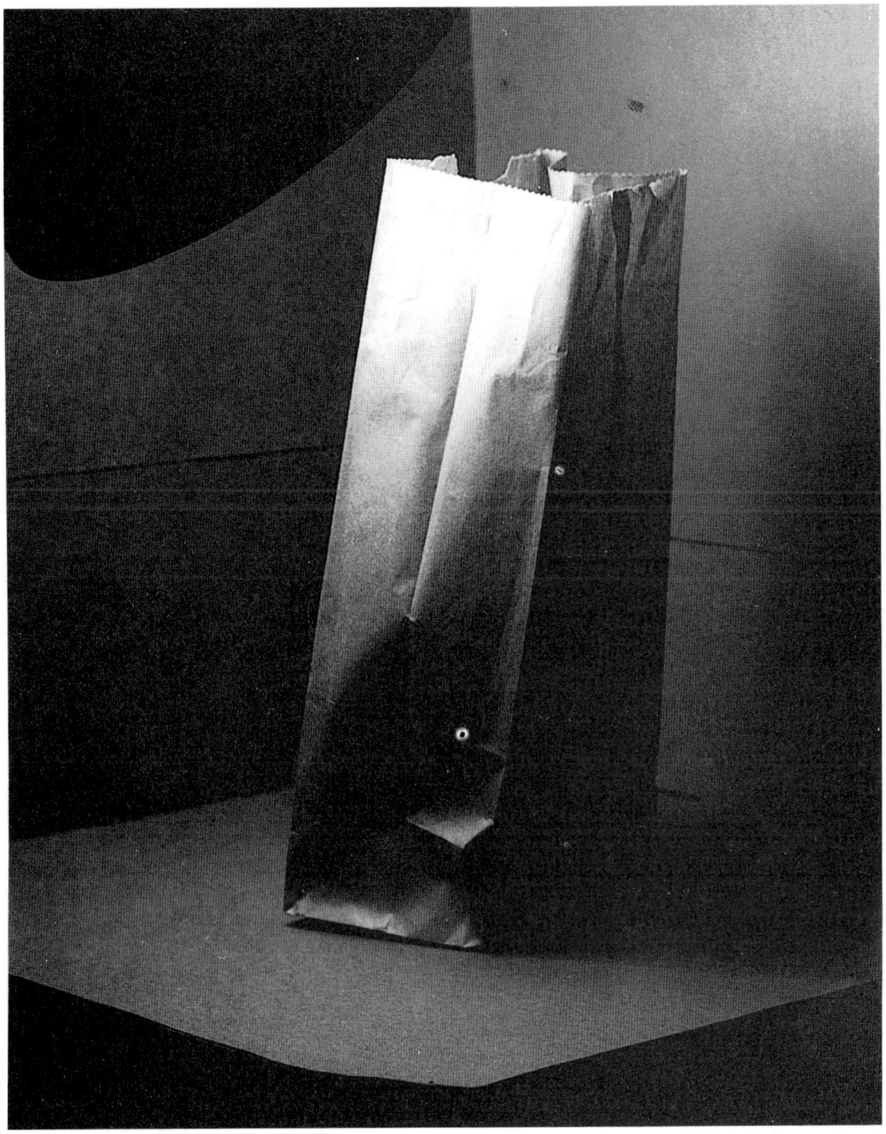

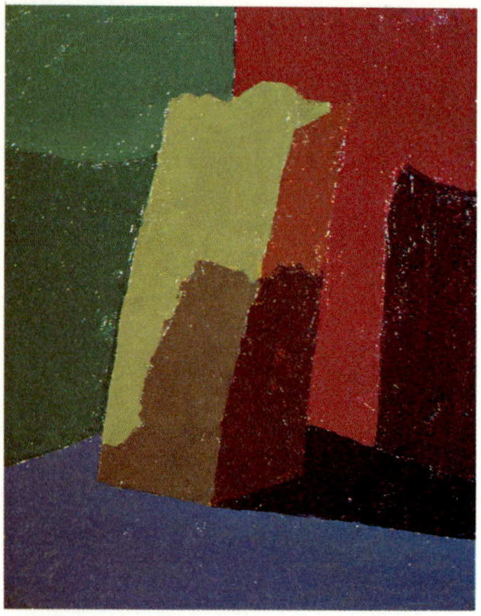

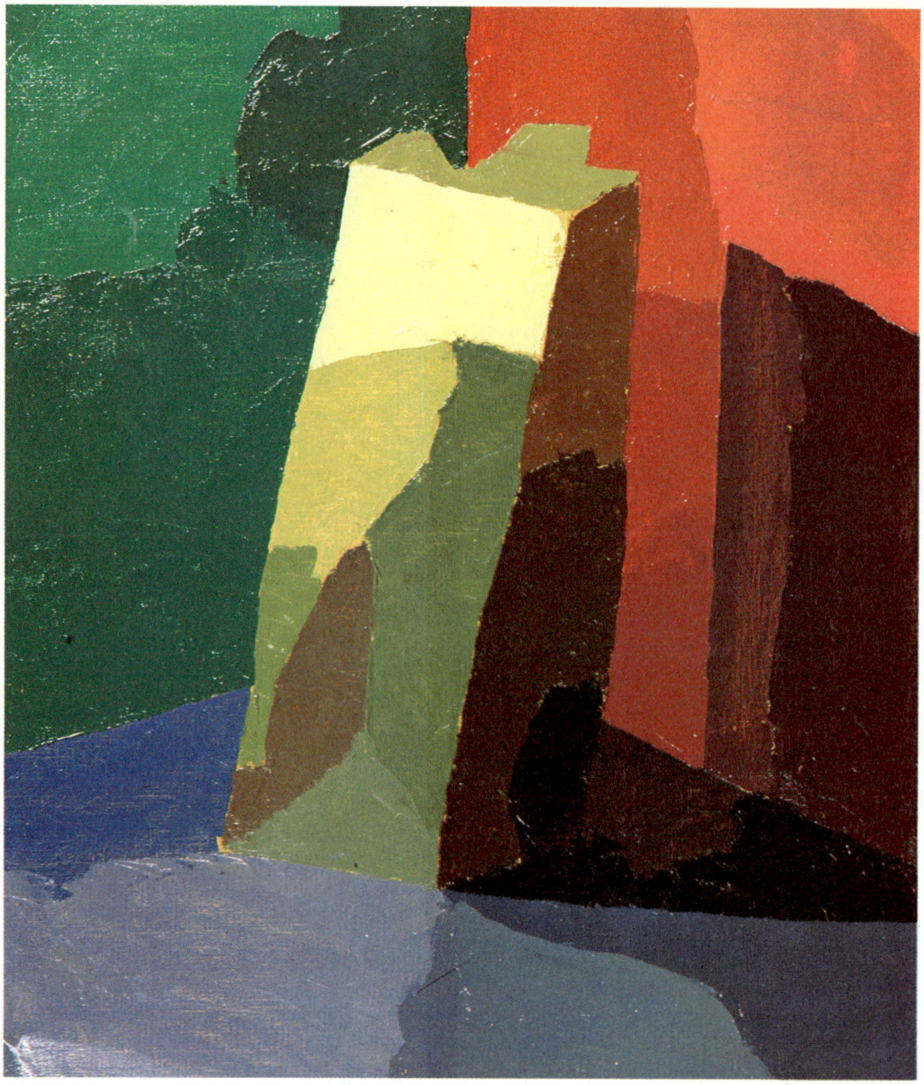

First Statement. Arthur Stern recommends using a full sheet of canvas paper, turned vertically. Use a 3:4 viewfinder to frame your composition, with the bag in the center. In painting this first statement, your goal is simply to establish the solidity of the object, without worrying too much about whether it looks like a paper bag yet. The bag is a fairly blocky object, and so concentrate on its planes, as well as those of the surrounding setup box. Also pay attention to the shapes of the shadows. In the statement illustrated here, student Richard Gleason summarized what he saw in just ten color spots: three for the lighted walls and floor of the setup box, one for the shaded area on the left wall, four for the lights and darks on the bag, and two for the shadow on the floor and wall.

The bag may not look like a bag yet, but it will look solid if you've put the right color spots in the right places. And it will look as if it occupies space, as any solid object should. Notice that his student's first statement captures not only the cast shadow that runs across the floor and up the right wall, but also a big patch of dark on the left wall. The upright bag isn't a simple arrangement of two planes, front and side. The folds of the bag actually break the front into two planes and the side into two more planes—which become four big color spots.

Second Statement. Now study the irregular folds and creases in the paper bag to find additional color spots. But don't consciously say to yourself: "The bag folds here, so this must be another color spot." Forget that what you're painting is a paper bag and just look for those color spots as areas with irregular perimeters that must be recorded as accurately as you can. If you make the right decision about the hue, luminosity, intensity, size, shape, and position of each color spot, then all the color spots, taken as a whole, will eventually register as a series of folds.

As you multiply the color spots—going back over the ten big color spots of the first statement—you're certainly learning the lesson that this supposedly "brown" paper bag can't be painted accurately with any color even vaguely resembling "brown." When you go through the process of naming, mixing, and matching each color spot, you can see why "brown" should be a forbidden word here: Every one of those mixtures turns out to be a subdued version of some very specific hue. The bag doesn't look like a bag just yet, but it's getting there. In the meantime, simply by painting each color spot as a flat area with its own unique character, you're making the bag look more solid, and you're creating a distinct sense of the space within the setup box.

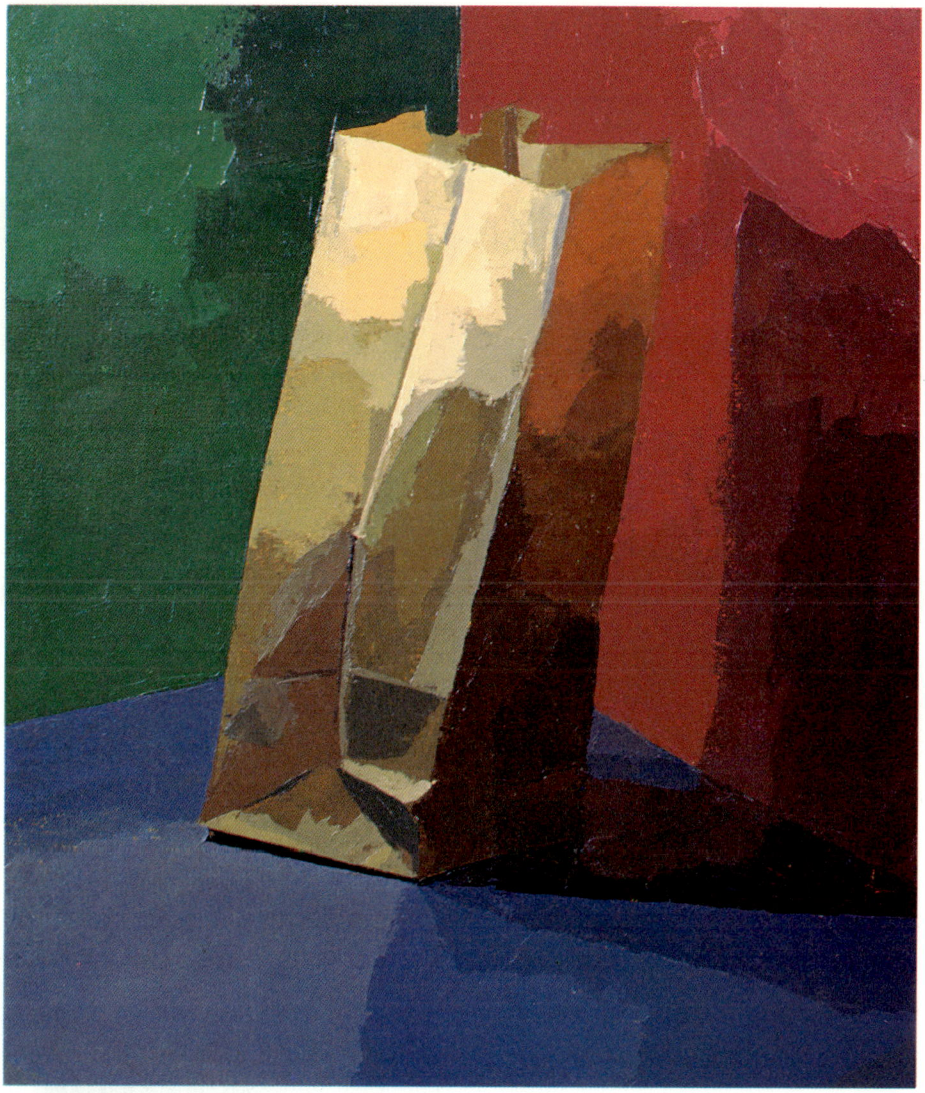

Extra Project. Now try the same project with an all-white paper bag, posed and lit in the same way. Change the colors on the walls and floor of the setup box to suit your taste. Carry the project through three statements. When you finish painting the white bag, try painting a single stripe of bright color around its middle and then start again.

Third Statement. At this stage, the bag should really come to look like a bag. But you must keep resisting the temptation to say to yourself: "Now I'm going to make the bag look more realistic by putting in all those nice creases and folds." As you add each new color spot, creating transitions and making corrections, focus your attention on that color spot alone. For example, as you get down to the complicated shapes at the bottom of the bag, just paint them as the ragged rectangles and polygons you see—and, almost all by themselves, they will become folds of paper. In the same way, as you put together the luminous color spots at the top of the bag, don't remind yourself that you're trying to capture the transclucent effect of the light shining through the paper; you should let the color spots do that job for you.

Your paper bag certainly is growing into a more complex subject than you might have expected when you started to paint it. Now look at the finished third statement and ask yourself some questions. Does the bag look solid enough, and does the surrounding space of the setup box look convincing? Do the bag and the setup box in your painting seem to fit with each other, and work together as well as their originals do in the actual setup? Does your bag boast as interesting a play of translucency and opacity as you see in the actual bag? Finally, has all of this been done with sufficiently smooth transitions and a minimum of false notes—that is, do the color spots seem to hold their place in the picture rather than leap out or fall back? If you can answer yes to all these questions, congratulations. If not, go back and try again.

Glass

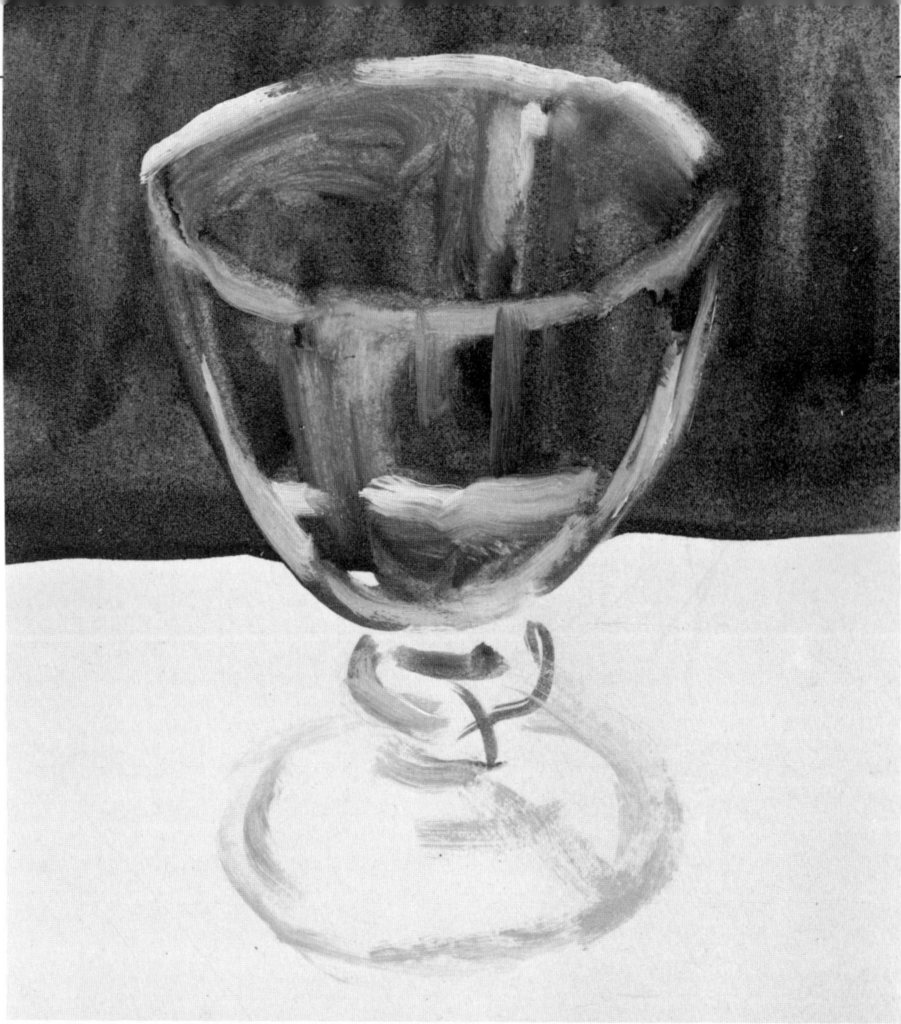

1. To paint glass well, you have to draw the glass accurately and also render its transparent quality. Artist Joseph Dawley recommends applying your oil paint thinly to allow for a great deal of delicate blending. Thicker paint would not enable you to achieve as high a degree of translucency. Mr. Dawley painted this glass against both dark and light areas to demonstrate how to handle glass against any kind of background.

Mr. Dawley's first concern was capturing the shape and proportions of the glass accurately. He left the lower area of the canvas unpainted for now and indicated the dark background roughly with raw umber thinned with turpentine. Next he used titanium white to draw in the upper outlines of the glass. He prepared a thicker white to show prominent reflections and highlights, such as those found on the rim and in the bowl. Then he drew the lower half of the glass on the canvas with a thinned blend of white and raw umber. Again, he indicated major reflections—such as those on the stem and base—by using thicker paint.

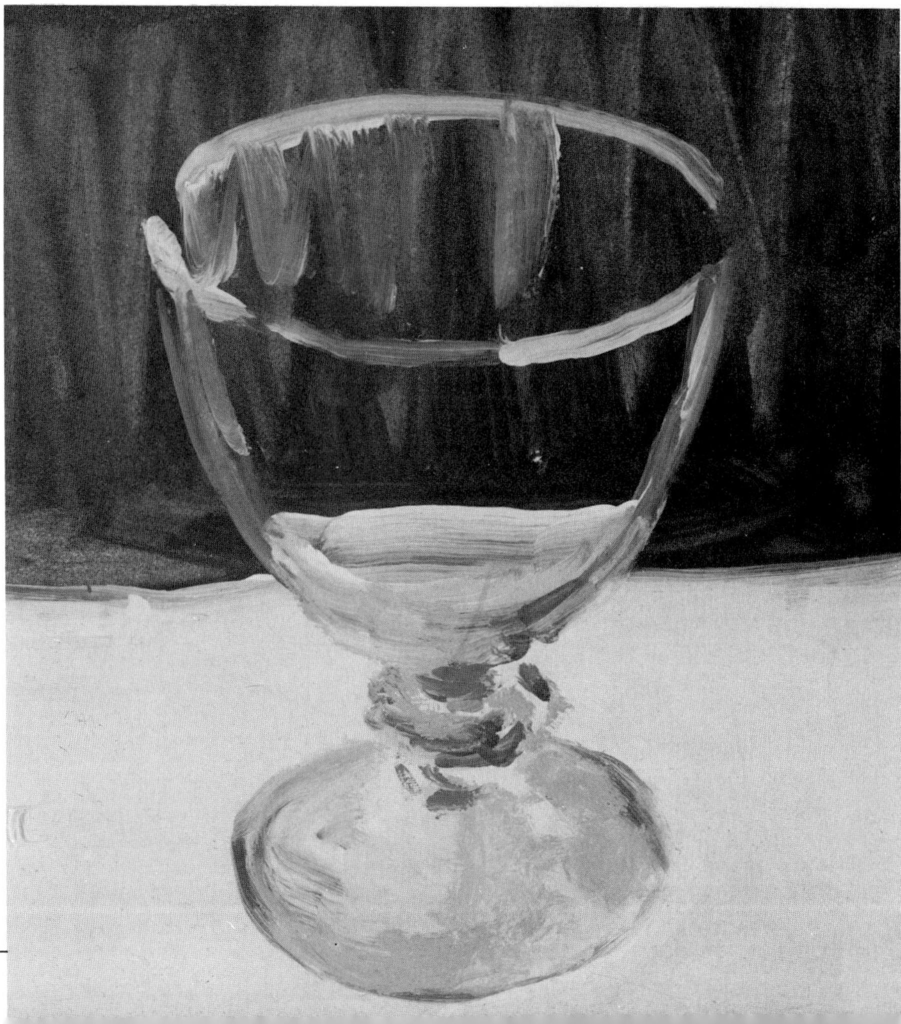

2. Leaving his guidelines undisturbed, the artist proceeded to fill the canvas with the approximate values of his composition. He used white for the tabletop beneath the glass and also to fill in its large reflection in the bottom of the bowl. Because he was painting into the raw umber background, this reflection was not pure white. He painted the stem and base of the glass in off-white tones so the final touches of pure white would really glitter by contrast. He used his lightest tone for the light areas in the base. For the darker areas in both the stem and the base, he deepened this tone with a bit more raw umber. The small, darkest reflections on the right side of the stem and on the perimeter of the base were done with pure raw umber. For the very lightest spots in these two areas, he used white and a no. 2 watercolor brush. For greatest precision, Mr. Dawley used a small brush to capture the minute but important value changes.

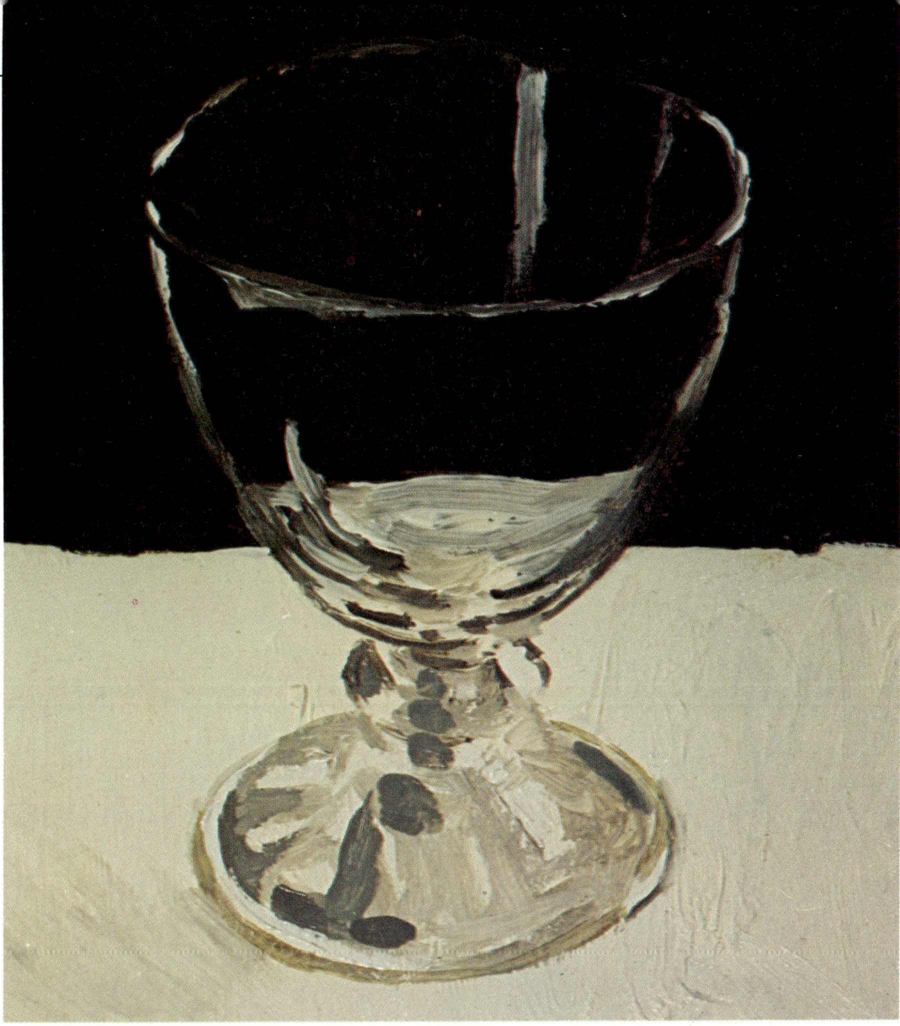

3. Mr. Dawley added ultramarine blue and yellow ochre to his palette. Then he laid in his final background of raw umber, sharpening the outlines of the rim and sides of the bowl. He used strokes and spots of white to accentuate the highlights and reflections on the glass. The bottom of the bowl, the stem, and the base housed a complex pattern of reflections, and for these he used his light and middle monochrome tones, as well as a combination of raw umber and ultramarine blue. He dabbed in a few spots of pure white for the highlights. He also combined yellow ochre and raw umber to outline the perimeter of the base where a yellowish reflection appeared. Then he painted the extremely faint shadow extending from the glass to the lower left with his lightest white–raw umber tone and brushed it very lightly into the white.

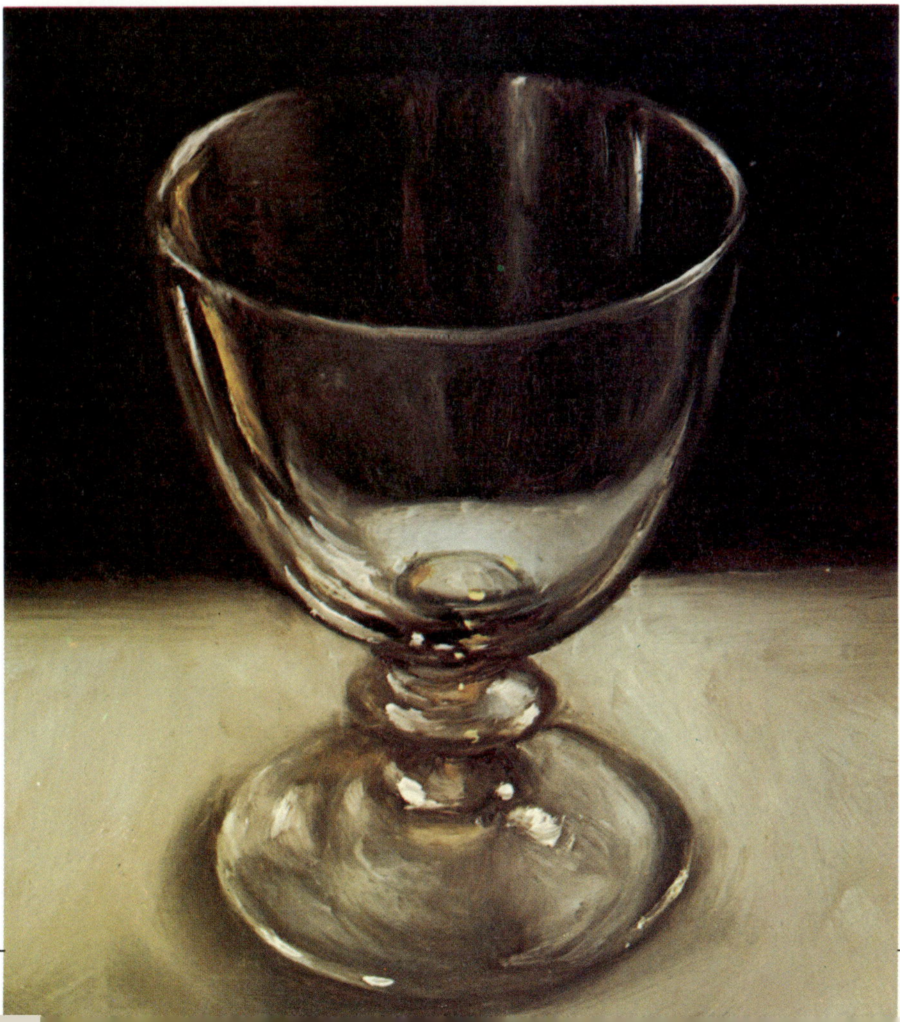

4. The artist added cobalt yellow (aureolin) to his palette to mix with yellow ochre for the warm reflections. Except for the final bright highlights, the entire process of creating a glassy effect consisted of blending together the tones he had already placed in the bottom of the bowl, stem, and base of the glass just well enough to merge them softly.

To show the translucency of the glass against the background in the upper portion of the bowl, Mr. Dawley used a sable brush to lightly blend the white rim and highlights into the raw umber already on the inside of the bowl. Notice that slightly more white is apparent in the front section of the bowl than in the rear due to the double thickness of glass. Now the artist was ready to add bright touches of highlights and reflections. These took the form of streaks or dots—such as the yellow streak on the left side of the bowl, and the dots of color in the bottom of the bowl. After changing the color beneath the glass to a bluish gray, he mixed raw umber and ultramarine blue for the shadow around the bottom rim on the right and the cast shadow extending from the left side of the rim.

Silver

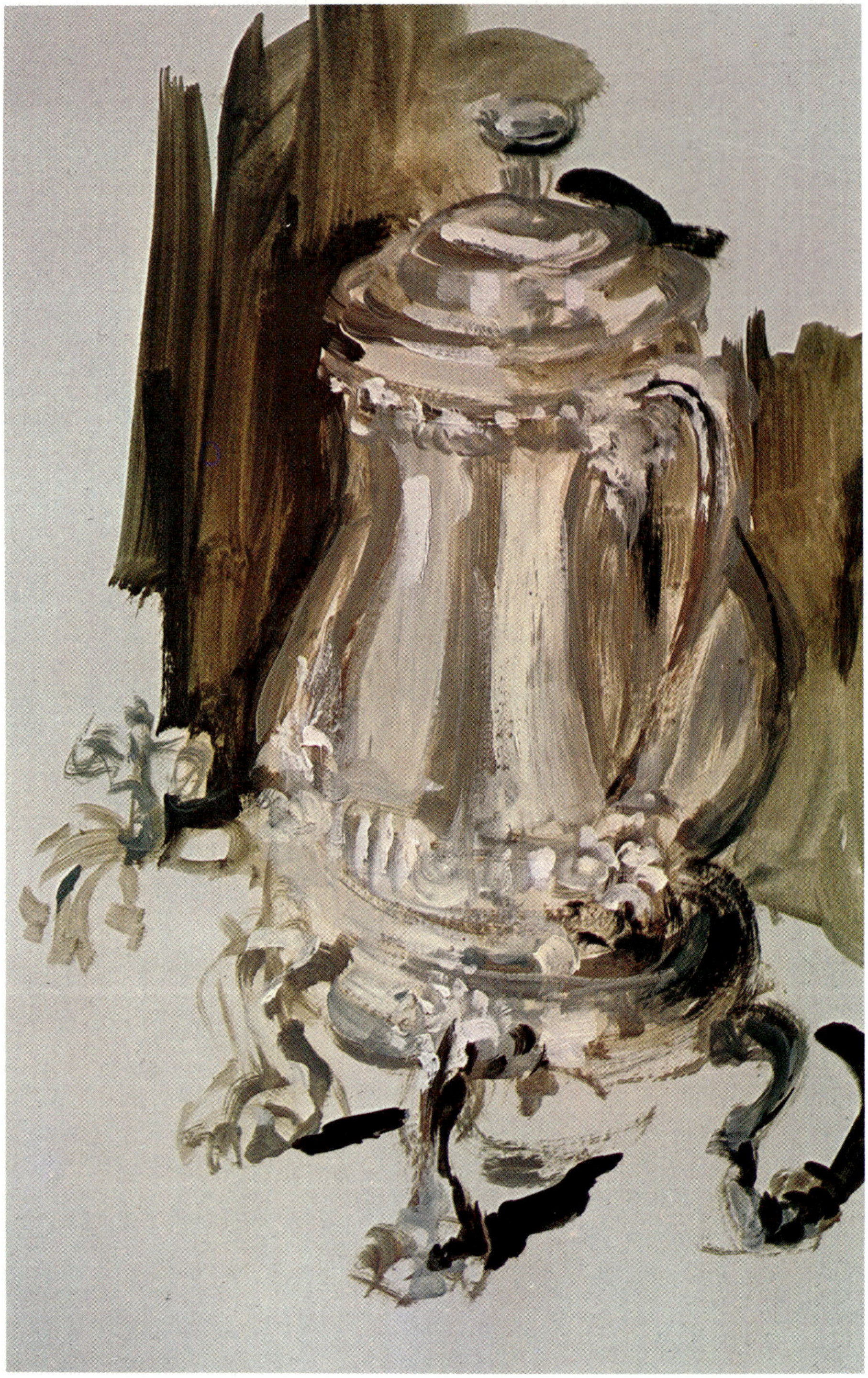

1. For this painting of a silver urn, Joseph Dawley began with a monochrome palette, using mixtures of white, raw umber, and phthalo blue to create three silver-blue tones of varying strengths. He loosely drew in the general shape of the urn and then roughly indicated all the values of the reflections in vague, broad strokes. He filled in the lightest and darkest silver tones in the urn and sketchily added the etched patterns found at both the top and bottom of the container. Then he added major shadows and indicated highlights. As these tonal values were filled in, his basic drawing became more refined. Now the artist expanded his palette to include yellow ochre, underpainting white, burnt sienna, and more phthalo blue. He began to concentrate more on refinement and accuracy. He mixed yellow ochre, blue, and burnt sienna, thinned with turpentine, to indicate the background and its reflections in the urn, adding white for coolness. For some warm reddish reflections on the handle and left side of the pot, he mixed yellow ochre, white, burnt sienna, and a little phthalo blue. Adding more blue to the original light monochrome, he filled in some areas on the right side of the pot, the lid, and the base. His darkest tones were a cool near-black mixed from phthalo blue and burnt sienna. Underpainting white was used for the pattern areas of the pot. Now he toned down all the other white areas by adding small amounts of burnt sienna and blue to obtain a bluish-gray tint.

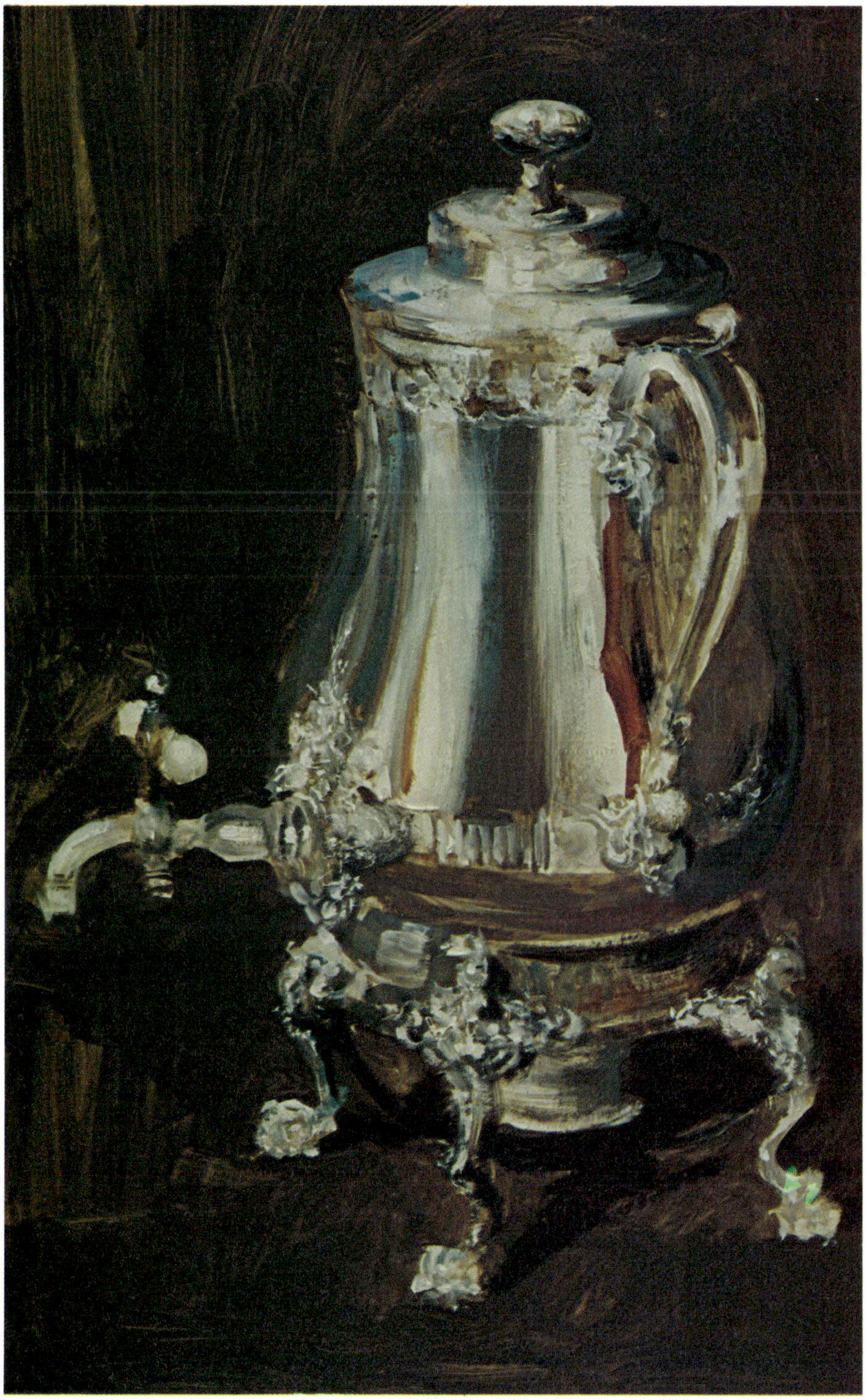

2. Now it became important to lay in precise colors in their proper locations to refine the shape of the urn and enable the artist to blend accurately. Blue was the predominant color reflection, and he used his original light tone with extra blue added for the spots on the lid, handle, and left side of the pot. Note that he has blended most of these blue reflections subtly. For the red reflections, such as the long streak by the handle, he used straight burnt sienna which he left unblended for intensity. He used phthalo blue and burnt sienna for the darkest portions of the urn on the right side and on the lid, and for the shadows at the bottom. He used underpainting white exclusively for the etched pattern areas. After being on his palette for half an hour or so, this white had become extra sticky and was even more suitable for this purpose. He applied it by twirling a no. 2 watercolor brush where he wanted to represent the pattern, thereby producing a raised brush stroke. Titanium white was used for the bright highlights such as those on the handle.

China

1. Joseph Dawley began his painting of a porcelain cup and saucer by drawing in their basic shapes with a thinned mixture of titanium white and a small amount of raw umber. He wanted to render them accurately before adding the various tonal values. The painted surface he was working on was pure white, and so he let this represent the whitest portion of the cup and just indicated the shadowed portion of the cup's interior on the left. He used a slightly darker mixture of the same colors for the dark exterior of the cup and swept a streak of white along the bottom of this area to show a reflection from the cup's base, which he filled in with his original turpentine-thinned tone. For the dark parts of the saucer he used his middle tone again, and then he went back to his first tone for the light area in the right center and surrounded the whole cup and saucer with this same wash.

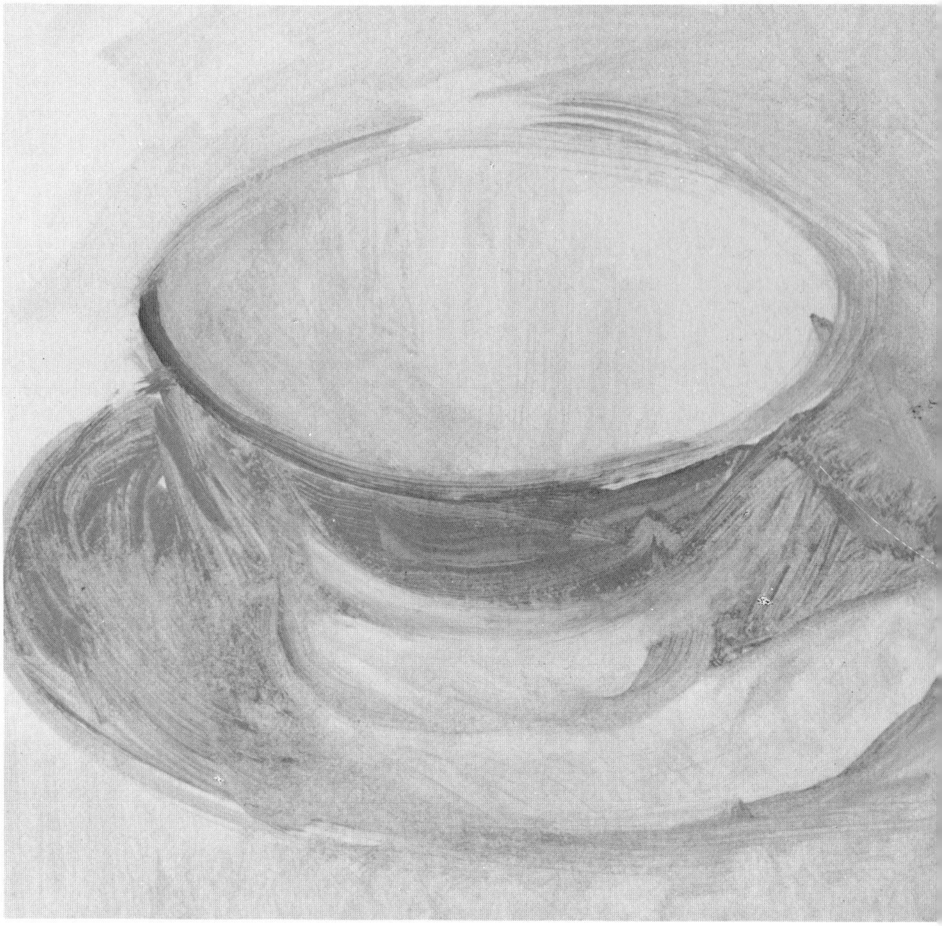

2. Mr. Dawley filled in the inside of the cup, the handle, and the cup base with light mixtures of white and raw umber. He added more of his light tone to the left shadowed side and blended it toward the center. Now he used his middle tone to fill in the exterior surface of the cup and for the saucer, applying it more densely on the left and allowing it to thin out as he approached the center and the right side. He used a darker blend for the dark shadow on the right side of the cup and for the large cast shadow. For the reflection between this shadow and the handle he placed a streak of his original light tone. He also saw shadows on the left front edge of the saucer and under the edge of the base of the cup, and he used his darkest tone for these. He made a background color by thinning his lighter tone with turpentine.

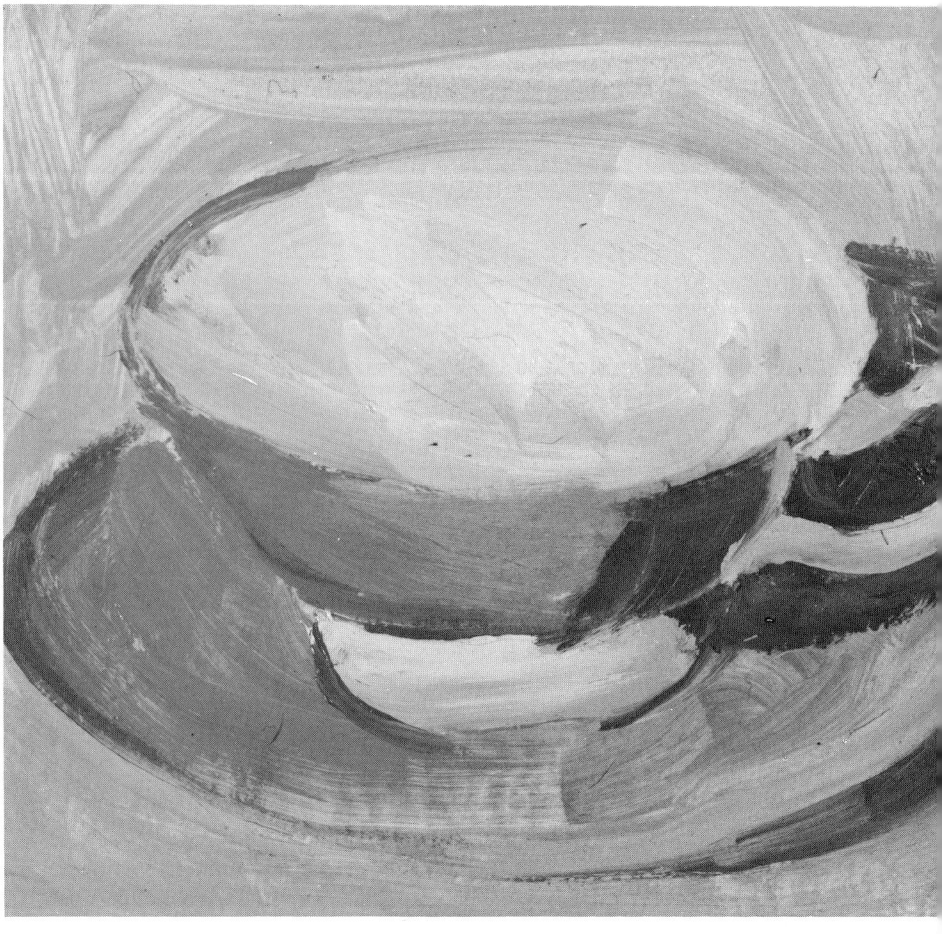

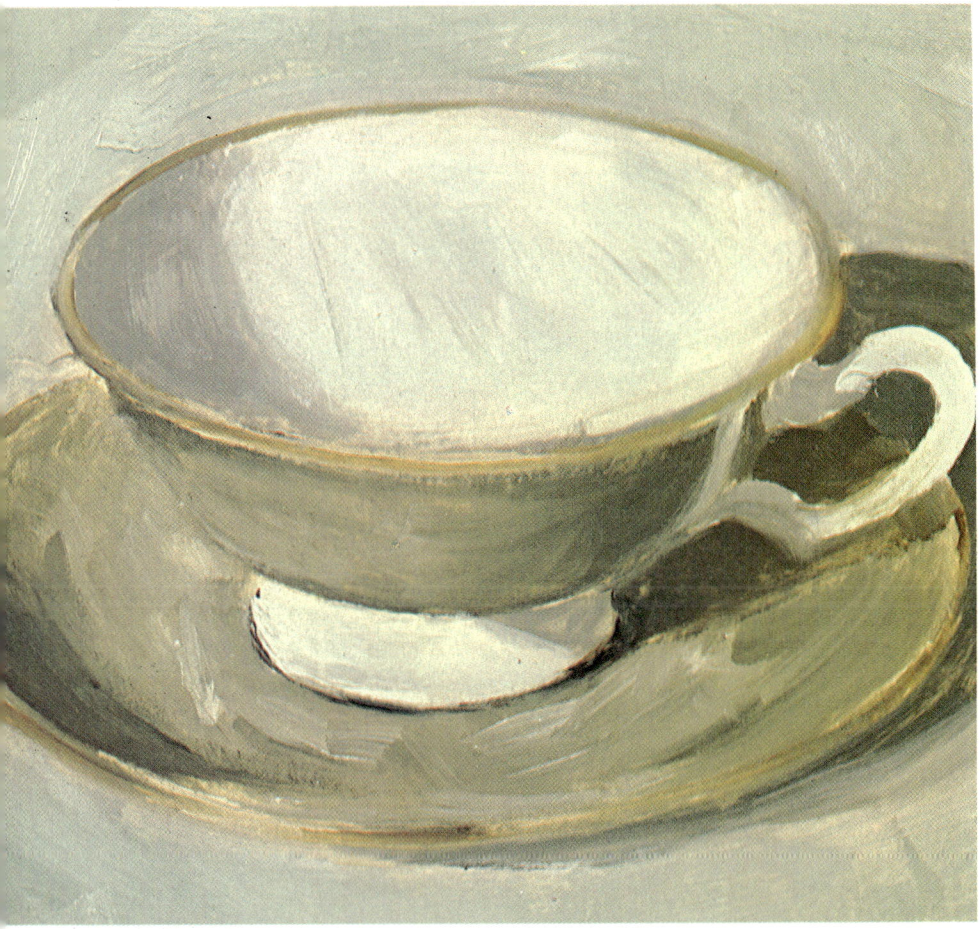

3. Now the artist added ultramarine blue, cobalt yellow, and yellow ochre to his palette. He made two mixtures of raw umber, ultramarine blue, cobalt yellow, yellow ochre, and white in different proportions to obtain one light greenish tone and one darker one. These would be used to simulate the color of the china. He refined the color of the cup's interior, base, and handle, toning down the white enough to permit bright highlights to be added later. With his middle tone he brushed in the shadows on the left side within the cup, the far right side of the base, and on the cast shadow on the left side of the handle. He painted the outside of the cup and saucer with the light green mixture, using the dark mixture for their shadows. The shadow under the base of the cup, however, was done with a combination of raw umber and ultramarine blue. He painted the gold bands with raw umber and yellow ochre, highlighted them with a blend of yellow ochre and white on the corner of a flat ¼″ brush, and then went over these highlighted areas with streaks of pure yellow.

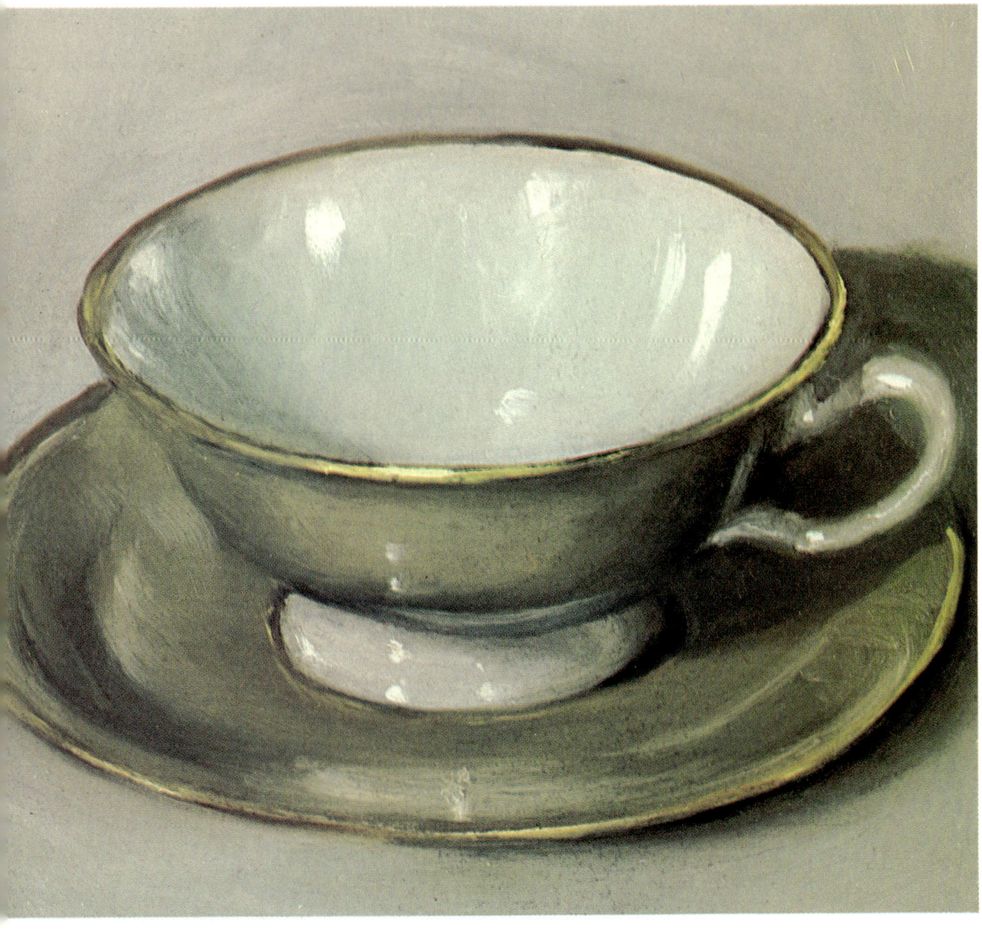

4. Now the artist blended and smoothed what had already been laid in. This included adding variations wherever needed, such as the streak of white highlighting the lower center of the saucer. On the outside of the cup and on the saucer, he lightly brushed a combination of raw umber and blue into the shadowed areas. The shadow on the right, beneath the saucer, was painted with raw umber. For the highlights on the top of the handle and other light areas, Mr. Dawley used white. For highlights in the shadows, he used his middle-value mixture of white and raw umber. He mixed cobalt yellow and white to get a medium deep yellow for the gold rims, and in various places he used pure cobalt yellow, as well as a mixture of cobalt yellow and white for highlights. The upper background was painted with white and raw umber, and the large cast shadow on the right was gently blended into it.

Shiny Fabric

1. Joseph Dawley's first step in painting the straight and broken folds of a length of shiny red taffeta was to establish the composition with a palette of monochrome tones. These were made from mixtures of white, Venetian red, and yellow ochre. He kept his colors subdued at this point so he could gradually increase the density of red and brighten the colors as he worked; there's no "super-bright" available once you've reached the peak of your color.

He drew in the fabric outline and then completely filled it in with his lightest tone. With a middle tone he indicated the largest and most prominent shadow areas.

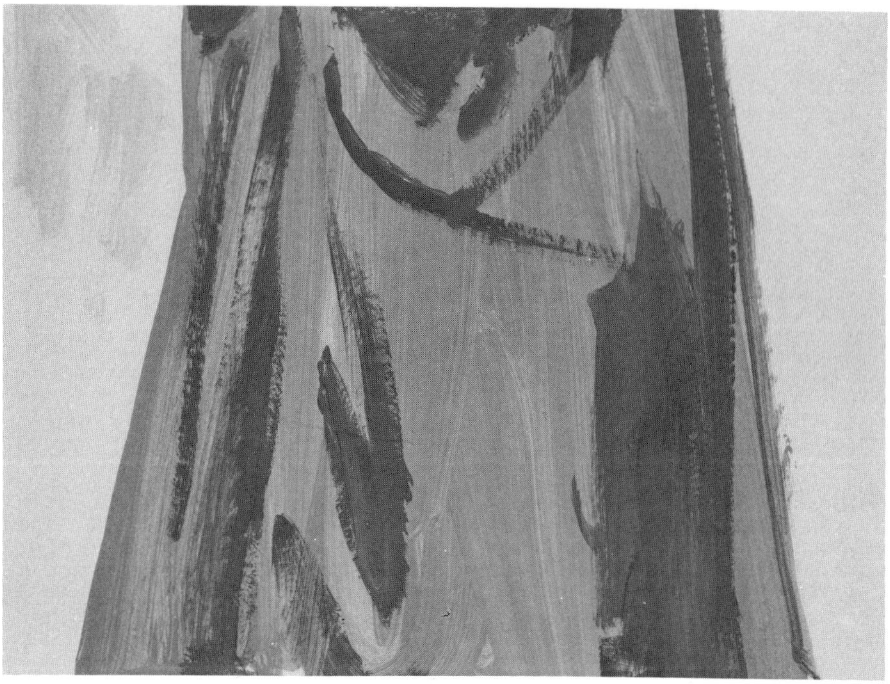

2. Next the artist completed the shadow areas, refining them to show depth and also indicating the largest areas of highlights. He continued to use his middle tone for the additional shadows. Deep folds in the fabric create especially dark shadows, and so he used a darker tone to define them. This depth can be seen in the vertical folds on both sides of the fabric. He used his very deepest tone for just a few areas. Mr. Dawley selected the main highlight areas—mostly along the top portions of folds catching the light—and laid these in with combinations of white and his lightest tone. An occasional bit of blending took place, but he preferred to leave the tones generally unblended at this stage.

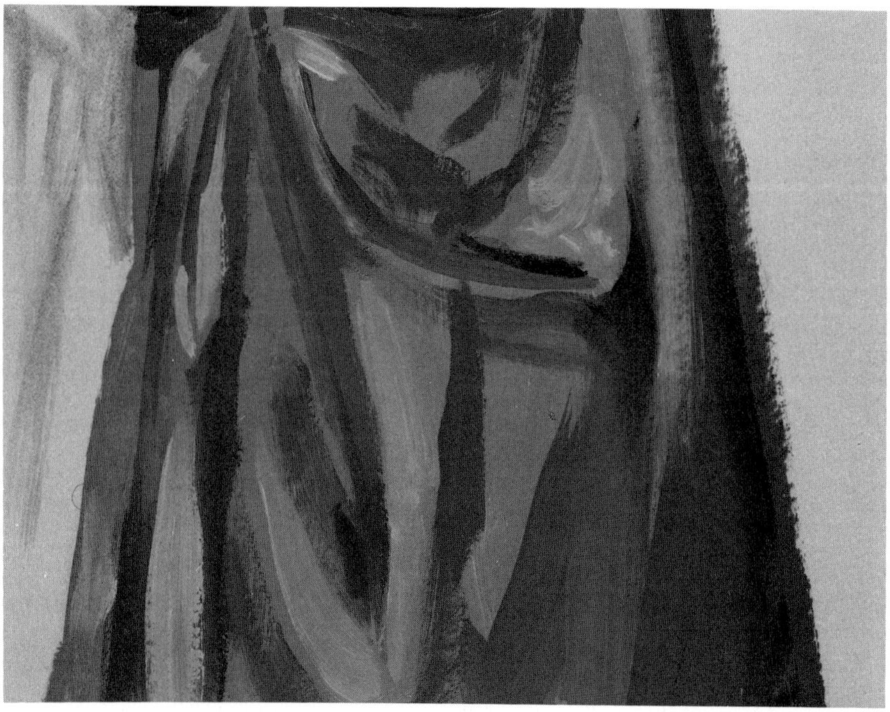

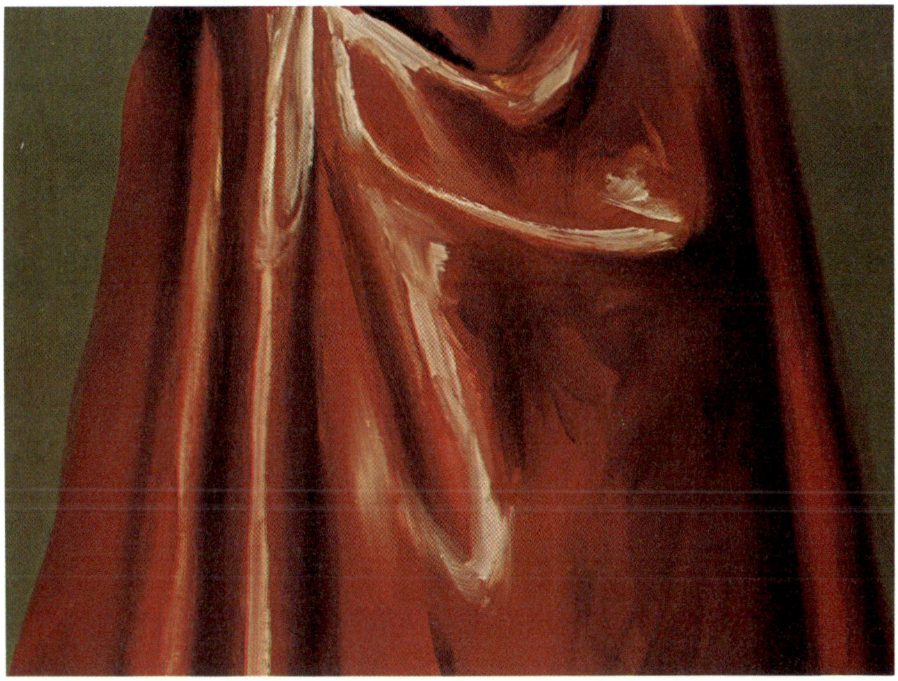

3. Cadmium red light, cadmium red deep, and raw umber were added to the palette at this stage. Then the artist mixed cadmium red light and deep together in equal amounts, adding a minute amount of yellow ochre to get the basic red color he wanted. He decided to add another fold on the far left side to balance the design. He continued to brush his basic red color into all areas of the drape. The undercolors automatically blended with the red as he brushed into them, maintaining a workable impression of the position of the light and dark areas.

The artist used a combination of cadmium red deep and raw umber in the shadow areas. Raw umber was brushed into the drape where the shadows were especially dark, and then this was blended into the red. In a few cases, the raw umber was left unblended. The very lightest areas were painted with white and areas that were not as light were done with a combination of white and cadmium red light.

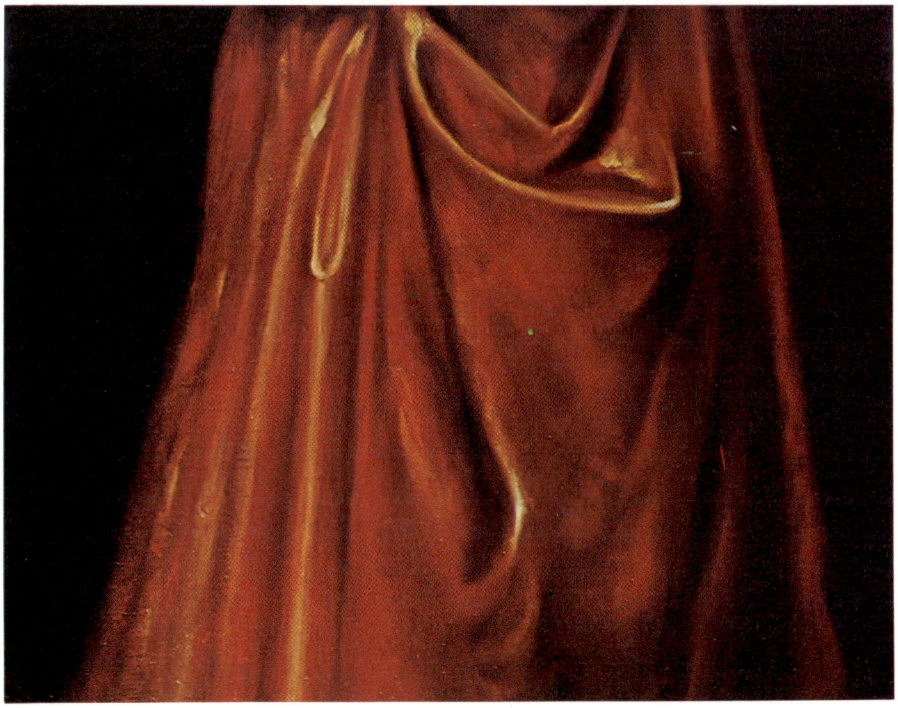

4. At this final stage all the necessary groundwork had been done, and so the artist needed to blend all the colors together and soften everything. During the blending process, the raw umber worked to tone down and mute the red, giving the artist the opportunity to blend in cadmium red light and deep wherever he pleased for additional color. The brightest highlights required further emphasizing with white after the drape was complete.

Lighted Candle

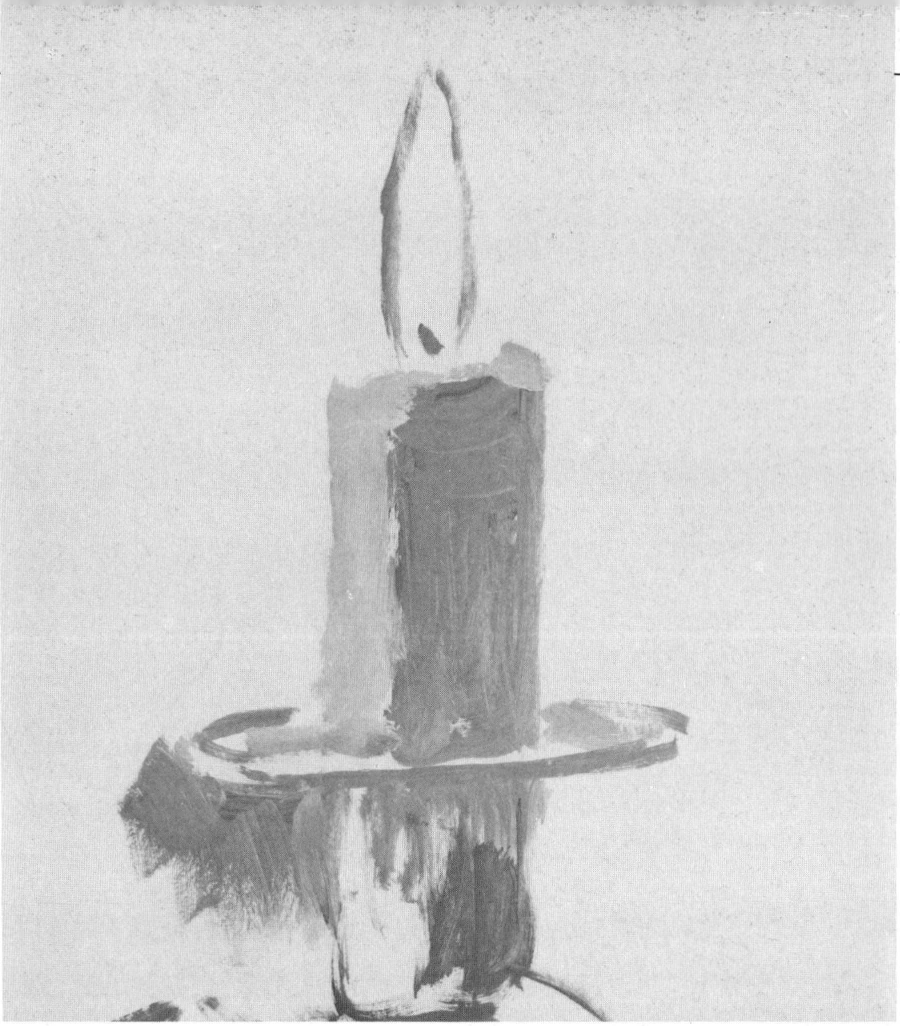

1. Joseph Dawley began this oil study of a lighted candle with a monochrome underpainting in tones mixed from white and a combination of raw umber and yellow ochre. The artist outlined the flame and the dot representing the wick with a middle tone, which he also used for the large, dark part of the candle and the rim of the holder. The lighter portions of the candle on the left and top were done with a lighter tone, which was also used for the shelf of the candlestick holder on either side of the candle.

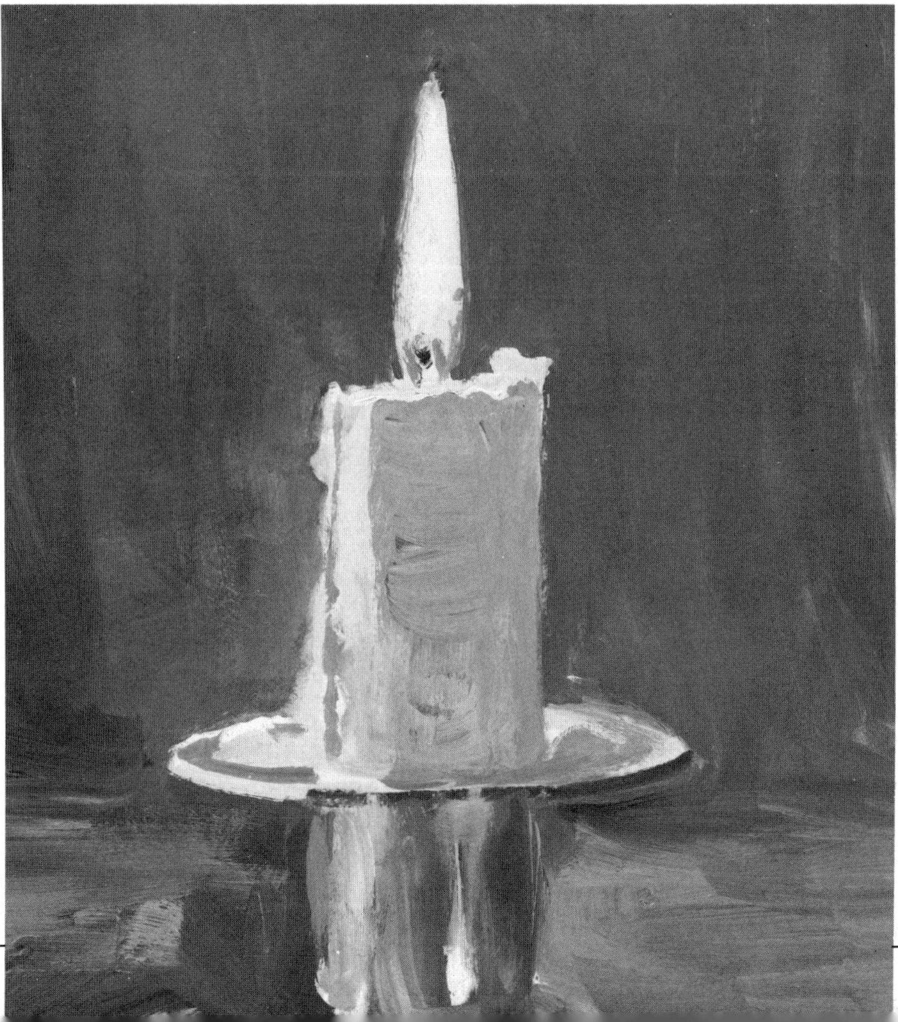

2. The artist filled in the background with a middle-dark tone, painted the flame white, and dotted the burned top of the wick with a dark tone. On either side of this dot, he placed a middle-value stroke to provide the impression of a halo of light surrounding the wick. He brushed white on top of the light areas on the left side of the candle, producing an off-white color. For the darker right-hand side of the candle, he brushed a light tone into the middle tone already there. He highlighted the rim with white and used a dark tone for emphasis along the center and right edge of the rim.

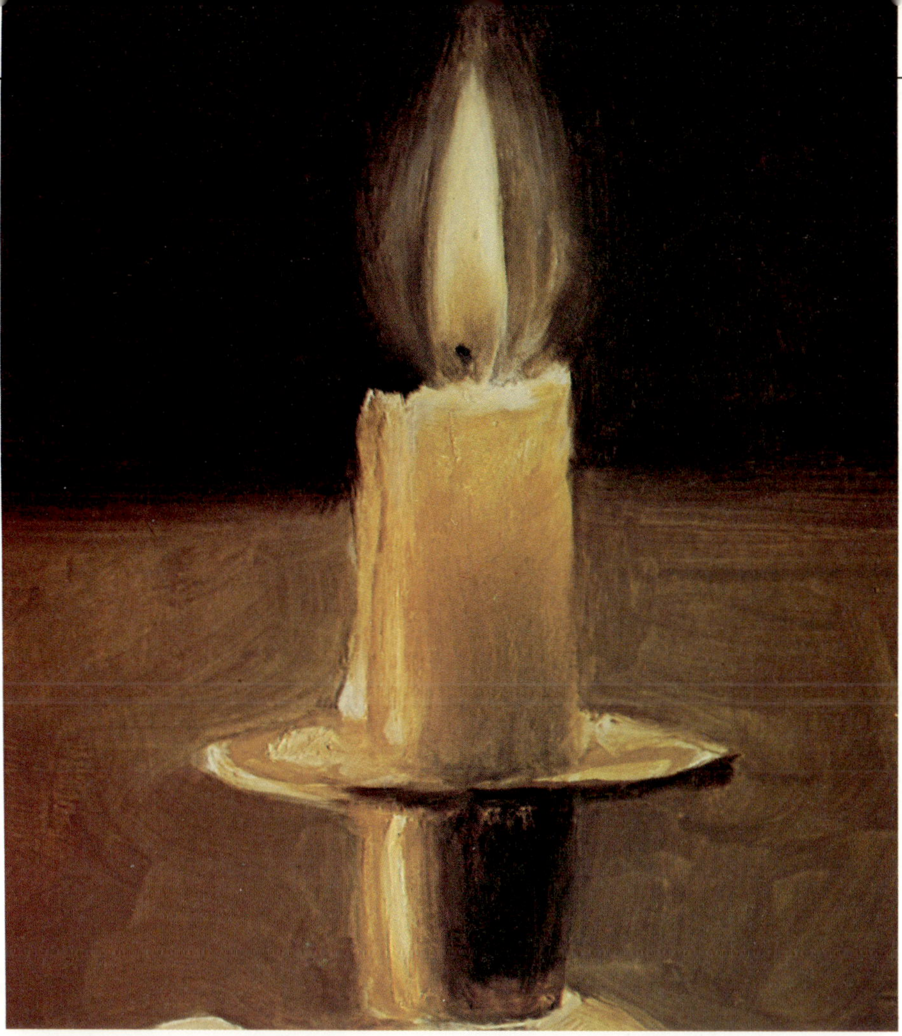

3. Now the artist added cadmium yellow, burnt sienna, raw sienna, yellow ochre, and phthalo blue to his palette. The tabletop was painted with a mixture of burnt sienna, yellow ochre, and phthalo blue. The background was done with raw umber. The artist lightly brushed white into the shimmery area around the flame, allowing the raw umber to remain dark all along the edge to emphasize its brightness. Next the artist lightly brushed raw umber into the bottom of the flame around the wick and used raw umber and raw sienna for the center area above the wick. Then he brushed a mixture of cadmium yellow and white into the brilliant upper portion, and blended it lightly into the white glow.

The artist filled in the candle with cadmium yellow and raw sienna and used yellow ochre and raw umber for the darker parts of the candle, and white for the melted wax. The candleholder was filled in with cadmium yellow and raw sienna; the shadow, with yellow ochre and raw umber; and the very darkest parts of the holder, with burnt umber. The artist used white for the lightest highlights.

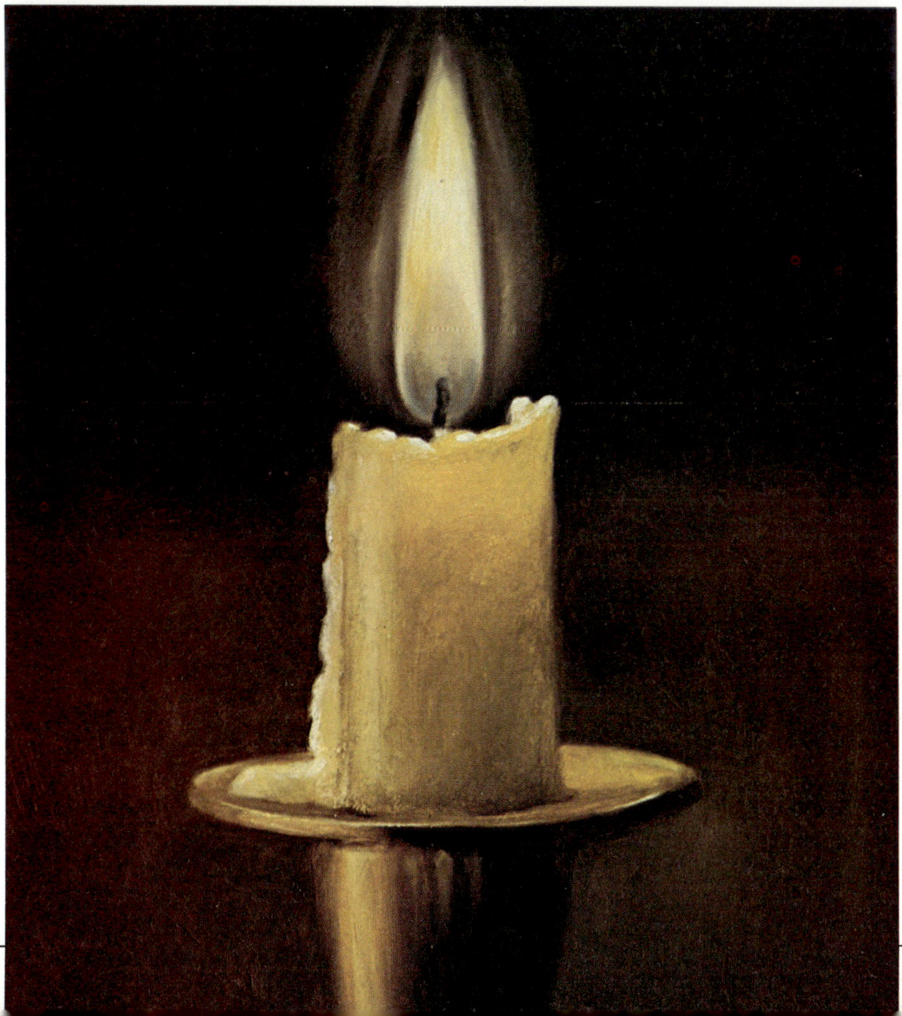

4. The flame was now basically complete except for blending a little ultramarine blue and white into the bottom of it. The wick was defined with black. The artist carefully blended the shimmering "ghost" into the background, allowing the less blended streaks to enhance the flickering effect. The edges of the flame were also lightly blended into the background. To render the transparent glow of the upper part of the candle, Mr. Dawley made the lower part more opaque by brushing a little more raw umber and white into the base. Raw umber was also laid in under the ridge of drippings at the top to show the pale shadow.

Attic Remnants

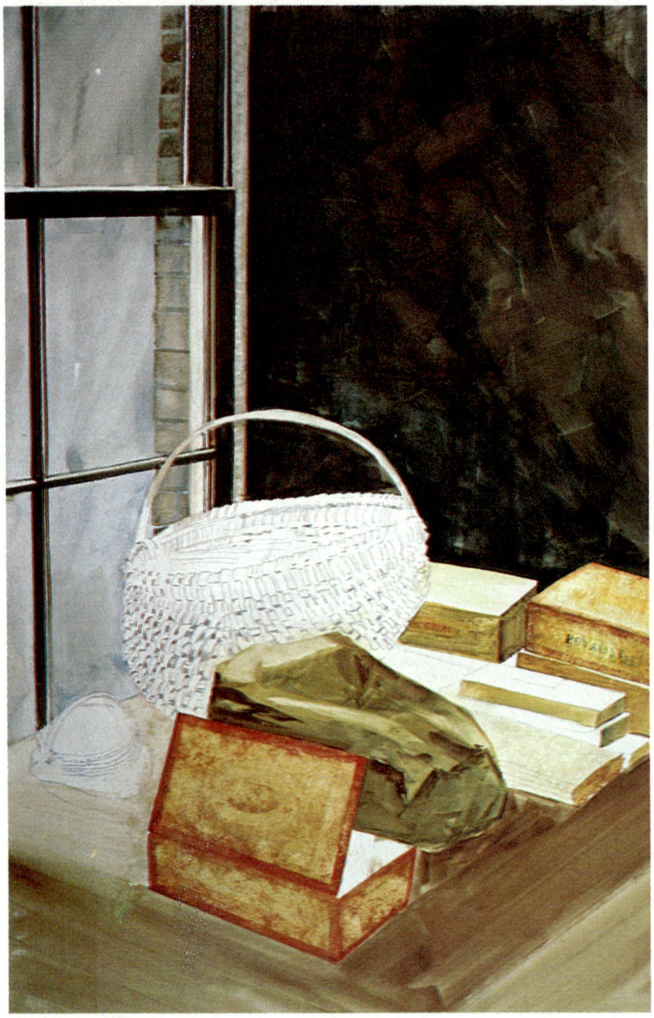

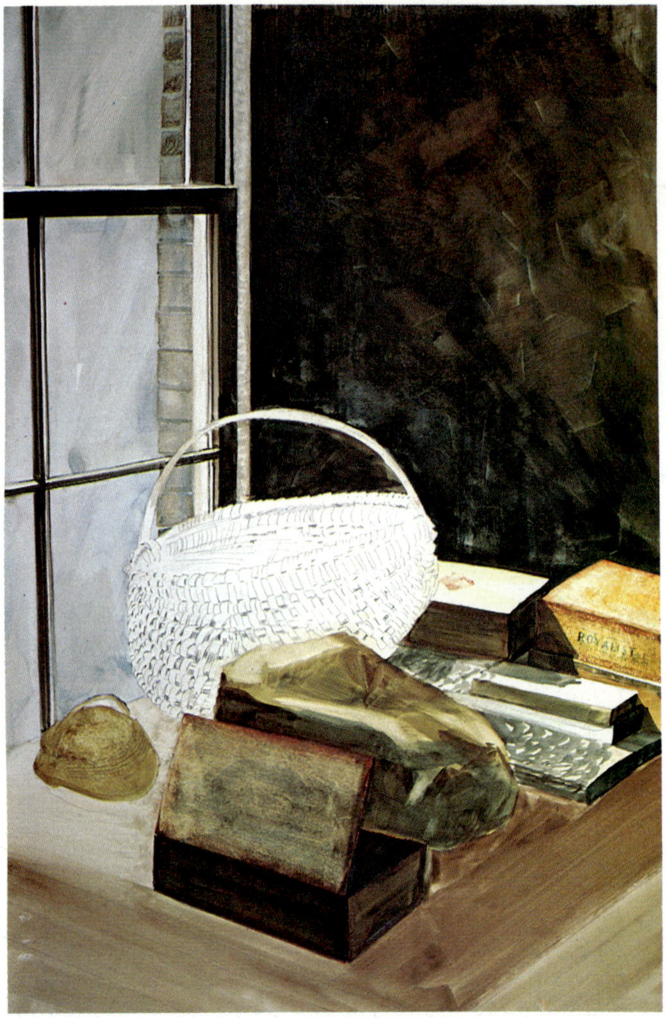

1. After completing an initial drawing wth a 2B pencil, Georg Shook established the darkest value with a mixture of Prussian blue and Van Dyke brown for the wall, using a ¾″ (19 mm) chisel-edged brush. Then he laid in more burnt sienna to interplay with the cool Prussian blue. Using a ¼″ (6 mm) chisel-edged brush, he painted the heavily shadowed window framework with Prussian blue and Van Dyke brown. Now he applied a dilute wash of Winsor blue and burnt sienna to the window itself, creating a diffused, translucent effect.

Now the artist blocked in the tabletop and cigar boxes with a very diluted wash of burnt umber. Then he loaded the same brush with raw sienna and burnt sienna to paint in the foreground cigar box, which he edged with pure burnt sienna in a ¼″ chisel-edged brush. With raw sienna and a little burnt sienna, he built up the cigar boxes in the foreground. Mr. Shook painted the paper bag with a mixture of raw umber and Winsor blue in a ¾″ chisel-edged brush, adding more Winsor blue to model its shadows and creases. Then he painted the brickwork outside the window with a mixture of Winsor blue, burnt sienna, and Van Dyke brown in a ¾″ chisel-edged brush. He softened the busy wall with clear water in a ¾″ chisel-edged brush and darkened the lower corner with an overwash of Prussian blue.

2. The artist developed the details and shadows on the boxes and bag, also filling in the shadow on the foreground cigar box, using a mixture of Van Dyke brown and Prussian blue in a ½″ chisel-edged brush. Then, with the same mixture in a ¾″ chisel-edged brush, he created shadows on the bag and boxes in the background. He painted the basketweave pattern on the books by applying cross-strokes with a ¼″ chisel-edged brush, using a dilute mixture of Prussian blue and Van Dyke brown. Finally, he blocked in the small basket on the left using raw sienna and burnt sienna in a ¼″ chisel-edged brush.

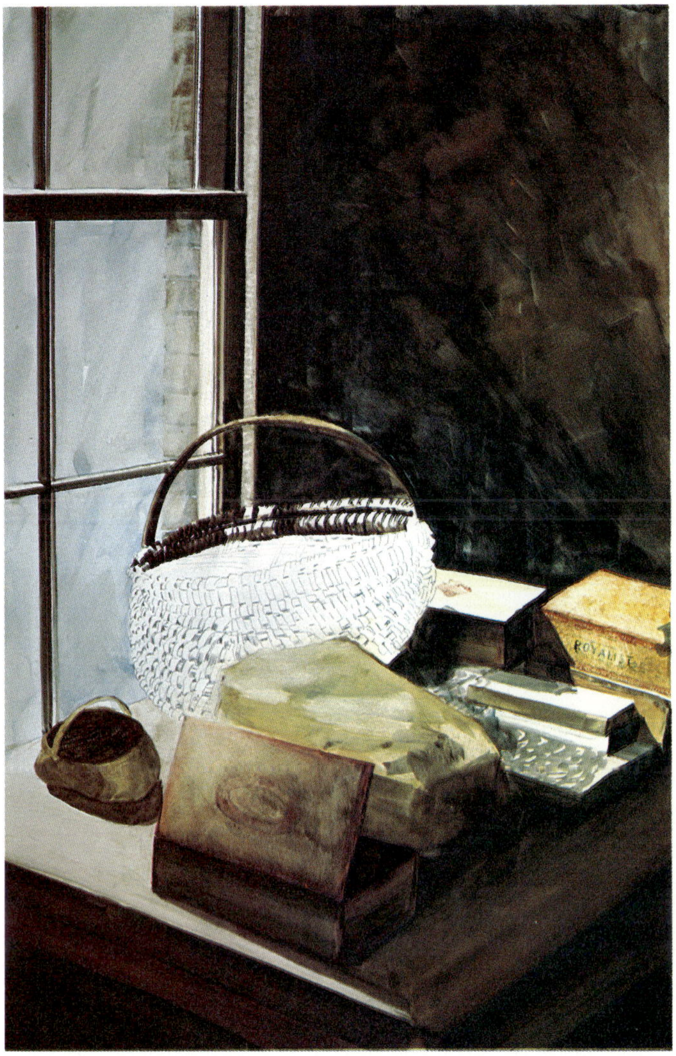

3. Now Mr. Shook developed the shadows on the table and the table edge with Prussian blue and Van Dyke brown in a ¾″ chisel-edged brush. Then he used the same brush dipped in clear water to lift some highlights from the unlit areas of the table. He further developed the deep shadow of the foreground cigar box and added density inside the box with Van Dyke brown. He treated the small basket on the left in the same manner. To further model the box, he lifted some of the color from the edge to reflect the sun from the table. Now he noticed that the bricks outside the window seemed too well defined, and so he lightened them with a sponge dipped in clear water and then blotted the area dry. Now he turned to the large basket, painting the handle with Van Dyke brown and Prussian blue in a pointed red sable brush. He used the same mixture to develop some of the shadow work on the basket.

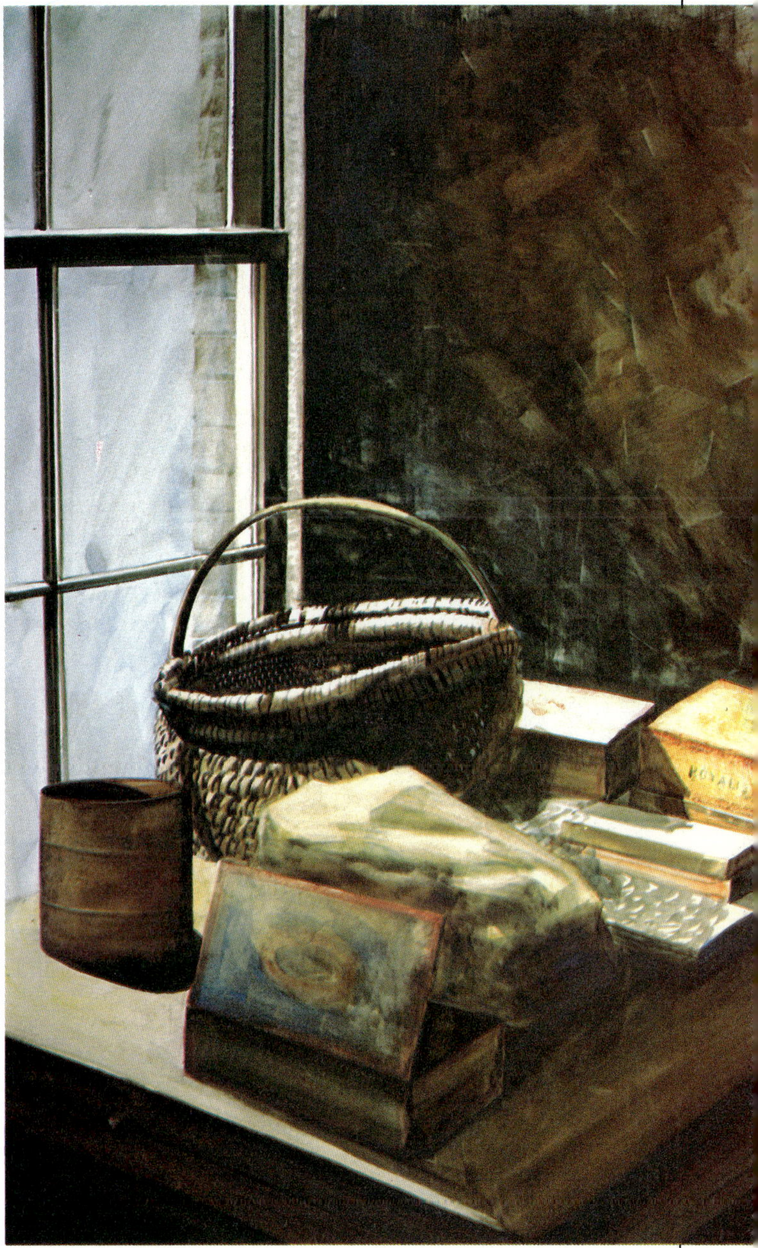

4. The artist lifted some color from the left side of the tabletop and deepened the shadows along the edges of the table and the background boxes. Now Mr. Shook removed the smaller basket by wetting it with a brush dipped in clear water and then blotting with a dry paper towel. Then he painted a tin can in its place, blocking it in with burnt sienna and Winsor blue and then adding shadows with Van Dyke brown and Prussian blue. Wetting his ¾″ chisel-edged brush in clear water, he lifted out the seams of the can. With a pointed sable brush he added detailing to the larger basket, using burnt sienna, Prussian blue, and Van Dyke brown. He rinsed his brush and loaded it with cerulean blue to paint the top of the foreground box. He warmed the box top with cadmium red. He lifted out highlights on the boxes, the bag, and the upper rim of the large basket, and finished the window frame.

Wicker Chairs

1. With a 2B pencil, Georg Shook made a detailed drawing of his subject. Next he brushed liquid masking resist over the chairs wherever he wanted highlights to be in the finished painting. He blocked in the wall with a ¾" (19 mm) chisel-edged brush loaded with Davy's gray and burnt sienna, using random strokes and then immediately blotting the entire area with a wet paper towel to give it texture. Next he used a heavy mixture of Prussian blue and Van Dyke brown for the dark interior. He painted the rear window by wetting the area and floating in a diluted wash of Winsor blue.

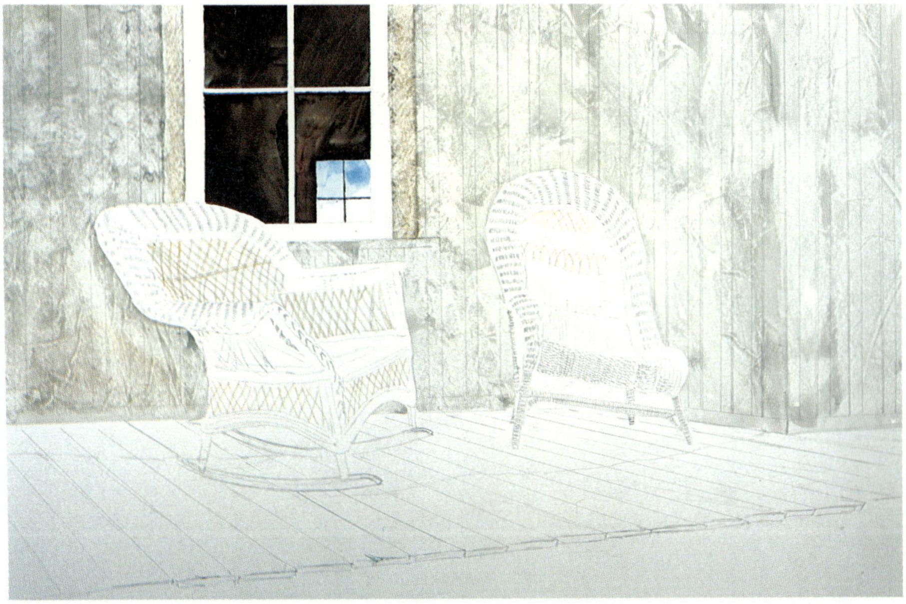

2. The artist applied additional texture to the weathered wall and then added vertical shadows with Davy's gray. Then he went over the same shadows with long, vertical strokes of burnt sienna and Winsor blue, using the Davy's gray as an undertone. Now he brushed a lighter mixture of Davy's gray, burnt sienna, and Prussian blue onto the floor area with a ¾" chisel-edged brush and added a highlight of burnt sienna on the left. Then he painted the dark diagonal shadow under the porch using Van Dyke brown and Prussian blue.

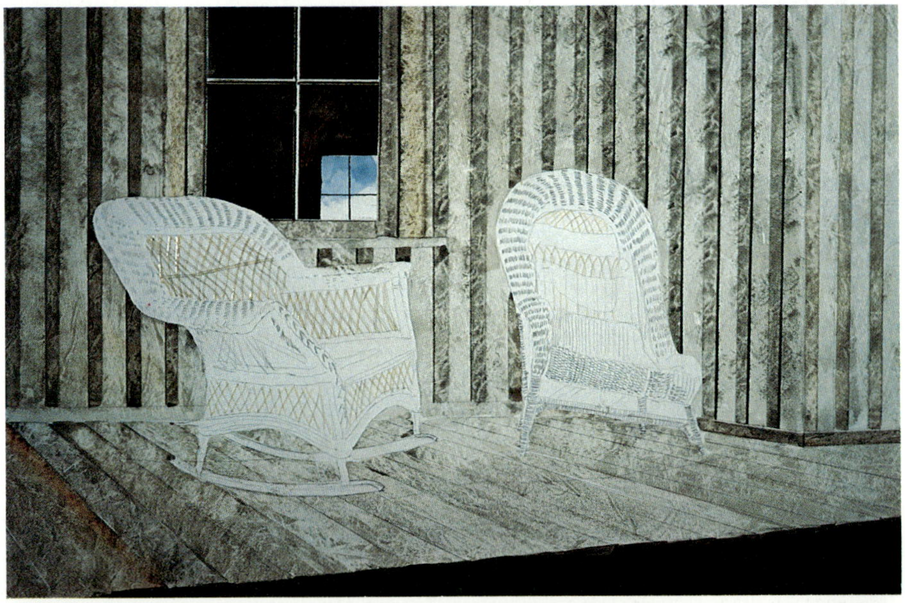

3. Mr. Shook added a cast shadow to the scene, drawing attention to the corner where the chairs are situated. With a chisel-edged brush, he painted each board of the wall and floor individually—some with Davy's gray, others with burnt sienna, and still others with Prussian blue—to represent the colorful hues of weathered wood.

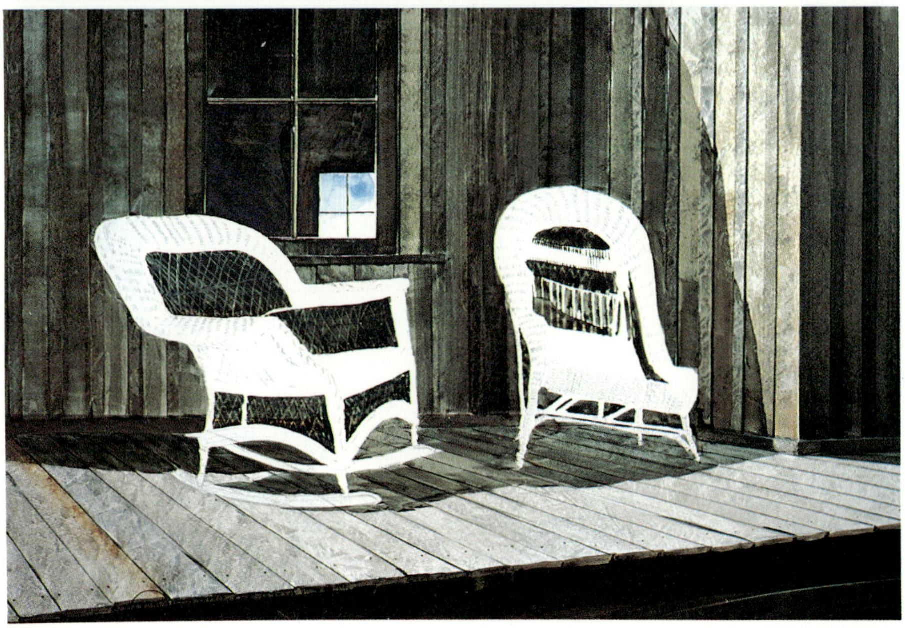

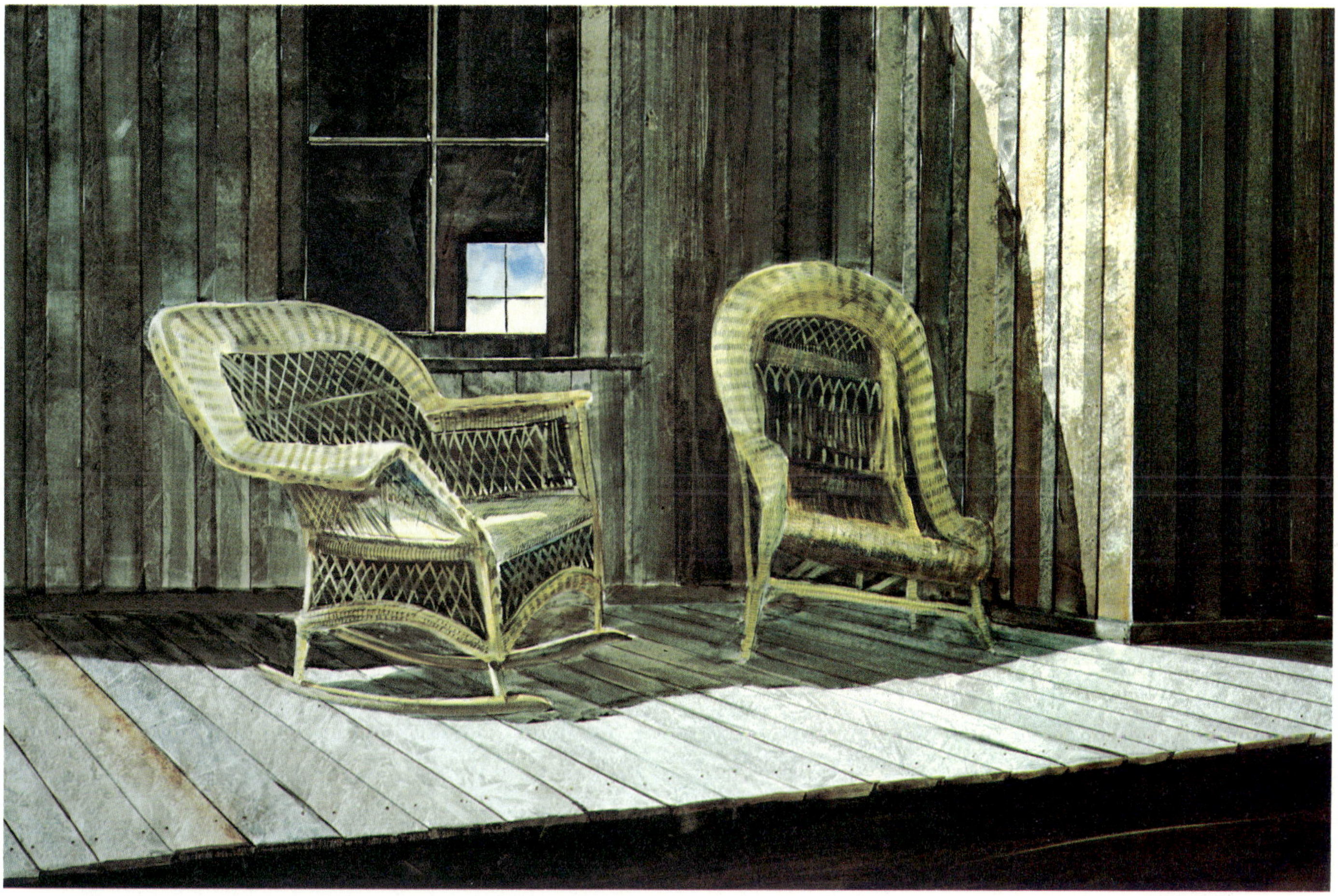

4. The artist rubbed the masking liquid from the chairs and then used a ¼″ (6 mm) chisel-edged brush to paint a wash of raw sienna mixed with a little burnt sienna and Winsor blue over them. He used the same brush to detail the chairs with Winsor blue to balance the warmer burnt sienna of the floor.

With a ¼″ chisel-edged brush he added further detail to the siding of the house and washed an additional shadow of Prussian blue and Van Dyke brown over the chair on the right. Then he increased the Prussian blue in the mixture and used a ½″ (13 mm) chisel-edged brush to pull this cooler overwash across the floor beneath the chairs. With Van Dyke brown in a ¼″ chisel-edged brush, he added detail to the sunlit area of the floor. Then he lifted color from the front edge of the floor with a ¾″ chisel-edged brush dipped in clear water. For a final touch, he added rusty nails with a pointed sable brush loaded with pure burnt sienna.

Sunlit Interiors

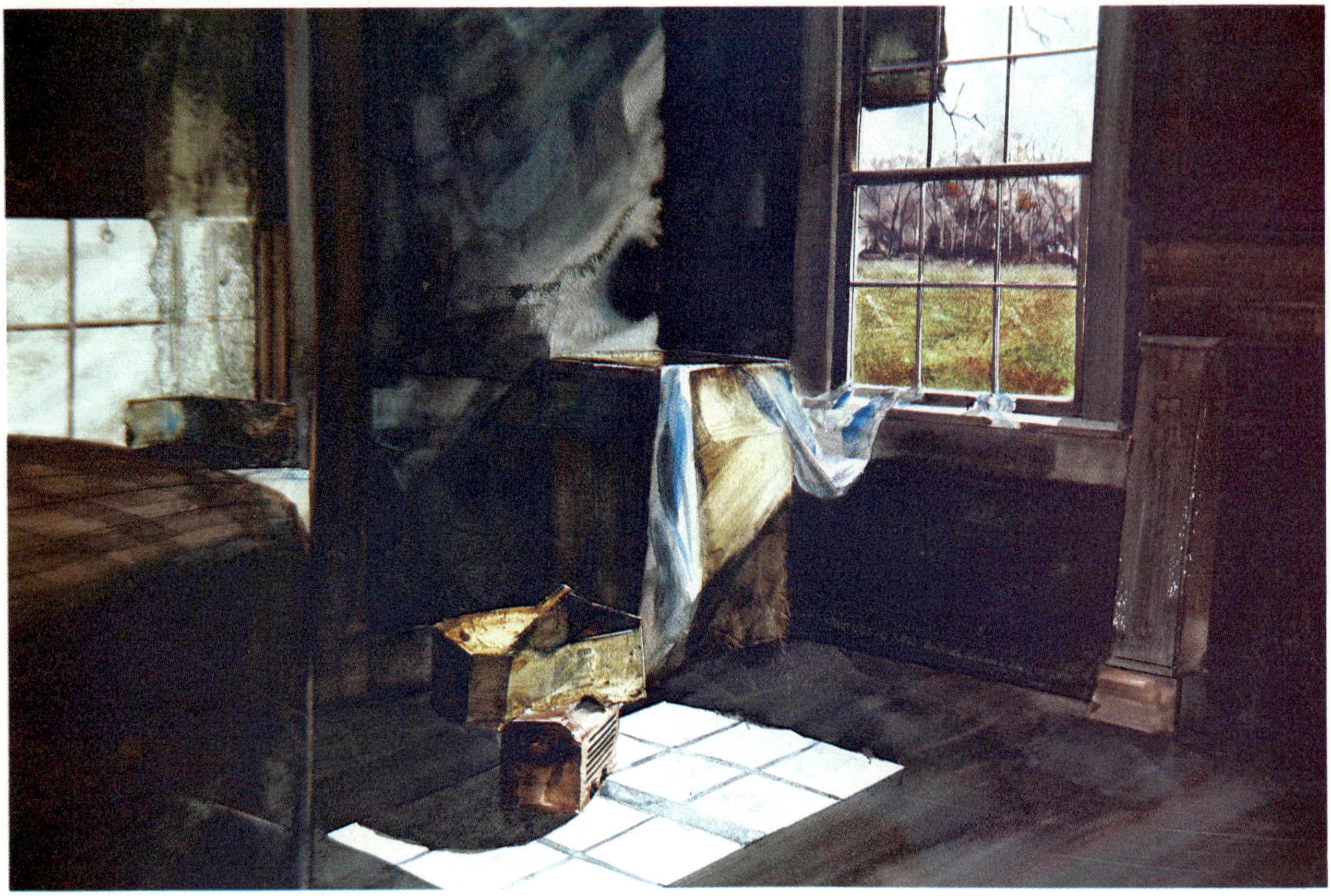

***Vacancy*, 30″ × 20″ (76 × 51 cm), watercolor, by Georg Shook.**

Bleak Interior. (Above) The artist wanted to create a bleak mood in his painting to add to the sense of abandonment in this desolate-looking scene with empty boxes, a ragged bedsheet, and an old radio. Yet, to allow the viewer an escape to a more pleasant scene, he also created a bright landscape outside. He placed strong sunlight patterns on the floor that create contrasting abstract shapes, and by doing this, he has built tension as well as allowed an escape from it. He began by making a preliminary drawing, and then he painted in the darkest darks using Prussian blue and Van Dyke brown. He worked up to the lighter areas, pulling in mixtures of burnt sienna and Winsor blue from time to time and lifting out the lightest spots with a sponge dipped in clear water. When he painted in the final details, Mr. Shook used burnt sienna and yellow ochre for the box and radio, and cerulean blue for the sheet that is draped over the large box by the window.

Nostalgic Mood. (Right) A photographer friend told the artist about this one-room schoolhouse in the Appalachian region of Tennessee. When he visited it, he was struck by the beauty of the sunlight streaming in through the only window and the interesting shadows that it created.

After sketching the scene, he blocked in the walls with a chisel-edged brush loaded with Prussian blue and Van Dyke brown, but he was careful to leave the window area unpainted. He used a mixture of burnt sienna and Prussian blue to paint in the back wall and the shelf, and then he used the same mixture to paint in the seats and floor. After he had painted in the cast shadows with Prussian blue and Van Dyke brown, he lifted out the sunlight on the seats and floor with a chisel-edged brush and clear water. Finally, he painted the scene outside the window and added a Winsor blue sky.

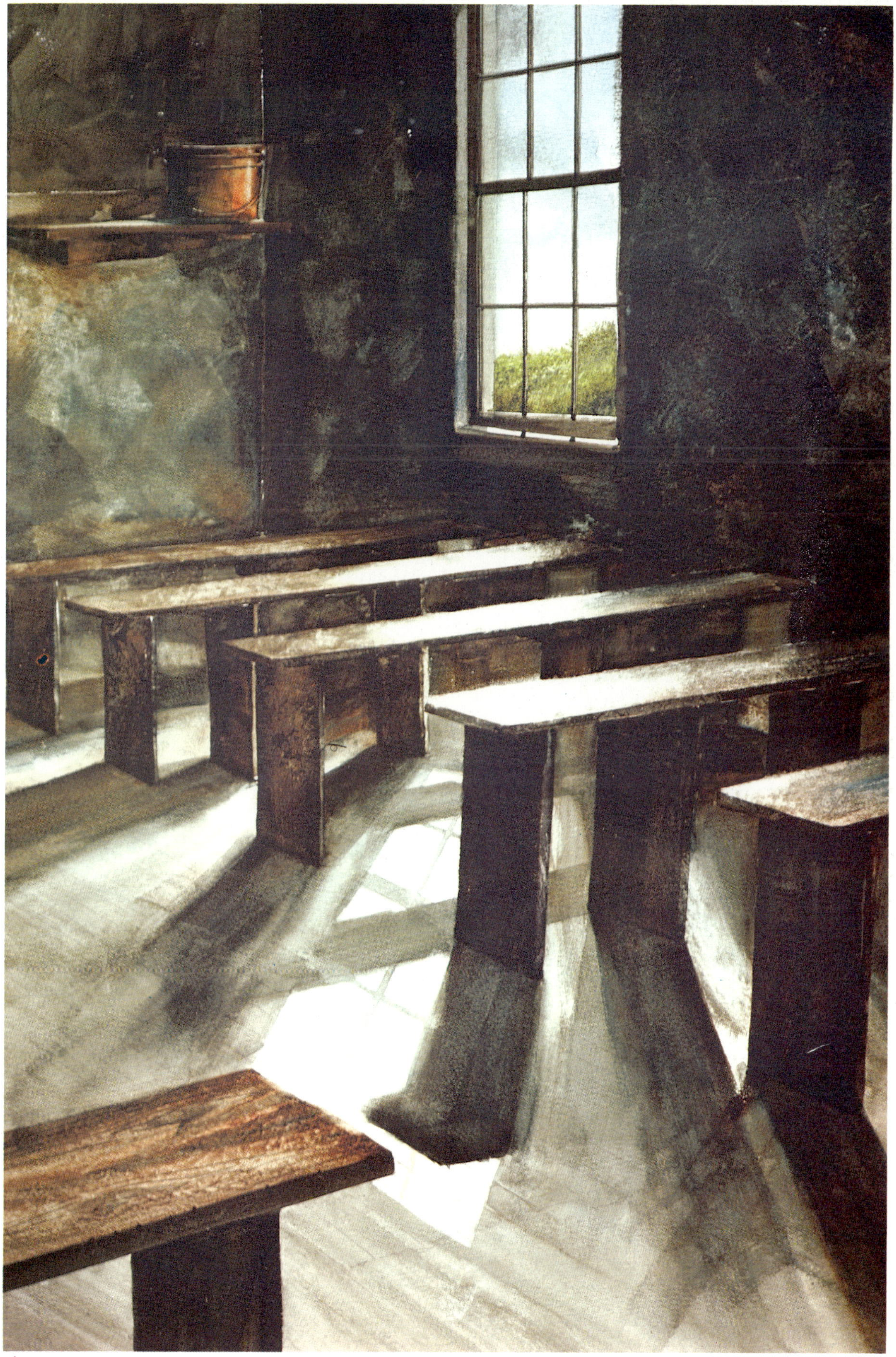

***The Common Place*, 20″ × 30″ (51 × 76 cm), watercolor, by Georg Shook.**

Latticework and Flag

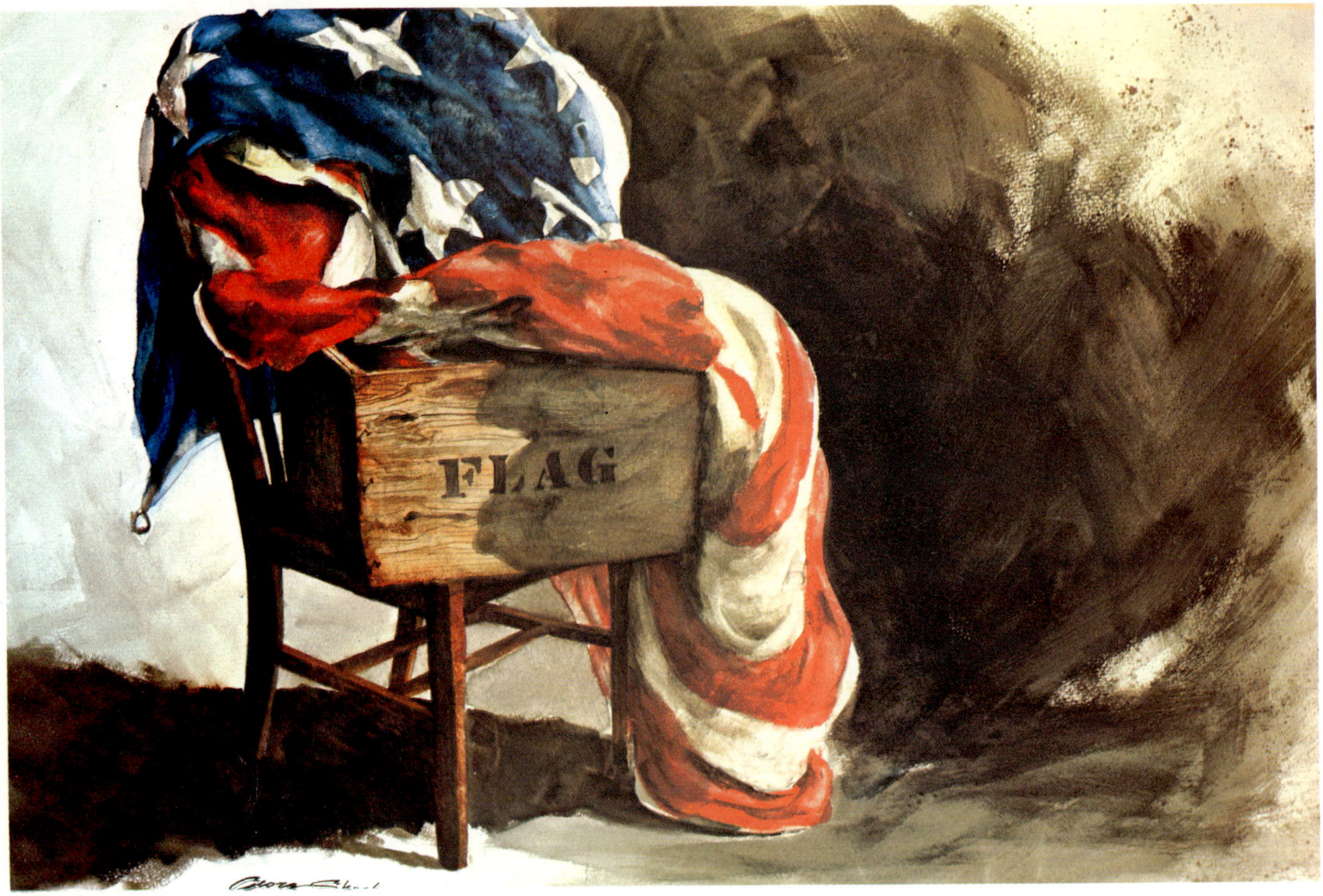

***Unconquered*, 30″ × 20″ (76 × 51 cm), watercolor, by Georg Shook**

Imaginary Light and Dark Background. (Above) To commemorate the retirement of the forty-eight star American flag, the artist wanted to emphasize its symbolic nature in this painting. He left the background neutral and created this imaginary scene: A tired old flag is draped over an antique wooden chair, having done its duty, and is ready to be packed away in a decrepit wooden box.

Mr. Shook began this painting with a fairly detailed drawing, carefully indicating the folds of the fabric as well as the position of the stripes and stars. Then he used Prussian blue to paint the field around the stars, pulling in some Van Dyke brown for the darker shadows. He used cadmium red for the stripes and burnt sienna for the chair and storage box. After the paint was completely dry, he blocked in a neutral background of Prussian blue and Van Dyke brown. Then, to complete the composition, he created a cast shadow beneath the chair, using the same neutral mixture.

Abstract Light and Shadow Patterns. (Right) As the artist visited a house in Jackson, Tennessee, one day, he noticed how the sunlight created an abstract pattern on the wall, railing, and steps leading to the porch. The scene was so warm and inviting that he did some sketches on the spot. To keep his impressions fresh, he began this painting within a day or so. His preliminary drawing simplified things by leaving certain objects out, but the complexity of the remaining composition with its intense spots of sunlight still posed quite a challenge. He covered the patterns of spots with masking liquid and then blocked in the porch with Davy's gray. To get the pinkish glow of aged wood, he underpainted the walls with very diluted cadmium red. After some detailing and work in the shadow areas, he added the table and chair, and he created a checkered tablecloth with cadmium red and Winsor blue in a pointed sable brush. After washing in the sky with Winsor blue and Davy's gray, and creating the tree line and grass in the lower left, he removed the masking material from the sunlit spots. Then he pulled a wet brush back and forth across these areas to get some color into them. This toned down the brilliant white of the board, yet preserved the intensity of these abstract patterns of sunlight.

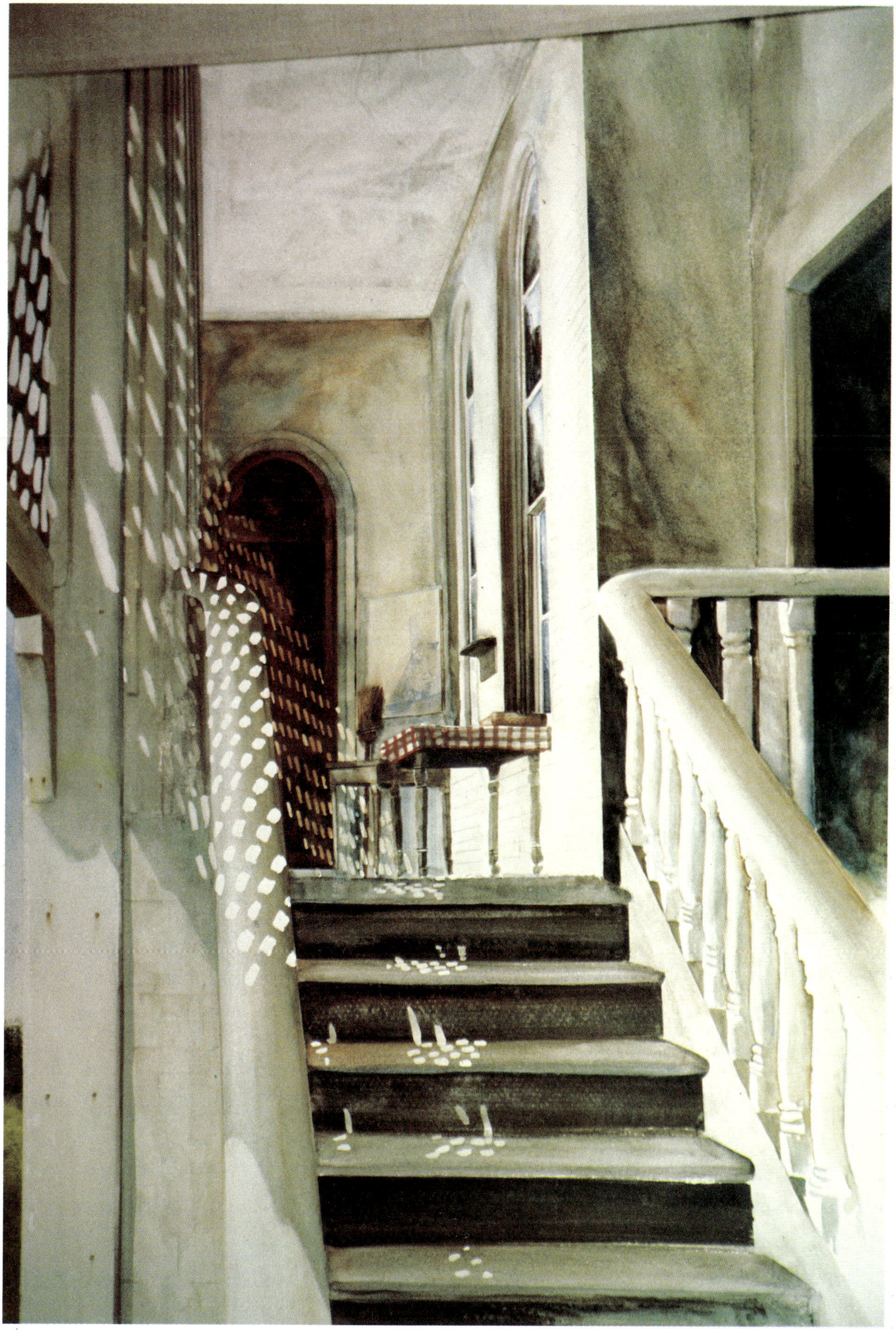

Lattice Work, 30″ × 40″ (76 × 102 cm), watercolor, by Georg Shook

Index